NEO-DISNEYISM

Inclusivity in the Twenty-First Century of
Disney's Magic Kingdom

Brenda Ayres and Sarah E. Maier (eds)

PETER LANG
Oxford • Bern • Berlin • Bruxelles • New York • Wien

Bibliographic information published by Die Deutsche Nationalbibliothek. Die Deutsche Nationalbibliothek lists this publication in the Deutsche Nationalbibliografie; detailed bibliographic data is available on the Internet at http://dnb.d-nb.de.

A catalogue record for this book is available from the British Library.

Library of Congress Cataloging-in-Publication Data:
Names: Ayres, Brenda, 1953- editor. | Maier, Sarah E. (Sarah Elizabeth), 1968- editor.
Title: Neo-Disneyism : inclusivity in the twenty-first century of Disney's magic kingdom / Brenda Ayres and Sarah E. Maier, [editors].
Description: Oxford ; New York : Peter Lang, 2022. | Includes bibliographical references and index.
Identifiers: LCCN 2022019903 (print) | LCCN 2022019904 (ebook) | ISBN 9781800797994 (paperback) | ISBN 9781800798007 (ebook) | ISBN 9781800798014 (epub)
Subjects: LCSH: Walt Disney Company. | Motion pictures--Social aspects. | Motion pictures--Political aspects. | Motion pictures--United States--History and criticism. | Animated films--United States--History and criticism.
Classification: LCC PN1999.W27 N46 2022 (print) | LCC PN1999.W27 (ebook) | DDC 384/.8/0979494--dc23/eng/20220613
LC record available at https://lccn.loc.gov/2022019903
LC ebook record available at https://lccn.loc.gov/2022019904

Cover Image: *Garden Angel* © Sue Greenfield.

Cover design by Brian Melville for Peter Lang Ltd.

ISBN 978-1-80079-799-4 (print)
ISBN 978-1-80079-800-7 (ePDF)
ISBN 978-1-80079-801-4 (ePub)

© Peter Lang Group AG 2022
Published by Peter Lang Ltd, International Academic Publishers,
Oxford, United Kingdom
oxford@peterlang.com, www.peterlang.com

Brenda Ayres and Sarah E. Maier have asserted their right under the Copyright, Designs and Patents Act, 1988, to be identified as Editors of this Work.

This publication has been peer reviewed.

Dedicated to
All the Elsas, Moanas, Mirabels, Lucases, Miguels, Hiros, Brunos, and
Other Disney Heroes in the Making

Contents

Figures

Tables

Acknowledgments

Our appreciation goes to Sue Greenfield of the Hanover Art Guild in Pennsylvania, for her permission to use her *Garden Angel* as the cover for this book.

Foremost, we would like to thank the contributors who wrote most of the chapters in this book: Michelle Chan, Amala Charulatha, Dalila Forni, Sheng-mei Ma, Elaine Morton, Korine Powers, Rritwika Roychowdhury, and Taylor Tomko. There were others who began this project but who had to withdraw because of dealing with COVID in their families. We appreciate the initial interest that we received when we placed calls for papers. Moreover, we really appreciate the contributors whose hard work and enthusiasm for Disney, informed by perspectives perhaps from those with non-Western ethnicities, have created a volume that we feel will be illuminating for readers and fans of Disney.

I (Brenda Ayres) want to thank the Penn State Library for its liberal access to material that expanded my research on Disney scholarship. I am also grateful to the Kaltreider-Benfer Library of Red Lion, Pennsylvania, for its loan of Disney films and books. As always, it has been a great boon to work with Sarah Maier. We are two editors that complement each other, and as a team, it is our hope that we have produced a collection of essays that will demonstrate both our appreciation and concern for Disney's evolving multiculturalism and multigenderism.

I (Sarah E. Maier) want to thank the Hans W. Klohn Commons Library staff at UNB Saint John who chase down books and bits of ephemera when I go off on a tangent much like Dory; and, as always, to my daughter and father who remind me to stop "blue fishing" when I am lost among too many ideas at once and forget where I started—my gratitude for reminding me to focus! I am always thankful for Brenda who is a fairy godmother of a friend who works her bibbidi-bobbedi-boo on our work; she is a magical woman full of kindness and intelligence.

Finally, we cannot say how much we treasure the films made by Disney, especially the more recent ones that encourage people to accept and value themselves and others, regardless of physical and mental challenges, body types, religion, gender, race, ethnicity, or any other variant, to appreciate "difference" as a bounty that strengthens the world and should make humanity a better behaved species than what we have been in the past. Disney's messages to the young gives us hope that future generations will do unto others as they would have done unto themselves. If they do so, they will truly produce a magic kingdom.

Brenda Ayres and Sarah E. Maier

BRENDA AYRES

Introduction: Walt Disney's Wonderful World of Color

In 2003 I generated a collection of essays that criticized the Disney industry for its global marketing of an ideology of Americana that, besides promoting WASP elitism, inculcated a strict adherence to gender binary and heterosexual, nuclear family formations. Eleanor Byrne and Martin McQuillan termed this ideology "duckology," asserting that "Disney has become synonymous with a certain conservative, patriarchal, heterosexual ideology which is loosely associated with American cultural imperialism" (1999, 2). I called it "The Emperor's Old Groove."

I did produce the book with misgivings because I grew up on Disney and have the fondest memories of its films. My all-time favorite movie is *Lady and the Tramp* (1955), and I am a better human being after having watched *Old Yeller* (1957) and *Pollyanna* (1960), to name just a few Disney films. When my family bought its first television in the 1950s, it was *The Mickey Mouse Club* that I watched. My first movie at a drive-in was *Snow White* (in 1958). In the 1960s, Sunday evenings always meant *Disney's Wonderful World of Color* in front of the TV. In 1964 I traveled with my Girl Scout Troop to New York City for the World's Fair where I came to sit in a boat and was enthralled by a Disney display of hundreds of dolls dressed in Indigenous costumes, singing "It's a small world after all" that encouraged us to be friends with everyone. The song was written by a brother team of Robert and Richard Sherman on the heel of the Cuban Missile Crisis. The words were a great comfort to me, for I was still upset over the assassination of President John F. Kennedy. Disney's exhibits at the World's Fair urged peace to hundreds of thousands of attendees from around the world and exuded hope for the future.

Therefore, while rendering *The Emperor's Old Groove*, it was often difficult to be critical of Disney but was warranted because of its proliferation of gender, racial, and ethnic stereotypes and their negative influence on children (including the adult child). I invited other scholars, who shared my concerns, to contribute essays that analyzed Disney's colonization tactics. Nearly at the same time, Douglas Brode was working on his *From Walt to Woodstock: How Disney Created the Counterculture* (2004), crediting Disney for creating the antiestablishment culture of 1967–72. Brode's stated "aim" was "to show that Disney's output—as experienced at the movies, on television, and in person at theme parks—played a major role in transforming mid-1950s white-bread toddlers into the rebellious teenage youth of the late sixties" (x). Brode attempted to argue his theory through identifying the "*anti-Establishment* values" in Disney (xi; emphasis in the original). He was accurate in making this declaration: "No other single figure of the past century has had such a wide, deep, and pervasive influence on the public imagination as Walt Disney. He did, after all, reach us first (and, therefore, foremost), at that very point in our youthful development when either an individual or a generation is most receptive (and vulnerable) to such forces and ideas" (x). But to say that the counterculture revolution occurred because of Disney's subliminal cultivation of rebellion against authority in his early films ignores the overwhelming evidence of Disney's propensity to promote a single conservative image of Americana, one that was deplorable to Hippies. Since I was one of those flower children, I cannot agree with Brode's theory, and although I love Disney's old films, I continue to cringe at what I am now calling "Disneyism," borrowing from Richard Schickel's description of "Disney's Americanism" as

> of the kind of clean, moral, simple and innocent stories he most often chose to present on the screen, of the right-wing politics of his later years, of his broad, gag-oriented sense of humor, containing no elements of social or self-satire, as entirely typical of the tastes of the region that formed him. The geographic center of the nation is also, broadly speaking, the most passionately American of the American regions. (1968, 72)

Most scholars agree: Disney is a powerful dynamo in its far-reaching proliferation of values especially to children through its films, theme parks, and merchandising. David Kunzle has made the deduction that Disney "may be the most widely known North American name in the world. He is, arguably, the century's most important figure in the bourgeois popular culture" (1984,

11). In their now well-known and widely quoted work on Disney, *The Mouse that Roared*, Henry A. Giroux and Grace Pollock confirm that Disney entertainment, through its extensive and effective influence, "wages an aggressive campaign to peddle its political and cultural influence" (2010, xiv). More specifically, Julie C. Garlen and Jennifer A. Sandlin, in their study of the influence of Disney on children, pronounce it to be "a major cultural force that shapes everyday life practices and identity formations through its representations of family values, gender, sexuality, race, class, ethnicity, 'Americanness,' childhood, pleasure, entertainment, education, and community" (2016, 2). The authors of *Animating Difference* consider Disney animation as "socializing agents ... that guide children (in the United States) through the complexities of highly racialized and sexualized scenarios, normalizing certain dynamics while rendering others invisible" (King et al. 2010, 11).

Scott Schaffer believes that "Disney plays a large part in this boundary denotation by allowing for the perpetuation of cultural stereotypes that portray, albeit in a 'cute' manner, the otherness of areas of the world the United States has come to dominate politically, culturally, or economically" (2016, 34). Keith Brooker concurs with this elaboration:

> That Disney films are so often taken (for better or for ill) to embody typical all-American virtues is a testament to the overall power of American ideology, which has so effectively instilled the vast majority of Americans with a confident belief that all things good and wholesome are associated with Americanness while anything opposed to the American way must be vile and depraved. (2010, 13)

When one considers the extent to which Disneyism has exponentially propagated as a global media, then an analysis of its *Weltanschauung* is timely in our current climate when xenophobia is a pole star, and it is in everyone's best interest to be at peace with one's fellow beings.

Disney is a multinational company that generates $48 billion a year (Iger 2014, n.p.). Disney's former chairperson and CEO, Michael Eisner, described the mass appeal of Disney and its proliferation in an article in 1995:

> More than 200 million people a year watch a Disney film or home video, 395 million watch a Disney TV show every week; 212 million listen to or dance to Disney music, records, tapes, or compact discs; 270 million buy Disney-licensed merchandise in 50 countries.

> More than 50 million people a year from all lands pass through the turnstiles of Disney theme parks in California, Florida and Tokyo, bringing the total since they opened to over half a billion people. (8)

In 1994 Disney earned over 14 billion dollars from products sold around the world (Wasko 2001, 21) and gleaned 20 percent of its total company revenue from international sales in 1998 (3). The Disney Company "represents the new face of neoliberal power, capable of not merely providing entertainment but also shaping the identities, desires, and subjectivities of millions of people across the globe" (Giroux and Pollock xv). The Disney Magic Kingdom is one of the most powerful and wealthy kingdoms in the world: "With Disney's ownership of Marvel, the *Star Wars* universe, and Pixar, in addition to its own animated and live-action movies, Disney has consistently been the most profitable studio in Hollywood; the first to gross over $5 billion consecutively for three years" (Dunn 2020, n.p.). Many of his films are based on published books, most of which have been widely read. Before the theater, the radio, and motion pictures, the major source of entertainment and education was provided by books. Oral fairy tales and literary *Kunstmärchen* used to be the staple of children's literature and illustrated morality: Adherence to moral lessons therein resulted in rewards while neglect or defiance guaranteed negative, unpleasant, and maybe even mortal consequences. Next to the Bible, they were the stories read to and read by children throughout the nineteenth century and first half of the twentieth century.

An increase in literacy in both Britain and the United States corresponded with or triggered or was triggered by the Golden Age of children's literature. In addition, Claudia Nelson asserts it to be a "truism" that "the Victorians were fascinated with childhood ... to an extent not shared by any previous culture" (2012, 1). *The Critic* called it "The Literary Cult of the Child" (Edwards 1901, 167). It was an age when, second to novels, the best-selling books in England were written for children. With very inexpensive publishing of children's books, including penny fiction and penny dreadfuls, Cassell and Company alone sold nearly 30 million copies each year in the 1860s (Ellis 1963, 80). In 1870 when the Education Act was passed, 695 juvenile books were published (66). A total of 180,000 copies of *Alice in Wonderland* were sold during Lewis Carroll's lifetime (66). "The literary marketplace swelled with children's books," so claims an article about the Golden Age of children's illustrated books reports from figures published in the *Bookman*, adding that they were "second only to novels in book production" ("Golden Age" 2006, 111).

But the children were not the only age group that read fairy tales, and fairy tales did not speak to just children. The growing religious doubt brought on by Darwinism affected the narrative in children's books that "had to speak simultaneously to adult readers who were increasingly anxious, as they grew older, to recover their own childhood selves, lost in time, in the children about and to whom they were reading" (McGavran 1991, 9). The modern age, with its wars wrought by divergent cultures and *Weltanschauungs*, cultivated literature that drew adults into escapism. Peter Coveney, in his *The Image of Childhood* (1967), was critical of Lewis Carroll (creator of Alice, 1865) and J. M. Barrie (creator of Peter Pan, 1902) for depicting childhood as

> an habitual means of escape, a way of withdrawal from spiritual and emotional confusion in a tired culture. In an age when it became increasingly difficult to grow up, to find valid bearings in an adult world, the temptation seems to have been for certain authors to take the line of least emotional resistance, and to regress, quite literally, into a world of fantasy and nostalgia for childhood. (1967, 32)

At nearly the same time, George Boas attacked the "cult of childhood" inherited from the Victorian period and deemed its ideology as anti-intellectualism and counterproductive for the modern age (1966, 11).

With the increase in literacy and childhood reading, even if not all Disney animations are based on fairy tales, they "function" as if they are because they offer "archetypal characters" and weave stories "which abound with themes of life, death, good versus evil, and the elevation of ideas such as devotion, loyalty, kindness, friendship, family, honesty, patience, tenacity, and the value of hard work" (Davis 2013, 7). Besides, Jack Zipes states that our current knowledge of fairy tales is flawed; the stories we know are not those penned by their originators and not those that reflect the culture and time in which they were written (1995, 21). Most twenty-first-century people are familiar with only those fairy tales filtered and reconstructed by Disney engineers. Furthermore, the Magic Kingdom built through computer-generated imagery makes it seem that animals and inanimate objects can really talk and sing. Magic happens on the screen and is more credible when technology portrays the Mouse King as a giant creature made of thousands of mice in Disney's *Nutcracker and the Four Realms* (2018). When one used to watch the ballet of Tchaikovsky's masterpiece and relied upon one's imagination and reasoning to figure out Clara's fantasy from E. T. A. Hoffman's short story (1816), Disney has, as if by magic, turned fantasy into reality, albeit a delightful, beautiful, and often terrifying phenomenon.

Of primary concern in *Neo-Disneyism* is what the more current Disney media are teaching today for, as Garlen and Sandlin put it, "a corporate, mouse-eared lens shapes the ways children understand the significant moments of their lives and make sense of the world around them" (39).[1] Although Disney's "clumsy depictions of racial stereotypes" (Byrne and McQuillan 97) have been detrimental to the acculturation of children who are to be progenitors and conservators of world peace, the contributors to this volume of essays have found affirming representations of people who were regarded as subalterns in Disney movies prior to the twenty-first century. Johnson Cheu also commends Disney for becoming more multicultural in its films, adducing Russell in *Up* (2009) as Asian American,[2] Tiana in *The Princess and the Frog* (2009) as the first African American princess, Buzz Lightyear in *Toy Story 3* (2010) as speaking with a Spanish accent, and Ken as being "ambiguously gay" in the same film (2013, 1–2). Because of Disney's prolific influence, we introduce *Neo-Disneyism* into the aesthetic movement in academe that revisits earlier cultures through contemporary lens, after the debut of neo-Victorianism.[3] Ours identifies a new Disney that is more inclusive, tolerant, and celebratory of the Other.[4] The Disney machine is manufacturing more positive messages that some scholars refer to as "colorblind."[5] A social and legal concept, colorblindness is the rejection of racial classification, a refusal to consider skin color in one's perception and treatment of others. It is a controversial term, extolled by some and argued by others that we have not reached the point of universal affirmative action, that there are plenty of groups based on gender, race, sexuality, creed, nationality, and ethnicity, both BIPOC and LGBTQ2+,[6] that are still underrepresented with equal opportunities with regard to education and employment.

Many Disney films since the 1990s tell children that race does not matter. Instead of being "colorblind," I would say that Disney's world is more colorful than ever before and what makes Disney entertainment more of a neo-ism is that it celebrates color in all its shades with regard to race, ethnicity, and gender. However, Sarah E. Turner, in her *The Colorblind Screen: Television in Post-Racial America*, would not concur as she discusses the Disney Channel's long-running *The Suite Life of Zack and Cody* (2005–8) and its spin-off, *The Suite Life on Deck* (2008–11). The latter drew 5.7 million viewers (Levin 2008) and was television's number one series for ages 6–11 as well as 9–14 in Canada, America, and the United Kingdom ("Disney Channel" 2008). Brenda Song, who is half Hmong Chinese and half Thai American, plays a wealthy teenager. Her character deliberately avoids the "stereotype of the cerebral and hardworking Asian," observes Turner; however, because she portrays a "wealthy, spoiled, and vacuous" and not very bright female (who needed 14 years to learn the American alphabet), Turner is uneasy about this depiction because the teen is "one of the only Asian actors on the Disney Channel," and her portrayal may lead viewers to think that she is a model for all Asians (2014, 241–42). To presume this is to also presume that we—especially children—are innately inclined to stereotype and that we deduce hasty generalizations based upon minimal exposure to information. I do believe that children enter this world with *tabula rasa* and that both acceptance and discrimination are taught. Children are very susceptible to believe what they are told and learn from television, but I am not convinced that they always pick up on physical differences between people and automatically discriminate against entire groups of people based on differences. I doubt that children assume that people just like themselves are superior to others.

In November 2019, Disney launched a streaming service, Disney+, which attracted over 10 million subscribers on the first day (Nunan, 2020, n.p.) and 73 million in the first year, and as of March 2021, over 100 million subscribers ("Fortune 500: Walt Disney," 2021). In 2020 Disney Media and Entertainment Distribution was formed, one of Disney's five major business groups. It now includes streaming services of Disney+, Hotstar that streams in India and Southeast Asia, Star+ that streams in Latin America, and other direct-to-consumer services. The mission of The Walt Disney Company, as stated at its website, is "to entertain, inform and inspire people around the globe through the power of unparalleled storytelling, reflecting the iconic brands, creative minds and innovative technologies that make ours *the world's premier entertainment company*" (2022; emphasis added).

The Walt Disney Company acknowledges and accepts its responsibility to positively influence its audience. Its website offers "Stories Matter, with this statement: "Stories shape how we see ourselves and everyone around us. So as storytellers, we have the power and responsibility to not only uplift and inspire, but also consciously, purposefully and relentlessly champion *the spectrum of voices and perspectives in our world*" (2022; emphasis added). Disney declares that "as part of our ongoing commitment to diversity and inclusion, we are in the process of reviewing our library and adding advisories to content that includes negative depictions or mistreatment of people or cultures" (2022). The company will not erase the products but will continue to provide them but with advisory notices. One example is the "racist caricature of East Asian peoples" perpetrated by a cat in *Aristocrats* (1970). Another is the crows in *Dumbo* (1941), who are caricatures of the black-face minstrel shows that "ridiculed enslaved Africans on Southern plantations" ("Stories Matter," n.p.). The stereotypes of Native Americans in Disney's *Peter Pan* (1953) and of Asian and Middle Eastern peoples in *Swiss Family Robinson* (1960) are also noted. An advisory council has been formed to oversee "cultural competency" in Disney's self-policing commitment to promote inclusivity.

How effective has Disney been in achieving these goals? This is the question that the contributors to this collection explore, beginning with a chapter ("Neo-Victorianism and Neo-Disneyism") written by coeditor Brenda Ayres that explains why this volume bears the title that it does and then investigates the neo-Victorianism in two renditions of *Lady and the Tramp* (1955 and 2019), identifying the positive and negative Disney borrowings from the nineteenth century that inspire children to participate in the world as peacemakers. Ann Heilmann and Mark Llewellyn have provided the seminal definition of neo-Victorianism; in their *Neo-Victorianism: The Victorians in the Twenty-First Century, 1999–2009*, the two scholars view neo-Victorian literature to be more than historical fiction. They encompass texts ("literary, filmic, audio/visual") that *self-consciously engage with the act of (re)interpretation, (re)discovery and (re)vision concerning the Victorians*" (2010, 4; emphasis in original). They have observed that contemporary works that are "re-reading and re-writing" the "Victorian experience" are more about critiquing the current culture as much if not more than critiquing nineteenth-century culture (4). Concurrently, neo-Victorianists often reinterpret and reinvent the nineteenth century through a corrective, twenty-first-century lens. Disney's nostalgia for the nineteenth century is well known; the man—and after his demise, his company—often resisted the changing moral climate of the modern world with preference to the values of the Victorians,[7] which is why Disney's neo-Victorianism is apropos to an examination of its influence on his film animation with its reconstructing values from the "good ole days."

In Chapter 2, "Transmedial Paratexts and Ideology in Disney's *Brave*, *Pocahontas*, and *Mulan*," Amala Charulatha applauds recent Disney films for their overt attempts to expand inclusivity in their portrayal of ideal beauty and womanhood, but their efforts are being severely undermined through merchandising dolls and other products derived from Disney's princesses in *Beauty and the Beast* (1991), *Pocahontas* (1995), *Mulan* (1998), *The Princess and the Frog*, and *Brave* (2012). These toy females have been designed to reflect old stereotypes that are misleading representations as to what children should regard as models of beauty and heroism. Disney heroines have been "portrayed as weak, pristine, and incapable of independent action" (Wasko 2016, 13). Marcia Lieberman argues that most of the princesses and heroines in fairy tales are portrayed as being beautiful but passive and self-sacrificial, even if they do have some active roles in the story (1972, 389). As "training manuals for girls," the stories define "femininity" as passive, and if the woman behaves in such a manner, she will be rewarded (395). Charulatha sees these images as being counterproductive to Disney's mission to give positive representation to females of diverse physiques, personalities, and cultures.

Besides merchandising, another vehicle that markets Disney's ideology are the Disney parks, resorts, and restaurants. Ayres' Chapter 3, "Imagineered Neo-Victorian American Real Estate: 'A clean, unspoiled spot,'" studies

Disney's nostalgia for the past as demonstrated in the construction of Main Street, U.S.A. with its multiple neo-Victorian-style buildings and establishments throughout the theme parks around the world. She identifies and analyzes the nostalgia for an ideal nineteenth century that proliferates through Disney's multi-billion-dollar enterprise of recreation; however, the chapter also notices an evolution and notes changes that have been made to reinvent the past to be more inclusive than it was once exhibited by Disney.

Michelle Chan, however, is dismayed that Disney fairy tales still lack color in their magic and beauty. Chapter 4, "Reiteration of Fairy Tales in the Twenty-First Century for a Global Market," suggests that Disney has been insistently and intentionally producing non-White animations, ranging from *The Princess and the Frog* and *Moana* (both 2016), and *Coco* (2017) to *Raya and the Last Dragon* (2021) as well as *Encanto* (2021). It is apparent that Disney does this for the global market, but the inclusion of non-White animations does reshape the ecology of fairy tales, a model of aspiration that is now seeking global recognition in the twenty-first century. Chan explores how the consolidated Disney that has become the defining authority of "fairy tales" has formulated a historically new set of diversified clichés while conducting pseudo-decolonization in their productions.

One of the major attacks upon Disney has been its disparaging stereotypes of Asians. Although gruffly repudiating any responsibility toward political complicity, in an interview for *Time*, Disney made the now oft-quoted remark: "We just try to make a good picture. And then the professors come along and tell us what we do" (1937). Regardless, Kimiko Akita and Rick Kenney have made this observation: "The equation of villain with Asian reinforces Western fear of and attempted dominance over the Other and potentially raises nationalistic levels of xenophobia and its consequences" (2013, 62). Many viewers have been scathing in their criticism of Disney's most recent revision of *Mulan* (2020). Sheng-mei Ma's Chapter 5, "Eastern Witch from the West: Xianniang in Niki Caro's *Mulan*," addresses these critical barbs, identifying the stereotypes and inaccuracies of Chinese history, literature, and culture in Caro's live-action film. Beginning with the "witch," named Hawk by film critics or Xianniang (Immortal Woman) in closed captioning, Ma criticizes her as a twenty-first-century "walk-on (fly-in?)" entirely absent in the genesis of the fifth-century "The Ballad of Mulan."

Nor does Xianniang exist in any previous reincarnations in the Chinese and English language, including Maxine Hong Kingston's ethnic classic *The Woman Warrior* (1975) or Disney's previous animation of *Mulan* (1998). Ma considers the character a Western wolf in Eastern sheep's clothing and questions the accuracy with which viewers can perceive a Chinese legend when they witness Hawk's power that possesses and zombifies victims.

Taylor Tomko is, too, critical of Disney's representations of Asians in Chapter 6, "The Hybrid Alice: Framing the Imperial Gothic in Tim Burton's *Alice's Adventures in Wonderland*"; however, her focus turns more to the neo-Gothicism in Burton's appropriation (2010) of Lewis Carroll's original text (1865). Unlike the horror caused by this "hybrid self" in the typical imperial Gothic, Alice's hybridity is a tool of political mobility that fashions an ostensibly anti-colonial storyline that is ultimately conscripted back into the imperialist narrative by her venture to China at the close of the film.

Korine Powers, in Chapter 7, "Peter Pan After the Blitz: Finding What Remains in *Return to Never Land*," likewise questions what the neo-Disney take is on the depiction of people of color. Nearly 50 years after *Peter Pan* (1953) debuted, Disney revised its animated past in *Return to Never Land* (2002), the third of Disney's animated sequels—following *Rescuers Down Under* (1990) and *Fantasia 2000* (1999)—fraught with post-9/11 anxieties in its restoration of traditional values. *Return to Never Land* is an attempt to repair violent trauma by asking its audience to believe in traditional "Disney magic" revised for the new millennium. Powers points out how these revisions often attempt to sidestep controversy by removing the bodies of people of color, a strategy that Disney has previously employed to reasonable success in its theme park adaptations of films like *Song of the South* (1946) and *Pocahontas* or making room for a "Lost Girl" among the adolescent masculine space of the "Lost Boys." In doing so, *Return to Never Land* presents an emptier world that leaves some World War II–sized scars across Never Land's surface.

The dominant theme in most Disney scholarship has been focused on the portrayal/betrayal of the womanly ideal, but outside of criticizing stereotypical, nameless (Davis 156), and "cardboard"-type princes (Cashdan 1999, 28), very few observations have been made about the recent efforts of Disney to complicate and authentic diverse characteristics of males. Chapter 8, "Neo-Disney's Reconstruction of Masculinities," cowritten by coeditors Maier and Ayres, explores the neo-Disney male, opening with an overview of gender misrepresentation in earlier films. Maier compares the 1937 Prince Charming in *Snow White* with Kit in Kenneth Branagh's live-action *Cinderella* (2015) and analyzes the realism of Kit as well as the equality between Ella and her prince, with both characters having full lives and backstories. The story was not just about a woman's waiting for her prince to rescue her. Her approach to the recent live-action remake of *Mulan* (2020) identifies the masculinity within the female as Hua Mulan becomes Hua Jun and discusses the breakdown of gender boundaries in the neo-Disney version. A similar break and demonstration of fluidity of gender are evident in *Brave*. Maier sees the depiction of Merida as a strong woman and challenges Disney to create men who are able to "keep up" with such women and to create new films that offer "alternate non-gender experiences."

In that same chapter, Ayres examines *Moana*, *Coco*, and *Encanto* in their refreshing, realistic depiction, both males and females. In the first film, for example, instead of being rescued by a male, Moana rescues Maui, the Polynesian demigod, and she releases her island from a curse. She does not end up marrying Maui or even needing him in her future calling to be the chief of her island. Nevertheless, Maui is an individual unto himself, with a strong personality and cultural identity that offers a unique, ethnic-specific image. As for *Coco*, although named for a matriarch in a large Latino family, the film is about three men: Miguel, the 12-year-old great, great grandson who defies the family by playing music which is forbidden. In the Land of the Dead, he searches for his father who, he mistakenly assumes, is Ernesto de la Cruz, "the most famous singer in Mexico" (00:05:15). He learns that his true father, Héctor, who wrote most of the music that made de la Cruz famous, is also a true hero, for he died for the sake of his family. As in *Moana*, the male characters are unique, and they are appropriate renditions of their ethnic identities. So are the characters in *Encanto*, with the hero being the outcast, the not-so-handsome, the quirky uncle Bruno. Both Bruno and Mirabel are family and community underdogs whose personalities and mental challenges resonate for viewers who identify with their "anti-heroic" natures but whose heroic actions save both the family and the community.

Both Ayres and Maier are optimistic and complimentary of the most recent neo-Disney films in their efforts to counter discrimination against ethnicities, gender, and mentally challenged peoples. Lin-Manuel Miranda's song "We Don't Talk About Bruno" became a No. 1 Billboard sensation because now is the time that people want and need to talk about Bruno.

In Chapter 9, "Disney's New Dance at the Ball: *Beauty and the Beast* and Bowing to Difference," Ayres compares the 1991 and 2017 versions of Disney's remake of a classic fairy tale, *Beauty and the Beast*. Her chapter locates myriad changes in the latter that embody a twenty-first-century reimaging of multiculturalism and gender. The earlier version certainly treated Belle, her father, and the Beast as the Other; they and the film's characters represented only a White, Americanized, heterosexual version of normalization, with the traditional paradigm of a plot that culminates in a heterosexual union between a man and a woman, rewarded with the promise of getting to live happily ever after. Ayres makes clear that the more recent, live-action version portrays people, not necessarily in a historically realistic manner for the film's setting, but realistic nonetheless in its myriad races, ethnicity, ages, religions, and genders. Although the basic plot might be the same, the twenty-first-century reconstruction emphasizes inclusivity, acceptance of those who are different, relationships with people not according to their physical appearance but to their interiority and behavior, and avoidance of the reduction and prescription of ethnic, class, religious, and gender identities.

Another affirming review of neo-Disney is in Chapter 10, " 'You must go on': The Neo-Disney Female and Her Mental Health," by Elaine Morton, which examines recent films that encourage well-being for women in ways that were lacking in earlier films. Besides more positive portrayals of females, Morton's chapter highlights the use of music and its lyrics to teach, especially young people, attitudes meant to promote good mental health. One example is in *Frozen II* (2019) when, destitute in her darkest hour, Anna sings, "You must go on / And do the next right thing" in order to motivate herself to persevere through challenges to free the people of the Enchanted Forest and destroy the dam. Morton analyzes the therapeutic modifiers in Disney in *Frozen* (2013), *Inside Out* (2015), *Zooptia* (2016), *Moana*, *Frozen II*, *Raya and the Last Dragon*, and *Encanto*.

Dalila Forni is interested in the evolution of Disney's animated villains. She has observed that, among those characters who deconstruct gender norms in Disney films, villains are the most powerful and intriguing figures who go beyond gender norms and sometimes reinterpret gender canons through a queer or nonbinary approach to be fluid or noncanonical. Chapter 11, "New Gendered Representations in Contemporary Disney-Pixar Villains," investigates the representations of Disney villains through a gender-sensitive approach to understand if their depiction is currently subject to change. The chapter offers an overview of recurrent trends focusing on a selection of antagonists in animated films produced between 2000 and 2020, for instance: *The Incredibles* (2004), *The Princess and the Frog*, *Tangled* (2010), *Brave*, *Frozen*, *Zootopia*, and *Coco*. Forni considers both physical and psychological features related to gender and literary canons, comparing villains' evolution to heroes and heroines' transformations to explore how positive and negative figures are perceived in relation to their gender and to gender experimentation.

A long-time *femme fatale* has been Maleficent. From its earliest inceptions as *La Belle au bois dormant* or *Dornröschen* and its inclusions in the fourteenth-century narrative *Perceforest*, Giambattista Basile's *The Pentamerone* (1634) and Charles Perrault's *Histoires ou contes du temps passé* (1697), there has long been interest in the beatified beloved—the sleeping princess—but very little has been thought of her supposed nemesis, the dark enchantress. Disney's 1959 adaptation of the Perrault tale centers upon a heteronormative love story between Aurora and Prince Phillip who seeks to free her from her spell with his sword of virtue. The patriarchal conventions are clear; a young virginal woman can only be saved by a young virile man of princely virtues. Chapter 12, "Maleficent's Rage," by coeditor Sarah E. Maier, engages feminist theorizing in relation to the new adaptations of Disney's *Maleficent* (2014) and *Maleficent: Mistress of Evil* (2019) to ask a simple question: Why is Maleficent so angry? The identity of Maleficent and her clear justification of her rage are suitably considered in the age of #MeToo. In these filmic adaptations, the narratives are focalized through the herstory of Maleficent who is a less evil enchantress and more dark fairy, who is—at the same time—a nurturing, fiercely protective maternal being matriarch who transgresses the entire patriarchal tradition of both the story's history and Disney's long-standing adoration of conventional storytelling. The humanity embodied in the posthuman casting of Maleficent's magnificence is in relation to the ethical depravity of the male-centered kingdom, the irresponsibility of the "good" fairy triumvirate and the exposure of the one true love as a mother's love reiterate the new narrative's embodiment of the insight of a natural woman/woman of nature, the power of environment versus biology, and the reclaiming of aggression from the passivity of the past.

Mothers certainly are supposed to be anything but villains to their children, but this is not the case in the 50th Disney animated feature film *Tangled*. In Chapter 13, "Beyond Perfection: Inclusion and Self-Exploration of Neo-Disney 'Beauties,' 'Beasts,' and 'Monsters,'" Rritwika Roychowdhury exposes layers of sociocultural underpinnings and deconstructing the character of Mother Gothel and Rapunzel. By applying Louis Pierre Althusser's theory of ideological state apparatuses, Roychowdhury demonstrates how family can manipulate children's minds to make them believe something that satisfies others' selfish desires instead of what is in the best interest of the child. Mother Gothel's liberal dosage of "ruler ideology" establishes a hierarchy within their relationship, insisting that "Mother knows best," which is a traditional, heterosexual ideology, but what happens when Mother is manipulative, cunning, and villainous? Rapunzel depicts a doubly colonized state; she is oppressed and exploited by another female and made to feel suffocated till she finds her way out of the captivity.

The volume concludes with an epilogue titled "Disney's Multifaceted Rainbow World" by Sarah E. Maier that commends Disney for its progress in representing multiple ethnicities, nationalities, genders, and individuals who might not be generally construed as either heroic or noble like Disney's traditional princes and princesses. She also describes further scholarship that can and should be done on Disney beyond what has been offered in *Neo-Disneyism*. In addition, Maier suggests ways that Disney still has work to do to be inclusive and accomplish its stated mission. After all, Walt Disney himself once said, "We share, to a large extent, one another's fate. We help create those circumstances which favor or challenge us in meeting our objectives and realizing our dreams" (quoted in Williams and Denney 2004, 107). That the world can enjoy the fate of hope and peace, that its people can dream and realize their dreams, that magic can create a better world for us all—this is all possible only if we people learn to get along with each other; respect, tolerate, and even champion differences to allow the pixie dust to free us all to be the individuals we were created to be.

Bibliography

Akita, Kimiko, and Rick Kenney. "A 'Vexing Implication': Siamese Cats and Orientalist Mischief-Making." In *Diversity in Disney Films: Critical Essays on Race, Ethnicity, Gender, Sexuality and Disability*, edited by Johnson Cheu, 50–66. Jefferson, NC: McFarland and Company, 2013.

Allan, Robin. *Walt Disney and Europe*. Bloomington: Indiana University Press, 1999.

Ayres, Brenda, ed. *The Emperor's Old Groove: Decolonizing Disney's Magic Kingdom*. New York: Peter Lang, 2003.

Ayres, Brenda, and Sarah E. Maier, eds. *Neo-Gothic Narratives: Illusory Allusions from the Past*. London: Anthem Press, 2020a.

———. *Neo-Victorian Madness: Rediagnosing Nineteenth-Century Mental Illness in Literature and Other Media*. London: Palgrave Macmillan, 2020b.

———. *Neo-Victorian Things: Reimagining Nineteenth-Century Material Culture*. London: Routledge, 2022a.

———. *The Palgrave Handbook of Neo-Victorianism*. London: Palgrave Macmillan, 2022b.

Boas, George. *The Cult of Childhood*. Dallas: Spring Publications, 1966.

Boym, Svetlana. *The Future of Nostalgia*. New York: Basic Books, 2001.

Brode, Douglas. *From Walt to Woodstock: How Disney Created the Counterculture*. Austin: University of Texas Press, 2004.

Brode, Douglas, and Shea T. Brode, eds. *Debating Disney: Pedagogical Perspectives on Commercial Cinema*. Lanham, MD: Rowman and Littlefield, 2016.

Brooker, Keith M. *Disney, Pixar, and the Hidden Messages of Children's Films*. Santa Barbara, CA: Praeger, 2010.

Byrne, Eleanor, and Martin McQuillan. *Deconstructing Disney*. London: Pluto Press, 1999.

Cashdan, Sheldon. *The Witch Must Die: The Hidden Meaning of Fairy Tales*. New York: Basic Books, 1999.

Chávez, Christopher. "Disney XD: Boyhood and the Racial Politics of Market Segmentation." In *From Networks to Netflix: A Guide to Changing Channels*, edited by Derek Johnson, 209–18. Oxon: Routledge, 2018.

Cheu, Johnson. Introduction: "Re-casting and Diversifying Disney in the Age of Globalization." In *Diversity in Disney Films: Critical Essays in Race, Ethnicity, Gender, Sexuality and Disability*, edited by Johnson Cheu, 1–8. Jefferson, NC: McFarland, 2013.

Coveney, Peter. *The Image of Childhood: The Individual and Society: A Study of the Theme in English Literature*. Middlesex: Penguin, 1967.

Davis, Amy M. *Handsome Heroes and Vile Villains: Men in Disney's Feature Animation*. Bloomington: University of Indiana Press.

"Disney Channel/Disney Channel.com Highlights for 2008." *PR-Inside*, December 24, 2008. <https://www.pr-inside.com/disney-channel-disneychannel-com-highlights-r992914.htm>.

Dundes, Lauren. *The Psychosocial Implications of Disney Movies*. Basel: MDPI, 2019.

Dunn, David. "Why Disney's Success Is a Growing Concern After *Star Wars* Acquisition." April 30, 2020. <https://filmdaily.co/obsessions/disneys-success-concern-for-film-industry/>.

Edwards, Louise Betts. "The Literary Cult of the Child." *The Critic* 29, no. 2 (August 1901): 99–192. <https://books.google.com/books?id=NXRBAAAAYAAJ>.

Eisner, Michael D. "Planetized Entertainment." *New Perspectives Quarterly* 12, no. 4 (Fall 1995): 8–10. <https://search.ebscohost.com/login.aspx?direct=true&db=ofm&AN=503360746&site=ehost-live&scope=site>.

Ellis, Alec. *A History of Children's Reading and Literature*. Oxford: Pergamon, 1963.

"Fortune 500: Walt Disney." *Fortune 500*, August 2, 2021. <https://fortune.com/company/disney/fortune500/>.

Garlen, Julie C., and Jennifer A. Sandlin. Introduction: "Popular Culture and Disney Pedagogies." In *Teaching with* Disney, 1–24. New York: Peter Lang, 2016.

Giroux, Henry A., and Grace Pollock. *The Mouse that Roared: Disney and the End of Innocence*. Lanham, MD: Rowman and Littlefield Publishers, 2010.

"Golden Age of Children's Illustrated Books." *Children's Literature Review* 113 (2006): 93–156. GALE|VZZIZT149034816.

Graves, Sherryl Browne. "Television and Prejudice Reduction: When Does Television as a Vicarious Experience Make a Difference?" *Journal of Social Issues* 55, no. 4 (1999): 707–25. doi:1.1111/0022-4537.00143.

Hegel, Georg Wilhelm Friedrich. *Phenomenology of Spirit*. 1807. Translated by A. V. Miller. Delhi: Motilal Banarsidass Publishers, 1988.

Heilmann, Ann, and Mark Llewellyn. *Neo-Victorianism: The Victorians in the Twenty-First Century, 1999–2009*. Basingstoke: Palgrave Macmillan, 2010.

Iger, Robert. The Walt Disney Company Fiscal Year 2014 Annual Financial Report and Shareholder Letter. Anaheim, CA: The Walt Disney Company, 2014. <http://thewaltdisneycompany.com/sites/default/files/reports/10k-wrap-2014_1.pdf>.

"It's a Small World." Composed by Robert B. Sherman and Richard Sherman. 1964.

King, Richard C., Carmen R. Lugo-Lugo, and Mary K. Bloodsworth-Lugo. *Animating Difference: Race, Gender, and Sexuality in Contemporary Films for Children*. Lanham, MD: Rowman and Littlefield Publishers, 2010.

Kunzle, David. Introduction to *How to Read Donald Duck: Imperialistic Ideology in the Disney Comic* by Ariel Dorman and Armand Mattlelart, 11–21. New York: International General, 1984.

Leaper, Campbell, Lisa Breed, Lauri Hoffman, and Carly Ann Perlman. "Variations in the Gender-Stereotyped Content of Children's Television Cartoons Across Genres." *Journal Applied Social Psychology* 32 (2006): 1653–62. doi:1.1111/j.1559-1816.2002.tb02767.x.

Levin, Gary. "Nielsens: Presidential Debate Fights for Numbers." *USA Today*, September 30, 2008. <https://usatoday30.usatoday.com/life/television/news/2008-09-30-nielsens-analysis_N.htm>.

Lieberman, Marcia R. "'Some Day My Prince Will Come': Female Acculturation Through the Fairy Tale." *College English* 34, no. 3 (December 1972): 383–95.

Li-Vollmer, Meredith, and Mark. E. LaPoint. "Gender Transgression and Villainy in Animated Films." *Popular Communication* 1 (2003): 89–109. doi.1.1207/S15405710PV0102_2.

McGavran, James Holt. *Romanticism and Children's Literature in Nineteenth-Century England*. Athens: University of Georgia Press, 1991.

Morris, Jill Anne. "Disney's Influence on the Modern Theme Park and the Codification of Colorblind Racism in the American Amusement Industry." In *Performance and the Disney Theme Park Experience: The Tourist as Actor*, edited by Jennifer A. Kokay and Tom Robson, 213–28. Cham: Palgrave Macmillan, 2019.

Müller-Hartmann, Andreas. "Is Disney Safe for Kids?—Subtexts in Walt Disney's Animated Films." *Amerikastudien/American Studies* 52, no. 3 (2007): 399–415.

Nelson, Claudia. *Precocious Children and Childish Adults: Age Inversion in Victorian Literature*. Baltimore, MD: The Johns Hopkins University Press, 2012.

Nunan, Tom. "5 Reasons Why Disney+ Is Breaking Records While Making History." *For bes* (August 5, 2020): n.p. <https://www.forbes.com/sites/tomnunan/2020/08/05/5-reasons-why-disney-plus-is-breaking-records-while-making-history/?sh=46621e6e2935>.

Report of the Commissioner of Education for the Year Ended June 30, 1911. Vol. 2. United States Bureau of Education. Washington: Government Printing Office, 1912. <https://books.google.com/books?id=O1U6AQAAMAAJ>.

Schaffer, Scott. "The Past, as Product in the Present: Disney and the Imagineering of Histories." In Brode and Brode 2016, 33–42.

Schickel, Richard. *The Disney Version: The Life, Times, Art and Commerce of Walt Disney*. New York: Simon and Schuster, 1968.

Singer, A. L. *Disney's "Beauty and the Beast."* Livonia, MI: Seedlings, 2017.

Spivak, Gayatri Chakravorty. *An Aesthetic Education in the Era of Globalization*. Cambridge, MA: Harvard University Press, 2012.

"Stories Matter." *The Walt Disney Company*. n.d. <https://storiesmatter.thewaltdisneycompany.com/>.

Towbin, Mia A. et al. "Images of Gender, Race, Age, and Sexual Orientation in Disney Feature-Length Animated Films." *Journal of Feminist Family Therapy* 15, no. 4 (2004): 19–44. doi:10.1300/j086v15n04_02.

Turner, Sarah E. "BBFFs: Interracial Friendships in a Post-Racial World." In *The Colorblind Screen: Television in Post-Racial America*, edited by Sarah Nilsen and Sarah E. Turner, 237–58. New York: New York University Press, 2014. <https://www.jstor.org/stable/j.ctt9qg55f>.

———. "Blackness, Bayous and Bumbo: Encoding and Decoding Race in a Colorblind World." In *Diversity in Disney Films: Critical Essays on Race, Ethnicity, Gender, Sexuality and Disability*, edited by Johnson Cheu, 83–98. Jefferson, NC: McFarland, 2013.

Wasko, Janet. "Challenging Disney Myths." In Brode and Brode 2016, 1–18.

———. "Is It a Small World, After All?" In *Dazzled by Disney? The Global Audience Project*, edited by Janet Wasko, Mark Phillips, and Eileen R. Meehan, 3–28. London: Leicester University Press, 2001.

"We Don't Talk About Bruno." Written by Lin-Manuel Miranda for *Encanto*. 2022.

Williams, Pat, and James Denney. *How to Be Like Walt: Capturing the Disney Magic Every Day of Your Life*. Deerfield Beach, FL: Health Communications, 2004.

Zornado, Joseph. *Disney and the Dialectic of Desire: Fantasy as Social Practice*. Cham: Palgrave, 2017.

BRENDA AYRES

1 Neo-Victorianism and Neo-Disneyism

If Peter Widdowson were invited to discuss Disney's appropriation of the Victorian in Disney's theme parks and films, he would probably label it "re-visionary fiction" (2006, 491), but I am calling it neo-Disneyism, following the academic and aesthetic trend of current neo-isms to characterize a regeneration of the past in art but infused with contemporary sensibilities that offer greater representation of diversity of cultures and complexities. Widdowson has argued that the Disney machine is not interested in "destroying myths and illusions about the past" but rather in "using fiction as history to explore how the scars of the past persist into the present, how the past's presence in the present determines the nature of that present." If not that, Disney may be "in fact making displaced and oblique comment on [its] own present by ironically counterpointing it with the past" (492). Widdowson does not discuss Disney, but he does offer an explanation that can be applied to the Disney Company's reproduction of Victoriana and its playing footloose and fancy free with historical accuracy. An example revision of history is Disney's versions of *The Beauty and the Beast* (1991 and 2017). In the mid-eighteenth-century ball scenes, everyone wears attire appropriate to the elaborate style of Rococo except Belle. Her gowns are Victorian with their décolletages, tight waists, and bouffant skirts in bell shape made full by crinoline or hoops. The 2017 Belle should be wearing gloves, either opera length or matinee. The coiffure of both Belles is modern; no eighteenth- or nineteenth-century woman would have appeared at a ball with her hair down when loose hair indicated a loose woman or prostitute.[1] Neither was it common for Black and Asian women to dance at the same balls with Caucasians. Since the themes of Disney's *Beauty and the Beast* are neo-Victorian (discussed in a later chapter) and not eighteenth century, then the Victorian gown combined with a modern hairdo reinforces their animus, but again, is not historically true. Disney has never been overly concerned with historical accuracy. The Disney mission has been "to portray life in places it depicts in its products to convey what America either was like or should have been, regardless of the historical specificity of the situation" (Schaffer 2016, 34). When *Squanto: A Warrior's Tale* (1994) was released, the *Globe* pointed out the films' license with history, concluding, "History is written by the winners, and you can't get much more victorious than Daddy Disney."[2] "Time and again," Scott Schaffer argues, Disney "reconstitutes [history] as the company's own, selling [it] as markers of American political, cultural, and imperial attitudes" (33).

Another aspect of Victoriana important to note about Disney's enterprises, Robin Allan points out that anthropomorphized animals originated mostly with nineteenth-century artists. Wilhelm Busch, for one, created the "mar-peace, or troublemaker … the dangerously vital, untrained, 'uncultivated' child, animal or rebel who challenges and ridicules the established order and the morality precarious constructed to sanctify it and uphold it."[3] "Mar" or *Mär* in German is the same as the English, but the phrase is unusual for English; it means someone or something that disturbs, disrupts, or impairs, so a "mar-peace" would be someone that disturbs the peace. Busch's cartoons from the nineteenth century inspired Disney to create Mickey Mouse and Donald Duck (Allan 1999, 18). Allan also lists Honoré Daumier (1808–79); Gustave Doré (1832–83); Jean-Ignace-Isadore Gérard (1803–47); John Tenniel (1820–1940), who illustrated Lewis Carroll's *Alice's Adventures in Wonderland* (1865) and *Through the Looking-Glass, and What Alice Found There* (1871); Edward Lear (1812–88); and Ladislaw Starevicz (1882–1965) as additional nineteenth-century artists who caricaturized people as animals.

Disney products were and are not so devoted to providing a counterpoint to the past, but *Lady and the Tramp* (2019) is ostensibly neo-Victorian in its reinvention of what the nineteenth century should or could have been like instead of what it actually was. The most flagrant illustration is that Darling is a Black woman married to Jim Dear who is White. The 1955

Lady, however, was like many other films that appropriated Victoriana with nostalgia, and both versions are examples of Disney Neo-Victorianism.

Cora Kaplan termed this emendation of Victorian as "Victoriana," defining it as the "self-conscious rewriting of historical narratives to highlight the suppressed histories of gender and sexuality, race and empire, as well as challenges to the conventional understandings of the historical itself" (2007, 3). To Ann Heilmann and Mark Llewellyn, neo-Victorianism is the production of texts ("literary, filmic, audio/visual") that *self-consciously engage with the act of (re)interpretation, (re)discovery and (re)vision concerning the Victorians*" (2010, 4; emphasis in original).

Especially for Disney, the practice of reinventing the past in nostalgic efforts to restore values and idealized peace from former eras began during World War I and accelerated after World War II. Just prior to the formation of opposing alliances by the ruling powers in 1914, there was a backlash against Victorian culture and its values, an overthrow brought on by the Age of Decadence, first women's movement, *fin-de-siècle* literature, death of Victoria, and reign of Edward VII that seemed to undermine Victorian morals and decorum at every turn. These historical events, coupled with the rise of socialism, communism, fascism, and discord in Ireland, India, and South Africa against British rule, undercut austerity and decorum, the pillars of Victorianism. Although maybe put too simplistically, the shot that killed Archduke Franz Ferdinand was the bullet that killed stability and peace throughout the world. The modern age experienced pandemic carnage and horror in two world wars and widespread suffering during the Great Depression.[4] Greatly shaken and fully expecting more devastation in the form of World War III, sure to be a nuclear war to end all wars along with civilization and the planet, the 1940s staggered into the 1950s, and many Westerners harked back to the Victorians with nostalgia, for, as Simon Joyce described it (2007), the majority of people were looking in their rearview mirrors and thought they were seeing a passing time of prosperity; positive advances in medicine, inventions, and scientific discoveries; and widespread well-being. Disney embodied this idealism in many of his films and theme parks.

So Dear to My Heart (1948) and *Ugly Duckling* (1939)

Disney's *So Dear to My Heart* was released in 1948 but is set at the previous turn of the century. It opens with an attic scene that zooms in on a Victorian scrapbook with a ribbon bookmark of 1903. The second page reads, "As the twig is bent so inclines the tree" (00:00:15). The third page is a Romantic scene of nature as the voice-over discusses "the small beginnings" that "shape our whole life" (00:00:13–20). As the theme song plays, the camera leads us in the scrapbook down a shady path where we see a one-room schoolhouse with a bell in a belfry (00:00:32–54). The next page is a snow-covered church with a steeple and cross on top and with two feathery birds happily singing in the foreground (00:01:02–22). As day turns into night, the church bleeds into the manger where Christ was born, and the steeple is now the beam from the star that leads the shepherds to Bethlehem (00:01:23–32). These premodern icons represent what is "dear to my heart"—to many Americans in 1948.

The plot is about the proverbial orphan (a stock character of Victorian literature), Jeremiah, who lives on a farm with his grandmother and uncle. The grandmother is played by Beulah Bond, readily recognizable as the ideal mother after her role as Ma Smith in *Mr. Smith Goes to Washington* (1939) and Mrs. Bailey in *It's a Wonderful Life* (1946). The uncle is played by everyone's uncle, Burl Ives, famous for singing ballads, folk songs, and songs for children.

In *So Dear to My Heart*, a mother sheep rejects her lamb because it has black wool, but Jeremiah adopts it and plans to show him at the Pike County Fair. The idea of appreciation and tolerance for someone who is different is a major theme for this film and one that is unusual for movies shown immediately after World War II. However, it reflects the same theme as Hans Christian Andersen's "The Ugly Duckling," first published in 1843, in *New Fairy Tales*. Disney produced a short of this story in *Silly Symphony* in 1939. As Mrs. Duck sits on her eggs, Mr. Duck paces like a human expectant father. When a flapper (baby swan) emerges from the egg, Mr. Duck apparently accuses Mrs. Duck of—to put it in the colloquial of the 1950s—being too friendly with the milkman (00:02:04–36).[5] Mrs. Duck and the ducklings reject the "ugly duckling." When he sees his reflection in the water, he recognizes how different he is from the other chicks and is disgusted with himself (00:03:55–4:09). Although a nest of bluebird chicks accept him, the mother kicks him out (00:04:41–5:24). It is only after a mother swan and her brood adopt him that he feels loved and accepted (00:06:48–8:38). Although swans do mate for life and the male shares in the protection and feeding of the offsprings, there is no father swan in the Disney short.

Neo-Disneyfied "Ugly Duckling" can be read in two ways: as a call for tolerance for those who are different, but more likely the postwar, twentieth-century message is Anita's song in the mid-1950 setting of *West Side Story*, "Stick to your own kind."[6] There was such a deliberate and ostensible effort by Hollywood and the American government to enforce conformity, as evident with McCarthyism. In many ways, the two decades that followed the wars in America were very neo-Victorian, a return to the values of the nineteenth century as if they would ensure peace and stability. This may have been the prominent ideology, too, because of the anticonformity urged by the Beat Generation of the 1950s and the counterculture movements of the 1960s, as well as the civil rights movement and the women's movement. More prevalent were movies that intentionally told women that Rosie the Riveter's time was over, and Rosie was needed back in the kitchen so that returning soldiers could have jobs and so that gender order could be restored. Just a few examples are Katharine Hepburn and Spencer Tracy in the 1942 *Woman of the Year* and in the 1949 *Adam's Rib*. Doris Day played in a number of films with Rock Hudson and Tony Randall, with a theme that a woman had no business being in business; she could be feminine and happy only after doffing her business suit for a shirtwaist dress and apron (when the shirtwaist came into vogue during the Edwardian period).

However, in *So Dear to My Heart*, the black sheep that does not receive fair treatment because of a superficial matter of color, and a young boy, who is not a part of a nuclear family, albeit a White boy, empathizes, accepts him, and endeavors to give him a home—actions that were counter to the treatment African Americans were receiving in the 1940s, including those who risked their lives in the wars.

In one segment, a wise, professorial owl sings, "It's Whatcha Do with Whatcha Got" with these lyrics: "It's what you do with what you got, / That pays off in the end," illustrated by a picture of David and Goliath from the Bible, pointing out what David could do "with a little old hunk of rock" (00:01:00–26). If at first you don't succeed and get knocked down, you got to get back up, the owl tells the lamb (00:01:35–2:10). The scrapbook turns another page to a picture of Joshua from the Bible: "Look how Joshua busted that wall down with a little old measly horn" (00:02:14). In 1948 referencing the Bible, Christianity, and the church was acceptable and expected, but to do so became unpopular by the beginning of the twenty-first century. The film is mostly unknown today.

Lady and the Tramp (1955)

In the background of the opening credits of the 1955 version of *Lady and the Tramp* are images of Victorian houses, a doghouse with gingerbread trim, a perambulator, an umbrella, and a train. They signal the significance of Victoriana in the movie, and not just its historical setting, but also the film's proclivity to perpetuate Victorian values of family with a hetero-sexual couple at its core, and along with it, the concept that "there's no place like home"—an ideology that will be woefully sung during the dog-pound scene by a crew of motley homeless dogs (00:53:54–54:37). The song "Home, Sweet Home!" was written by a New Yorker, John Howard Payne, who considered the song the "*ranz des vaches*" (Payne 1880, n.p.), meaning a melody that Swiss herdsmen sang or played on the alpenhorn to call cattle home. Payne heard a peasant woman singing a song similar to it in Italy (Payne; Harrison 1885, 108) and wrote down the notes and then wrote the lyrics. Afterward, English Sir Henry Bishop wrote its composition. The song was first performed in 1823 at the Covent Garden Theatre in Payne's opera titled *Clari: Or, the Maid of Milan* (Harrison 109). Ironically, Payne made very little money from it and continued to live in poverty and restlessly flitted from one European city to another, a man who could not afford a home, sweet home. He was not even given credit when it was published in London and sold more than 100,000 copies in the first year (107; Brainard 1885, 30–32). It became extremely popular during the American Civil War. In fact, one soldier wrote in a letter that at the Battle of Fredericksburg, a band of Yankees began to play and sing, "Home, Sweet Home!" and the Confederates joined in. "If it had not been for the officers," the letter writer said, "the war would have stopped that night and all the soldiers would have gone home" (quoted in Aubrecht 2009, n.p.).

Why does the film emphasize the value of home in a way it does in 1955 but not so much in 2019 when the song is omitted? Svetlana Boym defines "nostalgia" as *nostos* meaning "return home" and *algia*, as "longing" (2001, xiii), pointing out that one reason Victoriana became so popular in the 1950s was because of a nostalgic return to an idealized past during the post-war diaspora most demonstrated by the erection of the Berlin Wall (213–14). Kaplan describes this Victorian lingering a "cloying nostalgia" (6). The neo-Victorian adaptation of *Lady* then, in 1955 "retrieve[s] the certainties of the pre-modernist narrative and its attendant social structures" (Primorac 2018, 1), and in 2019, creates "critical rewriting and re-visioning" of the Victorian past to translate it "into a vocabulary understandable and relatable to contemporary audiences" (1).

After the credits and Donald Novis and the Disney Studio Chorus begin to sing "Peace on Earth," we see a village that appears to be in New England and staged to look like a Christmas card. At the center of the village is a single-steepled church; it signifies the centrality of religion in the nineteenth century (and in the 1950s), as if it is responsible for the peace enjoyed by the village (00:02:12). This message is further emphasized as the camera zooms in on the church that fills the frame, as a horse-drawn carriage passes by, again saying that it was in Victorian times when the church was the center of people's lives and by extension, a community's life that there was peace on earth. With the movie made in 1955, in the midst of the Cold War that threatened to escalate into World War III, peace on earth was the longing of the hearts of most people.

In *Lady*, as voices sing about peace and love, the camera zooms in on Victorian houses (00:03:04). Then it focuses on a Christmas tree (00:03:12). Celebrating Christmas with the lighting of a tree is often credited to Prince

Albert, Queen Victoria's husband. He presented one to her as a Christmas gift in 1841, which was the first Christmas tree in England (Hewitt 2007, 14). The Christmas tree did originate long before this however. Saint Boniface (675–754), an Anglo-Saxon who was appointed to be the archbishop of Mainz by Pope Gregory III, brought Christianity to Germania. While there, legend has it that he interrupted pagans preparing to sacrifice a child to an oak tree or else they were worshipping the oak tree. Either way, Boniface cut down the oak tree, and miraculously upsprung a fir tree. Because of its triangular shape, he identified it as a symbol of the Trinity, God, Christ, and the Holy Spirit (11–12). Legend also has it that Martin Luther was walking through a forest on a Christmas Eve and saw the stars through the fir trees. He took one of the trees indoors and put candles on it to symbolize God's light in the darkness (12–13). Although a German tradition to decorate a Christmas tree, it was not until Victoria became familiar with the custom through her German cousins and then with the gift from Albert (14) that the Christmas tree became a Victorian emblem, although the Germans had popularized it in the United States in the eighteenth century (13).

The Christmas tree is a major icon from the Victorian period with all its connotations of Victorian ideology of the centrality of religion and home, promising, as the song says, a world that "is calm and peaceful … bright and joyful."

The camera takes us inside the Victorian house and lets us see parts of people as we would if we were a puppy (00:03:12). Six months later we are to view two Victorian houses. The first is Jock's home in antebellum style, a boxed design upheld by Doric columns spaced around the house and a wrap-around porch perfect for a snoozing bloodhound, and a balcony on the second floor that wraps around short of the front door. Extended out from a green-shingled room are gable dormers. The windows are tall, plantation style. Surrounding the property is an ornamental fence with the traditional welcome pineapple on pillars at the entrance.

Jock's house is not so apparent, but with its large red blocks, it is most likely Georgian or early Victorian. When we do get to see Lady's house, it is New World, Queen Anne Revival that was very popular from about 1880 to 1910. It is a style that is extremely eclectic with asymmetrical façade, Dutch gables, polygonal towers, bay windows, dentils, and gingerbread.

The "official" address is 2137 Park Avenue, Old New England Town, USA ("Locations"), but most websites list it as 906 East Second Avenue in Rome, Georgia—the Claremont House built in 1882 ("Locations").[7]

Jock and Lady find Trusty snoring away on his porch. Given that all creatures in this movie—human and animal—are all ethnically stereotyped, Jock, the Scottish terrier, rolls the "r" and refers to people as lass or lassie or lad or laddie and uses such words as "bonnie." Trusty is the bloodhound with the lazy drawl of a Southern gentleman, who refers to Lady, as Miss Lady and in the traditional Southern stereotypical fashion nostalgically refers to his ancestors, particularly his grandpappy, Old Reliable. The two used to track criminals through the swamps (00:12:11–13). There is no mention of their having tracked runaway slaves.

On the surface, the magic kingdom in this move seems to celebrate multiculturalism or, more accurately, multiethnicity among the White race. Tramp, himself a mixed breed, tells Lady that he has multiple families, but none of them has him (00:43:56); on Mondays he enjoys Wiener schnitzel at the Shultzes and corn beef at the O'Briens on Tuesdays (or "Begorra," which means "Fine day, by God") (00:44:04–44:20). He stops when he remembers the Italian restaurant Tony's where two Italian stereotypes will serve them spaghetti (00:44:45–48:45). These stereotypes are positive ones though: These Disney Italians are "kind, hardworking, gentle, and incredibly generous" (Brode 2005, 106) at a time when most films projected Italians as being "out of control" (107). It is true that "Italian Americans excelled in organized crime in the 1940s through the 1960s, when they held dominant positions in many cities in the United States" (Iorizzo 2005 [2000], 158). I can still hear the ominous music and the deep-voiced narrator (Walter Winchell) who announced *The Untouchables* that came on TV on Thursday nights. The series that began in 1959 greatly denigrated Italians, and for those children who were allowed to watch the show, they witnessed many Italian criminals violently abusing children.[8] Randall Miller describes the "centripetal isolation of the Italian-Americans' slow rate of assimilation into the suburban, materialistic, and ethnically homogenized American middle class," and draws from the depiction of Italians in numerous Victorian novels in their portrayal of the "Italian male and female as sinister sexual, ethical, and religious threats to Protestant males" (1980,

75). Appropriately, then, Disney's Tony and Joe share an "affinity" with Tramp as being outsiders and thus treat him with kindness, acceptance, and understanding—unlike most of the other humans in the film (Brode 107).

In the dog pound, we meet a Russian stereotype, Bóris, who is a philosopher in the order of Karl Marx. M. Keith Booker asserts that this "Gorky-quoting Russian wolfhound ... associates the underclasses with Russians and communists" (2010, 25). Pedro, the Chihuahua, has a Mexican accent, has drooping lids as if he is too lazy to be awake, is stupid, and has a sister who is fast (given to loose sexual morals). When Bóris suggests that Tramp might have an Achilles heel, the uneducated Pedro misunderstands and says, "Pardon me, amigo. What is this 'chili heel'?" (00:57:56). His sister is Rosita Chiquita Juanita Chihuahua, (as if mocking the custom of having numerous names in Spanish-speaking families). Peg, a Pekingese, is portrayed as a floozy, like a Mae West type, with her out-of-control long bangs that seductively conceal/reveal sexy eyes (with blue beneath them as if either she had been abused with black eyes or else she did not get much sleep due to prostitute hours). When she sings, the camera focuses on her ample, swinging derriere (00:00:59:45–56). She informs Lady that Tramp is a womanizer. Dachsie, of course, is a Daschund, and says only "*und fifi* ....," as a German-speaker. "Although endowed with various cultural and national identities," Shen-mei Ma laments, "they are all, by blood, children of Disney" (2003, 150). What he means is that they are all stereotypes that may not be ostensibly racist, but they are nevertheless "composites based on images, stereotypes, and fantasies of the Other" designed to remove any association with alienation or hostility that does actually exist in the world (150). An appropriate example of this is the "sly, bucktoothed, cross- and slit-eyed, and pidgin-speaking Siamese cats that appear not only in the 1955 version of *Lady and the Tramp* but also in the 1970 *The Aristocats*" (150).

Kimiko Akita and Rick Kenney point out that Disney villains often "signal deviance" through positioning their bodies like a "well-bred lady" (as in Victorian times), moving with a "feminine gait" (2013, 59), as is illustrated by the swaying of derrieres in unison by the two cats in the early *Lady* film. Further, Alan Spector charges Disney films for "lump[ing] ethnic groups into a kind of undifferentiated mass—Asians, Chinese, Japanese, Siamese" (1998, 46). Besides the "denigrating humor in listening to the

Asiatic cats butcher the English language," Disney " 'educate[s]' millions of young Americans to embrace" a stereotype of "Asiatic as evil, but cunning, utterly deceitful without morals or principles" (96). Eleanor Byrne and Martin McQuillan perceive the cats as "wily, duplicitous, troublemaking, freeloading, Asia illegal immigrants," noting that the cats have infiltrated the domestic, secure American home, arriving "under cover in a basket" (1999, 97). They are distinctly different from the other animals that speak with Anglo accents and who are regarded as "morally good" (Brode 201).

Discrimination against Asians in America was widespread as demonstrated when it imprisoned Japanese Americans for fear of their divided loyalties during World War II. *Lady* was created shortly after the end of the war in the Pacific. This was followed by the Cold War with the threat of communism, which ignited more fear, especially about the Chinese, especially if they were immigrants, that they might infiltrate America with communist sympathies. After all, Disney was a witness in the House Committee on Un-American (oxymoron) Affairs in 1947, committed to expunge communism from Hollywood. Then, too, America was involved in the conflict between North and South Korea, with North Korea supported by China and the Soviet Union.

Aside from this "Yellow Peril," Byrne and McQuillan also assert that America was paranoid about the effect of immigrants on America, especially on American-born children, as illustrated by the baby in *Lady and the Tramp* when Lady is put on a chain outside, and a rat invades the home, where the rat, who will make the way for more rats, epitomizes an alien (97). Then there is the point that Booker makes about cats and their animosity with mice (28), when Mickey Mouse is the "emblem of the American spirit" (Apgar 2015). Additionally, Byrne and McQuillan mention that the setting of the film was at a time during Chinese exclusions (98). They also regard the pound as an "immigrant reception centre" with inmates from all countries that 1945 America did not want to adopt (99). The Disney cats represent "sinister foreigners" that pose a threat to not only the "domestic bliss" of Lady but also to Americans in the mid-1950s (Booker 27).

With a typical Victorian ending smacking of Jane Eyre's proverbial, "Reader, I married him," Tramp has been "assimilated into the stable domestic setting, adding extra protection against the future subversion of cats, or invasion by rats, and forever divorced from the ethnically and socially marginal, who are left to be purged by the elements, both natural and social" (Nadel 1995, 125). Alan Nadel most likely meant literally that the unadoptable dogs at the pound will be euthanized and figuratively, those who do not live according to the American way of life will be expunged. Acceptable Americans were exemplified in television shows like *The Adventures of Ozzie and Harriet* (1952–66), *Father Knows Best* (1954–60), *Leave It to Beaver* (1957–63), and *The Donna Reed Show* (1958–66).

In addition to the iteration of stereotypes, *Lady and the Tramp* is Victorian in its efforts to normalize heterosexual gender with the Victorian paradigm of the upper-class lady who falls in love with the lower-class fellow and inspires him to change his independent, restless, rogue ways, settle down, and become a family man. It must have been what people wanted to see and believe, for in 1987 when *Lady and the Tramp* was to be released on video, 2 million orders came in before one copy was ready for shipping (Gomery 1994, 81).

Lady and the Tramp (2019)

It seems as if Kari Granlund and Andrew Bujalski, who wrote the screenplay for the 2019 *Lady and the Tramp*, as well as the other producers of the film, meticulously removed most of the deleterious stereotypes from the previous film, and ostensibly reinserted diversity. Take the two stars: Lady's voice is Tessa Thompson, an actress who played in *Dear White People* and *Selma* (2014). She is the daughter of singer-songwriter Marc Anthony Thompson, who is Black and the founder of Chocolate Genius, Inc. Her mother is half-Mexican and half-European ancestry. Tramp, who obviously is a mutt of mix breeds, has a voice played by Justin Theroux, whose own ancestry is American of mixed heritage; he was born in Washington, DC, to a father of French-Canadian and Italian descent, and his mother is English and German, 1/64th Spanish, and distant Dutch.

The film opens like the earlier version, with a long shot of the village that shows Victorian houses and strikingly, a two-spire, neo-Gothic church, which is the Cathedral of St. John the Baptist in Savannah, Georgia. French Catholics came to Savannah shortly after the French Revolution that began in 1789 and after the first uprising in Haiti in 1791. The cornerstone for the church was laid in 1799 ("Cathedral" 2020). Noticeable are the Christmas lights strung across the streets. As a horse-drawn carriage emerges, the camera zooms in on the house and carriage and moves in through a three-sided bow window into a living room decorated with Victorian furniture and profuse knick-knacks (00:00:20:42–2: 23), with *Peace on Earth* being sung by Black American Kiersey Clemons. It is a remake of *Silent Night* composed in 1818 by Franz Xaver Gruber with lyrics by Joseph Mohr in Austria. *Peace on Earth* is the second song in the 1955 version and is sung by British-born tenor Donald Novis in the smooth, close-harmony style that characterized music in the 1940s and early 1950s.

Darling appears (00:02:23), and suddenly we should know that we are in a neo-Victorian movie for she is Black, played by Kiersey Clemons. Her husband is White, and their baby, Lulu, will be considered Black. It was not until 1967 that the US Supreme Court unanimously ruled that anti-miscegenation laws were unconstitutional. Supposedly *Lady and the Tramp* was to be filmed in New Orleans, which would explain the steamboat (00:42:25–46:01), the horse-drawn streetcar (00:16:24), and the prevalent mix of races and the presence of an Italian restaurant (00:47:55). Most of it was filmed in Savannah, Georgia, however (Das Biswas 2019, n.p.), especially evident with the close-up of the fountain in Forsyth Park. With its Spanish-moss-draped trees, the setting is in the nineteenth-century South when mixed-racial couples were an anathema in public. However, in 1799, Andrea Dimitry from the Island of Hydra (Greece) married Marianne Celeste Dracos, the daughter of a slave woman, and lived in New Orleans (du Bellet 1903, 167). There were at least, but only three interracial marriages in Savannah by 1880 (Blassingame 1973, 480).

As discussed above and in so many reviews and critical articles on the Siamese cats in the 1955 film, the later version was careful to get rid of Si and Me and the negative stereotypes of Asians. Those two cats were replaced by Devon and Rex. The Devon Rex cat has a "mad-cap personality within—a cross, some say, between a cat, a dog, a monkey, and Dennis the Menace" ("About" n.d., n.p.). They are not a Victorian breed, however, having originated in Devonshire England in the late 1950s ("About"). This information about the cat was posted by the Cat Fanciers' Association who includes this policy statement: "to promote equal participation without discrimination or harassment on the basis of race, color, religion, gender, sexual orientation, gender identity or expression, age, national origin or disabilities." The "Siamese Cat Song" with its racial stereotypes was replaced by a jazzy version of "What a Shame" written and sung by Black brothers Nate "Rocket" Wonder and Roman GianArthur, who have composed numerous songs for Janelle Monáe (the voice of Peg) who is Black and identifies with both bisexuality and pansexuality (Spanos 2018).

Despite the persistent title found in the remake, except for Peg's song that calls him *a tramp*, but does not call him *Tramp*, no one else in the movie, not even the dog himself, refers to him as Tramp. Why was this changed in 2019? In the early twentieth century, Nels Anderson reported that there was a "peculiar tramp problem" in the United States, and it was unique to the United States (1923, 290). There was an "army of perhaps two million homeless, wandering men" with "inadequate personalities, defective mentalities or physical defects" (290). Like Tramp, they were "exceeding unwieldy and undisciplined,"

> living anonymous lives, and generally … shifting and moving to avoid responsibility. They [were] a group of men with no home attachments and few interests that would identify them with any community. They [were] not burdened with the moral problems of any group nor are they even put in a position where their own conduct gives them much concern. (291)

By the twenty-first century, we have been taught to be more empathetic toward the homeless. In 2017 there were an estimated 553,742 people who were homeless or 17 out of every 10,000 people ("State" 2020, n.p.). In 2020 there were about 3,200 homeless people in the city of Atlanta, but a nearly 25 percent reduction since 2015, which reflects the city's concern and efforts to help this population ("Understanding" 2021, n.p.)

Further, the 1955 song referred to Tramp as a "rounder," which according to the *Oxford English Dictionary* was a popular term in the nineteenth-century North America that referred to "a person who is frequently imprisoned, or who frequents disreputable bars, nightclubs, etc.; a habitual criminal, idler, or drunkard" (*OED* 2020). We have since become more understanding of people, especially alcoholics, and it is now insensitive to marginalize them. The twenty-first century also urges compassion for criminals and for society to share in the responsibility of having made them criminals.

Furthermore, a "tramp" in the Victorian age was another term for a prostitute or a "sexually promiscuous woman" (Salvato 2006, 633). Nick Salvato associates "tramp" with "trash," calling the latter a "sister term" (638) and reminding us that an additional definition of "tramp" is to trample down and crush. He borrows from the *OED* in its Victorian usage of "to tread (sheets, blankets, etc.) in a tub of soapy water, as part of the process of washing."[9] One of the distinguishing class differences between the "street dog" and the "family dog" from "Snob Hill" mentioned several times throughout the 2019 version is smell, that Lady often is given baths and she is brushed every morning, unlike the street dog. As if cited in the Bible, which it is not, widely believed and quoted in the Victorian Period was "Cleanliness is next to godliness." The 2019 Tramp was extremely unkempt with hair out of place all over his face.

By the end of the movie, however, it is obvious that he has been groomed. Earlier in the movie Tramp says that he is nothing but trash, that people have treated him as if he is nothing but garbage. Unlike the 1955 version, Tramp recounts his painful experience with people, that he was once loved by a family, and then when they had a baby, the man, a White man, took an unsuspecting Tramp for a ride in his car, let him out, and then drove off (00:55:47–57:30). In short, Tramp was treated as millions of dogs are treated every year around the world; they are simply discarded as if they are nothing but trash. In 2017 according to the World Health Organization, there were more than 200 million stray dogs worldwide. It is even worse in America when its citizens have been trained to discriminate about trash, separating out the recyclable. When did Americans decide that it was acceptable to discard family members as if they are trash? The American Society for the Prevention of Cruelty to Animals says that there are more than 3.3 million dogs taken in by animal shelters in the United States every year (Raphelson 2017, n.p.).

Tramp tells Lady, "I'm just a street dog. I don't have much value to anyone" (2019, 01:15:50). Lady assures him that he has value to her and that he "deserve[s] to be loved." In the pound, the dogs say that they are unadoptable in contrast to Lady (2019, 01:01:36). In the current climate, children are taught that everyone is special and that there is no such thing as a reject or loser. In 2019, Peg and the English bulldog are adopted (01:12:43), and so are the two pups by Lady's next-door neighbors (01:33:54) as if to say to America: "Adopt a rescued dog and tell your neighbor to do likewise."

The 1955 Peg song envies Tramp his freedom, but by 2019, we are to be more sensitive to his plight, and instead of judging him, we are to judge ourselves as to our complicity in making him and other creatures "of the street" what they are.

There are two additional messages sent to children in this film that were nonexistent in the 1955 version. Firstly, unlike the traditional Victorian paradigm of a lady in distress needing to be rescued from a prince, even if he looks like a street rogue like Flynn Rider in *Tangled* (2010) or Jack Dawson in *Titanic* (1997), Lady and the other women in the film are strong characters. Even though Tramp teaches her to howl with borrowed language from Dawson in *Titanic* who teaches Rose how to spit (a particularly masculine skill as lauded by Gaston in *Beauty and the Beast*), when Lady is cornered by a dangerous street dog, Tramp does not battle him in the way he did in 1955. Instead, he enlists Lady's performance as a rabid dog to scare him away (00:26:36). Later when they board a steamboat, Tramp encourages Lady to make a precarious jump from the dock to the boat, but Lady uses her logic and wit to board (00:42:25), demonstrating an equal if not superior capability to perform in the world independently of masculine assistance. Even more significantly, Lady returns to the scene to help Tramp escape the dog catcher, which is when she gets caught. Tramp abandons her (01:00:45–1:00:55). It is Lady, and not Trusty, who stops the horses of the dog pound truck (01:30:15). These scenes tell little girls that they can save themselves and others; they are not dependent upon some male to rescue them or validate them.

Secondly, even though Tramp and Lady are in love, and they represent a heterosexual couple, unlike the 1955 version, the movie does not end with the message, "Because they are now a married heterosexual couple with children—the ideal nuclear family—only now do they get to live happily ever after." When Tramp and Lady are on their adventure, in the 1955 version there is a romantic scene at the top of a hill (00:49:49) that might hint to their having spent the night together. This is strictly neo-Victorian, for no lady would risk her reputation in such a way, and being dogs or humans, the implication is that the two had sex. If children do not assume that any sexual activity had been involved, then the scene.... the scene is also Victorian in utilization of the paradigm of the lady's taming of the tramp's "unruly masculine sexual energies" (Booker 27).

The even more neo-Victorian version (2019) refuses to encourage girls to be treated as sexual objects or to signal that the sexual act is essential for one's well-being. In the dog-pound scene, no one refers to Tramp as having sexual liaisons with females, not even Peg. At the end of the movie, Lady and the Tramp do not have pups.

There are two final observations to be made with this neo-Victorian treatment in the twenty-first century. The first is multiculturalism running through the entire movie in a way that is not historically possible in 1909 but endorses a form of tolerance that the more recent Disney inculcates for children. Besides the mixed-race marriage between Darling and Jim Dear, at Tony's, we see another mixed couple as if color does not matter at tall (00:00:34–35). The doctor who delivers Darling's child (who in this movie is a girl instead of a boy named after his father) is Korean American (00:25:30), played by Ken Jeong. Bull, just like the Rex cats, has a voice that cannot be identified by race; the voice belongs to Benedict Wong. The owner of a store that is being frequented by a stylish White woman is Black (00:16:00). The owner of the pet shop is played by Parvesh Singh Cheena. Although Joe should be Italian, his voice belongs to Arturo Castro, born in Guatemala. Tony's voice is the famous F. Murray Abraham of Syrian and Italian descent. Elliot, who plays the dog catcher, self-identifies simply as an American. There are other scenes in the film played by Black men and women in the mainstream of life. It is as if Disney is saying that ethnicity and race have nothing to do with who you are and what you can do and be.

The second observation has to do with gender. Jock—called Jocky Wocky by her eccentric mistress who constantly dresses him/her in costume and paints him—is played by Sottish actress Ashley Jensen. Unlike 1955, Jock is not strictly male. In fact, we don't know his gender from his voice or action. Although Trusty mocks him/her sometimes for wearing dresses, we don't know if his criticism is that Jock is a male wearing female clothes or if it is because he is a dog, and dogs don't wear clothes. Jock also wears a kilt, when traditionally, it was only a male attire. One scene shows completed portraits of Jock by his mistress. In two, his head is on the body of a woman in a lookalike of Johannes Vermeer's *Girl with a Pearl Earring* (1665) and DaVinci's *Mona Lisa* (1503–6). He is masculine in Van Gogh's *Self-Portrait* (1889) and Rembrandt's painting of George Washington (1854) (00:08:16). Jock seems to be bisexual.

When Tramp and Lady meet two poodles in town, they look like identical twins and females in that they both wear red ribbons. Tramp makes the mistake of asking if they are twins, and one, in a very deep bass voice replies, "I'm her husband, Pal" (00:13:25). The 2019 *Lady and the Tramp* practices a neo-Victorian rewriting of history that erases the boundaries between gender and ethnicity.

Bibliography

"About the Devon Rex." *The Cat Fanciers' Association*. <https://cfa.org/devon-rex/>.

Akita, Kimiko, and Rick Kenney. "A 'Vexing Implication': Siamese Cats and Orientalist Mischief-Making." In *Diversity in Disney Films: Critical Essays on Race, Ethnicity, Gender, Sexuality and Disability*, edited by Johnson Cheu, 50–66. Jefferson, NC: McFarland, 2013.

Allan, Robin. *Walt Disney and Europe*. Bloomington: Indiana University Press, 1999.

Anderson, Nels. "The Juvenile and the Tramp." *Law and Criminology* 14, no. 2 (August 1923): 290–312. <http//www.jstor.org/stable/1133620>.

Apgar, Garry. *Mickey Mouse: Emblem of the American Spirit*. Stockholm: Weldon Owen, 2015.

Arndt, Walter. *The Genius of Wilhelm Busch*. Berkeley: University of California Press, 1982.

Aubrecht, Michael. *The Civil War in Spotsylvania County. Confederate Campfires at the Crossroads*. Charleston, SC: The History Press, 2009.

Ayres, Brenda. Introduction: "'Hair Is the Woman's Glory'—Unless It's Red." In *A Vindication of the Redhead: The Typology of Red Hair Throughout the Literary and Visual Arts*, edited by Brenda Ayres and Sarah E. Maier, 1–17. Cham: Palgrave Macmillan, 2021.

Blassingame, John W. "Before the Ghetto: The Making of the Black Community in Savannah, Georgia, 1865–1880." *Journal of Social History* 6, no. 4 (Summer 1973): 463–88. <https://www.jstor.org/stable/3786511>.

Booker, M. Keith. *Disney, Pixar, and the Hidden Messages of Children's Films*. Santa Barbara, CA: Praeger, 2010.

"A Boy Like That." Composed by Leonard Bernstein. Lyrics by Stephen Sondheim. For *West Side Story*. 1957.

Boym, Svetlana. *The Future of Nostalgia*. New York: Basic Books, 2001.

Brainard, Charles Henry. *John Howard Payne: A Biographical Sketch of the Author of "Home, Sweet Home!"* Washington, DC: George A. Coolidge, 1885. <https://books.google.com/books?id=Mu9IAAAAMAAJ>.

Brode, Douglas. *Multiculturalism and the Mouse: Race and Sex in Disney Entertainment*. Austin: University of Texas, 2005.

Brode, Douglas, and Shea T. Brode, eds. *Debating Disney: Pedagogical Perspectives on Commercial Cinema*. Lanham, MD: Rowman and Littlefield, 2016.

Byrne, Eleanor, and Martin McQuillan. *Deconstructing Disney*. London: Pluto Press, 1999.

"Claremont House, 1882–Rome." *Old Georgia Homes: Every Old House Has a Story to Tell*, June 2019. <https://oldgeorgiahomes.com/2019/06/claremont-house-1882-rome/>.

Das Biswas, Shuvrajit. "Where Was *Lady and the Tramp* Filmed?" *The Cinemaholic*, November 14, 2019. <https://thecinemaholic.com/where-was-lady-and-the-tramp-filmed/>.

du Bellet, Louise Pecquet. *Some Prominent Virginia Families*. Vol. 4. Lynchburg, VA: J. P. Bell Company, 1903. <https://books.google.com/books?id=3iQSAAAAYAAJ>.

Gomery, Douglas. "Disney's Business History: A Reinterpretation." In *Disney Discourse: Producing the Magic Kingdom*, edited by Eric Smooden, 71–86. New York: Routledge, 1994.

Harrison, Gabriele. *John Howard Payne, Dramatist, Poet, Actor, and Author of "Home, Sweet Home!": His Life and Writings*. Rev. edn. Philadelphia, PA: J. B. Lippincott and Company, 1885. <https://books.google.com/books?id=iLxEAAAAYAAJ>.

Heilmann, Ann, and Mark Llewellyn. *Neo-Victorianism: The Victorians in the Twenty-First Century, 1999–2009*. Basingstoke: Palgrave Macmillan, 2010.

Hewitt, James. *The Christmas Tree*. Morrisville, NC: Lulu Distribution, 2007.

Iorizzo, Luciano J. "Crime and Organized Crime." 2000. In *The Italian American Experience: An Encyclopedia*, edited by Salvatore J. LaGumina et al., 151–59. New York: Routledge, 2005.

"It's Whatcha Do with Whatcha Got." Written by Don Raye and Gene de Paul. Sung by Ken Carson et al. For *So Dear to My Heart*. 1948. <https://www.yout ube.com/watch?v=ePR5vd7al7I>.

Kaplan, Kora. *Victoriana—Histories, Fictions, Criticism*. New York: Columbia University Press, 2007.

Kenna, Laura Cook. "TV Gangsters and the Course of the Italian American Antidefamation Movement." *The Italian American Review* 6, no. 2 (2016): 203–28.

Kennedy, David M. *Freedom from Fear: The American People in Depression and War, 1929–1945*. New York: Oxford University Press, 1999.

"Locations: Lady's House." *Lady and the Tramp Wiki. Fandom*. <https://ladyandtr amp.fandom.com/wiki/Category:Locations>.

Ma, Sheng-mei. "Mulan Disney, It's Like, Re-Orients: Consuming China and Animating Teen Dreams." In *The Emperor's Old Groove: Decolonizing Disney's Magic Kingdom*, edited by Brenda Ayres, 149–64. New York: Peter Lang, 2003.

Miller, Randall M. *The Kaleidoscopic Lens: How Hollywood Views Ethnic Groups*. Hollywood: Jerome S. Ozer, 1980.

"Mouse and Man." *Time* (December 27, 1937): 19–21.

Nadel, Alan. *Containment Culture: American Narratives, Postmodernism, and the Atomic Age*. Durham, NC: Duke University Press, 1995.

Payne, John Howard. *Home Sweet Home*. Boston: Lee and Shepard Publishers, 1880. <https://books.google.com/books?id=bpgUAAAAYAAJ>.

Pinksy, Mark I. *The Gospel According to Disney: Faith, Trust, and the Pixie Dust*. Louisville, KY: Westminster John Knox Press, 2014.

Primorac, Antonija. *Neo-Victorianism on Screen: Postmodernism and Contemporary Adaptations of Victorian Women*. Cham: Palgrave Macmillan, 2018.

Raphelson, Samantha. "No 'Easy Answer' to Growing Number of Stray Dogs in the U.S., Advocate Says." *NPR: Here&Now Compas Special Series*, December 29, 2017. <https://www.npr.org/2017/12/29/574598877/no-easy-answer-to-grow ing-number-of-stray-dogs-in-the-u-s-advocate-says>.

Reaves, Joseph A. *Taking in a Game: A History of Baseball in Asia*. Lincoln: University of Nebraska Press, 2002.

"rounder, n.2.d." *OED Online*. September 2021. Oxford University Press. <https:// www-oed-com.ezproxy.liberty.edu/view/Entry/167958?rskey=hIy54R&res ult=4&isAdvanced=false>.

Salvato, Nick. "Tramp Sensibility and the Afterlife of *Showgirls*." *Theatre Journal* 58, no. 4 (December 2006): 633–48. <https//www.jstor.org/stable/25069919>.

Schaffer, Scott. "The Past, as Product in the Present: Disney and the Imagineering of Histories." In Brode and Brode 2016, 33–42.

Schickel, Richard. *The Disney Version*. New York: Avon Books, 1969.

Shuttleworth, Sally. "Natural History: The Retro-Victorian Novel." In *The Third Culture: Literature and Science*, edited by Elinor S. Shaffer, 253–68. Berlin: Walter de Gruyter, 1997.

Spector, Alan. J. "Disney Does Diversity: The Social Context of Racial-Ethnic Imagery." In *Cultural Diversity and the U.S. Media*, edited by Yahya R. Kamalipour and Teresa Carilli, 39–49. Albany, NY: SUNY Press, 1998.

"The State of Homelessness in America." National Alliance to End Homelessness. 2020. <https://endhomelessness.org/homelessness-in-america/homelessness-statistics/state-of-homelessness-report-legacy/>.

"tramp, v. 1.b." *OED Online*. September 2021. Oxford University Press. <https://www-oed-com.ezproxy.liberty.edu/view/Entry/204519?rskey=jruZXO&result=3&isAdvanced=false>.

"Understanding the Numbers in Atlanta." *Midtown Atlanta*, October 7, 2021. <https://www.midtownatl.com/about/news-center/post/homeless-point-in-time-count>.

Widdowson, Peter. "'Writing Back': Contemporary Re-Visionary Fiction." *Textual Practice* 20, no. 3 (2006): 491–507. doi:10.1080/09502360600828984.

AMALA CHARULATHA

2 Transmedial Paratexts and Ideology in Disney's *Brave*, *Pocahontas*, and *Mulan*

Since what has been called the Disney Renaissance (1989–99), Disney has been making attempts to address concerns among audiences for its regressive portrayal of gender and race relations. Chris Pallant clarifies the term in *Demystifying Disney: A History of Disney Feature Animation* as a period characterized by "a return to the artistic ideologies of the Disney formalist period" (2011, 102), with emphasis on believability, life-like movement in the depiction of characters and contexts, and artistic sophistication.[1] The princess films that belong to this period are *The Little Mermaid* (1989), *Beauty and the Beast* (1991), *Aladdin* (1992), *Pocahontas* (1995), and *Mulan* (1998) (89)—narratives that shifted from unidimensional, passive women, to women who were more inclined to action (Hoerrner 1996, 225), and were more rebellious (Henke et al. 1996, 234).

Even as the introduction of racially diverse characters had more to do with gaining the loyalty of a multiracial population with disposable income (Valdivia 2008, 270) than social progressiveness, critical material on the films has since demonstrated how the movies that Disney produced in the 1990s were not as progressive as they were touted to be. *Mulan* was criticized for the superficial multicultural strategy of creating a Chinese-looking yet American-acting Mulan (Ma 2003, 162), for transforming a well-known story about filial piety and patriotism into one of personal growth, individualism, and independent spirit (Hains 2014, 150; Lit 187), for an exaggerated depiction of female oppression that is not historically accurate, and for the racist depiction of the Huns (Hains 221). *The Princess and the Frog* (2009) was criticized for its depiction of colorblind racism (Turner 2013, 91) that side-stepped any question of inequality or poverty. In that film, race continued to be depicted as of no consequence and was idealized unbelievably within the Jim Crow era, an age in the Southern United States notorious for its vicious racism, persecution of African Americans, and segregation. This hostility is nowhere present in *The Princess and the Frog* that is set in the Jim-Crow South.[2] *Pocahantas* was also criticized for trivializing the achievements of the historical figure, for reducing her story into a romantic tale, for mishandling history, and for race representation (Hains 221).

In response to such criticism, now in the twenty-first century, Disney is even more vocal in its claims of depicting progressive women as opposed to the helpless heroines of the past, and of being more culturally and racially sensitive in its depiction of non-White characters.[3] These changes are carried out mainly through its pre-release promotions that have the cast, in interviews, emphasize the progressiveness of the film. This spin happened during the promotion for the live-action film *Beauty and the Beast* (2017). Emma Watson, who played the role of Belle, insisted that by making Belle an inventor and an advocate of women's education, the film was offering a feminist take on the tale (quoted in Frost 2017, n.p.). She also drew comparisons between Belle and Hermione Granger (quoted in De Klerk 2017, n.p.), the intelligent bookworm from the Harry Potter series (also played by Watson). In doing so, she attempted to ensure that the discussions in the media surrounding the film supported this particular dimension of Belle's character (De Klerk).

Even when the films manage to depict an inclusive representation of gender and race, there are other texts related to the film that have the potential to undermine it. As has been the case with Disney for decades, even the neo-Disney films are merely the starting point for the consumer experience. The release of each film is followed by lucrative merchandise like princess dolls, music, coloring books, t-shirts, hats, totes, water bottles, video games, and so forth associated with the particular film. A Disney film, then, should be considered as just one narrative among many that can impact a consumer's understanding of the ideological makeup of the characters. Every piece of material brought out and marketed in connection with the film engages in an act of signification. Each of these princesses appear in one way on screen—often with an attempt to individualize the women—but off screen, Disney merchandise carry an image of beauty meant to appeal to young costumers (see Figure 2.1) and are often stereotypical.

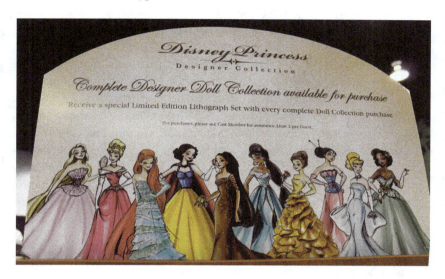

Figure 2.1. Designer doll collection based on the Official Princess Line. This image does not include the last two princesses Merida and Moana.

While ideological analysis of Disney film characters often overlooks the associated franchise material, the aim here is to give the merchandise an equal footing with the film (often considered the primary text) since they also play a vital role in shaping the ideological signification of texts. As Jonathan Gray opined, these paratextual[4] elements are not ancillary material but are rather material that should be looked at alongside the so-called main text (2010, 8). A contemporary theoretical concept useful for such an analysis is transmediality: nuanced and often overlapping, concepts like branding, franchising, and promotion which is not merely confined to individual characters, fictional worlds, and narrative/storytelling aspects but also pays attention to key expressions like sequels, franchises, spin-offs, novelizations, adaptations, and so on. Since these terms potentially carry pejorative connotations that disregard their ideological potential, it is more appropriate to consider them transmedia paratexts.

When the concept was initially formulated, Henry Jenkins described transmediality in relation to storytelling as "a process where integral elements of a fiction get dispersed systematically across multiple delivery channels for the purpose of creating a unified and coordinated entertainment experience" (2006, 1). Even though Jenkins foregrounded storytelling and world-building in his discussions on transmediality, narrative extension is not the only way in which content is deployed across media, nor is it the most common manifestation of transmedial expression.[5] Exploring transmediality exclusively through the additions to the narrative would, by default, exclude paratextual elements that do not add to the narrative of the story-world; however, it would be at the cost of neglecting the creative manifestations in different media that blur the line between telling and marketing a story. Disney is notorious for relying on the exploitation of multiple platforms for its revenue.[6] For a Neo-Disney production, it is nearly impossible to find one where the transmedia paratexts do not contribute significantly to the revenue. An era of media "convergence" (2),[7] coupled with horizontally integrated media platforms that hold interests across a range of what were once distinct media companies, is conducive to the simultaneous exploitation of different media platforms in order to tell and sell a story and is desirable from both a creative and economic standpoint.

The Disney Princess Line

One of the most profitable media franchises to date, the Disney Princess Line (hereafter DPL) features a cast of female protagonists from Disney movies (see Figure 2.1). The franchise sells "pastel products that includes animated films, DVDs, toys, fast-food meals, music CDs, books, interactive webpages, video games, costumes, clothing, bed linens, school supplies, makeup kits, and even Cinderella cleaning supplies" (Wohlwend 2011, 57), all materials based on the films associated with each princess. As of 2022, starting with Snow White and ending with Moana, there are 12 princesses in the official canon to date including Cinderella, Aurora,

Ariel, Belle, Jasmine, Pocahontas, Mulan, Tiana, Rapunzel, Merida, and Moana.

The DPL, which is the brainchild of the former chairman of Disney Consumer Products President Andy Mooney, capitalizes on the potential of the princesses combined. The statistics put forward by *Forbes* in 2012 listed the Disney Princess franchise at the top of the 20 best-selling entertainment products and generating a revenue of 1.6 billion dollars in retails in North America and a global revenue of 3 billion dollars (Goudreau 2012) attest to the pervasiveness and the popularity of the brand among children, who are the primary targets of the DPL. Children take up media narratives with which they are familiar and tend to explore familiar cultural material through narrative play (Dyson 1997, 34). Children rely on patterns drawn from storylines with which they are familiar, and they would utilize them in the games they play. The princess figure is nearly unavoidable in the early phases of a girl's development (Orenstein 2011, 2) and is a key element in their artwork (Westland 1993, 237). Some parents consider Disney princesses "safe" alternatives to other highly sexualized dolls available on the market (Orenstein 2011, 16) such as major popular dolls that flood the marketplace like Mattel's barbie and the Bratz dolls (10, 21). Both companies have gained notoriety for the highly sexualized bodies of its dolls as well as the revealing clothing that come with it (Gunter 2014, 74–75). When compared to these options, the Disney princess dolls are better alternatives. Even though Disney is better than Mattel and Bratz in its physical depiction of princesses, Disney still glamorizes passivity in women (Ehrenreich 2007) negatively impacting a child's understanding of gender relations. Children who are exposed to Disney princesses and princess products exhibit female-gendered stereotypical behavior (Coyne et al. 2016, 1907).[8] In some cases, the messages that the children receive from their play with the Disney princesses can be quite mixed (Bruce 2006, 15). Conducted by Alexander Bruce in 2006, with the intention of discerning the effect of Disney's portrayal of princesses in Disney films, a study on girls aged 7 to 9 years showed that while girls were very familiar with the plots, they were not blinded by marketing; they still wanted the life of a princess and not necessarily the happily ever after with the prince (7). The problem lies in their understanding of what it means to be a princess since achievements figure nowhere on their list of what it means to be one.[9] The unanimous opinion was that the princess is always beautiful; she also "lives in a castle," "wears pretty dresses," "gets whatever they want," and so on. They also "frequently associated material objects with princesses" and "equated 'beauty' with 'good' and 'ugly' with 'bad'" (14). Even though these children do not consider the prince as integral to their understanding of a princess, the former associations are still problematic.

In another significant study led by Benjamin Hine, on a group of 131 8- to 9-year-olds from the UK, the author examined how children identified and attributed gendered traits and characteristics in "new"[10] and "old" Disney princess movies as well as their gendered conceptualizations of princesses before and after viewing these movies. The results suggest that watching a "newer" Disney princess movie did not change their understanding of what it means to be a princess. Children still predominantly relied on visual cues to decide who is a princess and who is not. The progressive depictions in the films were not sufficient to get rid of "the gendered baggage attached to so many of the traditional princesses represented within this franchise" (Hine et al. 2018, 7). For instance, even though the children were able to identify and appreciate the androgynous traits of the newer heroines like Moana, they were reluctant to label her a princess or aspire to the level of agency she represents in the film (16); however, this perception could be positive because the traits that they associate with a princess are very regressive when compared to the agency embodied by Moana. In fact, the film hints that being a princess is not a desirable trait, with Maui's calling Moana a princess in a derogatory manner (00:52:10–53:40).

Given the pervasiveness of the Disney princesses among children, the role they play in learning stereotypical gender behavior and the tendency of children to absorb contradictory messages from the films and the merchandise, it is worthwhile to analyze the transmedial expressions of Disney films with the certainty that transmedial expressions cannot be understood in traditional ideological terms. The transmedial web of texts can either undercut or affirm ideologies offered by these films. For example, though a Disney princess film might appear to stand on its own with regard to its portrayal of gender identities, those themes are reconstructed through the DPL.

Although clubbed together in the DPL, the cast of princesses are ideologically varied in their films' characters. The earlier princesses in the pantheon (Snow White, Cinderella, and Aurora) are exemplary of extremely regressive patriarchal ideologies. In terms of character, this first wave of princesses is "not only passive and pretty, but also unusually patient, obedient, industrious, and quiet" (Stone 1975, 44) and they need to be saved by men (Ehrenreich n.p.). In terms of their physical appearance, being beautiful was a consistent requirement (Baker-Sperry and Grauerholz 2003, 725). These princesses were "stereotypically slender, beautiful and elegant, modelled after current stars and icons of the time" (Clapp-Itnyre 2010, 9). The princesses from the Renaissance period are more empowered compared to their predecessors (England et al. 2011; Lester 2019, 193–216). They are neither passive nor are they prim and proper (Do Rozario 2004, 45). They are shown to be rebellious figures even though their rebellious streak is more in line with postfeminist ideals that ultimately conform to gendered expectations (Leader 2019, 19). Post 2009, more positive changes were made: "princess characters are more androgynous … participate in more rescue behavior, and show greater variation in romantic outcome" (Hine et al. 74).

When launching the DPL, Disney wanted to ensure that each character was seen as distinct: "To ensure the sanctity of what Mooney called their individual 'mythologies,' the princesses never make eye contact when they're grouped" (Orenstein 2006, n.p.). However, as Caroline Leader points out, with their "Dream Big, Princess" campaign, Disney encourages cohesion and expansion of the princess idea. The Disney Princess brand image

> is one of independent, ambitious, kind, and spunky girls with unimpeachable characters and physically attractive features. The Disney Princess … balances her own needs with a pursuit of the greater good …. The Disney Princesses are promoted as role models, but they would also become the face of various consumer goods and experiences that did not necessarily adhere to the branding image presented above. (2019, 74)

The popularity still enjoyed by the first wave of princesses among children (Do Rozario 2004), despite Disney's attempt to be more progressive and varied with its filmic representations (England et al. 2011), is troubling because they carry very harmful as well as outdated ideas of what it means to be a woman. Though making these ideologically different princesses part of the same spectrum "creates an abiding immortality for the film, a viability and popularity long past their time of conception and lost past their time of cultural appropriateness" (Rothschild 2012, 89), this action has serious implications for the child consumers' understanding of the other more recent princesses in the franchise.

By including the first wave of princesses who exemplify "traditionally feminine traits" of "patience, obedience, and domestication" in the DPL, they are folded "into a later concept of girlhood that privileged postfeminism and girl power and offered more traditionally feminine options for consumers" (Leader 2019, 73). Postfeminism is a sensibility that arose after second-wave feminism and assumes that the goals of feminism have been achieved. It combines the contradictory messages of traditional femininity and feminism and includes "the notion that femininity is a bodily property; the shift from objectification to subjectification; an emphasis upon self-surveillance, monitoring and self-discipline; a focus on individualism, choice and empowerment; the dominance of a makeover paradigm; and a resurgence of ideas about natural sexual difference" (Gill 2007, 147). Postfeminism is sometimes tied to the concept of "girl power" as defined by Emilie Zaslow:

> An expansive media culture that encourages girls and women to identify both as traditionally feminine objects *and* as powerful feminist agents .... Rooted in a neo-liberal language of choice, girl power offers girls and women a sense that they can choose when to be girly and when to be powerful. (2009, 3)

Peggy Orenstein faults postfeminism for a misguided equating of "identity with image, self-expression with appearance, femininity with performance, pleasure with pleasing, and sexuality with sexualization" (2011, 4). It is this logic of postfeminism that informed Disney's purportedly feminist rebranding campaign "Dream Big, Princess" and is manifested in the catchphrases used to describe the princesses. Each princess on the *Shop Disney* page is introduced to the consumer using two sentences with the first one being specific to each princess and the second one common to all princesses. The description for the Pocahontas' page reads "This adventurer leads the way. Explore her doll, dress and costume collection" ("Pocahontas" 2022); Merida's page reads: "Adventures abound with the ultra-brave Merida. Add her costumes, dolls, and dresses to your arsenal" ("Merida" 2022); in Mulan's page the phrase is "A tough and fearless hero, it's an honor to know Mulan. Explore her dolls, dresses, outfits, and more" ("Mulan" 2022). In all these introductions, the first half alerts the consumer to what the character stood for in the film but the latter half of the descriptor calls the consumers' attention back to the dolls and dresses to undercut whatever political implications the first half might have had. Ultimately, these catchphrases in their totality reduce the princess to how she appears and what she wears instead of what she does and who she is.

As Rebecca Hains puts it, "when little girls love princesses, they become exposed to the princess behavior and attitudes that hearken back to the social norms of the 1930s, 1940s, and 1950s" (165). For the later princesses, from the Renaissance era (Ariel, Belle, Mulan, and Pocahontas) and the post-Renaissance era (Tiana, Rapunzel, and Merida), who are altered to fit in with the existing princesses, an induction into the pantheon has involved a retraction of the progressive strides made in the movies. As far as their appearance is concerned, the culturally diverse characters of this group were "Europeanized" by giving them lighter skin tones, changing the shapes of their faces, giving them bigger eyes, widened faces, and smaller noses (Cohen 2015, n.p.). By association, even the princesses from the post-Renaissance era are made to absorb the qualities of her sister princesses from the earlier period such as Cinderella, Snow White, and Aurora. According to Alisa Clapp-Intyre, "Combining the princesses erases any individuality among them" and when characters like "Pocahontas, Mulan, even Tiana is still shown much less often" than their White counterparts, it ends up "defeating the cultural strides the films had made" (10).

Brave

When *Brave* was released in 2012, Merida was praised for being a different and unique portrayal of a female character. According to the original and female director of the film, Brenda Chapman, Merida was intended to be a realistic role model for young girls, one of feminine strength (Cavna 2013, n.p.). Chapman described Merida as "a strong, confident, self-rescuing princess ready to set off on her next adventure with her bow at the ready. She was a princess who looked like a real girl, complete with the 'imperfections' that all people have" (quoted in Child 2022). The film's female producer, Katherine Sarafian, insisted on separating Merida from the tradition of Disney princesses before her. She argued "[Merida] is a Pixar hero. It is completely different from a Disney princess" (quoted in Whelan 2014, 184). Unlike other Disney princesses before her, Merida is not a damsel-in-distress or a mere love interest. The complete absence of a romantic male figure in her life sets her apart from earlier Renaissance heroines like Ariel, Jasmine, Belle, and Mulan. This move becomes significant because a romantic plot was traditionally the means through which the other princesses were brought back into the folds of patriarchy. Merida's physique and appearance rejects the regressive norms of feminine beauty put forward by other Disney princesses and the skill set she exhibits stand in opposition to the previous traits emphasized by Disney; Merida was the most "unlady-like" princess to grace a Disney princess film. The support that Disney received for the film took a turn with the release of the Merida doll and her induction as an official Disney Princess. The public's disapproval over the changes to the Merida doll was made clear through a petition on change.org, "Disney: Say No to the Merida Makeover, Keep Our Hero Brave," signed by over 258,905 supporters.

In its visual representation of the character, the merchandise reverted to an oversexualized image intended to give scopophilic pleasure instead of showcasing her warrior skills. The move was not well received by Chapman who argued that

> the redesign of Merida in advance of her official induction to the Disney Princess collection does a tremendous disservice to the millions of children for whom Merida is an empowering role model who speaks to girls' capacity to be change agents in the world rather than just trophies to be admired. Moreover, by making her skinnier, sexier and more mature in appearance, you are sending a message to girls that the original, realistic, teenage-appearing version of Merida is inferior; that for girls and women to have value—to be recognized as true princesses—they must conform to a narrow definition of beauty. ("Disney: Say No" n.p.)

The changes that were made in the process of merchandising took away from Merida the very attributes that made her a strong woman and a realistic role model (see Figures 2.2 and 2.3).

Figure 2.2. Merida in the film.

Merida's signature hair in the film is characterized by its unruliness (a visible signifier of her strong and nonconforming personality) and was replaced with luscious curls in the doll. In a discussion about how and why they created Merida's hair the way it is, the animation team had this to say: "Merida's hair is an important extension of her character. Like Merida, it is fierce, tempestuous, and unpredictable" (quoted in Leader 2018, 1096). Being that the hair is an indicator of her defiant personality (1087), the hair is given prominence in one of the most tradition-defying acts in the film; in the scene where she pulls off her cloak's hood to reveal her unruly hair before stating that she will be contesting for her hand in marriage (1092). The red hair and its ties to defiance are strengthened by

Figure 2.3. Merida in the merchandise.

its presence on the triplets, Merida's mischievous brothers, who also sport similar unruly hair: "locks indicative of their own defiance of rules of behavior and royalty, happy to raid the sweets as well as assist in disobedience for an extortionate price of a year's desserts" (Maier 2021, 231–32). Although Leader points out the meticulous work that went into creating the perfect "messy and natural" hair for Merida (2018, 1098) has to do with a postfeminist rhetoric, there is no denying that Merida's hair added diversity to the princess' hair profile. Transforming the messy hair into the luscious curls of the dolls strips away the defiance that it embodied in the film and instead imbues it with a seductiveness with the curls being visually suggestive of Medusa's snakes.[11]

The fact that the switch to tamed curls had to do with increasing sexiness as much as it did with conforming to the aesthetics of the already existing princess dolls is evident from the other alterations that were made to the doll's appearance; the doll's waist was slimmed down, bust enhanced, and hips expanded to give it a more lascivious appearance. The doe-eyed expression (a characteristic facial feature in the other princess dolls) was also made prominent and her smile made sexier. The most notable among these changes was the absence of her signature bow and arrow. Its significance to the character is set in the scene that introduces Merida, where a child Merida expresses an interest in her father's bow and arrow. Moments later he gifts her one (00:01:15–1:30) and it becomes for her a prized possession that she carries around and it is a bone of contention with her mother, Elinor. The bow and arrow represent not only her interest in a traditionally "un-feminine" activity but also her ability to physically fight for herself. Instead of the bow and arrow, the Merida doll is left with a hair brush just like the other princesses. With the doe-eyes, thin waist, luscious curls, and a sexualized appearance, the doll has more in common with the other fairy-tale princesses that went before her than with Merida from the film.

Figure 2.4. Classic Pocahontas collectible doll.

Pocahontas

Even though Disney was condemned for its refashioned merchandise of *Brave*, this mistake was not the first that Disney had made. A previous attempt by Disney to bring diversity into the physique of its princesses was with the character of Pocahontas, Disney's first Indigenous American princess. The film shows Pocahontas as a woman with a voluptuous and curvy body (see Figure 2.4). When the film was released, critics called out Disney for her Barbie-esque physique, for her overly sexualized appearance, and for sexual stereotyping that took away the power of the Indigenous woman (Ward 2002, 36). Although the concerns raised by these critics are valid, what this representation of Pocahontas brought to the DPL was diversity in terms of physique. The appearance of Pocahontas was toned down in the doll. The curvy figure was made less so and altered to resemble the other princesses of the pantheon. The figure of Pocahontas in the film stood in stark contrast to the skinny princesses that came before her. Pocahontas' wardrobe also received a makeover with the doll. Despite criticism for its highly distorted narrativization of an Indigenous American figure (Hains 12), the film did give the character a clothing ensemble that emphasizes her cultural roots. Contrary to this image, the art displayed on t-shirts and coffee mugs depicts a Pocahontas in a full-length gown with a flowing train and hair tied back in a long ponytail, an inappropriate, non-Indigenous sartorial aesthetic that is different from that in the film, an image popularized as part of the Disney designer doll collection (see Figure 2.1).

Mulan

Mulan's character has also been altered in the merchandise. Mulan is Disney's first warrior princess, an image that was emphasized in both animation and live-action versions (see Figure 2.5). Her storyline in 1998 depicted a level of agency and activity unprecedented in a Disney Princess. Changes were made to the narrative to make the 2020 film less racist, but there are certain key elements that unite both characters; Mulan wants to

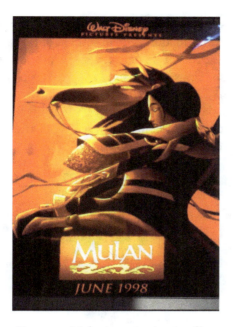

Figure 2.5. Mulan in 1998 animation film.

fight to uphold the honor of her family, but is also a woman who is not very feminine in her behavior, and a woman who shuns dressing up. In fact, the very first song in the animated film, "Honor to Us All," is dedicated to showcasing how much Mulan is against adorning herself with the accoutrements of femininity as contextually prescribed by society's conservative feminine roles. Her first act in the movie is to scribble notes on her hand ahead of her meeting with the town's matchmaker because she has difficulty remembering qualities expected of her like "quiet and demure, graceful, polite, delicate, refined, poised, punctual" (1998, 00:03:15–3:27). Having to write them down indicates that these traditionally feminine qualities are not innate to her but rather "they are to be learned and reiterated, to be placed on the body, just as the make-up and fancy dress, in order to designate her as female" (Limbach 2013, 116). While the other women who are there to meet the matchmaker smile and hope to bring honor to their families, Mulan is disconcerted (1998,

00:08:50). This same sentiment is echoed by her 2020 live-action counterpart. In the 1998 animation, Mulan sings about how she is forced into
many roles and the disjuncture between how she looks and who she really
is inside. When she sings "Why is my reflection someone I don't know"
("Reflection" 1998), Mulan is actually staring at the reflection of herself
all dressed and made up (1998, 00:12:05–12:10). It is this Mulan (someone
the character in the film does not identify as her true self) that finds its
way into the merchandise (see Figure 2.6).

Figure 2.6. Mulan and Li Shang doll set.

In the merchandise, Mulan is formally attired, wearing flowers and
holding a hand fan, the very things for which her character expresses a
complete disdain in both films. The doll's costume resembles the one that
the animated Mulan very reluctantly wears on her visit to the matchmaker.
Also available is a wardrobe for Mulan. A consumer of the merchandise is

likely to forget Mulan the warrior, as none of the outfits carry any signifiers that would associate Mulan with it. Unlike the doll and its accessories, some of the other merchandise does address her stature as a warrior in the form of tote bags that show Mulan defending her village or a watercolor mug that shows her with her sword in a warrior stance.

Even though dolled-up versions of Mulan are still sold on Disney's and Hasbro's official online shopping sites, with the release of the 2020 film, Hasbro made a warrior version of the Mulan doll available to the public. Hasbro obtained the license for the Disney Princess dolls in 2014 and released its first toys in 2016. In a highly publicized move from Mattel (which had been producing Disney Princess dolls since the 1990s), representatives of Disney and Hasbro explained that the move was part of a commitment to reimagining the princess franchise, to make empowered heroines rather than have them be damsels-in-distress, and to give more importance to its racially diverse princesses (Suddath 2015, n.p.; "Mattel" 2022, n.p.). Hasbro's new Mulan doll seems to live up to these claims since not only is she dressed as a warrior, but the set also includes a helmet, jacket, pants, chest armor, skirt armor, sword, dress, crown, collar piece, corset, dagger accessory, and two pairs of shoes. By placing the armor and weapons along with the dress and crown, it has given children the option of choosing whether or not they want to play with Mulan the princess or Mulan the warrior. Since the film emphasizes the warrior part of Mulan's personality, having battle accessories in the set increases the child's ability to embrace that part of her personality during play. However, the veracity of Disney's commitment to rebranding its princesses into powerful women and warriors remains to be seen since the company has re-entered into a deal with Mattel for its Disney Princess and *Frozen* franchises in January 2022.

Conclusion

When Mooney started the DPL, the mandate for depicting the princesses together was that "each stares off in a slightly different direction as if unaware of the others' presence" (quoted in Orenstein 2011, 15), ostensibly intended to emphasize their separation from each other; however, once the film is released and a princess is inducted into the Princess pantheon, her future representations are intricately linked not just to the film and the transmedial expressions associated with it, but also tied back to the larger narrative of the DPL. When consumed together, these princesses tell a story about what it means to be a princess in particular and a woman in general, but they are not in line with what is being depicted in the films. Even when the films manage to be progressive, the DPL has subsumed those messages using the rhetoric of postfeminism and girl power.[12] Even though transmedia paratexts like the princess dolls are brushed off in critical analyses as mere hype for the film, these iterations of, and additions to, the core text have the capacity to reshape our understanding of the films and their ideology depending on whether or not we are exposed to these materials. Disney's attempts to portray itself as "woke" will not work as long as the transmedial expressions of the films keep churning out material with contradictory messages and packaging them as part of a fairly standardized princess line.

Bibliography

Baker-Sperry, Lori, and Liz Grauerholz. "The Pervasiveness and Persistence of the Feminine Beauty Ideal in Children's Fairy Tales." *Gender and Society* 17, no. 5 (2003): 711–26. doi:10.1177/0891243203255605.

Bonilla-Silva, Eduardo, and David Dietrich. "The Sweet Enchantment of Color-Blind Racism in Obamerica." *The ANNALS of the American Academy of Political and Social Science* 634, no. 1 (2011): 190–206. doi:10.1177/0002716210389702.

Bruce, Alexander M. "Princesses Without a Prince: A Consideration of Girls' Reactions to Disney's 'Princess' Movies." *Children's Folklore Review* 28 (2006): 7–22. <https:// scholarworks.iu.edu/journals/index.php/cfr/article/view/25110/30984>.

Cavna, Michael. "No Merida Makeover? *Brave* Director Brenda Chapman on Disney Princess and 'Sexing Her Up.'" *The Washington Post*, 2013. <https:// www.washingtonpost.com/blogs/comic-riffs/post/no-merida-makeover-brave-director-brenda-chapman-on-disney-princess-and-sexing-her-up/2013/05/17/bf003d5a-bdd9-11e2-89c9-3be8095fe767_blog.html>.

Child, Ben. "Brave Director Criticises Disney's 'Sexualised' Princess Merida Redesign." *The Guardian*, 2022. <https://www.theguardian.com/film/2013/may/13/brave-director-criticises-sexualised-merida-redesign>.

Clapp-Intyre, Alisa. "Help! I'm a Feminist but My Daughter Is a 'Princess Fanatic'! Disney's Transformation of Twenty-First-Century Girls." *Children's Folklore Review* 32 (2010): 7–22. <https://scholarworks.iu.edu/journals/index.php/cfr/article/download/25090/30966/>.

Cohen, Philip. "The Trouble with Disney's Teeny, Tiny Princesses." *Times* (January 28, 2015): n.p. <https://time.com/3667700/frozen-brave-disney-princesses-heroes-and-sexism/>.

Coyne, Sarah M. et al. "Pretty as a Princess: Longitudinal Effects of Engagement with Disney Princesses on Gender Stereotypes, Body Esteem, and Prosocial Behavior in Children." *Child Development* 87, no. 6 (2016): 1909–1925. doi:10.1111/cdev.12569.

De Klerk, Amy. "Emma Watson on the Link Between Belle and Hermione." *Harper's Bazaar* (February 9, 2017): n.p. <https://www.harpersbazaar.com/uk/culture/culture-news/news/a39824/emma-watson-elle-uk-cover/>.

Dena, Christy. "Transmedia Adaptation: Revisiting the No- Adaptation Rule." In Freeman and Gambarato 2019, 195–206.

"Disney: Say No to the Merida Makeover, Keep Our Hero Brave." *Change.org* (2013): n.p. <https://www.change.org/p/disney-say-no-to-the-merida-makeover-keep-our-hero-brave>.

"Disney Updates Content Warning for Racism in Classic Films." *BBC* (October 16, 2020): n.p. <https://www.bbc.com/news/world-us-canada-54566087>.

Do Rozario, Rebecca-Anne C. "The Princess and the Magic Kingdom: Beyond Nostalgia, the Function of the Disney Princess." *Women's Studies in Communication* 27, no.1 (2004): 34–59. doi:10.1080/07491409.2004.10162465.

Dundes, Lauren, and Madeline Streiff. "Reel Royal Diversity? The Glass Ceiling in Disney's Mulan and Princess and the Frog." *Societies* 6, no. 35 (2016): 1–14. doi:10.3390/soc6040035.

Dunes, Lauren, ed. *The Psychosocial Implications of Disney Movies*. Switzerland: MDPI, 2019.

Dyson, A. H. *Writing Superheroes: Contemporary Childhood, Popular Culture and Classroom Literacy*. New York: Teachers College Press, 1997.

Ehrenreich, Barbara. "Bonfire of the Disney Princesses." *The Nation* (December 11, 2007): n.p. <https://www.thenation.com/article/archive/bonfire-disney-princesses/>.

England, Dawn Elizabeth, Lara Descartes, and Melissa A. Collier-Meek. "Gender Role Portrayal and the Disney Princesses." *Sex Roles* 64 (2011): 555–67. doi:10.1007/s11199-011-9930-7.

Freeman, Matthew, and Renira Rampazzo Gambarato, eds. *The Routledge Companion to Transmedia Studies*. New York: Routledge, 2019.

Frost, Katie. "Emma Watson Reveals Why She Turned Down Cinderella Before Accepting Belle Role." *Elle* (January 7, 2017): n.p. <https://www.elle.com/uk/life-and-culture/culture/news/a33458/emma-watson-turned-down-cinderella-before-belle/>.

Gagnon, Monika Kin. "Race-ing Disney: Race and Culture in the Disney Universe." PhD diss., Simon Fraser University, 1998.

Gazda, Courtney. "The (De)Evolution of the Disney Princess." *Dissenting Voices* 4, no. 1 (2015): 29–46. <http://digitalcommons.brockport.edu/dissentingvoices/vol4/iss1/6>.

Gehlawat, Ajay. "The Strange Case of *The Princess and the Frog*: Passing and the Elision of Race." *Journal of American Studies* 14, no. 4 (2010): 417–431. doi:10.1007/s12111-010-9126-1.

Genette, Gerard. *Paratexts: Thresholds of Interpretation*. Translated by Jane E. Lewin. Cambridge: Cambridge University Press, 2001.

Gill, Rosalind. "Post-Feminist Media Culture: Elements of a Sensibility." *European Journal of Cultural Studies* 10, no. 2 (2007): 146–66. doi:10.1177/1367549407075898.

Giovagnoli, Max. "Transmedia Branding and Marketing: Concepts and Practices." In Freeman and Gambarato 2019, 251–59.

Giroux, Henry A. *The Mouse that Roared: Disney and the End of Innocence*. Lanham, MD: Rowman and Littlefield Publishers, 2001.

Golden, Julia C., and Jennifer Wallace Jacoby. "Playing Princess: Preschool Girls' Interpretations of Gender Stereotypes in Disney Princess Media." *Sex Roles* (2017): n.p. doi:10.1007/s11199-017-0773-8.

Goudreau, Jenna. "Disney Princess Tops List of the 20 Best-Selling Entertainment Products." *Forbes* (September 12, 2012): n.p. <https://www.forbes.com/sites/jennagoudreau/2012/09/17/disney-princess-tops-list-of-the-20-best-selling-entertainment-products/?sh=4f55b22ab06a>.

Gray, Jonathan. *Show Sold Separately: Promos, Spoilers, and Other Media Paratexts*. New York: New York University Press, 2010.

Gunter, Barrie. *Media and the Sexualization of Childhood*. New York: Routledge, 2014.

Hains, Rebecca. *The Princess Problem: Guiding Our Girls Through the Princess-Obsessed Years*. Sourcebooks, 2014.

Henke, Jill Birnie, Diane Zimmerman Umble, and Nancy J. Smith. "Construction of the Female Self: Feminist Readings of the Disney Heroine." *Women's Studies in Communication* 19, no. 2 (1996): 229–49. <https://doig.org/10.1080/07491409.1996.11089814>.

Hine, Benjamin et al. "The Rise of the Androgynous Princess: Examining Representations of Gender in Prince and Princess Characters of Disney Movies Released 2009–2016." *Social Sciences* 7, no. 245 (2018): 1–23. doi:10.3390/socsci712.

Hoerrner, Keisha L. "Gender Roles in Disney Films: Analyzing Behaviors from Snow White to Simba." *Women's Studies in Communication* 19, no. 2 (1996): 213–28. doi:10.1080/07491409.1996.11089813.

"Honor to Us All." Composed by Matthew Wilder. Lyrics by David Zippel. Sung by Lea Salonga for *Mulan*. 1998. <https://www.youtube.com/watch?v=-1S9 pYmpkG8>.

Jackson, Victoria. " 'What Do We Get from a Disney Film if We Cannot See It?': The BBC and the 'Radio Cartoon' 1934–1941." *Historical Journal of Film, Radio and Television* 39, no. 2 (2019): 290–308. doi:10.1080/01439685.2018.1522789.

Jenkins, Henry. *Convergence Culture: Where Old and New Media Collide.* New York: New York University Press, 2006.

Johnson, Derek. *Media Franchising: Creative License and Collaboration in the Culture Industries.* New York: New York University Press, 2013.

Kennedy, Helen W. "Transmedia Games: Aesthetics and Politics of Profitable Play." In Freeman and Gambarato 2019, 72–81.

Leader, Caroline F. "Branding the Disney Princess: Femininity, Family and Franchise." PhD diss., University of Wisconsin-Madison, 2019.

———. "Magical Manes and Untamable Tresses: (En)coding Computer-Animated Hair for the Post-feminist Disney Princess." *Feminist Media Studies* 18, no. 6 (December 1, 2018): 1086–1101. doi:10.1080/14680777.2017.1390688.

Lester, Catherine. "Frozen Hearts and Fixer-Uppers: Villainy, Gender, and Female Companionship in Disney's *Frozen*." In *Discussing Disney*, edited by Amy M. Davis, 193–216. New Barnet: John Libbey Publishing, 2019.

Lester, Neal A. "Disney's *The Princess and the Frog*: The Pride, the Pressure, and the Politics of Being a First." *Journal of American Culture* 33, no. 4 (2010): 294–308. doi:10.1111/J.1542-734X.2010.00753.X.

Li, Jinhua. "Mulan (1998) and Hua Mulan (2009): National Myth and Transcultural Intertextuality." In *Heroism and Gender in War Films*, edited by Karen Ritzenhoff and Jakub Kazecki, 187–205. New York: Palgrave Macmillan, 2014.

Limbach, Gwendolyn. " 'You the Man, Well, Sorta': Gender Binaries and Liminality in Mulan." In *Diversity in Disney Films: Critical Essays on Race, Ethnicity, Gender, Sexuality and Disability*, edited by Johnson Cheu, 115–28. Jefferson, NC: McFarland, 2013.

Ma, Sheng-mei. "Mulan Disney, It's Like, Re-Orients: Consuming and Animating Teen Dreams." In *The Emperor's Old Groove: Decolonizing Disney's Magic Kingdom*, edited by Brenda Ayres, 149–64. New York: Peter Lang, 2003.

Maier, Sarah E. "Rebellious Royals: From Disney's Ariel to Pixar's Merida." In *A Vindication of the Redhead: The Typology of Red Hair Throughout the Literary and Visual Arts*, edited by Brenda Ayres and Sarah E. Maier, 223–42. London: Palgrave Macmillan, 2021.

"Mattel and Disney Announce Multi-Year Global Licensing Agreement for Disney Princess and Disney Frozen Franchises." *Mattel Newsroom*, January 26, 2022. <https://corporate.mattel.com/news/mattel-and-disney-announce-multi-year-global-licensing-agreement-for-disney-princess-and-disney-frozen-franchises>.

"Merida." *Shop Disney*. 2022. <https://www.shopdisney.com/characters/disney/disney-princess/merida/?originalTerm=merida&searchType=redirect&pdpRedirect=0>.

"Mulan." *Shop Disney*. 2022. <https://www.shopdisney.com/characters/disney/disney-princess/mulan/?originalTerm=mulan&searchType=redirect&pdpRedirect=0>.

Orenstein, Peggy. *Cinderella Ate My Daughter: Dispatches from the Front Lines of the New Girlie-Girl Culture*. New York: HarperCollins, 2011.

———. "What's Wrong with Cinderella?" *New York Times Magazine* (December 2006): n.p. <http://www.nytimes.com/2006/12/24/magazine/24princess.t.html>.

Pallant, Chris. *Demystifying Disney: A History of Disney Feature Animation*. New York: Continuum International Publishing Group, 2011.

"Pocahontas." *Shop Disney*. 2022. <https://www.shopdisney.com/characters/disney/disney-princess/pocahontas/?originalTerm=pocahontas&searchType=redirect&pdpRedirect=0>.

"Reflection." Composed by Matthew Wilder. Lyrics by David Zippel. Sung by Lea Salonga for *Mulan*. 1998. <https://www.youtube.com/watch?v=GcC3rYEZv90>.

Rothschild, Sarah. *The Princess Story: Modeling the Feminine in Twentieth-Century American Fiction and Film*. New York: Peter Lang, 2012.

Stone, Kay. "Things Walt Disney Never Told Us." *The Journal of American Folklore* 88, no. 347 (1975): 42–50. doi:10.2307/539184.

Suddath, Claire. "The 500 Million Dollar Battle Over Disney's Princesses: How Hasbro Grabbed the Lucrative Disney Doll Business from Mattel." *Bloomsburg Businessweek* (December 17, 2015): n.p. <https://www.bloomberg.com/features/2015-disney-princess-hasbro/>.

Turner, Sarah. "Blackness, Bayous and Gumbo: Encoding and Decoding Race in a Colorblind World." In *Diversity in Disney Films: Critical Essays on Race, Ethnicity, Gender, Sexuality and Disability*, edited by Johnson Cheu, 83–98. Jefferson, NC: McFarland, 2013.

Valdivia, A. N. "Mixed Race on the Disney Channel: From *Johnnie Tsunami* Through *Lizzie McGuire* and Ending with *The Cheetah Girls*." In *Mixed Race Hollywood*, 269–89. New York: New York University Press, 2008.

von Stackleberg, Peter. "Transmedia Franchising: Driving Factors, Storyworld Development, and Creative Process." In Freeman and Gambarato 2019, 233–42.

Ward, Annalee R. *Mouse Morality: The Rhetoric of Disney Animated Films.* Austin: University of Texas Press, 2002.

Westland, Ella. "Cinderella in the Classroom: Children's Responses to Gender Roles in Fairy-Tales." *Gender and Education* 5, no. 3 (1993): 237–49. doi:10.1080/0954025930050301.

Whelan, Bridget. "Power to the Princess: Disney and the Creation of the Twentieth-Century Princess Narrative." In *Kidding Around: The Child in Film and Media*, edited by Alexander N. Howe and Wynn Yarbrough, 167–91. New York: Bloomsbury, 2014.

Wohlwend, K. E. *Playing Their Way into Literacies: Reading, Writing, and Belonging in the Early Childhood Classroom.* New York: Teachers College Press, 2011.

Zaslow, Emile. *Feminism, Inc.: Coming of Age in Girl Power Media Culture.* New York: Palgrave Macmillan, 2009.

Zornado, Joseph. *Disney and the Dialectic of Desire: Fantasy as Social Practice.* Switzerland: Palgrave Macmillan, 2017.

3 Imagineered Neo-Victorian American Real Estate: "A clean, unspoiled spot"

Walter Elias Disney was a neo-Victorian American, with a view that Victoriana and Americana were synonymous and could and should be transported from the past into the present and future—a back-to-the-future venture. Disney came into the world on December 5, 1901, during a *fin de siècle* that was already in the process of rejecting Victorian values and turning toward a supposedly more progressive culture known as "modern." He was born in Chicago at a time when the Northwest hometown was changing rapidly and alarmingly, to the dissatisfaction of Disney's "strait-laced" father who blamed it on the "influx of immigrants from Italy, Ireland and Central Europe" (Burnes et al. 2002, 21); "the once-quiet suburb was suddenly alive with colorful street markets filled with a Babel of foreign tongues," and increasing crime prompted Elias Disney to lead a campaign to close barrooms. "Envisioning a life of rural virtues and God's bounty," he bought a 45-acre farm in Marceline, Missouri (21). Walt Disney would live there for only five years (from the age of 4 to 9) and after that idealize the small town. He told *The Marceline News* in 1938: "More things of importance happened to me in Marceline than have happened since—or are likely to in the future. Things, I mean, like experiencing my first country life, seeing my first circus parade, attending my first school, seeing my first motion picture."[1]

When Walt Disney visited Marceline in 1946, he was already envisioning the construction of Disneyland Park, although he planned to call it Mickey Mouse Park (Burnes et al. 166). His first theme park would materialize in Anaheim, California, but he always intended to return to Marceline and construct a park there but never did; the dream has since become known as the "Lost Park" (Bordsen 2018, n.p.). Nonetheless, the town in Missouri would be the inspiration of Main Street in his theme parks around the world and early films, such as *So Dear to My Heart* (1948), *Lady and the Tramp* (1955), and *Pollyanna* (1960) (Williams and Denney 2019, 32). Nearly all literature about Disney conveys the man's nostalgia for the nineteenth century during a time in America's history when Victorian values were under attack and threat of discard by modern liberalism and the twentieth-century cataclysmic historical events (two world wars, the Great Depression, and the Cold War) that threatened the very existence of civilization.[2]

In 1942 Vera Lynn made famous the song "(There'll Be Bluebirds Over) the White Cliffs of Dover," written a year after the Royal Air Force and the German Luftwaffe battled over the white cliffs of Dover. The words expressed the hope that "there'll be love and laughter / and peace ever after / tomorrow, when the world is free."[3] Peace was the prevalent yearning of a war-weary world, but when the Paris Peace Treaties in 1947 were signed, much like the Treaty of Versailles that closed World War I, the world gyred in uneasy, uncertain détente.

It was at this time that Disney sought peace, one that could comfort a beleaguered human race: He began making plans for a recreational escape into fantasy and a nostalgic turn back of the clock. For his first theme park, he was determined to create Main Street, U.S.A. as if it were a picture post-card of Marceline, Missouri—the one place and period in his life when he knew happiness as a boy. Robin Allan called Disney "a Biedermeier artist *par excellence* since he used realism to promote nostalgia for a romanticized past" (1999, 20). Throughout Central Europe the Biedermeier period was a reaction against industrialization from 1815 to 1848, and it eulogized the home life of the rising middle class. With British Romanticism that began a few years earlier, it also extolled nature, rustic life, and childhood, as illustrated in these lines from William Wordsworth's seminal poem: "My heart leaps up when I behold / A rainbow in the sky" and "The Child is father of the Man" (1802, 1, 2, and 7). Disney was a Romantic who, like Toby Tyler, sporting his bindle or blanket stick over his shoulder, was a runaway fleeing the modern era.[4] He was not alone in his uncertainty about twentieth century, and his bundle turned out to be full of gold.

Svetlana Boym explains the reason why nostalgia became so popular to moderns: "The rapid pace of industrialization and modernization increased the intensity of people's longing for the slower rhythms of the past, for continuity, social cohesion and tradition" (2001, 16). Paradoxically, she says, modern Europe considered nostalgia a "disease" and was determined to "escape the burden of historical time" (17). Even more paradoxical, nostalgic efforts to escape also created "an abyss of forgetting" and its "obsession with the past ... takes place in inverse proportion to its actual preservation" (16). Like many other nostalgic artists, Disney so idealized the past that he ignored its unpleasant realities. Disney especially romanticized the nineteenth century. Before he was rushed to St. Joseph Hospital on November 30, 1966, ten days before he would die of circulatory collapse caused by the cobalt therapy treatment of his lung cancer, he was finishing production of *Mosby's Marauders* about John S. Mosby who was a Confederate who led raids behind enemy lines. Mosby was played by Jack Ging, a debonair actor who came across as a hero, while two other actors, who were Disney staples and had played several roles as virtuous young men, Kurt Russell (who played a Confederate private) and James MacArthur (who played Union corporal), became friends when they were expected to be enemies. Disney's Civil War was all about amicability and adventures; there was no mention whatsoever of the horrors of war or slavery.

Why was Disney so surprised at the outcry against racism in the depiction of Jim Crow and his minstrel buddies in *Dumbo* (1941) and for Uncle Remus' singing about the "mighty satisfactual" good-ole days in *Song of the South* (1946)?[5] A film critic recently said, "We are in a polarizing time: Old wounds from the past—race, politics, gender equality, sexism and poverty—have all bubbled to the surface" (Tinubu 2019). Acknowledging that Disney+ is hiding some of its racist products, it is releasing still others without disclaimers as to "past atrocities" that need to be brought out into the open, discussed, and used to bring healing (Tinubu).

Boym suggests that there are two forms of nostalgia. Restorative nostalgia is about an arbitrarily defined truth and tradition, whereas reflective nostalgia "dwells on the ambivalences of human longing and belonging and does not shy away from the contradictions of modernity" (xviii). Disney, Joseph Zornado states, is all about "idealized images of a nation's past and the possibilities of a utopic future," based solely on "nonreflection" and "childhood innocence" (2017, 23). Zornado credits Disney for "institutionalized nostalgia" (23).

Disney most certainly did this, and his "institution" commercial-
ized into the most expensive "real estate" on the planet. As of 2022,
The Walt Disney Company has created twelve parks at six different resorts: Disneyland with its five themed lands opened in Los Angeles in 1955.
The Magic Kingdom, with six themed lands, opened in Orlando in 1971.
The next park, Tokyo DisneySea and Tokyo Disney Resort, opened in 2001,
followed by Disneyland Resort Paris in 2002, Hong Kong Disneyland in
2002, and Disneyland Resort in Shanghai in 2016. Expansions were made
in each, as other Disney enterprises burgeoned such as Disney Cruise Line,
Disney Sports Attractions, Disney World golf courses, restaurants, water
resorts, themed hotels, lodges, water parks, and so on.

Main Street U.S.A.

The entrance to these theme parks in California, Florida, Tokyo, Hong
Kong, Paris, and Shanghai all welcome visitors to first travel through a
neo-Victorian American town called Main Street U.S.A. Regardless of
countries, Disney's Main Street consists of a variety of Victorian-American
styles and establishments. Typifying most small towns in America at
the turn of the century, Main Street is also the commercial strip for an
ice cream parlor, emporium, confectionery, bakery, candy palace, and
cinema. In the Magic Kingdom, there is a barber shop complete with the
requisite pole of red and white stripes. Although the tobacco shop closed
in the mid-1980s, the Cigar Store Indian, Big Chief Seegar, has relocated
to the front of the Crystal Arts shop at the Magic Kingdom.

The ice cream eatery at Disneyland in Anaheim and Paris is called
the Gibson Girl Ice Cream Parlour, with "parlour" spelled in the old-
fashioned British way. "The Gibson Girl," with her puffed hair pulled up
to a bun on top with ringlets and tendrils hanging down, was the vision
of Charles Dana Gibson, an American illustrator who sent his first pen-
and-ink sketches of the ideal "New Woman" to *Life* magazine in 1886.
His Gibson Girls would also appear in *Harper's Weekly*, *Scribners*, and
Collier's[6]: "From the 1890s until World War I, the glamorous Gibson

Girl set the standard for beauty, fashion, and manners" ("The Gibson Girl's America" 2013, n.p.).

The Gibson Girl Ice Cream Parlour was a replacement in 1977 for what had been the Carnation Ice Cream Parlor that opened on Main Street in Anaheim in 1955. Carnation, now owned by Nestle, began in 1899 with its brand of evaporated milk. Founded by Elbridge Amos Stuart from North Carolina (but buried in Los Angeles), Carnation was known for a slogan about his milk coming from "Contented Cows" (Forbes 1923, 428). Stuart is an American rags-to-riches story about a man who worked hard, was driven by a vision, and had business smarts to found "the greatest evaporated milk enterprise in the world" (412). His career started as being a grocery boy and was at one time "a cripple on crutches" (412). Above his desk was framed this Victorian poem:

> Pluck Wins,
> It Always Wins
> Through days be slow
> And nights be dark
> 'Twixt days that come and go,
> Still pluck will win;
> Its average is sure.
> He gains the prize who can the most
>   Endure,
> Who faces issues, who never shirks,
> Who waits and watches,
> And who always works.[7]

Disney himself was "a rags-to-riches story like many others, in which some young male, born with no assets other than his own pluck ... becomes part of a specifically *American* aristocracy ... in a rat race that destroys the majority of his competitors" (Brode 2016, xi). An antique delivery truck traveled through Main Street, advertising, "Carnation Company: Fresh Milk Ice Cream Disneyland" and would sometimes be driven by Walt Disney himself. The Carnation Company was closed in 1997, but the new Carnation Café was opened in 2012 (Weiss 2018, n.p.).

In the earlier centuries, most towns were designed to have a town square, an open space where the public could congregate. Usually it would be a site for markets, concerts, and tree lighting at Christmas time. At

Disney's town square, Tony's restaurant from *Lady and the Tramp* (1955) is a place where one may enjoy meats-a-ball, hospitality, and socializing, regardless if one is a fine lady or a vagabond, canine or otherwise. Tony's is a *trattoria*, an Italian designation for an eatery that is less formal than a *ristorante*. The Tony's at the Magic Kingdom might remind one of the Crystal Palace in London where instead of walls, there are expansive windows, and the chairs are decorative wrought iron, an item that had become extremely popular in the nineteenth century. In Tokyo, Main Street is called Disneyland's World Bazaar, and it is covered by a giant Plexiglas canopy to protect visitors from Japan's frequent rainstorms. Significantly, Stephen Mills compared Disney's theme parks to the 1851 Crystal Palace Great Exhibition "which involved stupendous, seemingly indiscriminating display of British and Imperial artifacts" (1990, 69). The "ideological objective," thinks Mitsuhiro Yoshimoto in his analysis of Disney's theme parks, which he considers the same as empire building, "is to equate the commodification of daily life with the narrativization of American nationalism as a word of hegemonic power. The kernel of this articulation is Main Street USA" (1994, 192).

In addition to railways, iron was being used to build skyscrapers and bridges (especially in America) and providing ornamentation for Victorian houses. In America, the Bethlehem Steel Corporation mushroomed because of the world's demand for iron. The wrought-iron chairs at Tony's are a major American-Victorian symbol of progress and commercial vitality.

In both Disneyland in Anaheim and in Tokyo Disneyland is a themed land called New Orleans Square based on nineteenth-century New Orleans. Not exactly a square though, it is a series of streets similar to what can be found in the French Quarter, and nearly every house is decorated with intricately designed, lacey wrought-iron balconies. Once one enters the theme park in Paris, one sees a wrought-iron gazebo very similar to the one that is the center of the town in *Pollyanna* (1960) where a hometown band plays. There are also wrought-iron benches and wrought-iron fences around grassy areas with landscaped flora and statues of children.

Prevalent in England as well, iron was very important to building railroads that became a major form of mass transportation and the vehicle that facilitated distribution of products, all forms of commerce, and social mobility. Trains were a nostalgic entity for Walt Disney, who, as a child, would often put his ear on the tracks in Marceline to hear trains coming and going. Trains would appear not only in his theme parks but in many of his films (Allan 3). Zornado said something that is probably true about Disney's train, that it represented Disney's lost childhood, but insofar as it represented the cause of a desire of something ungraspable, it was constantly the object of his desire; as a toy train goes round and round, it never arrives anywhere (157). So was Disney's fetish for the past.

To Disney, Victorian was also synonymous with strong morals and American ideals such as the nuclear family with a saintly mother tending to the hearth and children and with a chivalrous father tilling the land or working in a tuppence-worshipping occupation that engaged the likes of George Banks in *Mary Poppins* (1964), protecting those weaker than he, and/or fighting the good fight for capitalism and commerce. Disney's early work inculcates a Victorian ideology of division of gender along the lines dictated in a lecture delivered at highly industrialized Manchester in 1865 by John Ruskin and then widely published throughout Britain and America. In this lecture Ruskin prescribed the man as performing "his rough work in the open world" where he "must encounter all peril and trial." His is "*always* hardened, But he guards the woman from all this; within his house as ruled by her" (1892 [1865], 136; emphasis in original). In blissful contrast, the home is "the woman's true place and power" where "[s]he must be enduringly, incorruptibly good, instinctively, infallibly wise,—wise not for self-development, but for self-renunciation" (137). The Victorian home is

> the place of peace; the shelter, not only from all injury, but from all terror, doubt, and division. In so far as it is not this, it is not home; so far as the anxieties of the outer life penetrate into it, and the inconsistently-minded, unknown, unloved or hostile society of the outer world is allowed by either husband or wife to cross the threshold, it ceases to be home. (136)

The ideal Victorian home is "a sacred place, a vestal temple, a temple of the hearth" (136).

Similarly, Mrs. Sarah Ellis, in her best-selling *Wives of England*, taught women to embrace her duty in serving her husband: "At home it is but fitting that the master of the house should be considered as entitled to the choice of every personal indulgence" (1846 [1843], 100). Thomas Carlyle said that he "never doubted but the true and noble function of a woman in this world was, is, and forever will be, that of being a Wife and Helpmate to a worthy man, and discharging well the duties that devolve on her in consequence as mother of children and Mistress of a Household—duties high, noble, silently important as any that can fall to a human being," which makes her the "Queen of the World."[8]

The prevalence of the Victorian-designed house (in many of Disney's movies) is, as Linda Hutcheon generalizes, "an unavoidably social act ... [that] reinstate[s] a dialogue with the past and—perhaps inescapably— with the social and ideological context in which architecture is (and has been) both produced and lived" (1988, 23). It may be "incorporated," as does Disney with its Victorian houses, but their ideological messages (of home and family) have been "modified, given new and different life and meaning" (24), so that the architectural style of Victorian houses in the 1955 *Lady and the Tramp*, may look the same as in 2019 *Lady*, but their symbolism means something entirely different from the nineteenth century in 1955, and then different again in 2019. It is, as Hutcheon says, a process of contradicting and subverting meanings attached to architectural styles (3), and it also demonstrates that memory (as in Walt Disney's memory) is "fictionalizing" (10). For Disney in 1955, the memory is nostalgic, a longing for an idealized past; in 2019, it is a revisioning of what the past should have been.[9]

Although there is a broad assortment of Victorian styles of houses on Main Street—with emphasis on "assortment" in that eclecticism is a key characteristic of Victorian architecture and furnishings—Casey's Corner is a perfect example of neo-Victorianism. It is a sprawling yellow Second Empire with terra-cotta tiles, including balconies, faux widow walks, bonneted dormers, elegant crestings, and elaborate ornamentation, in a way that Disney saw America, not as the proverbial melting pot, but more as a stew that was made all the hardier because of its bounty of variety.

The walls in the backroom of Casey's Corner are covered with Lincrusta, an embossed wall covering that was invented by Frederick Walton in 1860 but did not achieve popularity in America until Frederick Beck bought the patent rights and began producing it in a factory in Stamford,

Connecticut, in 1883 (Simpson 1999, 101–12). After that, it appeared in both upper- and middle-class houses and buildings throughout America. It can be found in several of the other Victorian houses on Main Street.

A large "C" is mounted in the front of the building, standing for the Cincinnati Reds, supposedly the first professional baseball team in America (Veness and Veness 2012, 103) in 1869 (Gilbert 2020, n.p.). Actually, baseball began to be popular in America in the 1850s first as recreational exercise and then later as a spectator event. Shortly after the American Civil War, baseball was being played and watched "from coast to coast" (Gilbert). In 1908 Jack Norworth wrote the lyrics to "Take Me Out to the Ball Game," and Albert Von Tilzer put it to music. Considered a Tin Pan Alley song,[10] it reflects the passion Americans had for the game and its form of escape as expressed in this line: "I don't care if I never get back."[11] The line previous to this is "Buy me some peanuts and Cracker Jack." An American snack of molasses, peanuts, and popcorn, the first Cracker Jack sold at a ball game was in 1896, so reports *Baseball's Greatest Hit* (Thompson et al. 2008, 125) and can be purchased at Casey's Corner as well as in Markham's (served with champagne), a luxurious restaurant in Walt Disney World's Golden Oak community (Thompson 2019, n.p.). In 1867 a newspaper in Washington, D.C. wrote: "Peanuts and Popcorn were not mixed up with piety when we first new camp meetings, nor cigar smoking nor Psalm singing.[12] But the times are changed and we with them." The times continue to change, however; with the rising allergies to peanuts, many ball parks have banned Cracker Jacks and peanuts.

By 1946 most Americans were home from the war, and the Boston Red Sox (representing the American League) with the famous Ted Williams was appearing for the first time since its championship of 1918. The team played against the St. Louis Cardinals (representing the National League).

In that same year (1946), Disney released *Make Mine Music*, a musical anthology of 10 segments that includes "Casey at the Bat," a retelling of the famous poem by Ernest Thayer, published in 1888. Like any good Victorian piece, it is didactic, teaching the biblical concept of "pride goeth before a fall" (Prov. 16:18). Casey, a forerunner of Gaston in *Beauty and the Beast*, is overconfident that he can win the game. While his confident male fans cheer and swooning female fans watch on, he strikes out.

Baseball had become fused with Americana. Baseball players had become national heroes. What baby boomer didn't collect baseball cards? As of 2021, there have been 175 movies made about baseball. Even in 2022, schools are let out so that kids can attend the World Series if their team is playing. But how did an American game become a world pastime? Some claim that the *New York World Telegram Newspaper* announced a game between the National League and the American Association to "decide baseball's 'World Champions'" (Lennox n.p.). Following that, other news-papers referred to the competition as "the World Series."

After arriving in the United States, Tal Barak was initiated into a long-standing American tradition of betting on the winning team in the World Series. He replied, "Sure …. What countries are participating?" The response left him feeling as if he were "the only person in the 'world'— a.k.a. 'United States'—confused by the notion of a World Series played entirely in North America" (2005, n.p.). Joseph Reaves, author of *Taking in a Game: A History of Baseball in Asia* (2002), told him:

> You really have to look back at the way most people in the United States saw the world in 1903—the year the "World Series" championship was created …. The Guilded Age was giving way to an era when the United States would dominate the glove militarily, economically and politically. No one could beat the United States militarily. And surely no one could beat the U.S. at its own game. (quoted in Barak n.p.)

Baseball, simply put, was America's pennant that boasted its competitive spirit, drive, might, and strength in global hegemony. It was democracy in action: Many baseball players came from dirt-poor farms and attained wealth and fame through sheer grit and force of will. It was American democracy in action when in 1910 the first President of the United States threw the ceremonial pitch, when in 1943 the All-American Girls Professional Baseball League was formed, when in 1947 Jacky Robinson became the first African American to integrate baseball, and when in 2020 an Asian American woman, Kim Ng, became the first woman to be a general manager of a Major League Baseball team (the Miami Marlins).

Casey's Corner is also in Tokyo Disneyland (as well as in Paris). In his fascinating *Transpacific Field of Dreams: How Baseball Linked the United States and Japan in Peace and War*, Sayuri Guthrie-Shimizu begins with: "'Whoever wants to know the heart and mind of America had better learned baseball,' Jacques Barzun famously wrote in 1954" (quoted in 2012, 1). The game was exported to Japan and was played for the first time in Tokyo in 1872 (13). It is now the most popular sport in Japan (Yazawa 2018, 132).

Inside Casey's corner in both countries is a plethora of Coca-Cola memorabilia. The title of Mark Pendergrast's book *For God, Country, and Coca Cola: The Definitive History of the Great American Soft Drink and the Company That Makes It* clearly identifies the concatenation of America and the soft drink. Credit is usually given to Georgia-born John Pemberton for inventing Coca-Cola in 1888, at a time of "America's metamorphosis from a land of farmers into an urbanized society of mills and factories ... arguably the most wrenching in its history" (Pendergrast 2000 [1993], 7–8). Pendergrast's theory is that "Coca-Cola emerged from this turbulent, inventive, noisy, neurotic new America," providing it with a "nerve tonic" that by 1938 became called "the sublimated essence of America" (9). It became even more popular when Pemberton advertised it as the Temperance Drink, as an acceptable substitute for gin (32)

Shortly after America entered World War II, the president of Coca-Cola announced: "We will see that every man in uniform gets a bottle of Coca-Cola for five cents, wherever he is and whatever it costs our company" (quoted in Pendergrast 195). A soldier wrote: "It's the little things, not the big, that the individual soldier fights for or wants so badly when away. It's the girl find back home in a drug store over a Coke, or the juke box and the summer weather" (quoted in Pendergrast 206). (Although there is no juke box in Casey's Corner, there is a piano with a pianist who plays American ragtime.)

Coca-Cola is sold in every country in the world except for North Korea and Cuba (due to US trade sanctions and embargos). Coca-Cola was instantly popular in China when it first arrived in 1927, but in 1949, when Mao Zedong came to power, both Coke and Pepsi and other Western imports were banned until 1979. In 2012 Pepsi built its largest innovation center outside of the United States in Shanghai ("PepsiCo Research," n.d., n.p.), which may be the reason that Shanghai is the only Disney park that serves Pepsi and not Coke, and there is no Casey's Corner. But Pepsi is also an American icon. It was developed in 1893 by Caleb Bradham who made it in his drugstore in New Bern, North Carolina, for the purpose of relieving dyspepsia (hence its name) (Tompkins 1994, 107). Further, Pepsi sponsored "It's a Small World" attraction at the UNICEF pavilion at the 1964–65 New York World's Fair, and it sponsored the Country Bear Jamboree for the first decade. It was the beverage of choice at the first Disneyland for the first three decades (Bricker 2017, n.p.). Competition, after all, is as American as apple pie.

Aside from baseball and soda pop, hot dogs are another American icon, and this is the main menu attraction at Casey's Corner. More recently nachos have been added to its menu, an indicator of multicultural changes in North America. The frankfurter was an American import as well, having originated in Frankfurt, Germany, as early as the thirteenth century. Still, the hot dog is an American invention: The story goes that Charles Feltman sold meat pies at Coney Island when in 1871 he got the idea that his cart could hold more if he could store thin links of sausage separate from oblong buns (Chetwynd 2012, 83). However, typical of American myths, this story has been often refuted and the credit given to a baker by the name of Ignatz Fischmann (Mercuri 2007, 12). Additional myths evolved as to how the sausage got its name, but so far, the most reliable is about a vendor who was selling "red hots" at a ballgame, which led to Yale students' nicknaming them further to "hot dogs," suggesting, in gest, that they were made of dog meat (Cohen 2004, 269–70).

"Ambiguity," Steven Watts has observed, "colored Walt Disney's attitude toward the past." The buildings on Main Street are not life-size, so that they offer an "intimate sense of comfort and security." Quoting Walt, Watts says, "every brick and shingle and gas lamp [has been] made five-eighths true size" (1997, 22–23).[13] In writing about Main Street U.S.A. in 1990, a reporter said that it was a "monument to an 'era of good feeling,' a born-again belief in the squeaky clean virtues of front-porch U.S.A., and nostalgia for a supposedly uncomplicated, decent, hardworking, crime-free, rise up and salute the flag way of life that is the stuff of middle America's dreams, an ersatz image of the past imposed within the here and now" (73). Disney's nostalgia for the past is not for the historically accurate past but for an idealized version of it that would satisfy the need in the present for one's belief system to be validated.

Not everyone agrees with that assessment though. When Disneyland became a place in Paris, first called EuroDisney, it was met with heavy protest, especially from "Communists and intellectuals" ("EuroDisneyland" 2006, 7). A theater director (Ariane Mnouchkine) labeled it a "cultural Chernobyl" (quoted in 7), while a reporter for *Le Figaro* wished that someone "would set fire to Disneyland," and another critic indicted Mickey Mouse for "stifling individualism and transforming children into consumers" (quoted in 7). Someone claimed that the park was "another attack on France's cultural landscape, already under siege from American movies and music" ("EuroDisneyland"). Still another swore, literally, that the park was "an example of American neoprovincialism," and did not mean that that was a good thing (7).[14] As for the Asian theme parks, Yoshimoto complained that Disney was a force of "cultural imperialism" that tries "to indoctrinate and brainwash the population of the periphery regions" (190).

The Haunted House

Victoriana, with its furnishings and architecture that symbolized the period, connoted more than just a time in history. The Victorian house has often been associated with hauntings. The Haunted House in Disneyland (see Figure 3.1) is antebellum in New Orleans Square, with its wrought-iron arches and Doric columns. The neo-Roman-style Gothic (popular in the Victorian period) with a Victorian glass atrium is in the Magic Kingdom (see Figure 3.2) and Tokyo Disneyland. In Disneyland (see Figure 3.3) Paris is the Phantom Manor (see Figure 3.4) with its Second Empire style that might remind one of the Bates Motel in Hitchcock's *Psycho* (1960). It is the same house that was used in *The Ghost and Mr. Chicken* (1966). Mystic Manor in Hong Kong (see Figure 3.5) is the most eclectic, fantastical Victorian house that includes onion domes, the likes of which one might associate first with St. Basil's in Moscow. Although onion domes, influenced by Muslim countries, appeared in Russia in the sixteenth century, they became very popular during the nineteenth century when most Russian churches were being built with them, not only for aesthetic purposes but for practical reasons, to prevent ceiling collapses caused by accumulated snow. Shanghai Disneyland refused a haunted house because many Chinese do believe that ghosts are relatives that help the living if they are treated with respect. To have a ride similar to the Haunted Mansion in Anaheim "would be a mockery of a serious fear" (Jennings 2016, n.p.). The point here though is that the Victorian house is often associated with a haunted house and is an image that recurs in film and theme parks.

Figure 3.1. The Haunted House at Disneyland.

Figure 3.2. The Liberty Square Haunted Mansion, Magic Kingdom.

Figure 3.3. Haunted Mansion, Tokyo Disneyland.

Figure 3.4. Phantom Manor, Disneyland Paris.

Figure 3.5. Mystic Manor, Hong Kong Disneyland Park.

Victoria & Albert's

Prior to the disruption of national identities caused by World War I, the British Empire was the largest empire in history and the greatest global power, covering over 13,700,000 square miles or 24 percent of the Earth (Taagepera 1997, 502). Just as surely as the British Victorian Empire colonized nearly one-fourth of the world with its Western perspectives and ways, so did and does Disney colonize the world with its own Western perspectives and ways, many of them adopted from British Victorians. As described in the previous section, Disney adapted British Victoriana in its definition of Americana and then promoted it in its theme parks and films that perpetrated the world with far-reaching influence that exceeded either the British or the Roman empire.

In tribute to Queen Victoria and the Victorian empire, Victoria & Albert's is a fine-dining restaurant at Disney's Grand Floridan Resort & Spa. Since its opening in 1988, it has become one of the most preeminent restaurants in America. The décor is Victorian, and the menu is global with specialties from around the world served on Bernardaud (French) china and Sambonet (Italian) silverware. Besides a dining room that is elegantly designed, there is a private dining room called Queen Victoria's Room complete with an oval portrait of the Victoria and Albert when they were young.

This restaurant is not Americanized: Diners are not allowed to wear jeans, shorts, capri pants, sandals, or even tennis shoes. Instead, men must wear dinner jackets with dress slacks and shoes, and women must wear nice attire as well (Tripadvisor). Propriety in all things must be preserved. Nevertheless, because it does also cater to Americans and is located in America, we might call the restaurant neo-Victorian or more accurately neo-Disney, in its reinvention of British Victorian to accommodate Americans as they offer hospitality to patrons from around the world.

Imagineered Neo-Victorian Real Estate

It can be said that there are other historical time periods represented in Disney's film and theme parks, but the Victorian period is the most prevalent, except in Shanghai Disney. Below (Table 3.1), is a list of nineteenth-century-related themes throughout the six parks.

The parks (as of 2022):

1 Disneyland Anaheim
2 Disneyworld Orlando
3 Tokyo Disney
4 Disneyland Paris
5 Hong Kong Disneyland
6 Shanghai Disney

Table 3.1. Neo-Victorianism in Neo-Disney Parks

Name	Victorian characteristics	Park(s)
Adventureland	Victorian Hunters, explorers, scientists, and missionaries were very active in Asia, Africa, South America, Oceana, the Caribbean Islands, and the Middle East. A lot of colonizing was going on as well. Edward Lane and Richard Burton translated *One Thousand and One Nights* in 1840 and 1882, respectively. Edgar Rice Burroughs published his first Tarzan novel in 1912.	1–6
Alice's Curious Labyrinth	A voyage into the White Rabbit's Hole from Lewis Carroll's *Alice's Adventures in Wonderland* (1865).	4
Alice in Wonderland Maze	Like Alice's Curious Labyrinth above.	6
The Bakery Tour	Boudin Bakery was established in 1849 in San Francisco by Isidore Boudin. It is the oldest continually operating business in San Francisco and claims to have been the first to offer sourdough to San Francisco.	1

Table 3.1. Continued

Name	Victorian characteristics	Park(s)
Big Thunder Mountain Railroad[a]	Reminiscent of Western mining in the Wild West.	1–4
Blue Bayou Restaurant	Nineteenth-century Louisiana setting.	3
Café Orléans	Like a café in the French Quarter of New Orleans.	3
Captain Hook's Gallery	Based on *The Little White Bird* by J. M. Barrie (1902).	3
Carriage House Refreshments	Horse-drawn carriages of the nineteenth century.	3
Casey Jr. Circus Train	Both trains and circuses were popular in the nineteenth century.	4
Cleo's	Based on *The Adventures of Pinocchio* by Carlo Collodi (1883).	3
Club 33	Private dining clubs with Victorian settings	1–3, 6
Cowboy Cookhouse	Wild West in America.	3
Crystal Palace Restaurant	The Crystal Palace opened in London in 1854.	3
The Diamond Horseshoe	Fancy saloon in the Wild West.	3
Discovery Arcade	Gadgets and inventions of the nineteenth century.	4
Disney's Davy Crockett Ranch	American folk hero who died at the Alamo 1836.	4
Eastside Cafe	Victorian setting.	3
Frontierland	American Wild West in the nineteenth century.	1, 2, 4
The Gazebo	A gazebo was in nearly every town square.	3, 4
Ghirardelli Soda Fountain and Chocolate Shop	In 1832, John Matthews of New York City and John Lippincott of Philadelphia began manufacturing soda fountains. Domenico Ghirardelli began exporting his chocolate to San Francisco in 1847 and opened his first store in Stockton in 1849 during the Gold Rush.	1

(*Continued*)

Table 3.1. Continued

Name	Victorian characteristics	Park(s)
Grizzley Gulch	Wild West—called Frontierland elsewhere.	5
Grizzly River Run	Old mining company.	1
The Haunted Mansion[b]	Variety of Victorian-designed houses.	1–5
Hotel Cheyenne	Facades: Saloon, Jail, Billy the Kid, Annie Oakley.	4
Hotel Sante Fe	Wild West.	4
Journey to the Center of the Earth	Based on Jules Verne's novel (1864).	3
Main Street	Victorian houses and shops and horse-drawn streetcars.	4
La Cabane des Robison	Based on *The Swiss Family Robinson* by Johann David Wyss (1812).	4
Liberty Arcade	Victorian setting and history of the French gift of the Statue of Liberty given to America in 1886.	4
Mad Hatter's Tea Cups	Based on a character in *Alice in Wonderland* (1865) and *Through the Looking-Glass* (1871).	4
New Orleans Square	Nineteenth-century New Orleans.	1, 3
Pecos Bill Café	Based on nineteenth-century cowboys found in books by Edward S. O'Reilly.	3
Peter Pan's Flight	Based on *The Little White Bird* by J. M. Barrie (1902).	4, 6
Phantom Manor	Victorian haunted house in Disneyland Paris.	4
Pinocchio Village Kitchen	Based on *The Adventures of Pinocchio* by Carlo Collodi (1883).	6
Queen of Hearts Banquet Hall	Based on Lewis Carroll's *Alice's Adventures in Wonderland* (1865).	3
Red Car Trolley	Modeled after the Pacific Electric Railway that began in Los Angeles in 1887.	1
Restaurant Hokusai	Nineteenth-century art and architecture in Japan.	3

Table 3.1. Continued

Name	Victorian characteristics	Park(s)
Royal Street Veranda	Nineteenth-century New Orleans.	3
Rustler Roundup Shootin' Gallery: Yee-Haw Partner	Wild West.	4
Selfie Spot with Disney Jungle Characters at Happy Circle	Characters from Rudyard Kipling's *The Jungle Book* (1894).	6
Sequoia Inn	Like Old Faithful Inn (1904).	4
Silly Symphony Swings	Based on Disney's *Silly Symphony* (1935), Mickey's band plays the *William Tell Overture* by Gioachino Rossini (1829).	1
Sinbad's Storybook Voyage	Edward Lane and Richard Burton translated *One Thousand and One Nights* in 1840 and 1882, respectively.	3
Soarin' Around the World	The middle and upper classes of the Victorians had the time and money to travel, so they would have seen the Eiffel Tower in Paris (first seen at the World's Fair in 1889) as well as the other marvels viewed on this ride. It was the age of exploration and safaris as well. Ivory was in great demand which resulted in the crazed killing of elephants in Eastern Africa and elsewhere.	1
Thunder Mesa Riverboat Landing	Nineteenth-century paddleboards and references to Mark Twain and Molly Brown.	4
Tower of Terror	Modeled after hotel in New York City; the owner mysteriously disappeared in 1899.	3
20,000 Leagues Under the Sea	Based on Jules Verne's novel (1870) and Disney's 1954 film.	1–3

(*Continued*)

Table 3.1. Continued

Name	Victorian characteristics	Park(s)
Victoria & Albert's	Victorian décor.	2
Les Voyages de Pinocchio	Based on *The Adventures of Pinocchio* by Carlo Collodi (1883).	4
Westernland	Wild West—called Frontierland elsewhere.	3

ᵃ Significantly, Hong Kong and Shanghai do not have any railroads in the parks. This may be because of the horrible treatment and exploitation of the Chinese in America in laying rails.
ᵇ See my comment above as to why Shanghai refused to allow a haunted house at its park.

The past to the Disney Company is what it does with an old castle, one that is too decrepit to patch up or renovate for, say, a wedding venue, apartments, or shops. It is no longer necessary as a fortress to protect a village, to house aristocracy, or to provide dungeons. Only piles of rocks remain and the artifacts of old have long since been excavated. One can hardly recognize it as a castle anymore, and it will not attract tourists. Having outlived its purpose and occupying space that is now prime real estate, it is razed and replaced with a Disney castle. This is what Disney has done with the past. When interviewed by Cecil DeMille, Walt Disney said that when his company produces, "We don't think of grown-ups and we don't think of children, but just of that fine, clean, unspoiled spot down deep in every one of us that maybe the world has made us forget and that maybe our pictures can help recall" (Jackson 2006 [1938], 14). Disney revitalizes the real estate of the past and appropriates it for the present and future, an enterprise that has gone global and is one of the richest in the world, with a revenue each year of over 69 billion U.S. dollars in 2020 (Stoll 2021, n.p.).

Bibliography

Allan, Robin. *Walt Disney and Europe*. Bloomington: Indiana University Press, 1999.

"Asaph Buck." In *The Biographical Dictionary and Portrait Gallery of Representative Men of Chicago, Iowa*, 401–2. Chicago: American Biographical Publishing Company, 1893.

Barak, Tal. "World Series? Wait a Minute …," *A Fresh Take on the All-American Game*. NPR, June 1, 2005. <https://www.rulesofsport.com/faq/why-is-the-world-series-called-the-world-series-if-only-american-teams-play.html.

Bordsen, John. "This Tiny Town Is the Site of Disney's 'Lost' Park." *CNN Travel*, June 12, 2018. https://www.cnn.com/travel/article/marceline-missouri-lost-disney-park/index.html>.

Boym, Svetlana. *The Future of Nostalgia*. New York: Basic Books, 2001.

Bricker, Tom. "Shanghai Disneyland Serves Pepsi." *DisneytouristBlog*. 2017. <https://www.disneytouristblog.com/shanghai-disneyland-serves-pepsi/>.

Brode, Douglas. "Introduction: Once Upon a Time at the Movies." In *It's the Disney Version! Popular Cinema and Literary Classics*, edited by Douglas Brode and Shea T. Brode, xi–xvii. Lanham, MD: Rowman and Littlefield, 2016.

Burnes, Brian, Robert W. Butler, and Dan Viets. *Walt Disney's Missouri: The Roots of a Creative Genius*. Kansas City, MO: Kansas City Star Books, 2002.

"Casey at the Bat." Recited by Jerry Colonna for *Make Mine Music!* 1946.

Chetwynd, Josh. *How the Hot Dog Found Its Bun: Accidental Discoveries and Unexpected Inspirations That Shape What We Eat and Drink*. Guilford, CT: Lyons Press, 2012.

Cohen, Gerald Leonard, Barry A. Popik, and David Shulman. *The Origin of the Term "Hot Dog."* Rolla, MO: Gerald Cohen, 2004.

"Dame Vera Lynn Takes on BNP Over White Cliffs of Dover." *The Daily Telegraph Online*, February 18, 2009. <https://web.archive.org/web/20090219163645/http://www.telegraph.co.uk/news/newstopics/politics/4687730/Dame-Vera-Lynn-takes-on-BNP-over-White-Cliffs-of-Dover.html>.

Eker, Nathaniel. "Everything You Need to Know About *Song of the South*." July 11, 2020. <https://insidethemagic.net/2020/07/song-of-the-south-ne1/>.

Ellis, Alec. *A History of Children's Reading and Literature*. Oxford: Pergamon Press, 1963.

Ellis, Mrs. Sarah Stickney. *The Wives of England, Their Relative Duties, Domestic Influence, and Social Obligations*. 1843. London: Fisher, Son, and Company, 1846. <https://books.google.com/books?id=GzVkAAAAcAAJ>.

"EuroDisneyland." *Thunderbird Case Studies*, A15-99-0007. August 30, 2006. <www. thunderbird.edu>.

Forbes, B. C. "Stuart's Fight for Success in the Old West and the New: Many a Thrill in Story of Carnation Milk President Who Went Through the Mill in Untamed West of Yesteryear." *Forbes* (July 7, 1923): 401–12, 427–28. <https:// books.google.com/books?id=Ka3D_Yrwf38C>.

Gibson, Charles Dana. *The Gibson Girl and Her America: The Best Drawings of Charles Dana Gibson*. Chelmsford, MA: Courier Corporation, 2012.

"The Gibson Girl's America: Drawing by Charles Dana Gibson." *Library of Congress*, March 30, 2013–August 17, 2013. <https://www.loc.gov/exhibits/gibson-girls-america/>.

Gilbert, Thomas W. *How Baseball Happened: Outrageous Lies Exposed! The True Story Revealed*. Boston: David R. Godine, 2020.

Guthrie-Shimizu, Sayuri. *Transpacific Field of Dreams: How Baseball Linked the United States and Japan in Peace and War*. Chapel Hill: University of North Carolina, 2012.

Hutcheon, Linda. *A Poetics of Postmodernism: History, Theory, Fiction*. New York: Routledge, 1988.

Jackson, Kathy Merlock. *Walt Disney: Conversations*. Jackson: The University Press of Mississippi, 2006.

Jennings, Ralph. "Two Disneyland Attractions You Won't See in China and Why." *Forbes*, June 15, 2016. <https://www.forbes.com/sites/ralphjennings/2016/06/15/two-disneyland-attractions-you-wont-see-in-china-and-why/?sh=67d1b4cd28d7>.

King, Richard C., Carmen R. Lugo-Lugo, and Mary K. Bloodsworth-Lugo. *Animating Difference: Race, Gender, and Sexuality in Contemporary Films for Children*. Lanham, MD: Rowman and Littlefield Publishers, 2010.

Lennox, Doug. *Now You Know—Giant Trivia Bundle*. Toronto: Dundurn Press, 2013.

Marcuse, Maxwell F. *Tin Pan Alley in Gaslight: A Saga of the Songs That Made the Gray Nineties "Gay."* Watkins Glen, NY: Century House, 1959. <https://babel.hathitrust.org/cgi/pt?id=uc1.31822013278122&view=1up&seq=6>.

Mercuri, Becky. *The Great American Hot Dog Book: Recipes and Side Dishes from Across America*. Salt Lake City: Gibbs Smith, 2007.

Mills, Stephen F. "Disney and the Promotions of Synthetic Worlds." *American Studies International* 28, no. 2 (October 1990): 66–79. <https://www.jstor.org/stable/41280772>.

Moore, Henry D. "Straitness in the Emerson Home." *Masonic Review* 69, no. 1 (February 1888): 21–22. <https://books.google.com/books?id=98ROAQAAMAAJ>.

Moses, Montrose Jonas. *Children's Books and Reading*. New York: Mitchell Kennerley, 1907. <https://books.google.com/books?id=vqkaAAAAMAAJ>.

Otis, James [Kaler]. *Toby Tyler; or, Ten Weeks with a Circus*. 1880. New York: Harper and Brothers, 1881. <https://books.google.com/books?id=_dgDAAAAYAAJ>.

paperbacklou. "Wacha Wacha Cracker Jack Rabbit Hole. 5 Reasons Why Tampa 8 NY 2 on 4-16-21." *Yankee Blue*, April 17, 2021. <https://www.yankee.blue/2021/wacha-wacha-crackerjack-rabbit-hole-5-reasons-why-tampa-8-ny-2-on-4-16-21/>.

Pendergrast, Mark. *For God, Country, and Coca-Cola: The Definitive History of the Great American Soft Drink and the Company That Makes It*. 1993. New York: Basic Books, 2000.

"Pepsico Research and Development Centre, Shanghai, China." *Food Processing Technology*, n.d. <https://www.foodprocessing-technology.com/projects/pepsico-research-development-china-shanghai/>.

"Pluck." *Life* 45, no. 1179 (June 1, 1905): 653. <https://books.google.com/books?newbks=1&newbks_redir=0&id=XIWlSGoeoGoC>.

Ruskin, John. "Of Queen's Garden." In *Sesame and Lilies*, 117–70. 1865. Philadelphia, PA: Henry Altemis, 1892. <https://books.google.com/books?id=mp85AQAAMAAJ>.

Schickel, Richard. *Walt Disney*. London: Weidenfield and Nicolson, 1968.

Simpson, Pamela Hemenway. *Cheap, Quick, & Easy: Imitative Architectural Materials, 1870–1930*. Knoxville: University of Tennessee Press, 1999.

Stoll, Julia. "Disney—Statistics & Facts." *Statista*, November 17, 2021. <https://www.statista.com/topics/1824/disney/#dossierKeyfigures>.

Taagepera, Rein. "Expansion and Contraction Patterns of Large Polities: Context for Russia." *International Studies Quarterly* 41, no. 3 (September 1997): 475–504.

"Take Me Out to the Ball Game." Composed by Albert Von Tilzer. Lyrics by Jack Norworth. New York: The New York Music Company, 1908.

"(There'll Be Bluebirds Over) The White Cliffs of Dover." Composed by Walter Kent. Lyrics by Nat Burton. Sung by Vera Lynn. November 1941.

Thayer, Ernest. "Casey at the Bat: A Ballad of the Republic, Sung in the Year 1888." *The Daily Examiner*, June 3, 1888.

Thompson, A. D. "Champagne & Cracker Jack: Peek into Markham's Disney World's Most Exclusive Restaurant." *News-Press*, August 15, 2019. <https://www.news-press.com/story/life/food/2019/08/15/peek-into-markhams-golden-oak-disney-worlds-most-exclusive-restaurant/1986470001/>.

Thompson, Robert, Tim Wiles, and Andy Strasberg. *Baseball's Greatest Hit: The Story of "Take Me Out to the Ball Game."* Milwaukee, WI: Hal Leonard Corporation, 2008.

Tinubu, Aramide A. "Disney's Racist Cartoons Won't Just Stay Hidden in the Vault. But They Could Be Used as a Teachable Moment: Unpacking How and Why Projects Like *Song of the Southern* Were Ever Made Could Offer an Opportunity for Growth, Conversation and Healing." *Think: Opinion, Analysis, Essays*, April 25, 2019. <https://www.nbcnews.com/think/opinion/disney-s-racist-cartoons-won-t-just-stay-hidden-vault-ncna998216>.

Tompkins, Vincent. *American Decades: 1900–1909*. Detroit, MI: Gale Research, 1994.

Turner, Richard, and Peter Gumbel. "Major Attraction: As Euro Disney Braces for Its Grand Opening, the French Go Goofy." *The Wall Street Journal*, April 10, 1992, A1.

Veness, Susan, and Simon Veness. *The Hidden Magic of Walt Disney World Planner: A Complete Organizer, Journal, and Keepsake for Your Unforgettable Vacation*. New York: Adams Media, 2012.

"Victoria & Albert's." *Disney.com*. <https://www.victoria-alberts.com/.>.

———. *Tripadvisor*. <https://disneyworld.disney.go.com/dining/grand-floridian-resort-and-spa/victoria-and-alberts/>.

Watts, Steven. *The Magic Kingdom: Walt Disney and the American Way of Life*. Columbia: University of Missouri Press, 1997.

Weiss, Werner. "The Original Carnation Ice Cream Parlor and Restaurant." *Yesterland*. 2018. <https://www.yesterland.com/carnation.html>.

Williams, Pat, and Jim Denney. *Lead Like Walt: Discover Walt Disney's Magical Approach to Building Successful Organizations*. Deerfield Beach, FL: Health Communications, 2019.

Wylie, William Howie. *Thomas Carlyle: The Man and His Books*. London: Marshall Japp and Company, 1881. <https://books.google.com/books?id=zWkqAAAMAAJ>.

Yazawa, Yutaka. *How to Live Japanese*. London: White Lion Publishing, 2018.

Yoshimoto, Mitsuhiro. "Images of Empire: Tokyo Disneyland and Japanese Cultural Imperialism." In *Disney Discourse: Producing the Magic Kingdom*, edited by Eric Smooden, 181–99. New York: Routledge, 1994.

Zipes, Jack. "Breaking the Disney Spell." In *From Mouse to Mermaid*, edited by Elizabeth Bell, Lynda Haas, and Laura Sells, 21–42. Bloomington: Indiana University Press, 1995.

Zornado, Joseph. *Disney and the Dialectic of Desire: Fantasy as Social Practice*. Cham: Palgrave Macmillan, 2017.

MICHELLE CHAN

4 Reiteration of Fairy Tales in the Twenty-First Century for a Global Market

Fairy tales are "told to create communal bonds in the face of inexplicable forces of nature, to the present" and "to provide hope in a world seemingly on the brink of catastrophe" (Zipes 2007, 1). While every culture has its own brand and interpretation of fairy tales, since the early twentieth century, Disney has become an influential storyteller of fairy tales for the global audience, beginning with its adaptation of Brothers Grimm's "Snow White" (1812). After *Snow White and the Seven Dwarfs* (1937), Disney has gradually gained "a cultural stranglehold" on contemporary fairy tales (Zipes 2013, 72), branding itself the "creator of and site of global narrative" of fairy tales (Anjirbag 2018, 3).

   Disney is not merely acclaimed for his fairy-tale adaptations; the company is also marked for its reinvention, reconstruction, and rebranding of fairy tales, adapting them for contemporary readers and thus creating its lineage of fairy tales for the modern age. However, its neo-nizing of narratives is not unique to the history of fairy tales, which invariably are reinvented as they pass from one generation to the next. One example of neo-Disneyism is its expansion of ethnic representations in *Princess and the Frog* (2009), which offers Disney's first African American princess, and its recreation of an Americanized version of the story of "The Frog Prince; or, Iron Henry" from an early German folk tale, collected by the Brothers Grimm in 1812. The Disney film revives the format of traditional fairy tale not only by modernizing its storytelling but also by visualizing through film and through a variety of visualization techniques suited to film. Disney's more recent multicultural works, such as *Moana* (2016), *Coco* (2017), *Raya and the Last Dragon* (2021), and *Encanto* (2021), intentionally unfold their stories as if, like fairy tales, recounting national legends and family histories intact with their authentic cultural contexts.

An effort to authenticate the story's source, an image of the storybook appears in many openings of Disney films (Haase 2006, 233; Zipes 2011, 88; Bacchilega 2013, 78–79; Mollet 2020, 8), such as in *Pinnochio* (1940), *Song of the South* (1946), *The Adventures of Ichabod and Mister Toad* (1947), *Cinderella* (1950), *Sleeping Beauty* (1959), *The Sword in the Stone* (1963), *Winnie the Pooh and the Honey Tree* (1966), *The Jungle Book* (1967), *Robin Hood* (1973), *The Many Adventures of Winnie the Pooh* (1977), *The Tigger Movie* (2000), and *Enchanted* (2007). The image of the book that appears as the films begin ties the adaption to its original source, and more importantly, to the oral narration and reading tradition of fairy tales. Additional artistic techniques appropriate to their cultural heritage are used, one example being the visualization of stained-glass art in *Beauty and Beast* (1991, 00:01:19–2:24). The backstory of Beast is told in his castle within the stained-glass windows, a form of narration that has been widely used in Gothic churches for a congregation who was illiterate and could learn the stories and messages of the Bible though the artwork of the windows. In *Moana* the tales given by Grandma Tala are aided by tapestries adorned with traditional patterns. Set in Mexico, the family story of Miguel Rivera in *Coco* is delineated with the changing patterns on the *papel picado*, the traditional cut paper folk art found throughout Mexico and other colonies of Spain, hung on string and draped across streets. The prologue of *Raya and the Last Dragon* is narrated with the aesthetics of the shadow puppet traditions, or *Wayang*. In the beginning of *Encanto*, Abuela Alma recounts the family history and the magic of the Madrigals. Her tale is accompanied by yellow butterflies, a well-known symbol used in *Cien Años de Soledad* (*One Hundred Years of Solitude* (1967)), written by the Columbian Nobel Laureate, Gabriel García Márquez. Inheriting from the traditions of fairy tale, those prologues refer to the transmission of heritage across generations. In line with the distinctive stories, the changes in the aesthetics of the storytelling exemplify the transition from Eurocentric tales and narratives in Disney to the stories from diverse cultural origins.

Focusing his studies on the productions before 1960s, Douglas Brode argues in *Multiculturalism and the Mouse* that Disney is one early proponent of diversity on screen (2005, 8). There is no dearth of multicultural characters and elements in Disney and asserts that those works do "challenge all those societal norms and once-unquestioned values in a way that no other filmmaker of the studio era dared" (19). Though Disney has been including multicultural characters, those representations are frequently composed of stereotypical portrayals, otherization of non-American cultures, and inaccuracy with the historical accounts. *The Three Caballeros* (1944), for example, depicts stereotypical partying Brazilians and sexualized Mexican women. In *Peter Pan* (1953), the Native Americans are portrayed with exaggerated and inaccurate customs, broken English, and caricatured images. Sung Gon, presuming playing the role of a Chinese cat, in *The Aristocats* (1970), parodies the Chinese as he speaks in a heavily accented voice, talks about fortune cookies, and plays piano with chopsticks. Since the 1990s, Disney has extended the range of inclusiveness. It sets *The Lion King* (1994) and *Tarzan* (1999) in Africa, *Aladdin* (1992) in a fictional Arabian city and *Mulan* (1998) in Asia. Non-White characters are no longer the side characters and a number of non-White princesses such as Princess Jasmine of *Aladdin*, Pocahontas of *Pocahontas* (1995), and the eponymous *Mulan* are included in feature-length films. Still, controversies and great insensitivities are manifested in those same films. Jasmine's story arc ends in an "American style romance" that frees her from a "restrictive Islamic gender codes" (Wasko 2001, 141), and the film vilifies Islamic law that entraps figures like Aladdin, Jasmine, and Genie (Wise 2003, 106). Jasmine enacts a "pseudo-feminist image" because the film asserts that a woman's liberation is gained only through romance (Addison 1993, 19). *Pocahontas* depicts only the period of John Smith's visit and dramatizes the scene in which Pocahontas saved Smith, a scene that is considered in the historical account as a ritual but not an actual killing of Smith (Wood 2016, 75). In the film, Pocahontas becomes the peacemaker of the two parties (Edgerton and Jackson 1996, 94). Disney, however, sugarcoats British colonization and ignores the historical facts that Pocahontas was abducted by the British, remarried to John Rolfe, and was converted to Christianity. *Mulan* is based on a sixth-century Chinese poem "The Ballad of Mulan," which narrates Mulan's filial piety and her hardship in warfare. Like all the other princesses before her, Mulan is given a romantic interest in Disney's version, even though the original poem mentions nothing about her marriage and romantic prospect.

Neo-Disney Ethnic Inclusivity: *Princess and the Frog*

Before *Princess and the Frog*, overt racial discrimination against BIPOC (Black, Indigenous, and People of Color) individuals are found in the early animated productions of Disney. In *Midnight in a Toy Shop* (1930) and *Santa's Workshop* (1932), a doll that has dark skin repeats "Mammy," a racist mockery of African-American woman. In *Mickey's Nightmare* (1932), a Venus bust is turned into an African parody after the young Mickey has splashed it with dark paint, and an imbecilic African is found in *Mickey's Man Friday* (1935). Worse still, *Fantasia* (1940), which Brodes calls "decidedly democratic" (13), depicts the master-servant relationship between white centaurettes and dark-skinned ones in the segment of "The Pastoral Symphony." Two young black centaurettes, Sunflower and Otika, are caricatures of Africans. They are the servants who are busily grooming the centaurettes. Two sexualized black zebra centauresses, similarly, are subservient to other centaurs and centaurettes. While the latter are celebrating the Dionysian festival, they just serve food and wine to Dionysus. In *Dumbo* (1941), a crow is named Jim Crow for the period by that name of segregation, persecution, discrimination, and repression of African Americans practiced in the Deep South in the United States. This casual naming poignantly reflects Disney's indifference to the hardship of African Americans during the Jim Crow era. As these examples have evidenced, Disney has promoted stereotypes of Black people through caricatures and unchallenged and uncritical expectancy of subservience to White people.

The Disney Company is now consistently demonstrating its increasing sensitivity toward the misrepresentations in its earlier films. On its webpage, "Stories Matters" of Disney, the company claims that "we can't change the past, but we can acknowledge it, learn from it and move forward together to create tomorrow that today can only dream of" (2020). Ever since 2020 on *Disney+*, prior to the playing of some works that have been heavily criticized for misrepresentations (such as *Dumbo* and *The Three Caballeros*), the following disclaimer appears:

> This programme includes negative depictions and/or mistreatment of people or cultures. These stereotypes were wrong then and are wrong now. Rather than remove

this content, we want to acknowledge its harmful impact, learn from it and spark conversation to create a more inclusive future together. (2020)

Disney demonstrates its recognition of the inappropriate portrayals in the past although it simultaneously makes it clear that it cannot rectify all of them. With this disclaimer, the company declares that is now attempting to be more sensitive toward issues of race and culture and that future films will be scrutinized carefully by the company to avoid any stereotypical portrayal and harmful impact.

Princess and the Frog is one major attempt by Disney to display its ethnic inclusivity by introducing its first African-American princess, Tiana. Set in the 1920s in New Orleans, racism permeates and underlies the social context, which is rather appropriate because New Orleans was still very racist at the time. However, in the film, racism is displayed in a silent background, as if Disney admits its existence but refuses to voice any comment on it. Tiana's mother, Eudora is portrayed as being content to be the seamstress of Charlotte's family; there is no hint of the oppressive mistreatment and exploitation of non-White domestic maids that was rife in the 1920s in the Deep South. In the scene of the tram-taking (00:03:35–3:56), a White man is sitting in the front row of the tram when Tiana, Eudora, and another Black woman are sitting behind him. Here, the scene alludes to the segregation between the Black and the White but without censure. The film depicts the unlikely friendship between Tiana and a White, wealthy girl named Charlotte La Bouff. There is a huge gap between the financial income and living conditions of the two girls. The scenic transition from La Bouff Estate to Tiana's shotgun house, in particular, marks the massive disparity between the life of the White and Black. Later, when Tiana is struggling to save up for her restaurant, the money that Charlotte casually gives Tiana for making and serving beignets in her masquerade ball can instantly fill the desperate need of Tiana. The most explicit and audible evidence of demeaning African Americans is articulated by the estate agents, the Fenner Brothers, who tell Tiana that "a little woman of your background would have had her hands full trying to run a big business like that" (00:24:34–24:47), asserting that because she is of "that" race, she is incapable of achieving her goals, not because of outside discrimination but because African Americans were simply incapable of handling "big business," and thence, it is impractical to give them opportunities for class mobility, or so the Whites believed. At the end, when Tiana's restaurant welcomes customers from all walks of life, Tiana is still serving food to Charlotte and her father, indicating that her success is still not good enough to elevate her status to the wealthy White.

In line with the silent racism in the background, the repetitive claims of Tiana's virtues and qualities seem to propose a colorblind reading of *The Princess and the Frog*. The film invites the audience to dig deeper and see beyond the surface, expressed in the song that Mama Odie sings, "You got to dig a little deeper / Find out who you are" (01:03:33–3:37; "Dig a Little Deeper"). John Lasseter, the former Chief Creative Officer for Walt Disney animation, states that "In *Princess and the Frog*, we did want to have a princess character, but we want her to be a princess for today. And Princess Tiana is the princess for today" (2009, 00:26:54–27:04). Likewise, in *The Art of "The Princess and Frog,"* Jeff Kurtti introduces Tiana as a heroine who is "miles away from any royal maiden in the Disney canon" (2002, 26). To become a princess of today, Tiana is not following her predecessors who harbored romantic interests and dreams restricted to domesticity and marriage. Tiana is an industrious American who strives toward her goal. She longs to open her own restaurant, makes good use of her cooking talent, and supports her family well. She becomes the first neo-Disney female lead to pursue the American dream. The supervising animator Mark Henn explains that Tiana is outstanding because she "has her own motivating desire and decisions that drive her and make her interesting and sympathetic" (quoted in Kurtti 26), marking Tiana with a strong work ethic, entrepreneurial aspiration, and dedication to her parents. Yet, these emphases on the spectacular qualities of Tiana encourage not only to compliment Tiana but also to avoid truly recognizing Tiana as an African American in New Orleans in the 1920s. It is as if Disney wants to convey that "while princess Tiana is clearly [B]black, that is not the point of the test—she is simply a princess who 'happens' to have black skin but is not representational of blackness or racially-prescribed tropes" (Turner 2012, 84).

To be precise, this colorblind reading is problematically selective. Disney ostensibly visualizes the racism in the background, while it requires the colorblindness to the color of Tiana and the restraints and glass ceiling that she has encountered. Lauren Dundes and Madeline Streiff consider Tiana's restaurant as a mundane wish in comparison to the glamorous royal lives of the previous princesses (2016, 35). As evidenced by the ample reminders of Tiana's lower social class, she is clearly limited by the glass ceiling constructed for the African Americans. Tiana is pathetically outstanding because she has made the best of a restrictive environment, hostile and obtrusive to the vocational success of Blacks. Given that Tiana's restaurant is guaranteed only by the financial support provided by Prince Naveen, the hard work of Tiana fails to safeguard her dream. There are two times that Tiana is praying to the wishing star for her restaurant. The first time, Tiana's father said, "the old star can only take you part of the way. You got to help it along with some hard work of your own, and then, yeah, you can do anything you set your mind to" (00:05:30–5:40). In the second time, Tiana makes the prayer after she has been rejected by the estate agents (00:26:38–26:55). On both occasions, a frog is present; the frogs seem to mock Tiana's wish upon a star and hard work, that they will never suffice to help Tiana realize her dream. It is only through the frog, which is the prince in this case, that Tiana's dream can come true. Chris Ayres calls *The Princess and the Frog* the first "[B]lack fairytale" of Disney (2009) as the film assimilates the other princess films of Disney, a widely recognizable representation of its fairy tales. Yet, there are limits in this Black fairy tale. It can only provide as much as the fictional context permitted for an African American princess. Ultimately, *Princess and the Frog* accentuates the impotence of the African Americans that not even a princess can make any changes to their predicament in 1920s New Orleans. The relatively financial success of Tiana is a result of her marriage with Prince Naveen. Hence, the story of Tiana will only, sadly, "further disenfranchise other minorities who have yet to attain that success because that ideology posits that hard work allows everyone to access the American Dream while ignoring social, economic, educational, or political inequities that might actually limit that access" (Turner 91).

The gumbo that Tiana makes signifies the unity of all races and classes, and her restaurant serves as a melting pot of all ethnicities and all classes: "Disney's gumbo represents its utopian vision of a colorblind New Orleans which blends individuals from different cultures, races, and classes who are able to live and play together" (Gregory 2010, 438). Considering that the film is a significant response to the dearth of ethnic representation in Disney, this colorblind reading only exacerbates the images of the marginalized in the major media. Joe Edwards claims, "We wanted to show that the forces were against her—it could be sexism, racism, classicism. But we didn't want this story to be one that teaches people about racism" (quoted in Ayres n.p.). The ethnic representation in this film is made, but it is intentionally undermined. As Ilan Mitchell-Smith argues, the ethnic identities presented in Disney are "descriptive" depictions rather than a "prescriptive" one, since these representations are often "conflicted" in mass media (2012, 222). Though Disney may want to address the need of including an African American princess, it does not want to risk the loss of White viewers. The film expurgates the contemporary racism that is rooted in Tiana's social context in favor of a colorless discourse and narration. It displays "sanitized notions of identity, difference, and history in th seemingly apolitical, cultural universe of the Magic Kingdom" (Giroux and Pollock 2010, 96). Being a company of family-friendly films, it seems that Disney finds that it is too heavy to discuss the ethnic matters rooted in in its films. As Richard M. Breaux observes, the film is interrelated with plenty of contemporary historical facts and incidents. By labeling itself as a "racially neutral colorblind company," Disney remains silent to their racial misrepresentation and, as what Breaux surmises "After 75 years of magic ... Walt Disney Pictures ... Answers Its critics, Rewrites African American History and Cashes In on its Racist Past" (2010, 413–14). Nonetheless, here in this film, Disney has, at least, given a comparatively impartial portrayal of African Americans. It proposes a silenced yet visible colorblindness in *Princess and the Frog*, where the racism can be seen but not heard, while discrimination and the limitation endured are evincible but intentionally neglected.

Recreating the Myths: *Moana* and *Raya and the Last Dragon*

The creation of *Moana* was inspired mainly by the cultural practices of the Pacific Islands: Samoa, Fiji, and Tonga (Julius and Malone 2016, 10), and *Raya and the Last Dragon* limn the cultures of a number of Southeast Asian countries: Thailand, Vietnam, Cambodia, Laos, Indonesia, Malaysia, and Singapore (Hurley and Shurer 2021, 12). Ron Clements and John Musker, who contributed to the storytelling of *Moana*, took their inspiration from a tale told nearly 3,000 years ago about the voyaging feats of the Pacific Islanders and the halt to their practice of traveling the high seas have been put for a thousand years. The islanders developed a fantasy of a demigod by the name of Maui and his theft of the heart of Te Fiti, goddess of fertility, which in turn jeopardized the perpetuity of the Pacific Islands. In the Disney version Moana courageously travels beyond the reef into the unknown, finds Maui, and asks him to return Te Fiti's heart.

Raya and the Dragon is grounded in the belief of *Nāga* in Southeast Asian culture. The *Nāga* is a "class of ancient Indian serpent deities associated with water and therefore fertility; they were later appropriated as guardians by the great Indic religions, sometimes a serpent king or queen" (Kossak and Watts 2001, 118). Raya, as the chief's daughter of the Heart Tribe of Kumandra, undergoes a journey to search for the last dragon, Sisu. She intends to save the entire country from the consumption of Druun, an evil force that petrifies anyone it touches. The writer of the film, Qui Nguyen of Vietnamese heritage, states that "[the movie] is our chance to create our [Southeast Asian] Excalibur and our [own] Arthurian legend" (quoted in Koeppel 2021).

Faithfulness and credibility are some major concerns in the remaking of the myth of Maui and Nāga. The producer of *Moana*, Osnat Shurer states, "We're making a Disney animated film full of fantasy and imagination, not a documentary. But we tried to honor the people and be respectful of the Pacific cultures that inspired the movie" (quoted in Julius and Malone 13). Shurer, who is also the coproducer of *Raya and the Last Dragon*, expresses the same respect for the Asian countries that she is working on: "The world of Kumandra is a fantasy, filled with otherworldly creatures and unique environments, but underneath it all, our goal is for the audience to sense an authentic 'fragrance' of Southeast Asia" (Hurley and Shurer 60). Her claim on the respect and truthfulness to the origin attempts to safeguard Disney from criticisms that it has been receiving over the years. Many critics have accused Disney of obfuscating the ownership of the text (Leitch 2007; Zipes 2013), refusing to give credit to the original writers, being unfaithful to the original texts (Wood 1996), and repeating the same message and structure of its stories from one film to the next (Wasko 2001; Zipes 2011). Disney has also been criticized for monopolizing the presentation of its adaptations and pay only limited attention to the authenticity of the representations.

With *Moana* and *Raya and the Last Dragon*, Disney creates contemporary ancient heroines from the Pacific Islands and for Southeast Asians, respectively. Both Moana and Raya are considered to be royal members in their stories as Moana is the daughter of the Chief Tui, leader of Motunui, and Raya is the daughter of Chief Benja, leader of Heart tribe in Kumantra. The two title characters are marked by their independent and strong characterization. They differ from those in previous princess series also because they put their homeland before their personal pursuit. They are both adventurous, with Moana desiring to be a voyager and Raya being trained to be a warrior. Moana is determined to restore the heart of Te Fiti to save her island. Raya undergoes a journey to search for the last dragon who saved the Kumantra 500 years ago. Her image and characters are inspired by the Vietnamese heroines the Tru'ng sisters, who took part in reforming the nation: They were military leaders who led a rebellion against the first Chinese domination of Vietnam (Goscha 2016, 21). When the two stories are set in ancient times, the two heroines consequently become the legendary saviors of their homeland. Yet, Justin Chang deduces that "in these dark times, onscreen as well as off, 'happily ever after' isn't as simple as a preposition as it used to be" (2021). Moana and Raya bear the image of an independent and courageous teenager, and they do not follow the conventions of Disney nor having the conventional "happily ever after" ending as other Disney's princesses have. Though Moana and Raya do have male companions, they are not motivated by romantic interest, and their heroism is mainly accomplished by themselves. In the case of Moana, Maui teaches her the skills of sailing and later, protects her from Te Kā, but it is Moana who restores the heart of Te Fiti. Likewise, the male companions of Raya—Boun and Tong—are periphery characters; the main actions are conducted by Raya. She is the first one in her pack to trust Namaari, the princess of Fang who once betrayed her. The characterization of Moana and

Raya correspond to the contemporary interest of female empowerment. Furthermore, the heroines have prioritized the communal survival before their individual wants, thus faithfully indicating the prime importance of familial and social solidarity in their corresponding cultures.

An additional cultural facet, both *Moana* and *Raya and the Last Dragon* accentuate the relationship between humans and nature, and notably the restoration of order. Maui removes the heart of Te Fiti for humans so that he can fulfill what they desire. This removal incites the dark power that will gradually devour the islands. His act also gives birth to the volcanic monster, Te Kā, who, as the story unfolds, is the darker side of Te Fiti. Te Kā configurates the result of offending the natural order that will consequently provoke the annihilation of humans. Similarly, the fall of Kumantra and the resurrection of Druun are triggered by humans' greed. It is because those who have attended the banquet in the Heart tribe have broken the gems of Sisu that they have released the soul-consuming Druun. He is the concretization of the ever-growing vices of mankind, standing for discord and extermination. Te Kā and Druun may appear to be the villains in the two films, but their behavior originated from the vices and aggression of humans. It is as Raya narrates in the prologue, "people being people—they all fought to possess the last remnant of dragon magic" (00:02:43–02:50). These aforementioned vices and aggressions of people have led to the crumbling of the homelands. Both Moana and Raya are indeed rectifying the past mistakes of mankind and attempting to reestablish a connection with nature. Moana shows great compassion to Te Kā and returns her heart with respect, while Raya places her trust in Namaari and asks her to complete the gem for the benefit of all. As it appears, the two heroines are not merely the saviors of their homeland, they revive trust and integrity among mankind. They demonstrate the principles of survival and the essential need of keeping harmony between humans and nature.

The mythical figures Maui and Nāga accompany the heroines and assist them in their tasks of correcting human's mistakes and restoring the natural order. Although a nod to authentic cultural essence, the images of these two figures have provoked some concerns among critics. In Arman Manookian's drawing "Maui snaring the Sun" (1927), Peter Gossage's *How Maui Slowed the Sun* (1982), and Preston McNeil's animated short film

Maui and the Sun (2012), Maui appears to be a lean, strong, young man. But Disney's Maui is "basically a square, and his legs are less than half the length if he were a normally proportioned person" (Julius and Malone 87). Additionally, Hannah Dittmer points out that Disney "simplifies and homogenizes Pacific belief systems, as Maui does not play such an important role as demigod on each of the Islands" (2021, 55). Likewise, Vincente Diaz claims, Disney disneyfies that Polynesian culture and portray a colonial fantasy about "noble savagery": Moana "elides and erases real diversity in the Pacific, which only betrays Disney's imperialist roots and longings" (2016). Shurer explains the depiction of Maui that, "In animation, we're not literal. You're trying to find the essence of the character. We always felt that the audience needed to know" (quoted in Ito 2016). She claims that even if Disney tried to stay true to the ethnic representations, it fails to faithfully represent the exact legends. The company does succeed though in producing a believable narrative that is strongly identified with the corresponding culture. *Raya and the Last Dragon* is founded on the myth of Nāga. In Hinduism, Buddhism, and Jainism, Nāgas are "powerful, mythical beings of Southeast Asia who are often able to manifest as a serpent or human and are usually associated with bodies of water" (Hurley and Shurer 2021, 42). Though there are various versions of Nāga's stories, Nāga is widely considered a guardian of river and treasure. Peter Debruge (2020) criticizes Sisu's image as "weird, like someone stuck a plastic 'My Little Pony' head on a floppy feather-boa body" (2020, 93), suggesting that Sisu looks like a caricature of a dragon. Besides, Nāga is a belief shared by the areas near the Mokong river. In the film, the compromised practice of worshipping the Sisu and her siblings among the five regions of Kumantra seems to have homogenized the belief of Nāga in Southeast Asia as well (Hefner 2015, 7–8; Johnson 2019, 390–91).

Michelle Anjirbag defines Disney's fairy tales that "though the films are respectively adapted from legend and folklore of their originating source and are not originally fairy tales as understood within a Western literary context" (2–3). The inclusivity of Disney's productions in recent decades will only expand its own brand of fairy tales, no matter how much compromise it has to make with the corresponding cultures. The heroines, the mission of order restoration, and the recreation of the image of the mythical creature can be taken as Disney's rebranding of the mythical elements of the Polynesian and Southeast Asian culture for its commercial use. Katherine Whitehurst complains that Disney "colonizes Polynesian mythology and culture to promote American myth-building" (2021, 159), demonstrating that Disney is aggressively creating an American myth by exploiting the myth of Polynesians. Whitehurst compares how Moana inherits the traditions from her older generations, Grandma Tala and Maui, and recrafts the tradition of voyager with the way Obama's politics restructures American exceptionalism and foreign policy (166). Raya may not respond to any particular political statement between Southeast Asia and America. Still, the mythmaking of Raya can also be read as a recontextualization of the myth of Nāga with an American interpretation. The fact that Disney has blended the heterogeneous cultural practices of a number of Southeast Asian countries into one is indeed a rather bewildering gesture. Arguably this is caused by a Pan-Asian impression or a disrespect to distinctive national communities or simply a matter of convenience.

Diaz places the onus on Disney to accurately represent other cultures: "It is Disney that now administrates how the rest of the world will get to see and understand Pacific realness, including substantive culture material that approaches the spiritual and the sacred" (2018). Nonetheless, despite the potential colonization of the Polynesian practices and the appropriation of the culture for box office, A. Mārata Keterkri Tamaira and Dionne Fonoti (2018) find the cultural representations in *Moana* exhibiting "a willingness to expand beyond their [Disney and Oceanic story trust] own proclivities and expectations to meet the middle, even if that middle—the zone of contact—was already always going to be unstable" (2018, 321), even if the inclusion may remain controversial. As it appears, despite their simplification, generalization, or homogenization, or even unfaithful and inaccurate depictions of the original mythical elements, the two recreations of myths in *Moana* and *Raya and the Last Dragon* shed a positive light on the underrepresented Polynesian and Southeast Asian cultures to the world. Disney has taken the liberty of creation in these two films while it makes a specific claim on its inclination of authenticity and respect. To be certain, Disney's overt declaration to be more inclusive cannot alter the fact that it has rearranged the cultural elements into a specific form of presentation, or this will only solidify the dominance of Disney in the portrayal of some cultural groups. After all, Disney's fairy tales are entrapped in the business of representation, since there is no barometer to assess the balance between Disney's liberty of creation and the faithfulness to the original source. This struggle is similar to Henry Giroux and Grace Pollock's argument on Disney's trademarking innocence that the company is entangled in the paradoxical combination of innocence and business (2010, 92–96). Perhaps, Disney has earned the position of the global narrator of fairy tales, as mentioned by Anjirbag, but this title comes along with the inherited complexity of adaptations and recreations. Particularly when Disney is expanding its reach to global market that involves multiple cultures, customs, and ethnicities, its fairy tales will be intrinsically subjected to controversies and unsettlements.

Consolidating Cultural Icons: *Coco* and *Encanto*

Sharing the setting in Latin America, *Coco* and *Encanto* are developed from some long-established icons of Mexico and Columbia, respectively. *Coco* is based on a Mexican festival, *Día de los Muertos* (Day of the Dead). It is a time when families commemorate deceased family members. They believe that souls will return to the earth during the festival. In *Coco*, a soul will be posthumous affected by the memory of the living. If the deceased is no longer remembered by any living people, their soul will eternally disappear in the Land of the Dead. The title character, Miguel Rivera, is the only one who likes playing music, while the rest of his family remain hostile to it. *Encanto* makes clear reference to *Cien Años de Soledad* (1967; *One Hundred Years of Solitude*), written by the Columbian Nobel Laureate, Gabriel García Márquez: The novel depicts the family of Buendía, who lives in a fictional place, Macado, where magic is normalized. Like Márquez's novel, in *Encanto*, Mirabel lives with her family in a magical house, *Casita*, in a hidden town. Except for Mirabel Madrigal and the two characters who marry to the family, all Madrigals are naturally born with magical power. Both *Coco* and *Encanto* aim at illustrating the odd members in a family and thus depicts the conflicts between individuality and diversity in families and cultures.

Jessica Wax-Edwards thinks that *Coco* has revolutionized the representation of Mexican culture on screen by redefining *Mexicanidad*, the Mexican identity on visual images (2020). Before *Coco*, there is a similar celebration of *Día de los Muertos* in *The Book of Life* (2014), produced by 20th Century Fox and then purchased by Disney, in which a museum guide narrates the story to a group of American students. Here, Mexico is just a storybook, and the Mexican characters are materialized into a set of figurines. The story presents the Mexican culture as an "exotic other," an outsider perspective that reasserts the "us" and "them" binary and fails to narrow the gap between cultures. In *The Art of "Coco,"* deliberate explanations are made to show that Disney and Pixar are trying to create a believable fantasized Mexican story (Lasseter et al. 2017). Plenty of photos of *Día de Los Muertos* are included to demonstrate the similarity between Mexico and the settings in *Coco*. Specific attentions are paid to the *ofrendas* at home as well as the cemetery. The Land of the Dead is developed from the architectural style of the hillside city of Guanajuato and Mexico City. The design of the skeletons is inspired by the works of José Guadalipe Posada. A number of Mexican celebrities are found on the Land of Dead including Frida Kahlo, a well-known painter. El Santo, a wrestler, is found at the entrance of a party (00:57:01–14). Pedro Infante and Jorge Negrete (01:01:53–1:01:56), Maria Felix, and Cantinflas (01:01:59–2:00) are all invited to De le Cruz's party. *Coco* presents itself as a valid and reliable display of Mexican culture. It is a story *of* the Mexicans but not the one about them. As claimed in *The Art of "Coco,"* "It was incredibly important to the *Coco* team to create an environment and a story that was not only vivid and beautiful, but also respectful of and true to the traditions of the people and the holiday" (Lasseter et al. 7).

Representations of Mexicans and Mexico itself are nothing new to Disney, but the company ensures that that the culture in *Coco* is illustrated without otherization. The prolific use of Mexican music, aesthetics, architecture, or even deceased celebrities creates a believable Mexican fantasy. When *Coco* was released in 2017, Mexicans were being defiled severely by Donald Trump's American government and accused of immigrant criminalization.

Héctor, who has been seen by the family as a defiled figure in the first half of the film, proves to have been a victim all along because he was murdered and robbed by De La Cruz. Héctor—like many immigrants—has been misunderstood and falsely criminalized. The Riveras are taught by Mama Imelda that Héctor irresponsibly abandoned his family, leaving her to take care of their child alone. In the Land of the Dead, Héctor consistently disguises himself in order to deceive customs. The clarification and justification of Héctor subvert the misrepresented image of the Mexicans in much American media. Though the film does not make a political statement related to the vilification of Mexicans, it does, as Jacqueline Avila (2020) compliments, create "a positive and inspiring representation of Mexican culture for audience in and outside of Mexico" (16). The positive reception of *Coco*, indeed, "marks a compelling attempt to challenge false narratives and portray Mexican people and culture with greater complexity" (Wax-Edwards 126). Released coincidently in a turbulent time when President Donald Trump was pursuing building a wall between the borders of the United States and Mexico, *Coco* successful and ironically empowered Mexican cultural icons, demonstrating how the people of Mexico celebrate their family, friends, music, and tradition in the production of a mega American corporation. In effect, the concurrence of the film and the political struggle fortifies the cinematic representations, and turning *Coco* into a contemporaneous tale of Mexicans.

In the case of *Encanto*, Disney attempts to develop a fantasy that is authentic and relatable enough but remains true of the culture and history of Columbia. The film is developed with magic realism and the fictional world of Márquez. Since "Columbia is often thought of as the home of magical realism," the directors state clearly that *Encanto* is intended to explore reality "through a unique lens: heightened moments and emotions combined to invoke a feeling, to explain a complicated world, to deal with a painful past" (quoted in Pablo and Jones 2021, 8). Director Byron Howard further explains that the magic in *Encanto* is specific to Columbia, "not European magic—not wizards and wands—but magic that's tied to emotion and part of a tradition called magical realism" (quoted in Jefferson 2021). Intent upon authenticating *Encanto*, Disney filled the film with items that are closely related to Columbia and South America. These include

Antonio's animals (a jaguar, capybara, keel-billed toucan) and Isabella's flowers (the carnivorous *drosera*, the *Jacaranda mimosifolia*, and *Cattleya trianae* orchids, the national flower of Columbia). The colorful river where Abeulo Pedro is killed as well as where Abuela Alma and Mirabel reconcile is inspired by a river called Cãno Cristales in Columbia.

While American racism appears to be too heavy for a fairy tale like *Princess and the Frog*, comparatively speaking, *Encanto* offers a much more honest discussion of the unpleasant history of the Columbian civil war, The Thousand Day's War (1899–1902). In the visualization of Abuela Alma's recollection (01:18:13-1:20:21), Abuela Alma and Abuelo Pedro are fleeing from their home because their town is being attacked. This short reference to the civil war explains not only the death of Abuelo Pedro, but also the origin of the magic in the Madrigal family, and more importantly, the trauma of Abuela Alma. It is because she has experienced the pain of losing her husband and home, and so she is afraid that if the magical power is gone, the family will have to undergo the same predicament as she has gone through. Disney does not explain any details of the war nor make any political statement about it. Instead, *Encanto* focuses on the agony of Abuela Alma, a refugee who runs from extreme violence. It stresses on overcoming generations of trauma with family unity. It also encourages the practice of empathy toward the older generations who have experienced warfare and displacement while accentuating the importance of cherishing the new changes brought by the younger generations. Indeed, taking an overview of Disney's animated films, even if the subject of death is often included, painful history, such as the colonialization in the account of *Pocahontas* is not usually kept. This allusion to actual history in *Encanto* is significant as this is a proper recognition of the atrocities in distinctive cultures. Instead of sugarcoating or ignoring them, Disney proposes an optimal solution, and that is to heal the wound with family unity and the mutual understanding among the members.

In addition to the historical reference to the Thousand Days War, the Spanish version of *"Dos Oruguitas"* is played in the scene where Abuela Alma recalls the civil war (01:18:13–23:17; *"Dos Oruguitas"*). The song is recorded in Spanish and translated into English. Given that Disney has been using English as its primary language of production, the priority to provide

the Spanish version of *"Dos Oruguitas"* expresses respect for Columbia. To
be sure, while the story is given a stronger taste of Columbian culture, it
is still a narration of Disney. Yet, there is a compromise between the cultures: Like many Disney's films in which the leads are royals or royals-to-be,
the Madrigals are the special ones in its community. Regardless, the main
characters are still the "special chosen celebrities and elite groups" who
"are destined to rule and administer just social codes that will make people
happy and keep them in their proper places" (Zipes 2011, 26). Although
Disney's conventions and frameworks are kept in the new productions,
the company attempts to accommodate the tales with the corresponding
culture. Tracey L. Mollet reminds us that Disney's fairy tales are fundamentally American, an engagement in American values, history, and dream
(5–9). Nonetheless, it is clear that there is a growing diversity in the films.
Coco and *Encanto* have unfolded how Disney has attempted to produce
responsible representation. These two recent productions demonstrate that
cultural diversity is genuinely and gradually embraced by the company.

Disney's Fairy Tales: Representations and Authority

Since the 1990s, Disney has exhibited a rising sensitivity toward ethnical
and cultural representation, and it has demonstrated such inclination
consistently through its animated films. As exemplified in *Princess and
the Frog, Moana, Coco, Raya and the Last Dragon*, and *Encanto*, in the
twenty-first century, Disney has been actively portraying believable and
realistic narratives of the corresponding cultures. Thematically, instead
of following the conventions of individual pursuits, romantic interests,
or usual binaries, the inclusivity reinvigorates Disney's fairy tales by re-
inforcing the importance of individual independence, solidarity in family
and social community, and the respect to cultural and mythical icons.
Inevitable complexities are embedded in the process of creating fairy tales
for a global audience. Disney will have to come across the difficulties like
references to painful history, struggles between creativity and authenticity, compromises between cultural features and Disney's conventions.

Each of the above films may also be subject to a wide range of challenges, including, for example, the accuracy of historical background, the faithful recreation of mythical figures, the homogenization of heterogeneous cultural representations, or dilemmas among recontextualization, adaptation, and creation. Nonetheless, these problems are constant and invariably involved in fairy tales. It is only that the concern of global audience seems to have complicated and multiplied the complexities. Still, even if the aforementioned issues persist, the growing inclusivity has refashioned the domination of Disney and once again consolidated its defining power on fairy tales. Indeed, more significantly, by producing international narratives, Disney has not limited itself as the storyteller of fairy tales, but has crowned itself the hegemonic narrator of *global* fairy tales.

Bibliography

Addison, Erin. "Saving Other Women from Other Men: Disney's *Aladdin*." *Camera Obscura* 31 (1993): 4–25.

Anjirbag, Michelle Anya. "Mulan and Moana: Embedded Coloniality and the Search for Authenticity in Disney Animated Film." *Social Science* 7, no. 230 (2018): 1–15.

Avila, Jacqueline. "Memorias de Oro: Music, Memory, and *Mexicanidad* in Pixar's *Coco (2017)*." *Americas: A Hemispheric Music Journal* 29 (2020): 1–23. doi:10.1353/ame.2020.0009.

Ayres, Chris. "*The Princess and the Frog*: Disney Black Fairytale." *The Sunday Times*, December 12, 2009. <https://www.thetimes.co.uk/article/the-princess-and-the-frog-disneys-black-fairytale-lcpnw3pj3jc>.

Bacchilega, Christina. *Fairy Tales Transformed?: Twenty-First-Century Adaptations and the Politics of Wonder*. Detroit, MI: Wayne State University Press, 2013.

The Book of Life. Directed by Jorge R. Gutierrez. Feel FX Animation Studios and 20th Century Fox Animation. 2014.

Breaux, Richard M. "After 75 Years of Magic: Disney Answers Its Critics, Rewrites African American History, and Cashes In on Its Racist Past." *Journal of African American Studies* 14 (2010): 398–416.

Brode, Douglas. *Multiculturalism and the Mouse: Race and Sex in Disney Entertainment*. Austin: University of Texas Press, 2005.

Chang, Justin. "Review of *Raya and the Last Dragon*, Featuring Disney's First Southeast Asian Heroine, Is a Moving Adventure." *The LA Times*, March 1, 2021. <https://www.latimes.com/entertainment-arts/movies/story/2021-03-01/raya-and-the-last-dragon-review-disney-plus>.

Debruge, Peter. "Raya and the Last Dragon." *Variety Magazine* 351, no. 9 (March 4, 2020): 93.

Diaz, Vincente. "Disney Craps a Cute Grass Skirt: Unpacking Insidious Colonial Power and Indigenous Enabling in Disney's *Moana*." *The Hawaii Independent*, September 29, 2016. <https://thehawaiiindependent.com/story/disney-craps-cute-grass-skirt>.

———. "Don't Sallow (or Be Swallowed by) Disney's 'Culturally Authenticated *Moana*.'" *Indian Country Today*, September 12, 2018. <https://indiancountrytoday.com/archive/dont-swallow-or-be-swallowed-by-disneys-culturally-authenticated-moana>.

"Dig a Little Deeper." Composed by Randy Newman. Sung by Jennifer Lewis, Anika Noni Rose, and the Pinnacle Gospel Choir for *The Princess and the Frog*. 2009. <https://www.youtube.com/watch?v=2v7QQbJO6aw>.

Dittmer, Hannah. "Moana Made Waves: Discussing the Representation of Pacific Islanders in the Disney Movie *Moana*." *Pacific Geographies* 55 (2021): 25–29.

"*Dos Oruguitas*." Written by Lin-Manuel Miranda. Sung by Sebastián Yatra for *Encanto*. 2021.

Dundes, Lauren, and Madaline Streiff. "Reel Royal Diversity? The Glass Ceiling in Disney's *Mulan* and *Princess and the Frog*." *Societies* 6, no. 35 (2016): 35.

Edgerton, Gary, and Kathy Merlock Jackson. "Redesigning Pocahontas: Disney, the 'White Man's Indian,' and the Marketing of Dreams." *Journal of Popular Film & Television* 24, no. 2. (1996): 90–98. <https://doi.org/10.3390/soc6040035>.

Giroux, Henry A., and Grace Pollock. *The Mouse That Roared: Disney and the End of Innocence*. Lanham, MD: Rowman and Littlefield Publishers, 2010.

Goscha, Christopher. *Vietnam: A New History*. New York: Basic Books, 2016.

Gossage, Peter. *How Maui Slowed the Sun*. New Zealand: Lansdowne Press, 1982.

Gregory, Sarita McCoy. "Disney's Second Line: New Orleans, Racial Masquerade, and the Reproduction of Whiteness in *The Princess and the Frog*." *Journal of African American Studies* 14, no. 4 (2010): 432–49.

Haase, Donald. "Hypertextual Gutenberg: The Textual and Hypertextual Life of Folklore and Fairy Tales in English Language Popular Print Editions." *Fabula* 47 (2006): 222–30.

Hefner, Carol J. "Tempting the Naga: Local Knowledge and Mysteries of the Mekong." In *At Home and in the Field: Ethnographic Encounters in Asia and the Pacific Island*, edited by Suzanne S. Finney et al., 7–11. Honolulu: University of Hawaii Press, 2015.

Hurley, Kaikolehua, and Osnat Shurer. *The Art of "Raya and the Last Dragon."* San Francisco, CA: Chronical Books, 2021.

Ito, Robert. "How (and Why) Maui Got So Big in *Moana*." *The New York Times*, November 15, 2016. <https://www.nytimes.com/2016/11/20/movies/moana-and-how-maui-got-so-big.html>.

Jefferson, Camille. "A Behind-the-Scenes Look at Walt Disney Animation Studio's *Encanto*." Walt Disney Animation Studio, October 26, 2021. <https://news.disney.com/encanto-behind-the-scenes>.

Johnson, Andrew Alan. "The River Grew Tired of Us: Spectral Flows Along the Mekong River." *Journal of Ethnographic Theory* 9, no. 2 (2019): 390–404.

Julius, Jessica, and Maggie Melone. *The Art of "Moana."* San Francisco, CA: Chronical Books, 2016.

Koeppel, Kari. "Southeast Asian Cultural Representation in Disney's *Raya and the Last Dragon*." *Walt Disney Animation Studio*, March 10, 2021. <https://news.disney.com/southeast-asian-culture-in-raya-and-the-last-dragon>.

Kossak, Steven, and Edith Whitney Watts. *The Art of South and Southeast Asia: A Resource for Educators.* New York: The Metropolitan Museum of Art, 2001.

Kurtti, Jeff. *The Art of "Princess and the Frog."* San Francisco, CA: Chronical Books, 2002.

Lasseter, John. *Dreams Come True: A Celebration of Disney Animation.* American Broadcast Company. December 4, 2009. <https://www.youtube.com/watch?v=bzBTAuOoSZs>.

Lasseter, John, Lee Unkrich, and Adrian Molina. *The Art of "Coco."* San Francisco, CA: Chronicle Books, 2017.

Leitch, Thomas. *Film Adaptation and Its Discontents: From "Gone with the Wind" to the "Passion of the Christ."* Baltimore, MD: Johns Hopkins University Press, 2007.

Manookian, Arman. *Maui Snaring the Sun.* Pen and Ink. 1927. Honolulu Academy of Arts. *Wikimedia.* <https://commons.wikimedia.org/wiki/File:Maui_Snaring_the_Sun,_pen_and_ink,_circa_1927,_Honolulu_Academy_of_Arts.jpg>.

Maui and the Sun—Ko Maui me te Ra. Directed by Preston McNeil. Mofresh Productions. 2012. <https://www.youtube.com/watch?v=wgLWdCrgR7w>.

"Maui and the Sun—*Ko Maui me te Ra*." *ACMI: "Moana" Learning Resources.* n.d. <https://www.acmi.net.au/education/school-program-and-resources/moana-learning-resource/>.

Mitchell-Smith, Ilan. "The United Princesses of America: Ethnic Diversity and Cultural Purity in Disney's Medieval Past." In *The Disney Middle Ages: A Fairy-Tale and Fantasy Past*, edited by T. Pugh and S. Aronstein, 209–24. New York: Palgrave Macmillan, 2012.

Mollet, Tracey L. *A Cultural History of the Disney Fairy Tale: Once Upon an American Dream*. Cham: Palgrave Macmillan, 2020.

Pablo, Juan, and Reyes Lancaster Jones. *The Art of "Encanto."* San Francisco, CA: Chronical Books, 2021.

"Stories Matter." The Walt Disney Company. 2020. <https://storiesmatter.thewaltdisneycompany.com/>.

Tamaira, A. Mārata Keterkri, and Dionne Fonoti. "Beyond Paradise? Retelling Pacific Stories in Disney's *Moana*." *The Contemporary Pacific* 30, no. 2 (2018): 297–327.

Turner, Sarah E. "Blackness, Bayous and Gumbo: Encoding and Decoding Race in a Colorblind World." In *Diversity in Disney Films: Critical Essays on Race, Ethnicity, Gender, Sexuality and Disability*, edited by J. Cheu, 83–98. Jefferson, NC: McFarland, 2012.

Wasko, Janet. *Understanding Disney: The Manufacture of Fantasy*. Malden, MA: Polity, 2001.

Wax-Edwards, Jessica. "Re-Animating Mexicanidad: Mexican Cultural Representations in *The Book of Life* (2014) and *Coco* (2017)." *Interdisciplinary Mexico* 9, no. 18 (2020): 112–29.

Whitehurst, Katherine. "Youth Films and the Nation: Imagining Obama's US Foreign Policy in Disney's *Moana*." *Narrative Culture* 8, no. 1 (2021): 155–74.

Wise, Christopher. "Notes from the *Aladdin* Industry: Or, Middle Eastern Folklore in the Era of Multinational Capitalism." In *The Emperor's Old Groove: Decolonizing Disney's Magic Kingdom*, edited by Brenda Ayres, 65–78. New York: Peter Lang, 2003.

Wood, Karenne. "Prisoners of History: Pocahontas, Mary Jemison, and the Poetics of an American Myth." *Studies in American Indian Literatures* 28, no. 1 (2016): 73–82.

Wood, Naomi. "Domesticating Dreams in Walt Disney's *Cinderella*." *The Lion and the Unicorn* 20, no. 1 (1996): 25–49.

Zipes, Jack. *The Enchanted Screen: The Unknown History of Fairy-Tale Films*. New York: Routledge. 2011.

——. *Fairy Tale as Myth/ Myth as Fairy Tale*. Lexington: The University Press of Kentucky, 2013.

——. *When Dreams Came True: Classical Fairy Tales and Their Tradition*. London: Routledge, 2007.

5 Eastern Witch from the West: Xianniang in Niki Caro's *Mulan*

Reviewing Niki Caro's live-action *Mulan* (2020), film critics such as Peter Debruge in *Variety* and Brian Truitt in *USA Today* associate the witch character (played by Gong Li) with the hawk on account of her metamorphosis into the raptor during key scenes. The IMDb film website and closed captioning simply identify her as Xianniang, which means "Immortal Woman." Remaining unnamed other than the "witch" diegetically, that is, so addressed by characters within the film, she is alluded to, extradiegetically, by reviewers and subtitlers in two diametrically opposed ways for the Anglophone global cinema. To call her by the shorthand Hawk underlines the dark animal kinship; to call her Xianniang risks alienating the non-Sinophone audience, who most likely would not have turned on closed captioning and who would have missed the deification implicit in xian (translates as immortal) even if they had. Either name removes the character from the centrality of humanity, leaning to bestiality or to beatification. The former name resonates with the tangibility of cinematic special effects of a soaring hawk and the flock of bat-like birds; the latter is largely occluded because of the unintelligibility of the romanized Xianniang.

Ironically, the visible materiality of the hawk and batty birds is constituted by digital mirages in a technological sleight of hand. The impenetrable Xianniang encrypts two concrete Chinese ideograms 仙娘, an abstract mess sourced from a solid mass of fifteen brushstrokes, five to form 仙, ten to form 娘. However, in a world where traditional calligraphy and penmanship have been flattened into romanization via keyboards, the five brushstrokes of 仙 are cut down to the four keystrokes of xian in pinyin, and the ten brushstrokes of 娘 to the five keystrokes of niang. Translation converts the meaning or soul as much as it casts off form or body. What if the meaning rests solely in the form? What if the spirit of the character—both the fictional person and the words pointing to that person—resides in the letter of the character? Contrary to Walter Benjamin's utopian prophecy, "The Task of the Translator"—not only subtitlers but cultural translators of film reviewers and filmmakers like Niki Caro—may unwittingly amputate the source culture in exchange for the mighty prosthesis and filmic gadgetry to win over the target culture.

To proceed with the name of "least resistance" yet most fraught in English, the witch Hawk is a twenty-first-century "walk-on" (fly-in?), entirely absent in the genesis of the Mulan legend, the fifth-century "The Ballad of Mulan." Nor does she exist in any previous reincarnations of the Mulan legend in the Chinese and English language, including Maxine Hong Kingston's novel, the ethnic classic *The Woman Warrior* (1976) or in the earlier Disney animation, *Mulan* (1998). The closest existence one can find is the animation's monstrous, gorilla-like Hun leader Shan Yu with his barrel chest, long arms, sharp fangs, and slant eyes. Given their shared predator attributes, Caro casts the witch as a familiar, "a slave" to her Shan Yu character, Böri Khan, complete with an umlaut over "o." The diacritical mark ousts the character from the English language and culture, while effecting no change in its pronunciation. Purely decorative, the "ö" is for looks only, aiming to rub off on the character played by Jason Scott Lee, made up to look Central Asian, almost Arabic, as do his dark-clad, masked, and turbaned cohort of shadow warriors. That the Khan's horde debut by multiplying from one Khan on horseback to many like a mirage out of the desert validate their Central Asian or Near Eastern association. Drawing not only from the long Chinese dynastic memory against northern nomadic "barbarians," Caro also taps into post-9/11 worldwide paranoia in pop culture where villainy carries an odious Orientalist, Muslim tone.

The witch's same-sex lookalike is the shaman or "Great Wizard" (Figure 5.1) in *Matchless Mulan*, one of a handful of Chinese media conglomerate iQIYI's rush productions during the lull of *Mulan*'s delayed global release, bumped off by Covid-19 from Wuhan. Two letters apart, albeit with identical vowels, Wuhan and Mulan resemble Sino-ese twins, one born at the close of 2019, the other all but aborted the following year. Mulan is female, yet that initial "m" signals the historical male impersonator.

Figure 5.1. The shaman or "Great Wizard" in *Matchless Mulan*.

By contrast, Wuhan's "w" points to female, yet the city's homegrown, airborne bug ravages the world like a historic, masculine conqueror.

Given the absence of the witch before 2020, is Caro's addition to the cast a Western wolf in Eastern sheep's clothing, speaking in English to boot, swallowing whole the gullible Anglophone audience? Is Caro affixing, fixating on, a feminist, homoerotic tail to an imperial, heteronormal Chinese tale? Is Caro a Western neo-imperialist bewitching—pun intended—the world in the name of a liberal, all-Asian performance?

Mulan Who?

Before turning to the supporting actress Hawk, the spotlight ought to stay a while longer on the leading actress Mulan. It is high time for a paternity test for Mulan: What is her last name? Is it the Chinese tradition's Hua, although her literary debut in "The Ballad of Mulan" does not exactly spell that out? Is it the Cantonese-inflected Fa, as in Kingston's *The Woman Warrior*? Kingston's ethnic classic introduced this crossdressing heroine who, as Chinese legend has it, took her ailing father's place in the conscription for battle against invasions along China's northern borders. Is her surname Disney when the 1998 animation absorbs

Kingston's ethnic angle into its multicultural lineups of teenage girl power? Grounded in the whiteness of Ariel in *The Little Mermaid* (1989) and of Belle in *Beauty and the Beast* (1991), Disney adroitly expands to and whitewashes the Arab girl, Jasmine, in *Aladdin* (1992); the Native American young woman, Pocahontas (1995) in the eponymous animation; the Gypsy woman, Esmeralda, in *The Hunchback of Notre Dame* (1996); and finally, the Chinese or Asian daughter in *Mulan*.

For decades, the Chinese performing arts and film industry have produced their own heroines. As opposed to Mulan Hollywood, China proudly presents Mulan Huallywood *à la* the second syllable of *zhonghua* for China, eerily punning its very own *hua* (flower, prosperity) with her surname. *Hua Mulan* (2009), featuring China's lead performers Wei Zhao and Kun Chen, arrives almost as a delayed response to the popular Disney animation. Under the auspices of the Magic Kingdom, Niki Caro turns Mulan Disney into a feature film with an Asian and Asian American cast in 2020. The global release of Mulan Caro, so to speak, having been postponed due to Covid-19, leaves iQIYI in the meantime to cobble together *Matchless Mulan* and *Mulan Legend*, both of which were streamed online in the summer months of 2020. An animation *Kung Fu Mulan* by Leo Liao follows on Caro's heels in being released in October 2020. Ian Shepherd directed *Hua Mulan*, a short documentary for children, which was distributed as a DVD in November 2020. American children were ill-served by opportunists like Shepherd, whose narrator pronounced "Hua" in two separate syllables—"HU-A." This mispronunciation is a mistake as basic as English learners whose native tongues are monosyllabic turning "Ian" into two distinct words: "I-AN." Ultimately, a paternity test may prove futile in the face of so many serial sperm donors: Hollywood, Huallywood, Disney, Caro, iQIYI, Liao, and Shepherd.

At the heart of the original Mulan legend, "The Ballad of Mulan" (木蘭辭 *Mulanci* circa 400 AD), lies twin binarities of gender and race. A female pretends to be her father in a border conflict between China's majority Han people and another unnamed race to the north. That the breach comes from an unidentified source arises from centuries-old Chinese anxiety over the amorphous umbrella term of northern nomadic "barbarians," who have made relentless incursions into China, culminating in two dynasties—Mongolians' Yuan and Manchurians' Qing—both eventually establishing their capitals in Beijing. "The Ballad of Mulan" betrays, however, the porousness of a dichotomy between Chinese and non-Chinese. Answering the imperial conscription, Mulan in "The Ballad," describes it as having been handed down from "the Khan," which segues subsequently to "the Son of Heaven," the traditional Chinese address of respect for the emperor. In her triumphant homecoming, Mulan is granted an audience with the Son of Heaven, which changes in no time to "The Khan asks what she wants." To call China's emperor "the Khan" after chieftains of northern nomads is not only bewildering but verging on blasphemy, as if one nomadic Khan bent on offense meets Beijing's Khan in defense. Arguably, the Ballad's switch stems from a fluid tribal perception of the nation's leader, one that flips between northern Khans and Chinese emperors. Mulan is likely to be a member of the northern minorities retaining residuals of tribal linguistic habits, despite having been assimilated and sinologized. Proper nouns for concrete things, ranging from daily objects to human relationships of naming such as the Khan, are the last to go anyway in any assimilation.

The Disney animation glosses over the Ballad's racial blurring by pitting the northern Huns, commanded by the ape-like Shan Yu, against the Han army stationed along the Great Wall. At the outset, the imperial decree mobilizes male conscripts in response to the Hun incursion. Disney identifies the villain's race as "Hun" whereas the Ballad does not. The clarity of Disney is cartoonish, given the Ballad's historical ambiguity. Not only narrowing down the umbrella term Huns to Rourans, Caro's film also takes leave of the Ballad in the setting of Mulan's village. Her family lives in the renowned tourist site of Hakka adobe roundhouses in Fujian and southern China, over a thousand miles away from the northern borderland of the Ballad. The Hakka, suffice to say, is one of the most ancient Han ethnic groups, entirely different from tribal nomads, sinologized or not, along the Great Wall.

To a vigilant Chinese reader, the racial obfuscation would cry out from the text. Yet another obscuring concludes the Ballad. The male impersonator, Mulan, after 12 years of military service, returns to her parents, changes back to her female costume and makeup, and shocks her comrades. The last lines read: "The male rabbit's feet are kicking, the female rabbit's eyes squint, almost closed / Both rabbits running side by side, how can you tell whether I am male or female?" "Kicking" and "squint[ing], almost closed" comprise a Chinese maxim, *pushuo mili* ("kicking, hopping" and "misty, unclear"), to illustrate the confusing and mysterious state of things. In China's patriarchal, heteronormative tradition, that unsettling haze is never meant to include sexual orientation. A dozen years of gender-bending aberration in the military constitute an extreme condition with the express purpose of extoling filial piety in a family and patriotism to a nation. The female serves at the pleasure of the father or the father figure.

The racial, national division of Han and Hun has already been deconstructed by the Ballad's internal evidence. Conceivably, even the gender division is subject to debate as to whether we take the Ballad's last word at its word. The rhetorical question at the end, "How can you tell whether I am male or female?" is literal because Mulan defies gender binarism. Rather than either-or, she is both-and as well as neither-nor. Instead of two rabbits—a female Mulan and her male colleague—running alongside each other, kicking barbarian butts, pardon the expression, the cross-dresser inhabits both rabbits, both roles, in Freudian terms. The buck's kicking of hind legs symbolizes phallic erection; the doe's squinting eyes acquire a vaginal likeness or orgiastic expression. Or the other way around at the moment of orgasm: female leg muscles spasm; male eyes swoon. Ideally, *la petite mort* culminates lovemaking of two bodies and consciousnesses into one climax, bridging Eros and Thanatos, equating Self and Other. The various Freudian scenarios circle back to Kingston, who capitalizes on androgyny when General Fa Mu Lan alters her armor to mask her pregnancy. The most masculine moment of killing happens to be the most feminine moment of gestation.

Hawk Caro

Hawk the witch materializes out of left field of the Mulan legend or, geopolitically, to the left of China all the way to the West—Europe and

America and Australia, from which Niki Caro hails. Hawk performs black magic on the battlefield, courtesy of special effects and computer-generated imagery. Occidental, Hollywood media technology conjures up the ghost of a phantasmagoric Orient, except this Orient is possessed by the Anglo-European mania over sorcery. How is one to read Hawk's power, which includes possessing, merging, and zombifying her victims of a Central Asian caravan merchant, an imperial soldier, and the imperial chancellor? Taking control of these victims' bodies and minds resonates with Western—not Eastern—vampire lore, which ties in with the repeated *mise en scène* of swarms of bat-like birds in flight cross-dissolving into the witch on foot. Vampiric possession and bats fall within Western popular culture. Hawk is empowered by Orientalism, harking back to Bram Stoker's *Dracula* from across "the most Western of splendid bridges over the Danube ... [taking] us among the traditions of Turkish rule" (2013 [1897], 1). Turkish or Transylvanian, Dracula transports himself in a coffin to England, bringing Eastern despotism and death to individual sentience. In reverse, the Chinese witch's agency flows from the Australian Caro and the Western mythology of witchcraft.

Long before Hawk graces the screen, the stigma of the witch is already introduced by Mulan's mother, but in reference to Mulan. The mother fears that neighbors would "call her a witch" had Mulan failed to conceal her inborn *chi*, a supernatural power manifested in her gliding through air or letting her weapons fly. In fact, villagers do curse Mulan as a "witch" after she gives chase to a chicken, her gravity-defying prowess surpasses any mortal male. The two women warriors of Hawk and Mulan are inextricably intertwined through the indeterminacy of the witch and the warrior Mulan in the eye of patriarchy, one that colors women's perception right from the outset. This *chi* is essential for military exploits, hence it is celebrated in male heirs. Misplaced in a female body like Mulan's, this mysterious force of the chosen boy damns her instead. Women's sole avenue to "bring honor to the family" is through arranged marriage, one of many places where Caro follows verbatim the animation's stilted lyrics and dated plot. Such Orientalist stereotypes span the two decades of Disney's animation and Caro's feature film. Amidst the millennial maelstrom over racial and gender injustice, Caro has not disabused herself of Orientalist vocabulary and milieu. Rather, she recycles the plotline and the high points of the animation to cater to millennial audience who had grown up on Disney animations. The live-action feature film constitutes a collage of Orientalist banalities.

One such cliché concerns Chinese families; Caro's retelling of *Mulan* hinges on a Confucian-style family. Beyond reiterating the stereotypical virtues of loyal, brave, and true carved on Mulan's sword, the Hua family heirloom, a fourth inscription is added to the back of the emperor's sword bequeathed to Mulan in the closing moments after she has saved the empire. The fourth word is *xiao*, filial piety, rendered as "devotion to the family." This commends Mulan's dedication to "honor," to borrow the Orientalist buzzword again, her biological family as well as the collective family headed by the emperor.

Family becomes the point at which Hawk's and Mulan's destinies diverge. In their confrontations, Hawk sees through Mulan's disguise. "We are the same," urges Hawk at joining forces, "we will take our place together" (Figure 5.2). While their *chi* or innate abilities that are housed in female bodies are similar, Hawk is practically an orphan, shunned by all except the Khan, a cruel adoptive father who exploits her talents. The Khan, in turn, rages against the Chinese emperor (played by Jet Li) as if he were a rebellious, even parricidal, son about to set aflame the bound yet composed father figure. The Khan seethes in fury in the name of avenging his own father of the same name, slain in the past by the emperor. Whereas Mulan replaces her father in battle to keep him alive, the Khan wishes to kill and replace the emperor as the master of the land. That he does so under the guise of revenge veils his desire to be the father; that Böri Khan is what both the father and the son are called suggests the identical impulse of the alpha male, always singular after displacing the biological or symbolic patriarch. Despite his grotesque scars and weathered countenance, the Khan looks almost churlish, so childish as he strikes two scimitars to generate fiery sparks that alight on and burn the emperor's unruffled face, a silly child's game, a "warm-up" for the imminent burning at the stake. The Khan's lame bluster promises no paternal patronage to Hawk or any of his followers. By contrast, Mulan's loving biological family comes under the wings of the Father of China, the emperor, the Son of Heaven. By corollary, Mulan becomes the beloved granddaughter to Heaven.

Figure 5.2. Hawk urges Mulan to join forces in Niki Caro's *Mulan*.

Absent a family, Hawk's power seems corrupted into *maleficium* in opposition to Mulan's *chi*. In their skirmishes, Caro performs a shotgun marriage of Western demonology and Eastern mysticism. However, both witchery and *chi* remain so ambiguous and ill-defined that they are presented as not only alike but causal. Mulan's repressed *chi* comes to fruition on account of Hawk's "mercy killing" of the male imperson-ator in her to free her *chi*. Feeling spurned by Mulan's refusal to be true to her feminine core, Hawk flings a dart at Mulan's heart, disposing of this "toy" soldier who could have been so much more. Yet that dart is stuck in Mulan's tight, breast-flattening wrapping: Mulan is saved by her disguise (Figure 5.3). Having fainted from this near-death experi-ence and gradually coming around, Mulan 2.0 sheds all pretense of masculinity, including armor and helmet, her long black hair flowing in the wind, riding to the rescue of her comrades. Letting go of the masquerade clearly empowers her, but the logic escapes the viewer. If the corset-style wrapping has shielded her, then she ought to take on more—not less—protective gear, including gender. Caro romanticizes to win over the viewer's heart, not the head. The rush of a feeling of tri-umph, along with the crescendo of music and tracking shots, is designed to overwhelm emotionally the audience.

Figure 5.3. Hawk's dart is stuck in Mulan's tight, breast-flattening wrapping.

Hawk's demise reprises this scene of mercy killing to birth Mulan, but in reverse. Hawk dares to challenge her master the Khan, inspired by the heroine Mulan, a model for what Hawk could have been, if only she had lived in a more tolerant world, a.k.a., imperial China. Sensing a greater threat, the Khan turns his arrow aimed at Hawk toward Mulan. To save Mulan a second time, Hawk dives down to take the arrow (Figure 5.4), making possible the subsequent duel between Mulan and the Khan. Nevertheless, Caro's triumphant plotline proceeds from one narrative cage to another, from racial stereotypes of nomadic and marauding Huns to those of patriarchal and compassionate Hans. Despite their seeming antagonism, both Mulan and Hawk gravitate to the same Confucian patriarchal center. Hawk's realization that "they accept you, but they will never accept me" pivots on "they," the world of men that adjudicates between heroism and hedonism, between the flight of the phoenix and the fall of the hawk.

Their closeness is foreshadowed by their avian avatars: the hawk and the phoenix. The difference rests in the fact that Mulan is blessed by the phoenix soaring well above her, an ancestral spirit watching over her. Indeed, in her showdown with the Khan on bamboo scaffoldings—yet another trite kung fu tableau from King Hu's bamboo grove in *A Touch of Zen* (1971)— where the emperor is manacled, the phoenix rises up in the distance behind Mulan, its wings extending from Mulan's shoulders as though endowing

Figure 5.4. Hawk dives down to take the arrow in order to save Mulan.

her with aerial *chi* (Figure 5.5). The phoenix is conjured up out of nowhere as much by Mulan's desperation after losing her sword as by the emperor's exhortation: "You are a mighty warrior. Rise up like a phoenix!" Mulan is enabled by Chinese mythology regarding the phoenix, the counterpart to the dragon embodied in the emperor, as well as by Western mythology over the birth of phoenix out of the cauldron that has incinerated her sword into ashes. The phoenix' wings over Mulan's shoulders is the brief moment when the corporeal splicing occurs. In Hawk's case, either the raptor or the bat-like throng metamorphoses into Hawk on foot. Whereas Mulan's humanity remains intact with a fleeting image of two-in-one high up on the bamboo scaffoldings, Hawk's identity collapses into the animals. The divergence notwithstanding, their *chi* keeps them aloft. The male principle seems bound to the earth. The emperor is in bondage; the only martial act he completes is to catch the arrow shot by the Khan. Even the arrow returned to pierce the Khan's heart is aerially kicked and redirected by Mulan, after being flung high by the emperor. The Khan, of course, breathes his last breath once prone on the ground.

Figure 5.5. The phoenix rises up with wings extending from Mulan's shoulders.

The witch and the warrior differ only in terms of social acceptance, which debunks the neoliberal notion of individual meritocracy. Hawk, rejected by all, turns to serve the Khan like a slave; by contrast, Mulan finds herself through male impersonation first and subsequently through male-rescuing, but only after the rebirth of her femininity at the hands of Hawk. Since the male she saves happens to be the Chinese emperor, Mulan is not only spared for transgressions against military code of conduct and gender roles, but she is well-nigh apotheosized. The witch dies; the warrior flies high. Mulan in history fades; Mulan in Disney learns English and does a bit of queerbaiting with her fellow witch in what Caro intimates as "a love scene."

Niki Caro's addition of Gong Li as the witch culminates gender instability throughout centuries of retelling in the East and the West. In Robert Ito's *The New York Times* review on September 3, 2020, Caro notes: "And there's a scene between Mulan and Gong Li's character that's literally directed like a love scene. It's all conscious, and yet the movie can also live for a general audience quite happily." Caro consciously fashions a homoerotic tease that has remained repressed in textual subconsciousness owing either to the absence of other females, as in "The Ballad of Mulan," or to the dominance of heterosexual romance, as in Mulan and Shang of the Disney animation and Wei Zhao and Kun Chen of *Hua Mulan*. Nevertheless, Caro hastens to promise that the LGBTQ 2+ motif lends itself to a heteronormal cooptation by Disney's general audience. Caro's proviso suggests a balancing act between commercial interests and artistic visions. Caro visualizes what is hiding in plain sight for almost two millennia: Mulan cross dresses not to replace her father but to be herself, a self that is both female and male.

To keep the general audience happy, Caro continues to veil Mulan's sexual orientation, favoring her femininity. The casting of Yifei Liu as Mulan has undermined any possibility of gender destabilizing because Liu has been catapulted to fame by playing lead roles in TV adaptations of *wuxia* (swordsman) novels by Jing Yong (pen name of Louis Cha), the preeminent wuxia novelist, one given to unabashed male fantasy in the proverbial *jianghu* (River and Lake), the alternate universe of swordplay akin to the lawless Wild West of Hollywood's Westerns. In fact, Liu has been designated by Jing Yong as the perfect candidate for his female protagonists in *Demi-Gods and Semi-Devils* (2003), *Chinese Paladin* (2005), and *The Return of the Condor Heroes* (2006). Treasured for her willowy femininity by Jing Yong and Caro, Liu pales in comparison to a number of other choices whose physique, carriage, and elocution problematize gender divisions, such as China's Yao Chen or Taiwan's Megan Lai. (Incidentally, Yao Chen is one of the three celebrities of the spotlight squad, along with Charlize Theron and Misty Copeland, featured in the Breitling women's watches ad in *The New York Times Style Magazine*. Apparently, many Chinese, women and men alike, purchase this status symbol.) Truth be told, it may be Liu's teenage years in the United States and English proficiency that landed her this Disney role.

Thus, the question "Mulan Who?" suggests, racially and paternally, Mulan Hu, with "Hu" a double entendre for a Chinese surname as well as a term that lumps together all northern "barbarians," for she may well have been of non-Chinese descent. With regard to gender, it veils the question "Whose Mulan?"—a phallic fetish into which the Chinese and the West, the male and female director and film industry, project longing for power, so long as this symbol returns to traditional femininity and commercial viability.

Gong Li, who plays the witch, rose to stardom in Zhang Yimou's *Red Sorghum* (1988) and several other films by the Chinese director. Gong Li of late has turned to international productions, ranging from the English-mangling Madame Hatsumomo in *Memoirs of a Geisha* (2005) to Lady

Murasaki in *Hannibal Rising* (2007) to Isabella in *Miami Vice* (2006) to Anna Lan-Ting in *Shanghai* (2010). The first two roles are Japanese, and the latter two are Chinese. Hawk's white face paint serves as a mask, accentuating the character's enigmatic, otherworldly aura. The face paint brings to mind the Great Wizard's Maori-style facial tattoo in *Matchless Mulan* (figure 5.1). A true, unadorned face would show oneself plainly. Masquerading lends itself to mystification, either the supernatural Hawk who transforms into a torrent of bats or the Great Wizard who dispatches a flood of rats against the matchless Mulan's garrison. Ultimately, the Eastern witch and the Orient are shadows thrown by Niki Caro and Disney on the cave wall of, by, and for the West.[1]

Bibliography

"The Ballad of Mulan." 386–535 AD. <http://www.tsoidug.org/literary_comp.php>.

Benjamin, Walter. "The Task of the Translator." 1955. In *Illuminations: Essays and Reflections*, translated by Harry Zohn, Shocken and edited by Hannah Arendt, 11–25. New York: Schocken Books, 1969.

Breitling Women's Watches Ad. "Women's Fashion." *The New York Times Style Magazine*, February 21, 2021: 69. <https://www.youtube.com/watch?v=9tLEI-o.NFi4>.

Chinese Paladin. Directed by Wu Jinyuan, Liang Shenzhi, and Mai Guanzhi. CTV (Taiwan) and CBG (Mainland China). 2005.

Debruge, Peter. "Review of *Mulan*." *Variety*, September 3, 2020. <https://variety.com/2020/film/reviews/mulan-review-live-action-adaptation-1234758090/>.

Demi-Gods and Semi-Devils. Directed by Yu Min, Kuk Kwok-leung, and Zhou Xiaowen. CCTV. 2003.

Hannibal Rising. Directed by Peter Webber. Performed by Gaspard Ulliel, Rhys Ifans, and Li Gong. Dino De Laurentiis Co. 2007.

Hua Mulan. Co-directed by Jingle Ma, Wei Dong. Performed by Wei Zhao and Kun Chen, Starlight International Media Group. 2009.

———. Directed by Ian Shepherd. Children's Documentary Film. 2020.

Ito, Robert. "Mulan, a Most Adaptable Heroine: There's a Version for Every Era." *The New York Times*, September 3, 2020. <https://www.nytimes.com/2020/09/03/movies/mulan-history.html>.

Kingston, Maxine Hong. *The Woman Warrior: Memoirs of a Girlhood Among Ghosts.* 1976. New York: Vintage, 1986.

Kung Fu Mulan. Directed by Leo Liao. Performed by Danny Fehsenfeld and Vivian Lu. Gold Valley Films. 2020.

Matchless Mulan (無雙花木蘭). Directed by Chen Cheng. Performed by Xue'er Hu, Wei Wei, and Jarvis Wu. New Studio Media. 2020. <https://www.iq.com/play/19rykyxerk>.

Memoirs of a Geisha. Directed by Rob Marshall. Performed by Ziyi Zhang, Ken Watanabe, Michelle Yeoh, and Gong Li. Columbia Pictures. 2005.

Miami Vice. Directed by Michael Mann. Forward Pass. 2006.

Mulan. Directed by Yuxi Li. Performed by Chuxuan Liu and Mo Li. iQIYI. Starlight International Media. 2009. <https://www.iq.com/play/owds1dsqvg>.

Mulan. IMDB. 2020. <https://www.imdb.com/title/tt4566758/mediaviewer/rm3506086401/?ref_=tt_ov_i>.

Mulan Legend. Directed by He Jia Nan. Performed by Zhang Dong. iQIYI. 2020. <https://www.iq.com/play/1d39j9ta5ik>.

Red Sorghum. Directed by Zhang Yimou. Xi'an Film Studio. 1988.

The Return of the Condor Heroes. Directed by Yu Min and Zhao Jian. Ciwen Pictures. 2006.

Shanghai. Directed by Mikael Håfström. Phoenix Pictures. 2010.

Stoker, Bram. *Dracula.* 1897. London: Penguin, 2013.

A Touch of Zen. Directed by King Hu. Union Film. 1971.

Truitt, Brian. "Review of *Mulan.*" *USA Today*, September 3, 2020. <https://www.usatoday.com/story/entertainment/movies/2020/09/03/mulan-review-disney-live-action-remake-improves-upon-animated-original/3451042001/>.

TAYLOR TOMKO

6 The Hybrid Alice: Framing the Imperial Gothic in Tim Burton's *Alice's Adventures in Wonderland*

In James Bobin's *Alice Through the Looking Glass* (2016), Alice's past suitor and now employer, Hamish Ascot, declares his concern for her mental state after her return from a trade voyage in Asia because she is dressed in a brightly colored Chinese garment; indeed, "she had spent months upriver. Dressed like she'd gone native" (00:12:55).[1] Alice's departure on this imperial venture closes *Alice in Wonderland* (2010), Tim Burton's adaptation of Lewis Carroll's *Alice's Adventures in Wonderland* (1865).[2] In Burton's film, Alice is now a young woman who has repressed the memories of her childhood adventures in Underland (which she, at the time, called Wonderland), Burton's canny stand-in for Wonderland. A substantial change that Burton makes is the addition of Alice's career as a ship captain, positioning the film as feminist, especially for the nineteenth-century setting in which women were rarely employed at all and certainly not within the imperial project; as Brenda Ayres reminds us, nineteenth-century women were meant to be "submissive, self-denying, modest, childlike, innocent, industrious, maternal, and angelic" while men were "the explorers, inventors, and negotiators of the world 'out there'" (2003, 39).[3] In Burton's retelling, the adaptability, determination, and grit that Alice harnesses in Underland allow her to break the glass ceiling by entering the business of imperial trade after her return to England, another (ad)venture that implicitly links her overthrow of the tyrannical Red Queen.

The progress that should be associated with Alice's feminism is thus complicated by the broader implications of her desire "to be the first to trade with China," itself a false historicization, as trade between Britain and China had been ongoing since the eighteenth century (Burton 01:38:55). Alice's remark that they "have a foothold in Hong Kong" situates the film post-1842 after the conclusion of the 1839 Opium War (01:38:49). This erasure of colonial violence highlights contradictions within the film's seemingly anti-colonial depiction of liberation from the Red Queen and reclamation of power for the White Queen. The reinstatement of the White Queen accompanied by Alice's return to England and expansion of imperial trade negates the revolutionary efforts of Alice and her side-kicks, such as the Mad Hatter and Tweedledee/Tweedledum, and actually reinforces nineteenth-century Western models of civilization.

By framing Alice's adventure in Underland with her trade voyage, Burton's film combines English imperialism with the strangeness and otherness of Underland, a union that typifies the imperial Gothic. Patrick Brantlinger writes that the imperial Gothic merges "the seemingly scientific, progressive, often Darwinian ideology of imperialism with an anti-thetical interest in the occult" revealing the contradictions between the triumphant rise of the empire with imperial anxiety signified by the un-known (1988, 227). In this reading, Alice becomes a figure of colonial hybridity who possesses a dual English-and-Underlandian subjectivity that empowers her to perpetuate the colonial project in both realms. The application of the imperial logic that drives Alice's feminist plot in England reveals a distinctly Western perspective in the Underland rebellion. Burton's film thus commodifies the ethos of imagination and liberation offered by Carroll's *Alice* texts into an expansion of the European imperial project, wherein the struggle for liberation in Underland conversely replicates both nineteenth-century colonization and Disney's repeated pattern of cultural appropriation.

While the contradictions between the liberation of Underland and Alice's feminism-through-imperialism in Burton's film deserve sustained critical attention, reading Carroll's *Alice* texts as colonial is not a new per-spective. In both Carroll's *Alice's Adventures* and their frequent appearance in adaptations, the mad tea party and the Caterpillar's hookah point to the ongoing spice and opium trades between Britain and various parts of the Eastern world, particularly India and China. Alice's adventure itself, as scholars have noted, replicates the discovery and civilizing process enacted by European colonizers.[4] Carroll's sequel, *Through the Looking-Glass, and What Alice Found There* (1872) also replicates foreign adventure, as the text depicts Alice "surveying" the geography of the looking-glass world and encountering a variety of strange creatures on her road to being crowned queen (Carroll 2009 [1872], 148). Burton's suggestion of a feminism that is made possible through imperial participation is not a new addition to the Alice universe, but one that is made most explicit by the expansion of Alice's imperial journey into the real world.[5] This negotiation between types of oppression is typical within the larger tradition of neo-Victorianism, which Sonya Fritz and Sara Day argue "intended to promote diversity [but] also runs the risk of only shoring up problematic nineteenth-century discourses" (2018, 9). Elizabeth Ho further has observed that neo-Victorian fiction "engages in a meta-dialogue with its own appropriative impulses and strategies" by "exhibit[ing] a need to recover and recover from the atrocities of empire in the past [that] demonstrate[s] an imperative to delineate neo-imperial and neo-colonial arrangements in a globalized present" (2012, 10, 9). In Burton's film, Alice's ability to embark on her commercial venture reorients the globalization of women in the nineteenth century, but in doing so problematically re-establishes imperial authority. This dynamic is reiterated by the conclusion of Bobin's film, in which Alice and her mother (Lindsay Duncan) establish the "Kingsleigh & Kingsleigh Trading Company" and Alice cuts her hair short, which is revealed in a shot of her poring over a map of the "whole world" (Bobin 01:41:52). The emphasis that Burton and Bobin place on Alice's imperial plot dramatizes the implicit analogy made by Carroll's texts between Wonderland/Looking-Glass World and the Eastern territories on earth that were the targets of imperial expansion.

Underland's framing as a discoverable territory positions it in binary opposition to England, binarism being a staple in Gothic literature and fundamental to Edward Said's concept of Orientalism (Said 2003 [1978], 206).[6] Underland's opposition to England is emphasized by Alice getting stuck on the ceiling of the room she falls into from the rabbit hole, implying she is in an upside-down version of England (Burton 00:13:47). Said argues that European imperialism has historically used this rhetoric of opposition to frame the "Orient," or the pan-East, as a "contrasting image, idea, personality, [and] experience" to Europe, positioning Western culture as superior (2003 [1978], 1–2, 7). Orientalism thus grants the Western world symbolic authority over the pan-East; however, it is an especially tenuous grasp on authority that is created (and displaced, as we will see further on) by discourse. The imperial Gothic emerges in these moments of tenuousness, wherein the rhetorical binaries between colonized and colonizer are exposed as porous and fragile. For Brantlinger, the imperial Gothic highlights the "atavistic character" of both imperialism and spiritualism, "shadowing forth the larger, gradual disintegration of British hegemony," and "express[ing] anxieties about the ease with which civilization can revert to barbarism or savagery" (253, 229). This possibility of "reversion" back to "savagery" is an offshoot of Charles Darwin's theories of evolution which were essential to taxonomical sciences in the nineteenth century and shaped popular opinions regarding race and species that justified colonial activity. While Darwin did not put forward the idea of regressive evolution, degeneration theory was a nineteenth-century pseudoscience that took up his theory from *The Descent of Man* (1871) that the human races have separate evolutionary lineages, and therefore differing physiological and mental characteristics, to maintain that humans were also subject to *de*volution (Darwin 1886 [1871], 241). Degeneration theory thus offered a pseudoscientific basis for claims that certain groups, such as racial Others, women, the disabled, and criminals were less biologically and/or morally advanced than the ideal European subject.

The imperial Gothic novel dramatizes social, if not scientific, anxieties surrounding evolutionary backsliding, questioning the stability of Englishness as a subjective category. This anxiety is related to "Englishness tak[ing] its place as an essential nineteenth-century value and a key element in Victorian self-representations [wherein] comparative and negative definitions of English selfhood are invoked with greater frequency as the empire comes into contact with and subdues more and more foreign peoples" (Schmitt 1997, 13–14). The unexpected result of this comparison can be "an internalization of the foreign … that results in an uneasy awareness of a hybrid, deeply fractured, and contradictory self" (14). The most famous example of the imperial Gothic in literature is Joseph Conrad's *Heart of Darkness* (1899), which depicts the final stages of the idolized British agent Mr. Kurtz's descent into madness, seemingly due to a combination of close contact with the locals at his trading post and first-hand experience of imperial cruelty. Chinua Achebe writes that the linked portrayal of the Thames and Congo rivers in Conrad's novel professes a Gothic "lurking hint of kinship" that is further displayed by Kurtz' degeneration after having "gone native" (2016, 15) the same phrase Hamish applies to Alice after her first voyage (00:12:55). As Hamish notes, spending time with colonized groups is known "to do strange things to a man's mind, let alone a woman's" (00:55:56). Taken together, Hamish, Conrad, and Achebe identify an essential kinship between colonized and colonizer, one that opens the colonizer to a kind of "contamination" if he spends too long in the company of colonized peoples, an otherness that can be brought back to English society. In Underland, Alice is opening herself up to atavistic contamination that threatens to destabilize the empire.

Burton's Alice is unable to fit into English society even before she falls down the rabbit hole. At the engagement party, she questions notions of English propriety ("who's to say what is proper? What if it was agreed that 'proper' was wearing a codfish on your head?") and displays such imagination that Hamish thinks that "it would be best if [she] kept [her] visions to [her]self" (Burton 00:03:30, 00:06:09). Importantly, Alice's resistance to the oppression of the Red Queen is foreshadowed by her interactions with Lady Ascot, who is tied to the former by her rage that the gardeners have planted white roses in her garden instead of red. In her efforts to instruct Alice in being the ideal wife to Hamish, whom Alice does not want to marry, Lady Ascot asks, "do you know what I have always dreaded?" to which Alice responds, "the decline of the aristocracy?" (00:08:24). Alice's dual critique of gender and class oppression here not only prefigures her future struggle against the Red Queen but also marks Alice as an outsider for making these connections at all. As Alice spends little time in England in Carroll's texts, the expanded presence of English society in Burton's adaptation emphasizes Alice's ostracization, a difference that the audience knows comes from her childhood experience in Underland, though Alice herself will not become aware of this until the climax of the film. The dangers that Alice represents as an outspoken, unconventional female in England plays into the imperial Gothic, as she seems to be contaminated by a mysterious Other; Alice is strange, but the source of this alterity, Underland, is unknown.

The marked strangeness or "muchness," that keeps Alice from prop-
erly fitting in with English society hearkens to the mysterious "occult"
that Brantlinger reads as a threat to triumphant imperialism (227). As the
Hatter's claim that Alice has lost this "muchness" correlates to her refusal
to slay the Jabberwocky, "muchness" seemingly refers to the qualities that
made Alice stand out as a Victorian character: perseverance, bravery, and
a willingness to break gender expectations (Burton 00:38:13). That Alice
lacks this "muchness" upon arriving in Underland indicates that she has
been contaminated by England in the time since her childhood visit. By
maturing and becoming assimilated into English society, even if she is
somewhat marginal, Alice possesses less of the otherness that is desirable in
Underland. She is contaminated in two directions—Underland has made
her too unusual for England and England has made her not unusual enough
for Underland. This hybridity causes her identity to be questioned, especially in Underland; she is constantly accused of being the "wrong" Alice.
She does not become the correct Alice until she remembers her childhood
experience in Underland and affirms her own "muchness."

In the *Alice* universe broadly, this "muchness" connects to a willingness
to experience otherness that manifests in her obsession with the impossible.
Here, the impossible conflates with the Other to represent the occult aspect
of imperial Gothicism. Imperialism is explicitly connected to "muchness"
in the figure of Alice's father Charles Kingsleigh, who tells his partners in
commercial trade that "the only way to achieve the impossible is to believe
it is possible" (00:01:18). This enthusiasm for the impossible is inherited by
Alice; Hamish criticizes her for thinking "impossible" thoughts, to which
she replies: "My father said he sometimes believed in six impossible things
before breakfast" (00:06:35).[7] We learn that this attitude toward impos-
sibility is very Underlandian, as the Hatter finds the consideration of six
impossible things before breakfast to be an "excellent practice" (01:26:00).
Once Alice recognizes that the events in Underland are the impossible
manifested in real life, and not a product of her imagination, she is able
to harness her full power. Indeed, just before killing the Jabberwocky, she
lists six impossible things, the last of which is "I can slay the Jabberwocky"
(01:27:54). Upon returning to England, she is able to leverage this vision
of the impossible into what seems like female liberation, refusing Hamish's

offer of marriage and instead becoming an apprentice in the trading company owned by Lord Ascot. In this position, Alice is able to see that Ascot's traders have not gone "far enough," uncovering opportunities for economic growth that were previously deemed impossible (01:38:43).

While this conclusion may signal a win from feminist perspectives, it undermines the anti-colonial message that is seemingly offered by the victory over the Red Queen. Alice's "muchness," while allowing her to participate in the masculine public sphere, is reinscripted by the English empire. The ideas of imagination and adventure-for-its-own-sake that were espoused by Carroll's original text are commodified by the end of the film, wherein Alice participates in a different type of adventure by using her belief in the impossible as a means to economic and political ends; her ship is, almost too cannily, named "The Wonder." Alice's hybridity, too, is neutralized; while Homi Bhabha describes the colonial hybrid subject as one that "disturbs the visibility of the colonial presence and makes the recognition of its authority problematic," Alice only commits this "strategic reversal of the process of domination through disavowal" in the case of her gendered oppression (1994, 159). In this regard, Burton's Alice takes after the most famous hybrid figure in nineteenth-century imperial literature, the title character of Rudyard Kipling's *Kim* (serialized 1900–1901). Kim, too, is a cultural hybrid by being assimilated enough in India to pass as an Indian citizen, despite being orphaned by two Irish parents; however, his hybrid racial identity is celebrated because he uses it to imperial advantage in his role as a British secret agent. Similarly, Alice's "muchness," her ability to see outside of convention, is permissible only on the condition that she uses it to further the imperial project in both England and Underland.

The replication of Eurocentric imperial storylines is more insidious in Underland, as the population of Underland is certainly violently oppressed under the Red Queen's ruler; however, there are several contradictions within Underland's version of the colonized/colonizer binary that call the legitimacy of the anti-colonial plot into question. Of particular interest here are the names of certain characters, particularly Charles Kingsleigh and Absolem (played by Alan Rickman); the connections between the Hatter's insanity and colonial victory, which manifest in the figure of the Jabberwocky, and the characterization of the White and Red Queens according to nineteenth-century conventions of gendered behavior and physiological sciences. While they are relatively minor characters, it is worth noting the choice of the names "Charles Kingsleigh" for Alice's father and "Absolem" for the Caterpillar not only because they are both introduced by Burton in this film but also because these names connote failed historical and biblical uprisings. Charles Kingsleigh is likely a reference to Charles Kingsley, a priest in the Church of England, social reformer, historian, and novelist. While he never went on any imperial missions himself, Kingsley has multiple links to British colonization; aside from being a proponent of Darwin's theories of evolution, Kingsley was a vocal supporter of colonial administrator Edward Eyre, who was instated as Governor of Jamaica in 1854 and threatened with incarceration after his violent suppression of the 1865 Morant Bay Rebellion (Handford 2008, 836). Similarly, the Caterpillar's new name "Absolem" is a homophone for the biblical Absalom. In the second book of Samuel, Absalom is the third son of David, the King of Israel, who is remembered for leading an unsuccessful revolt against his father in an effort to usurp the throne (2 Samuel: 13–18 King James Version). These naming choices are especially notable as Kingsleigh and Absolem are essential to Alice's victory: Alice's final conversation with Absolem is the film's peak of self-actualization, which symbolically occurs during Absolem's literal transition from caterpillar to butterfly. During this sequence, Alice has an extended flashback that causes her to realize that she has actually been to Underland before (though she called it Wonderland, as Absolem reminds her) and the recurring nightmares she describes to her father at the opening of the film are memories, not dreams.

This transition from abstract to concrete is what inspires Alice to take the action she never imagined was possible, both in slaying the Jabberwocky and rising against the domestic married life that is expected for her in England. Importantly, alongside Absolem, it is her late father who helps her come to this realization; in defending her status as the correct Alice to Absolem, she declares: "My father was Charles Kingsleigh. He had a vision that stretched halfway around the world, and nothing ever stopped him. I'm his daughter. I'm Alice Kingsleigh" (Burton 01:20:51). While it is ultimately Alice who sets course for China and captains the ship, her achievement is couched within her father's vision, Absolem's encouragement, and the finances of Lord Ascot, Hamish's father and the new owner of Charles Kingsleigh's company, whose name is also a sly reference to British material culture. Despite the victory of Alice and her compatriots, the names Charles Kingsleigh and Absolem both hint that the success of Underland's revolution is ultimately a failure, especially given the imperial frame that surrounds said rebellion. The trend of undermining this seemingly anti-colonial plot continues in the figure of the Hatter, who utilizes Bhabha's language of colonial nonsense as a form of resistance. In Underland madness is "not an insanity but a necessary condition for freedom under the tyranny of the Red Queen" (Callen 2012, 121).

One advantage of the Hatter's revolutionary madness is that it allows him to assume a guise of unaccountable insanity in the face of authority, destabilizing the power relations between oppressor and oppressed. This power shift is evinced by the Knave of Hearts threatening that the Hatter and his companions will lose their heads for hiding Alice, to which the Hatter replies "already lost them" and the Hatter's risky choice to tell the Red Queen that he's been "considering things that begin with the letter 'M.' Moron, mutiny, murder, malice" which is luckily dismissed by the Red Queen as the ramblings of insanity (Burton 00:34:47, 00:50:56). The Hatter's guise of madness neutralizes the Red Queen's threat to him (up until his death sentence), an act that Jeffrey Callen says "destabilizes [and] deterritorializes the privileged position and, in turn, 'revalues all value," (123). This questioning of absolute imperial authority offers an "in-between space of self and other, a space haunted by specters of liberation, where one forgets what is impossible" (123). The effect of this nonsense as an "ominous silence" that responds to the also silent assumption of colonial power and "utters an archaic colonial 'otherness,' that speaks in riddles, obliterating proper names and proper places" (Bhabha 176). For Bhabha, colonial nonsense is a hybrid signifier that displaces the fragile rhetorical binaries of self/Other that Said, Brantlinger, and Schmitt argue are essential to Western imperial subjectivity, by "mock[ing] the social performance of language with their non-sense" (177). In using nonsense so strategically, the Hatter becomes a hybrid figure; like Alice, his ambivalence allows him to fit into the mad ethos of Underland, while also being able to seem harmless enough that the Red Queen does not perceive him as a threat. In doing so, he destabilizes (or at least delays) the enactment of the Red Queen's violent power.

While the Hatter's employment of colonial nonsense is a mode of resistance toward the Red Queen, this nonsense language is nevertheless tied to English imperialism. The dialect of the Hatter's mantra of resistance, "downal wyth Bluddy Behg Hid!" ("down with Bloody Big Head!") is repeated in his recitation of Carroll's poem "Jabberwocky," which appears in the text of Carroll's *Looking-Glass* (2009 [1872], 134–36) (Burton 00:32:06). In Burton's film, the Jabberwocky is a symbol for Underland's oppression under the Red Queen, and therefore the Jabberwocky's defeat should symbolize liberation. However, the final battle taking place on a field of black-and-white square tiles, which are diagonally arranged to represent a chessboard, couches Alice's defeat of the Jabberwocky as imperialist (Burton 01:23:38). The chessboard motif alludes to both *Looking-Glass*, in which Alice plays an extended chess game against the Red and White Queens, and to the "Great Game," the diplomatic confrontation between the British and Russian empires over control of Afghanistan and connected South and Central Asian territories (1830–1907).[8] In the context of this conflict, Alice's trade target, China, along with Tibet and Mongolia, were subjects of Victorian political contention. The seemingly anti-colonial message of the Red Queen's defeat is called into question by this visual reference, likening the White Queen's ascension to a British imperial victory, while undermining the role of nonsense as an act of political rebellion.

The aforementioned details of naming, nonsense language, and the allusion to the great game urges us to reevaluate the role of the White Queen who ultimately represents a more Eurocentric female ideal than her sister, the Red Queen. Despite the extensive and damning (for the Red Queen) comparisons that Burton's film makes between these two characters, the fact that they are siblings offers the same Gothic hint of kinship that Achebe sees in Conrad's depictions of the Thames and Congo rivers. Still, the White Queen is positioned as the "good" sister, and the ideal English woman, in terms of temperament and physiology. Kathleen E. B. Manley identifies a positioning of women as a "civilizing force" in Disney films, a tradition that is incorporated into the Disney canon through heroines reforming male characters to Western standards of behavior, serving as a "model of acceptable behavior for people in Western culture" (2003, 79, 80). While Alice does most of the legwork in the liberation of Underland, she is less of a "civilizing force" than the White Queen, who is the ultimate symbol for European heteronormativity. When Alice meets the White Queen for the first time, the Queen makes a potion that returns Alice from too tall to regular size. This event takes place in the kitchen, and the White Queen uses a recipe that positions potion-brewing as an Underland equivalent of cooking. The White Queen not only acts as a regulator of abnormality but does so through domestic means, making her an Angel in the House, the Victorian ideal of domestic and submissive womanhood. Alice, in contrast, is too masculine by most Victorian standards, being an explorer and, to borrow Ayres' phrase, "negotiator of the world 'out there'" (39). Physiologically, too, Alice oscillates between being too large and too small, an issue corrected by the White Queen through the magic of appropriate womanhood.

During the potion-making sequence, the White Queen is sure to position the Red Queen as the opposite of this domestic ideal by noting that her sister "preferred to study dominion over living things" (01:08:47). Unlike the White Queen, who we see lead with mercy by choosing to banish the Red Queen instead of having her put to death, the Red Queen leads through violence, evinced by the petrified bodies of her victims, including that of her late husband, which fill the moat of her castle. That these differences in conduct are matched by the White and Red Queens' physiologies reinforces the positioning of the White Queen as the correct ruler. If Alice's adventures in Wonder/Underland are of a fundamentally imperial nature, then her descent down the rabbit hole depicts a journey backward in evolutionary time to a land of atavistic beings, such as the speaking nonhuman animals, physiologically unconventional humans (Tweedledee and Tweedledum), or the mentally unstable Mad Hatter, whose brightly colored eyes and hair Johnny Depp attributes to mercury poisoning.[9]

No one is more degenerate than the Red Queen; what differentiates her from the other denizens of Underland is that nineteenth-century pseudoscience would directly link her degenerate physiognomy to her criminal behavior. One of the contemporary pseudoscientific offshoots to Darwin's evolutionary theories was physiognomy, the practice of judging a people's character based on their physical appearance, particularly the face.[10]

Physiognomy was popularized in Italian criminologist Cesare Lombroso's "ground-breaking" work *The Criminal Man* (1887), in which physiognomy is posed as a method for determining the typical physiological features of criminals. Darwin's influence on Lombroso is clear because the latter theorizes that the criminal "reproduces physical, psychic, and functional qualities of remote ancestors," or past evolutionary iterations (1911 [1887], 8). Thus, criminal physiologies, even those of the White criminal, are aligned with animals or racial Others. While the White Queen's proportionate physiognomy excludes her from this criminal type, the Red Queen, and, if their disguises are believed, the members of her court who wear artificial large noses, stomachs, and cheeks, are not so lucky. According to Lombroso, features such as enlarged orbits (skull bones) and hooked noses "often impart to criminals the aspect of birds of prey, the projection of the lower part of the face and jaws … found in negroes and animals" (7). Further, exaggerated temples, such as the Red Queen's, are "correlated to an excessive development of the temporal muscles, a common characteristic of primates and carnivores" (12). The alignment with animals and other races positions the Red Queen as a hybrid of colonizer and colonized; while she enacts a version of colonization in Underland, she most resembles the English depiction of colonized Other.

That the Red Queen is so animalized by her behavior and physiognomy is especially interesting within the taxonomical politics of Underland, wherein the imperial reduction of racial Others (among other marginalized groups) to nonhuman animals is seemingly neutralized by the removal of the language barrier that separates human from nonhuman creatures; yet, the traditional human/nonhuman animal hierarchy is upheld in the Red Queen's court, where animals primarily serve as labor, such as her frog footmen, her pig footstools, and the monkeys that hold up chair cushions (00:26:00, 00:48:30, 00:48:46). In a universe where humans and nonhuman animals exist on the same ontological field, the continued subjugation of animals in the Red Queen's regime is analogous to the labor extraction that colonized peoples were subject to under European rule. It is no surprise that when the Hatter encourages "the abused and enslaved in the Red Queen's court" to rise up against her, we are shown several animals emerging from between sets of human legs (01:14:19). Naturally, the

White Queen also employs nonhuman animals in her court, such as the March Hare and Bayard the bloodhound, but the White Queen's attitude toward these animals is far more merciful; while the Knave of Hearts lies to Bayard about releasing his family in exchange for his efforts in finding Alice, the White Queen praises him and tells him to rest (00:28:19, 00:53:35).

This dynamic between humans and nonhuman animals is important not only for the purpose of comparing the two queens but also for assessing the species-ontological landscape of Underland. Among the animalized humans and the nonhuman animals, the White Queen stands alone as the only character in Underland who is untouched by degeneration and is entirely pure, with no trace of physiological, intellectual, or cultural hybridity. The White Queen is therefore the only suitable ruler for Underland from a Western imperial perspective. Alice would not be allowed to reign because she is less ideally English than the White Queen in terms of gender expectations, which are surprisingly consistent between England and Underland. Like the rest of the White Queen's supporters, Alice is just a pawn (or, perhaps a knight?) in the restoration of the appropriate ruler to the throne. In a *New York Times* review of Burton's film by Larry Rohter (2010), the screenwriter Linda Woolverton is quoted as saying this narrative "comes down to good and evil ... there are people who represent the positive and those who have fallen into a dark, more evil value system," with this "evil" value system seeming to refer to those who do not fit in with nineteenth-century imperial norms (para. 22). The depiction of the great game in Burton's film marks a female victory that is ultimately linked to the restoration of British imperial order. These connections are solidified by the image of the White Queen giving Alice blood from the slain Jabberwocky, a symbol for the resources extracted from colonized peoples, which gives Alice the ability to return to England to continue establishing colonial power (Burton 01:34:23).

Alice's time in Underland, especially after she recognizes that it is real and not a product of her imagination, shifts from an exercise in fantasy to an imperial training ground. She learns how to harness her hybridity for the sake of colonial adventure and to identify and support the Underland equivalent of Western values, before taking a symbolic victory in the Underland great game. The imperial Gothicism that characterizes

Alice's unconventionality in England is remedied by an education in how to further imperialism, even if she must break gender norms to do so. The connection between Alice's time in Underland and her newfound colonial prowess in England is encapsulated in Absolem's appearance on her shoulder in the final moments of the film, as she is about to embark on her first voyage (01:39:54). The connection between Absolem, Alice, and her imminent adventure is evinced by the color match between the coat she is wearing over her seafaring uniform and Absolem's blue wings. Absolem's presence here is a reminder that Alice's experiences in "Wonderland" as a child, and Underland as a young adult, have prepared her to break gendered boundaries within the frame of imperial ideology. The ending concludes that Alice's experiences of wonder, imagination, and otherness in Underland will be economized into foreign trade potential, her participation in imperialism thus resolving her contact with this otherness. As Kamilla Elliott reminds us, "Alice's realization that her childhood dreams are not dreams but memories of her childhood visits to Underland flattens the possible and impossible—the imagined possibilities of a dream are unveiled to be what is actual" and therefore "for Alice 'to kill the Jabberwocky is to kill nonsense,'" silencing the resistant nonsense of Underland and all possibilities for legitimate colonial liberation (2010, 194).

Alice's scandalous promotion to ship captain solidifies Burton's *Alice* as a feminist film, as this plotline allows her to rise above the policing of her behavior in England by her mother, sister, Hamish, and Lady Ascot; however, her commercial venture and its connotations of violent resource and labor extraction position Alice as a participant in the Western misogynistic tradition that oppressed other nineteenth-century women, especially non-European women. The problematic politics of Alice escaping gendered oppression by instead participating in racial oppression is reminiscent of the critiques third-wave feminism has received regarding racial diversity both within and outside the Disney universe. Critical race theorist Kimberlé Crenshaw, who coined the term "intersectionality," contends that "when [feminist] practices expound identity as 'woman' or 'person of color' as an either/or proposition, they relegate the identity of women of color to a location that resists telling," which ultimately results in women of color being marginalized within both discourses (1991, 1,241 and 1,244). Intersectional feminism views the White feminist as the feminist par excellence, defining itself through difference to the feminist of color and offering "woman of color" as an intersectional category through exclusion from the "subject X," the White female, the original feminist; accordingly, women of color are often situated as "new arrivals" within feminism (Puar 2012, 52).

Similar issues of racial exclusion being excused by feminist achievement haunt the Disney cinematic canon. Michael Macaluso reasons that female achievement in Disney films is permissible because it is couched within Disney-specific ideologies, usually heteronormative notions of success (2016, 77). In Burton's adaptation, this ideology is Disney's imperialistic pattern of cultural appropriation. The irony of Alice's being released from gendered restrictions, only to be forced to further the colonial project, is that the latter ultimately still subsumes the former. Woolverton explains that in the screenplay, she set out to create an image of female empowerment, of a role model who has "an opportunity to make [her] own choices, difficult choices, and set out on [her] own road" and White Queen similarly claims that Alice "cannot live [her] life to please others" and thus the choice to slay the Jabberwocky "must be [hers]" (quoted in Rohter para. 6). Yet, the Oraculum has foretold Alice's slaying the Jabberwocky on Frabjous Day and thence it is not her choice at all but is written into history. The Oraculum is "the most damning limitation on Alice's free will" (Siemann 2012, 184). Absolem's insistence that the Oraculum is a compendium that "tells of each and every day since the beginning" echoes Victorian imperialism by narrativizing a timeline, casting the ascension of the White Queen as a marker of progress. Alice's victory reinforces not only colonial success in England but also gendered and imperial conventions in Underland.

By attempting to depict the White Queen's victory as an anti-colonial effort, Burton's film enacts the trap of futility into which Western media, Disney in particular, so often falls when attempting to write anti-colonial narratives. Sotirios Mouzakis (2019), Lan Dong (2010), and Richard Pells (2004), among others, have written about Disney's history of racial stereotyping and pattern of cultural appropriation, with the company basing many of its animated films from the 1930s onward on either ahistoricized or Americanized versions of the mythologies of other places.[11] Mouzakis highlights the ambivalence of scholarship on American globalization, a field divided between those who position cultural globalization as a co-lonial act and others who are more apologetic about America's dominant role in the global marketplace (2019, 63). In support of the first line of thought, Mouzakis cites Pells' argument that "American culture spread throughout the world because it has habitually drawn on foreign styles and ideas," meaning that "Americans have specialized in *selling the fantasies and folklore of other people back to them*" (emphasis in original).[12] The hybridity of global culture demonstrates that Disney's animation *Mulan* (Dong 2010), which was criticized for being both insufficiently Chinese and insufficiently American, offers Mulan as the Oriental Other who yet represents Americanized values in order to appeal to American audiences (228–29). As Mouzakis suggests, Disney's take on the female role in globalization has less to do with racial authenticity but is reduced to the commodities of film production and merchandising, creating a dissonance between "the aggressiveness with which Disney enters the global markets" and "the often innocent and likable characters of the film franchise[s]," such as Mulan herself (64).

The *Alice in Wonderland* cultural property is not exempt from this commodification; Carroll's texts are in fact one of the greatest victims of Disney absorption. Walt Disney consistently has tried to align the imaginative ethos of Wonderland with that of Disney, from the 1923 release of *Alice's Wonderland* the first of 57 animated/live action shorts starring Virginia Davis as Alice, in which the curious young Alice visits Disney studios and encounters Walt Disney himself, to the appearance of Carroll's *Alice in Wonderland* on a bookshelf during the title sequence of *Pinocchio* (1940). Despite his enthusiasm for Alice, Walt Disney seemed to have issues with her; the more Disney worked on the animated film, the more he thought of her as "a prim and prissy little person, lacking in humor and entirely too passive in her role in the story" (Schickel 1997, 295). Disney's 1951 animation particularly emphasizes the "clueless little girl" aspect of Alice's character relative to Carroll's texts, making it more stereotypically Victorian than the nineteenth-century originals (Ross 2000, 207). This dissonance illustrates that the issue with Alice is not passivity, but an excess of activity; she was already capable of colonization without Disney's commodification of her character, a power imbalance corrected by the 1951 film.

While Burton's adaptation certainly offers a more feminist narrative, we have seen that it is ultimately subsumed by the Disney pattern of
imperialization. A producer of Burton's adaptation, Richard D. Zanuck,
foreshadows that the film will perpetuate this Disney tradition of
ahistoricization, describing it as "a piece of entertainment where you have
a heroine off to another adventure at the end, and unless I'm wrong, people
of all nationalities will just enjoy it as an entertainment and not try to
interpret it" (quoted in Rohter para. 10). The assumption that the film
will be uncritically enjoyed by viewers of all nationalities, including those
persons who may still feel the traumatic repercussions of British colonization, demonstrates the ability of an ambivalent Western perspective to
view the film as harmless fun. This perspective is especially appropriate
for the *Alice* universe which was constructed by Carroll as a haven for imagination without tangible real-world consequences. Elliott highlights the
self-consciousness of Burton's introduction of nineteenth-century English
reality into *Alice*, arguing that "Burton's film adapts the all-star casting
from prior Alice films and is even thicker with theatrical layering that
keeps peeling off to reveal what lies beneath. Alice's costumes drop from
her body; fake body parts drop from courtiers near the end of the film;
and the Red Queen's lips remain visible beneath the heart-shaped painted
ones" (199). These markers, along with the film's hybrid production of live
action, computer-generated images, and 3D, "investigate not so much a tension between nonsense and sense as between fantasy and reality: they aim
to make the fantastic seem real and the real seem fantastic" (Elliott 199).
This dichotomy is a sign that Burton's adaptation is reinscripting Alice's
role within the Disney canon: "Whereas Carroll's books subvert and mock
authority figures and social structures," Elliott writes, "Disney's film makes
the historical Western conquest of Eastern nations as its happy ending,
an apt adaptation of its own colonising enterprises" (200). Despite these
feminist intentions, the introduction of English imperialism to Burton's
Alice in Wonderland begs for a more critical analysis of the ostensibly anti-
colonial overthrow of the Red Queen than the film can survive. Here, as
in the Disney animated adaptation, the wonder, imagination, and liberation that are offered by Carroll's Wonderland are framed as the forms of
contamination that mark the imperial Gothic and are reappropriated to
serve Disneyfied ideological ends.

Bibliography

Achebe, Chinua. "An Image of Africa: Racism in Conrad's *Heart of Darkness*." *The Massachusetts Review* 57, no. 1 (2016): 14–27.

"Alice Through the Looking Glass Press Conference: Johnny Depp, Mia Wasikowska, Sacha Baron Cohen." *YouTube*. Uploaded by the Upcoming. May 8, 2016. <https://www.youtube.com/watch?v=APL3iPA9vIY>.

Ayres, Brenda. *The Emperor's Old Groove: Decolonizing Disney's Magic Kingdom.* New York: Peter Lang, 2003.

———. "The Poisonous Apple in *Snow White*: Disney's Kingdom of Gender." In Ayres 2003, 39–50.

Bailey, Jessica. "Exclusive: Inside Mia Wasikowska's Costume Trunk." *Grazia Magazine* (2016): n.p. <https://graziamagazine.com/articles/inside-mia-was ikowska-alice-through-the-looking-glass-costume-trunk-2016/>.

Bhabha, Homi K. *The Location of Culture.* New York: Routledge, 1994.

Brantlinger, Patrick. *Rule of Darkness: British Literature and Imperialism, 1830–1914.* Ithaca, NY: Cornell University Press, 1988.

Butler, Jess. "For White Girls Only? Postfeminism, and the Politics of Inclusion." *Feminist Formations* 25, no. 1 (2013): 35–58.

Callen, Jeffrey C. "Impossible Things: An Investigation of Madness as Resistance in Tim Burton's *Alice in Wonderland.*" *Administrative Theory & Praxis* 34, no. 1 (2012): 120–24.

Carroll, Lewis. *Alice's Adventures in Wonderland.* 1865. In *"Alice's Adventures in Wonderland" and "Through the Looking-Glass"*, edited by Peter Hunt, 9–113. Illustrated by John Tenniel. New York: Oxford University Press, 2009a.

———. *Through the Looking Glass, and What Alice Found There.* 1872. In *"Alice's Adventures in Wonderland" and "Through the Looking-Glass"*, edited by Peter Hunt, 123–250. Illustrated by John Tenniel. New York: Oxford University Press, 2009b.

Cheu, Johnson, ed. *Diversity in Disney Films: Critical Essays on Race, Ethnicity, Gender, Sexuality and Disability.* Jefferson, NC: McFarland. 2012.

Ciolkowski, Laura E. "Visions of Life on the Border: Wonderland Women, Imperial Travelers, and Bourgeois Womanhood in the Nineteenth Century." *Genders* 27 (1998): n.p. Wayback Machine Internet Archive.

Conrad, Joseph. *"Heart of Darkness" and Other Tales.* 1899. Introduction by Cedric Watts, xi–xxviii. Oxford: Oxford University Press, 2002.

Crenshaw, Kimberlé. "Mapping the Margins: Intersectionality, Identity Politics, and Violence Against Women of Color." *Stanford Law Review* 43, no. 6 (1991): 1241–99.

Darwin, Charles. *The Descent of Man*. 1871. In *The Principal Works of Charles Darwin*. 151–470. New York: John B. Alden, 1886.

Dong, Lan. "Mulan: Disney's Hybrid Heroine." In *Beyond Adaptation: Essays on Radical Transformations of Original Works*, edited by Phyllis Frus and Christy Williams, 156–67. Jefferson, NC: McFarland, 2010.

Elliott, Kamilla. "Film Review: Adaptation as Compendium: Tim Burton's *Alice in Wonderland*." *Adaptation* 3, no. 2 (2010): 193–201.

Fritz, Sonya Sawyer, and Sara K. Day. *The Victorian Era in Twenty-First Century Children's and Adolescent Literature and Culture*. New York: Routledge, 2018.

Graner, Emma D. "Dangerous Alice: Travel Narrative, Empire, and *Alice's Adventures in Wonderland*." *CEA Critic* 76, no. 3 (2014): 252–58.

Handford, Peter. "Edward John Eyre and the Conflict of Laws." *Melbourne University Law Review* 32, no. 3 (2008): 822–60.

Ho, Elizabeth. *Neo-Victorianism and the Memory of Empire*. New York: Continuum, 2012.

Kipling, Rudyard. *Kim*. 1901. Introduction by Alan Sandison, xiii–xxviii. Oxford: Oxford University Press, 1991.

Lombroso, Cesare. *Criminal Man: According to the Classification of Cesare Lombroso*. 1887. New York: G. P. Putnam's Sons, 1911.

Macaluso, Michael. "The Postfeminist Princess: Public Discourse and Disney's Curricular Guide to Feminism." In *Disney, Culture, Curriculum*, edited by Jennifer Sandlin and Julie Garlen, 73–86. New York: Routledge, 2016.

Manley, Kathleen E. B. "Disney, the Beast, and Woman as Civilizing Force." In Ayres 2003, 79–89.

Manning, Kara M. "'That's the Effect of Living Backwards': Technological Change, Lewis Carroll's *Alice* Books, and Tim Burton's *Alice in Wonderland*." *Neo-Victorian Studies* 4, no. 2 (2011): 154–79.

Mouzakis, Sotirios. "Princess of a Different Kingdom: Cultural Imperialism, Female Heroism, and the Global Performance of Walt Disney's *Mulan* and *Moana*." In *Heroism as a Global Phenomenon in Contemporary Culture*, edited by Barbara Korte et al., 61–80. New York: Routledge, 2019.

Pells, Richard. "From Modernism to the Movies: The Globalization of American Culture in the Twentieth Century." *European Journal of American Culture* 23, no. 2 (2004): 143–55.

Puar, Jasbir K. "'I Would Rather Be a Cyborg Than a Goddess': Becoming Intersectional in Assemblage Theory." *Philosophia: A Journal of Continental Feminism* 2, no. 1 (2012): 49–66.

Rohter, Larry. "Drinking Blood: New Wonders of Alice's World." *The New York Times Online*, February 26, 2010. <https://www.nytimes.com/2010/02/28/movies/28alice.html>.

Ross, Deborah. "Escape from Wonderland: Disneyland the Female Imagination."
    Marvels & Tales 18, no. 1 (2004): 53–66.

———. "Home by Tea-Time: Fear of Imagination in Disney's *Alice in Wonderland.*"
    In *Classics in Film and Fiction*, edited by Deborah Cartmell et al., 195–207.
    London: Pluto Press, 2000.

Said, Edward. *Orientalism.* 1978. London: Penguin Books, 2003.

———. "Orientalism Reconsidered." *Race & Class* 27, no. 2 (1985): 1–15.

Schickel, Richard. *The Disney Version: The Life, Times, Art and Commerce of Walt
    Disney.* Chicago: Ivan R. Dee, 1997.

Schmitt, Cannon. *Alien Nation: Nineteenth-Century Gothic Fictions and English
    Nationality.* Philadelphia: University of Pennsylvania Press, 1997.

Siemann, Catherine. "'But I'm Grown Up Now': *Alice* in the Twenty-First Century."
    Neo-Victorian Studies 5, no. 1 (2012): 175–201.

Spurzheim, Johann, and Franz Josef Gall. *The Physiognomical System of Drs. Gall and
    Spurzheim.* London: Baldwin, Cradock, and Joy, 1815.

Stover, Cassandra. "Damsels and Heroines: The Conundrum of the Post-Feminist
    Disney Princess." *LUX: A Journal of Transdisciplinary Writing and Research
    from Claremont Graduate University* 2, no. 1 (2013): 1–10.

Yapp, Malcolm. "The Legend of the Great Game." In *Proceedings of the British
    Academy: 2000 Lectures and Memoirs*, 179–98. Oxford: Oxford University
    Press, 2001.

7 Peter Pan After the Blitz: Finding What Remains in *Return to Never Land*

All this has happened before and it will all happen again. But this time it happened in London—it happened on a quiet street in Bloomsbury. That corner house over there is the home of the Darling family, and Peter Pan chose this particular house because there were people here who believed in him.

—Opening narration to Disney's *Peter Pan* (1953)

Mary Martin, leader of the Lost Boys,
when you flew across the stage in drag,
in your tattered forest suit, teasing Hook,
some of us recognized you. Girl-boy, darling,
you refused to grow into any version
of manhood, while we cheered at the play
in New York, 1960, tomboys pulled from play
to put on dresses and sit among the feckless boys.
—Robin Becker (1996)

Fifty years after Disney's *Peter Pan* (1953) debuted in theaters, *Return to Never Land* (2002) opens with a fairy light flitting between the clouds in the London night sky, illuminating silhouettes from the original film: The Darling children taking flight, a crocodile with a clock glowing in its stomach, Skull Rock, Captain Hook's profile, a totem pole with the sound of war drums in the background, swirling mermaids, marching Lost Boys, and, finally, the real Peter Pan aboard the Jolly Roger hanging in the shadow of the moon. The montage zooms out to young Wendy gazing up at the moon from the nursery window, stepping away, and returning with her husband and young children, Jane and Danny. In place of the original film's authorial voice assuring the viewer that "all this has happened before and it will all happen again," *Return to Never Land* begins with a more direct evocation of the audience's nostalgia. *Return to Never Land* is not a "new" Peter Pan story but a continuation of the previous film. Never Land and Pan are as they have always been, and the adult Wendy, like her mother before her, is raising a new nuclear family in the beautiful corner townhouse where she and her brothers played as children. In her blue dress and white apron, grown-up Wendy strongly resembles *Beauty and the Beast*'s (1991) Belle, just as Mrs. Darling's hair and pink ball gown in the original *Peter Pan* echo Cinderella in her mice-made ball gown. *Return to Never Land* begins with an evocation of its Disney identity, both as a sequel to a specific animated Disney classic, and as a descendant of the more recent Disney Renaissance of 1989–1999. That evocation of a nostalgic joy for an uncomplicated, shared imaginary past—the heightened feeling of childhood adventure as translated through stunning, familiar animation and merchandise tie-ins—is integral to "Disney magic."

While the opening of *Return to Never Land* steeps images of the original *Peter Pan* film adaptation in classic "Disney magic" and cozy Edwardian nostalgia, *Peter Pan*'s production takes place during rapid periods of change for the Walt Disney Company and global culture. The process of adapting J. M. Barrie's 1904 play—and subsequent 1911 novel—spans the 1930s, when Disney first had the idea to adapt *Peter Pan*, carries into the start of World War II when Disney obtained the animation rights, and continues through the postwar period from 1948 to 1952 (Ohmer 2009, 153). Between Walt Disney's idea to make a *Peter Pan* film and its eventual release, the company had its first financial failures with *Pinocchio* (1940) and *Fantasia* (1940), produced war shorts for the US government, released its first live-action films, and began exploring the possibility of building a theme park in California (158, 153).

Peter Pan was the beginning of a formalized early storyboard and animation screening process that permitted—and recorded—the reactions of women to films in development. While women had worked on animated Disney films as inkers and painters since the studio's inception, *Peter Pan* was the first film where women on the Disney staff were asked to review a film in process and share their thoughts on its animation, characters, and songs as they were produced (160–61). As a story in which Wendy Darling is forcibly removed from the childhood nursery by her father only to return to her family three hours later at peace with her role as a young woman (and mother-to-be), *Peter Pan* was in one sense building an argument for the importance of motherhood and the nuclear family in the postwar era, a position that seemed to come less from an anxiety about women joining the work force—as mentioned, women were a critical part of Walt Disney Studios well before the war—than Disney's own "strict and quite Victorian views" on women's roles (Johnson 1988) and their perceived interest in "the little sentimental things" that make up stereotypical domesticity (quoted in Ohmer 167). At the same time, Disney was determining how to make Pan, in Disney's words, "a real boy," voiced and modeled by American child actor Bobby Driscoll (174) rather than "such fraudulent, if beguiling, facsimiles as Miss Adams, Betty Bronson, Marilyn Miller, Eva LeGallienne, and Jean Arthur" who had occupied the Peter Pan role on stage ("Peter Pan: Real" 1953, 96). The concern seemed in part a desire to make Pan traditionally masculine for an American audience now used to the rugged heroes of television serials. Even the racist portrayal of American Indians or "Injuns,"[1] was "clearly intended to appeal to children caught up in the television craze for Westerns" (Ohmer 171), to say nothing of its literalization of the Cold War's "Red Scare" and Congressional attempts to resolve "the Indian problem" by eliminating reservations and dismantling the Bureau of Indian Affairs.[2] The success of Disney's adaptation efforts was debated then and now,[3] but it unambiguously presented Barrie's stories with an eye toward an American postwar Disney audience.

Disney's *Return to Never Land* is no less marked by its own time. In an era that saw a swath of poorly received animated films like *Atlantis: The Lost Empire* (2001) and *Treasure Planet* (2002) intermixed with cheaply animated made-for-video sequels and television show tie-ins like *The Buzz Lightyear of Star Command: The Adventure Begins* (2000), *Lady and the Tramp II: Scamp's Adventure* (2001), and *The Hunchback of Notre Dame II* (2002), *Return to Never Land* is a more ambitious endeavor. It was only the third of Disney's animated sequels to earn a theatrical release, following *Rescuers Down Under* (1990) and *Fantasia 2000* (1999), and draws heavily from the popular cachet of *Peter Pan*. The movie poster features Pan's shadow on an emerald-green background with his name emblazoned over top like an A-list celebrity, so that it reads:

PETER PAN

in

Disney's

Return to Never Land

An All-New Adventure Only in Theatres February[4]

The use of Peter's shadow—the impetus for Peter's intrusion into the Darling home in the first film—combined with the promise of "an all-new adventure" highlights Disney's effort to both profit from and revise its own history. While Tinkerbell still arcs over the Disney Castle that precedes its animated features, the original film's emphasis on jealous women, its concerns with motherhood, and its offensive depictions of Native Americans already chafed against viewer sensibilities in the early 2000s. *Peter Pan* was not yet packaged with a warning about its use of slurs and stereotypical depiction of Native peoples as it is on Disney+ (Doody 2021), but the studio was increasingly aware of its problematic past. Critics' mixed reactions to *Pocahontas* (1995)—to say nothing of the disastrous *Pocahontas II: Journey to a New World* (1998)—highlighted an increasing diversity and cultural awareness in Disney's audience. As one of the earliest films made in the age of neo-Disneyism, *Return to Never Land* attempts to quietly address the overt racism and sexism of its past without upsetting its fundamentally traditional (i.e., conservative) brand image.

Return to Never Land moves the story from the turn of the twentieth century to the start of the 1940s, when Walt Disney was beginning to consider his *Peter Pan* adaptation in earnest. The sequel tells the story of Wendy Darling's[5] 12-year-old daughter, Jane, as she reckons with the realities of World War II. Her father has left to fight the Nazis, she and her brother are the imminent subjects of a forced evacuation from London as German planes terrorize the city and reduce its skyline to rubble, and Jane is too grown up to make time for her mother and younger brother's stories about Peter Pan and pixie dust. This depiction of wartime instability and general uncertainty carries additional meaning in 2002, especially as Disney expanded its market influence, and the digital age afforded underrepresented groups greater opportunities to voice their concerns about Disney's cultural and political power. *Return to Never Land*'s contradictory desire for Jane to find a temporary community within the adolescent male space of the Lost Boys but ultimately serve as a surrogate mother for Danny reflects commercial feminism's insincere nods to "girl power"; it is the illusion of empowerment mapped onto a traditional story. The film is no less conflicted in its attempts to deal with the original *Peter Pan*'s racism, as it leaves a hodgepodge of teepees and totem poles on display but removes Never Land's Indigenous inhabitants. In short, *Return to Never Land* is an attempt to address the political turmoil within Disney classics and its own historical moment by asking its audience to believe in traditional "Disney magic" revised for a new millennium. These revisions attempt to sidestep controversy using two strategies that Disney continues to employ today: the "corrective absence" of people of color—a strategy Disney previously employed in its theme parks—and Jane's temporary access to masculine modes of behavior as a would-be soldier and "Lost Girl." The incomplete and superficial appeals to feminism and inclusivity efforts in *Return to Neverland* foregrounds the core of the modern neo-Disney approach to representation. Ultimately, *Return to Never Land* presents a fleeting and anxious escape from the troubling realities of the adult world; Jane's trip to Never Land is only ever in service of preparing her to believe—and repeat—the same Peter Pan stories as Wendy and Danny.

"There's trouble brewin' on the island: women trouble"

Return to Neverland returns to a London much transformed by World War II. After the cloudy opening montage of the original *Peter Pan* adventures and introduction to the adult Wendy's family, the narrator warns, "Our story begins in difficult times. England is threatened with war, and many men have been asked to leave their families to protect their country" (00:02:55–3:06). Jane's father, Edward, says goodbye to his children while clad in British battledress and boards an army truck. Jane, aged 7 or 8, begs to come with him, but Edward tells his "big girl" that she is needed at home "to take care of your mom and Danny" (00:03:13–24). Jane agrees, and somberly takes her mother's hand to return to the house. There is no mention of the Darling boys, but presumably they, too, are away at war. As the lights to the Darling house are clicked off and the film pans away to the wreckage and the whistling sound of falling bombs, the narrator continues: "But the war lasted much longer than anyone could have imagined. Bombs fell from the sky and tore at the very heart of London. ... In times such as these, it is no wonder that some discard childish things like Peter Pan. And Never Land." After a pan through a scene of tearful children waving goodbye to their parents and boarding packed train cars to the countryside "for safekeeping" (00:04:00–15), we see Jane, aged 12, racing through the destroyed streets of London carrying a paper package and clad in a British "tin hat" and wool great coat. Her loyal dog, Nana II, runs alongside with a helmet and gear pack of her own, rushing with Jane through rubble, splashing over dirty puddles covering an old hopscotch play area, and darting across spotlights meant to reveal German bombers. An alarm blares through the city and, realizing bombings are imminent, Jane and Nana II find a hiding place amidst the wreckage to avoid the fallout. At the same time, Wendy scoops up her young son Danny and carries him to their backyard bomb shelter. As she slowly shuts the door on their shelter, the film makes it clear that there is no guarantee Jane will escape her trek into the city alive.

Inside the bunker, Wendy tells Peter Pan stories to transform the frightening sound of the falling bombs into Captain Hook's cannons, and Danny loses his fear in pirate play. Jane breathlessly returns during this commotion and presents Danny with the package she has risked her life to secure for him: a birthday present of two mismatched socks. "How very ... practical," Wendy notes with some disappointment, making up for Jane's mature gift by turning the socks into Pan and Hook puppets. Jane, for her part, takes out her field notepad and busies herself with military reports on the radio, though her own attention drifts to Wendy's Peter Pan stories before she catches herself and grows irritated with her mother's "poppy-cock" (0:008:40–48). Jane is too serious, too adult, and too modern for childish nonsense.

Jane proves an interesting contradiction in *Return to Never Land*, as Disney showcases her independence and discomfort with traditional gender roles and simultaneously identifies these qualities as a problem that must be corrected. On the one hand, Jane is outgoing and adventurous; she has taken her father's words to heart and adopted the masculine role of provider for her family. Clad in military uniform, she risks her life to get clothes for her brother and puts together a "Things We Need" list for the family. The nursery has been converted to her own room, and it is mostly bare save for toys from Wendy's childhood and a poster for the Auxiliary Territorial Service promoting the women's branch of the British Army pinned above her bed.[6] On the other hand, Jane's maturity leaves her little time to delight in the whimsical, magical stories that have come to define Disney's animated films. It is difficult to imagine Jane going to the cinema to watch *Pinocchio* (1940) or *Dumbo* (1941) in between scouring rubble for spare socks. The same qualities that make her a complicated heroine also make her a poor Disney audience member. As she removes her army coat to reveal her lilac nightgown, we see that the problem with Jane is that she is at once too adult and too unfeminine. Jane is, in the words of a *Chicago Defender* article announcing the release of *Return to Never Land*, a "hardened girl" (2002, 24), and it is up to Peter Pan, Tinker Bell, and the Lost Boys to "soften" her. She must—as she does before bed—strip off her military uniform and embrace her youthful femininity.

The grim specter of war adds a further complicating pall to the project. Jane's frustration and dissatisfaction comes to a head when Wendy reveals that she and Danny are being sent away to the British countryside. Abandoning her post in London as head of the house proves much more threatening to Jane than German bombs. It is here where she fights her mother the most, even as Wendy begs Jane to be mindful of the Peter Pan stories for Danny as much as for herself: "He needs them, Jane. And so do you" (00:10:57–11:05). Wendy understands the stories as an extension of both Jane's childhood *and* Jane's role as a mother-surrogate to Danny during their forced separation. In Jane's determination to take the place of their absent father, she is not prepared to occupy Wendy's role as maternal playmate. In wartime, there is no room for entertainment, and Jane, unlike her mother, must be dragged into the magic of Never Land by force.

Following her fight with Wendy about her upcoming evacuation, Jane is embroiled in a different war between Peter Pan and Captain Hook. Instead of being swept away by Peter Pan, Jane is abducted by Hook's crew in a failed attempt to kidnap "Wendy." In this conflict, too, Jane is made to fill Wendy's role; one British girl-child is the same as the next.

We might assume that the conflict between Hook and Pan parallels World War II—and it does, to a degree—but *Return to Never Land* resists a simple correlation between Hook and the Nazis. In fact, part of the confusion between Jane and Wendy is the result of Hook's haste to escape the London skyline. Even his magic ship is at risk as the Germans prepare for another round of bombings, and the Jolly Roger bobs between thin London streets, upsetting tanks and dodging planes. With his nineteenth-century British blustering "Great Scott!" (00:27:58–28:00), Captain Hook is an extension of the Empire; however, his piratical behavior becomes emblematic of self-serving adulthood. He is manipulative and untrustworthy, and values objects more than his people.

Of course, Never Land is not generalized make-believe either but a confabulation of British colonies covered in tropical fruits, rhinos, and lions, Fez-wearing pirates, and—most significantly—a conflation of Hollywood-style Native iconography and American-accented Lost Boys. In this New World, Jane still does not fit. She is too serious to fly even with the aid of pixie dust and finds the Lost Boys too coarse and clamorous. As in London, Jane's problem is contradictory; Peter suggests that Jane, like Wendy, should be their mother and "tell stories" but also expresses his shock at Jane's "grown-up" reactions to the Lost Boys' pranks and boisterous antics (00:26:15–20). Unlike Wendy, who explicitly travels to Never Land in the original film to play (temporarily) mother to Peter and the Lost Boys, Jane rejects the role of mother-storyteller even as she falls into the role of mature disciplinarian. As the Lost Boys excitedly yell about playing treasure hunt, Jane stops them in their tracks with a stern "No!" before her face softens at Tootles, the smallest, preverbal Lost Boy. "You remind me of someone I know," Jane says, hugging him tightly to her chest before declaring that she must go back home to London (00:25:45–26:07). The Boys are shocked into silence by her mature behavior, and Jane clearly sees her return home as a duty to Danny. She is split in her duties to Danny as surrogate father-soldier *and* mother-caregiver, but in either case, Jane has resolved to return home because she already has a child to parent.

Unable to fly, Jane sets to work finding a nonmagical means of escaping Never Land. As in London, she approaches the problem like a young cadet by crafting a raft, storing provisions for the journey, and even finding a Union Jack to fly on her makeshift vessel. The raft sinks, but Jane stays focused on her goal of getting home. In her goal-oriented world, Peter and the Lost Boys' games and traditional Disney hijinks become increasingly frustrating and insensitive. After dropping Jane off a cliff and failing to catch her, Peter and the Lost Boys then play a game of keep-away with Jane's field notes. Jane tries and fails repeatedly to get back the notepad until it is at last destroyed. This final dismissal of Jane's notepad—the physical embodiment of her responsibility to her family and her soldier duties—leads to an eruption of anger at Peter, the Lost Boys, and Tinkerbell:

> JANE: "Everything is just a game to you, isn't it? Well, I'm tired of playing!"
> PETER: "Gosh Jane, we didn't mean to make you mad."
> JANE: "Oh grow up, you did so! You're just a bunch of silly, ridiculous children—" (*At Tinkerbell, who pulls her hair in retaliation.*) "Leave me alone! I don't believe *any* of this. And I *especially* don't believe in fairies!" (00:34:58–35:23)

Disney's *Peter Pan* excised the scene from the original play where Peter directly appeals to the audience to clap their hands if they believe in fairies out of concern with what Bosley Crowther identified as "some anxiety that the mention of pixiness in the modern American movie theatre might provoke some embarrassment" (1953, 23). Jane, as a child living in times much more reflective of the early 1950s than the turn of the twentieth century, reflects the same anxiety that there is no room for fairies in wartime. Peter's inability to change with the times or reflect on the reasons for Jane's behavior beyond a childish, repetitive, "why?" highlights the question of how classic Disney stories like *Peter Pan*, literally a "fairy" tale, can remain relevant in a modern, war-torn world. Disney returns to the question of belief as lifeforce to highlight the weight of war on one's childhood; Jane *cannot* believe in Tinkerbell even as the fairy yanks at her hair for recognition. Practical, self-serious characters like Jane do not belong in Disney's magical, colorful animated worlds. In rejecting Tinkerbell and the very same pixie dust that Disney sprinkles over its animation logo, Jane-as-audience-surrogate threatens to reject the Disney brand as incompatible with her modern reality.

The negative consequences of Jane's lack of belief are stressed further as she distances herself from Peter's gang. Hook offers to get Jane back to London without "harming a single hair on Peter Pan's head" in return for Jane's alerting him to the location of his stolen treasure (00:40:28–50). Hook's bargain is a lie, of course, and a revealing one. As a representative of self-serving adulthood, Hook, too, does not believe in other people. In the context of Jane's too-rapid maturity, Hook suggests that one of the dangers of lack of belief is a lack of loyalty. In her urgency to explore the streets of London for socks of her own, to singlehandedly provide for what her family needs, and finally to escape from Never Land without the help of magic, Jane demonstrates a self-reliance that could quickly give way to a lack of faith in traditional family roles or traditional national governance. When she rejoins Peter's group, Jane must learn not only how to have fun but also to reconfirm her loyalty to a community. The montage where Jane earns her place as the "first ever Lost Girl," complete with white cat hood, by paddling across rivers on a log-turned-boat, scouting wildlands with the Lost Boys, and skipping rocks to find the hidden treasure, abruptly ends with one of the Lost Boys accidentally summoning Hook's men to their location. Jane, newly an official member of Pan's community, is then mistakenly branded a traitor by Peter and the Lost Boys as the pirates take them hostage.

In order to establish her loyalty to Pan and save the day, Jane must hurry back to the Lost Boys' hideout to save Tinkerbell. However, *Return to Never Land* resists the impulse to unite Jane and Tinkerbell through—or for—Peter, and briefly but radically departs from previous Disney efforts. Jane appears to arrive too late and, while mourning Tinkerbell, momentarily forgets Peter Pan and the Lost Boys as she stands vigil over the fairy's body. This moment of belief and care brings Tinkerbell back to life, and she announces her return by pulling Jane's hair—affectionately this time— and nuzzling her nose.[7]

Up until this point, Jane has been asked to choose between two male factions: Hook's pirates or the Lost Boys. Apart from the vain, violent, and territorial mermaids, there are no women-controlled spaces in Never Land. The first *Peter Pan* imagines Never Land as a boys' paradise that replicates the rigid gender structures of 1950s television serials, where girls and women exist on the margins to be rescued or to perform domestic labor. When Jane first mentions Tinkerbell's hostility toward her, Pan offhandedly replies, "Oh, she's just jealous. All girls get like that around me" (00:24:00–04). Peter is right, at least so far as the original film is concerned: The mermaids, Tinkerbell, and Wendy all express a competitive antagonism with other women for Peter's affections. The silent Tiger Lily is the sole exception, even though her loyalty to Peter at risk of death, as well as her betrothal, and their shared "nose kisses," were points of focused consternation for Wendy. In a rejection of this competitive female space, Jane responds with a rather dismissive, "How very nice for you" (00:25:05–09). Disney first attempts to correct the traditionalist gender constructs of *Peter Pan* by making Jane "one of the boys." Instead of occupying the rarified space of mother and would-be love interest, Jane becomes "the first ever Lost Girl," but this position proves to have its own gender troubles. The value of being the "first ever" Lost Girl lies in part in its singularity; Jane is the only girl permitted equal status in this adolescent male space. The title of "Lost Girl" notes that she has met the requirements to belong with the boys as an exception to the prevailing gender rules.

In having Jane give up her Lost Boys' animal hood to bond with Tinkerbell outside of their relationships to Peter, Disney raises the possibility of female relationships within Never Land—and Disney's twenty-first-century animated films more broadly—free of competition over male affection. Their friendship also affords Jane a far more powerful position than the one she earned as a Lost Boy. As Hook binds Peter to an anchor and forces him to walk the plank with the promise that the Lost Boys will follow, Jane assumes the heroic Peter Pan role herself. "Not so fast, you old codfish, or you'll have to answer to me!" she cries (00:00:51:50–55). Jane and Tinkerbell collaborate to unbind the Lost Boys and fight off the pirates, first working with the Lost Boys to slingshot treasure, and finally freeing Pan from his ropes. In this single scene, Jane flies weightlessly through the air to the cheers of Tinkerbell, the Lost Boys, and even Hook's crew. Rather than serving as an elevated sidekick, love interest, or singing damsel to be rescued, *Return to Never Land* momentarily explores the possibility of exploring Disney/Never Land magic beyond the gender binary.

Both Jane and Peter crow to the Lost Boys as she and Pan defeat Hook and sink the Jolly Roger. The moment works in part as a connection back to the staged productions where Pan is traditionally played by a woman, a tradition begun with Nina Boucicault at the Duke of York's Theatre in 1904 and cemented in modern American minds with Mary Martin in the 1954 Broadway musical version. Yet there is something especially exciting about Jane's occupying the role of Peter as an undisguised "girl"; in her effortless, joyful flight, the films hints at the possibility of more complicated gender politics. In the time between the mid-century's anxieties about making Pan a "real boy" and the turn of the millennium, a queer community had embraced Peter Pan as a figure beyond easy gender confines. In 1996, Robin Becker's poem "Peter Pan in America" spoke to a "Girl-boy, darling, /[who] refused to grow into any version /of manhood" (31), and here is a possibility of occupying the role of Never Land hero with neither motherhood nor (lost) boyhood involved. Jane has managed to make herself Peter's equal—or his feminine shadow—even in the eyes of Tinker Bell. For the briefest moment, *Return to Never Land* contemplates a version of the *Peter Pan* story free of romantic tension or traditional gender roles, something more fantastic than even the original film could imagine.

But it is only a moment. Never land "is defined by an eventual desire to go home" (Isojärvi 2021, 16), and *Return to Never Land* cannot end with its protagonist abandoning her family to join Peter's gang. Jane cannot find herself among the lost and eternally boyish; she must go home and take her place as playmate-mother to her brother Danny. Never Land, like a trip to Disneyland or a Disney film, is not a permanent residence, and Jane—as a new convert to the power of magic and childish play—must return home to pass on the value of Peter Pan stories to other children. *Return to Never Land* is in part an argument for the value of returning to the original *Peter Pan* story; Jane's progressive qualities are second to her role as a Wendy's modern echo. While the film can tease the possibility of revising Disney stories to incorporate radical gender play, the nostalgic power of Disney magic demands that she—and the film—ultimately embrace their fundamentally conservative past.

Peter and the Lost Boys are disappointed to have lost a friend but are immediately comforted by Jane's promise to tell stories all about them. The power of storytelling—and a belief in Peter's power to escape every problem, no matter how dire—becomes Jane's lesson despite its damage to her characterization in the rest of the film. Jane's adventure began with her insistence that she is not Wendy nor any other mother, but it ends with Jane's accepting that this adventure in Never Land, like Wendy's, is ultimately just a fairy tale to share with her own children. Peter identifies that the role of a mother is to "tell us stories" (00:24:54–59), and the stories she tells Danny immediately reframe her adventure as one where she plays the rescued rather than the rescuer: "Captain Hook kidnapped me! Stuffed me into an old dirty bag, he did! He took me off to Never Land. He took me off to Never Land and tried to feed me to a giant octopus!" (00:59:55–1:00:06). Upon the release of *Peter and Wendy* (1911), Barrie's novelization of the 1904 play, a *New York Times* review was titled, "Peter Pan, with Wendy Grown Up: When She Can No Longer Fly He's Just as Happy with Her Children" (1911, LS650). Nearly a century later, the same can be said for *Return to Never Land*. Jane's adventure ends with her excitedly scooping Danny into her arms and filling Wendy's role with brand new Pan stories. Wendy, for her part, seems content to have daughter replace her. In the final moments of the film, Peter and Wendy are briefly reunited. "You changed," Peter says accusingly. "Not really," Wendy replies, "Not ever" (01:00:50–56). Jane is spared from mandatory evacuation as her father returns home, and her adventures beyond London, like her mothers before her, are now just stories to be recited as Danny's maternal playfellow.

Americanizing the Blitz

Just as Walt Disney Studios updated the original *Peter Pan* to suit the perceived tastes of 1950s American audience, *Return to Never Land* makes several attempts to update Barrie's world for its twenty-first-century

American audience. At least superficially, much about *Peter Pan* and *Return to Never Land* is deeply British. Beyond its source material, the films' use of iconography like Big Ben and London Bridge, the sequel's evocation of the London Blitz, and the mass evacuation of London's children employ a history of destruction far removed from America's World War II experience. However, within the context of British nationalism are overreaching arguments for Western patriotism. For all the uncertainties the film has about Jane, she is unequivocally a patriot. Jane is loath to abandon the nation's capital, eager to join her father in serving her company, duty-bound to protect women and children (namely Wendy and Danny), and even seems to keep a Union Jack in her pajamas to fly at a moment's notice. Hook primarily serves as a foil to Jane's patriotism. His attempts to manipulate Jane are grounded in stories of faux-homecoming and desperation to keep his men on his side, as he claims that he, too, is attempting to return home to his "own dear mother" and only wants the treasure back because his men "would mutiny if I so much as tried to leave without it" (00:00:39:10–35). When his deception is uncovered and Jane boards the ship to rescue Peter, she pointedly tears Hook's pirate flag in two, an act that serves to underline her own patriotism and her rejection of Hook's right to lead. In this, at least, *Return to Never Land* is much more traditional than it is neo-Disney; Jane's allegiance to her country is no more complicated than Donald Duck's patriotism in Disney's anti-Nazi short film *Der Fuehrer's Face* (1943).

The connection between Jane's British loyalties and questions of modern American identity may seem tenuous. While Disney was not yet the mega-empire it has become with the acquisition of Pixar, Marvel Studios, *Star Wars*, and 20th Century Fox, confining Disney's power in the turn of the twenty-first century strictly to America grossly undervalues its global reach. But Disney's Peter Pan and Never Land have powerful associations with America. Pan's aged-up teenage bravado, his insistence on individualism, and his (and the Lost Boys') American accents draw Never Land into an American context.[8]

Never Land is further connected to American mythology at the end of the *Return to Never Land* when Peter guides Jane back home. Even before arriving in Never Land, the film is largely outside of time, and connecting when the film takes place to a clear historical moment proves challenging. The narration tells viewers that London is in throes of a mandatory evacuation that separated children from their parents. While millions of London children were evacuated and separated from one or both parents in the process, neither the evacuation nor the children-only restriction was mandatory. Disney's decision to make the evacuation a forced measure in that necessarily separates parents from their children allows *Return to Never Land* to better explicitize the relationship between London and the adult world. In direct contrast to Mr. Darling's insistence that Wendy is too old to remain in the nursery in *Peter Pan*, Jane's "last night in the nursery" is ironically an attempt to reassert her toehold onto maturity as compared to the children's countryside. However, tying this evacuation to a specific historical moment is nearly impossible. The majority of London evacuations took place between 1939 and early 1940 (Clouting 2022), but the images of Jane running through the city rubble suggests that she is in the heat of the Blitz, sometime between September 1940 and May 1941. The return of Jane's father at the end of the film would push the date back further, most likely to the summer of 1944, during Germany's use of V 2 flying bombs or *Vergeltungswaffen* on London following Britain's D-Day occupation of France ("Terrifying" 2022). In that case, Jane and Danny would have already survived the Blitz and the bulk of the German attacks, and the "mandatory" evacuation would have taken place during the final optional evacuation after the bulk of damage and civilian death in London had already happened ("Terrifying"). This historical looseness allows for a joyful family reunion while strengthening the relationship between Peter Pan and American forces. Peter's return to London coincides with the end of World War II and allows for another form of implied patriotism, as Peter's American-accented presence ushers in the end of a global conflict wherein Peter—and pro-American mythos—are stronger than ever.

Return to Never Land also repeatedly makes use of racist Native American iconography as filtered through Hollywood Westerns, even as the film carefully hides Native peoples from view: A totem pole and the sound of "war drums" appear in the cloud montage. Peter Pan flies Jane through a Native site punctuated by a confusing blend of the Plains' teepees of nomadic nations and a large, very permanent Pacific Northwest-style totem pole. The credits, too, feature several Indigenous icons that evoke the missing Native peoples, including a return of the totem pole, teepees, and rawhide drums.

The choice to make repeated reference to Indigenous nations but include no glimpse or mention of Tiger Lily, her father, or any other Native characters is odd. However, Disney's ventures shortly before *Return to Never Land* provide some practical explanations for this incomplete erasure of Indigenous people. *Return to Never Land* was released only four years after *Pocahontas II*, and Disney's Virginia and Never Land have some subtle connections. Mike Gabriel's original concept art for *Pocahontas* featured an image of Tiger Lily from the infamous "What Made the Red Man Red?" sequence, transposed into a woodland scene with "Walt Disney's POCAHONTAS" emblazoned atop it in stylized lettering (Rebello 1995, 14–15). Tiger Lily is traced over to become Pocahontas and disappears from Never Land.

Disney used a version of this partial erasure at its theme parks only a few years before *Return to Never Land*, with reasonable success. Most notably, Splash Mountain, a lavish $80 million Disneyland flume ride built in 1989 based on *Song of the South* (1946), includes animatronic versions of cartoon characters Brer Rabbit, Brer Bear, and Brer Fox, but excises Uncle Remus and the Tar Baby (Sperb 2005, 933–35). Like *Return to Never Land*, the ride attempts to address its racist past by retaining the film's songs and iconography but removing "people of color." The ride leaves Uncle Remus' language as disembodied quotes along the ride's entrance, replaces the Tar Baby with a pot of honey, and closes with a merry refrain of faux-minstrel song "Zip-a-Dee-Doo-Dah" (Longworth 2019). In 2020, Disney announced plans to retheme the ride to tie-in with *The Princess and the Frog* (2009), a film that itself went under fire for "the recurrent vacillations throughout the film, in which race and class are alternately made visible and then erased" (Charania and Simonds 2010, 69). As of March 2022, Splash Mountain is still playing "Zip-a-Dee-Doo-Dah"; whether the ride will replace Brer Rabbit with a Tiana the frog rather than Tiana the Black woman remains to be seen. For now, the neo-Disney approach to its racist past remains erasure.

For a more explicit example of *Return to Never Land*'s approach being replicated in modern day, Disneyland Paris' "Pocahontas Indian

Village" was constructed in 1996 and quietly renamed in 2020, features "Indigenous" climbable structures like fishing racks, teepees, canoe slides, and a *Pocahontas*-themed totem pole (2022). Any physical reminders of people of color have been removed, as have any efforts toward giving the play area the veneer of historical accuracy. The area was quietly renamed "Frontierland Playground" in 2020 but continues to make use of the same strategy of contradictory Native iconography seen in *Peter Pan's* Never Land. One might assume that the playground is undisturbed in part because it is France rather than the United States; after all, Disneyland Paris was also home to a Disneyfied recreation of Buffalo Bill's Wild West Show (with Mickey and Friends) until COVID-19 closures in March 2020 (Michaelsen 2020). However, an approved March 15, 2022 Magic Kingdom performance of the Port Neches-Groves High School's "Indianettes" chanting "Scalp 'em Indians, scalp 'em" in fringe, feathers, and cowboy boots (Nicholson 2022) suggests that the neo-Disney approach to representation and inclusivity remains more concerned with obscuring its participation in colonization rather than attempting to meaningfully remediate it. Like Jane's feminism, Disney's efforts toward racial diversity and inclusion often feel fleeting, superficial, and insincere.

Return to the Never Land foregrounds this strategy, opting to remove Native peoples' bodies rather than correct the images it employs. Never Land's "Injuns" are a conflation of different cultures and artifacts beyond any clear tribal identity, and viewers are invited to come to their own conclusions about the village's emptiness. While Never Land's tribe is elsewhere or annihilated is left unanswered,[9] there appears to be nothing about racist modes of speech and physical appearance that is safe for Disney to acknowledge without addressing the ugliest parts of the studio's past. The racist universalization of Native identity has always suggested in that Indigenous people are "the vanishing Indian who resides on in a distant, pre-modern past, or in a Neverland [*sic*] next to the pirates of bygone days" (Purdy 2008, 243). With *Return to Never Land's* choice to employ images of "Indian-ness" as represented in the original *Peter Pan* but avoid peopling these structures, the film implies that Indigenous peoples are being killed or displaced even in Never Land. In its "corrective absence," *Return to Never Land* echoes a history of genocide and ethnic cleansing made extra potent as World War II—and the horrors of the Holocaust—lie just beyond Never Land's borders. Disney's slow efforts to reckon with the theme park relics of their racist past—and their willingness to reduce and erase token efforts toward greater inclusion in other areas, most notably queer representation (Laman 2021)—suggests that neo-Disney's efforts remain regressive.

Lost No More: Returning to *Return to Never Land*

As Peter Hollindale notes in a centennial retrospective of J. M. Barrie's play, "*Peter Pan* enacts the eternal paradox of time and growth" (2005, 211), Disney's *Peter Pan*—with its double-insistence on Disney magic and pixie dust—perhaps more so. *Return to Never Land* is a frequently overlooked piece of the Disney *Peter Pan*-theon. It is a film at a crossroads of identity, preoccupied with how to hold onto a traditional childhood in a state of national turbulence and the strength of "classic Disney magic" as questions of gender and race were increasingly part of the public consciousness. In 2002 the wreckage of London invokes images of New York City after September 11th, and Jane's reaffirmed patriotism is an aspirational reaction to the uncertainty of war and terrorism more broadly. At the same time, Jane's willingness to satisfy herself with a one-time adventure in Never Land suggests that questions of gender identity or empowerment are a phase to be explored and then abandoned before reassimilating to life in a traditional nuclear family. *Return to Never Land* can never quite escape grouping women and children together, nor can it accept Jane's "hardness." The "corrective absence" of its Native peoples further reinforces cultural misconceptions about the extinction of the monolithic "American Indian." In trying to capture the never-changing Never Land in 2002, the film imbues its viewers with the same foreboding emptiness as its teepees. Disney's Never Land has been transformed into a more anxious, uncertain place in the new millennium, as neo-Disney attempts to hold onto a "classic" past points to baggage that is not so easily excised from our cultural memory.

Bibliography

Becker, Robin. "Peter Pan in North America." In *All-American Girl*, edited by Robin Becker, 31–32. Pittsburgh: University of Pittsburgh Press, 1996.

Brown, Noel. "Individualism and National Identity in Disney's Early British Films." *Journal of Popular Film and Fiction* 43, no. 4 (October 2015): 188–200.

Charania, Moon, and Wendy Simonds. "The Princess and the Frog." *Contexts* 9, no. 3 (2010): 69–71.

Clouting, Laura, ed. "The Evacuated Children of the Second World War." *IMW*. Imperial War Museums. 2002. <https://www.iwm.org.uk/history/the-evacuated-children-of-the-second-world-war>.

Crafton, Donald. "The Last Night in the Nursery: Walt Disney's *Peter Pan*." *The Velvet Light Trap: A Critical Journal of Film and Television* 24 (Fall 1989): 33–52.

Crowther, Bosley. "The Screen: Disney's *Peter Pan* Bows." *New York Times*, February 12, 1953, 23.

Doody, Kieran. "Disney+ Make Dumbo, Peter Pan and More 'Adult-Only'—This Is Why." *Northern Echo* (Darlington, UK), March 12, 2021. <https://www-proquest-com.ezproxy.bu.edu/docview/2501264076?pq-origsite=primo>.

Gilbert, Sarah. "Second World War British Propaganda Posters—In Pictures." *The Guardian*, November 3, 2014. <https://www.theguardian.com/artanddesign/gallery/2014/nov/03/-sp-second-world-war-british-propaganda-posters-in-pictures>.

Hollindale, Peter. "A Hundred Years of Peter Pan." *Children's Literature in Education* 36, no. 3 (September 2005): 197–215.

Imperial War Museums. "The Terrifying German 'Revenge Weapons' of the Second World War." <https://www.iwm.org.uk/history/the-terrifying-german-revenge-weapons-of-the-second-world-war>.

Isojärvi, Aino A. T. "Ambivalent Visual Cues: The Setting and Background as Narrative Nods of Postwar American Culture, Domesticity, Family and Fatherhood in the 1950s Walt Disney Feature Animation." *Quarterly Review of Film and Video* (September 2021): 1–30.

Johnson, David. "Not Rouge, Mr. Thomas!" *Animation Artist*. 1988. n.p. *WayBackMachine Internet Archive*, May 10, 2000. <https://web.archive.org/web/20080828234755/http://www.animationartist.com/columns/DJohnson/Not_Rouge/not_rouge.html>.

Laman, Douglas. "Why Disney Is Failing at LGBTQ+ Representation." *Collider*, August 8, 2021. <https://collider.com/why-disney-queer-representation-is-failing/>.

Longworth, Karina. "Six Degrees of *Song of the South*: Splash Mountain." *You Must Remember This*. Podcast, November 25, 2019. <http://www.youmustremember thispodcast.com/episodes/tag/Splash+Mountain>.

Meyers, Eric M., Julia P. McKnight, and Lindsey M. Krabbenhoft. "Remediating Tinker Bell: Exploring Childhood and Commodification Through a Century-Long Transmedia Narrative." *Jeunesse: Young People, Texts, Cultures* 6, no. 1 (Summer 2014): 95–118.

Michaelsen, Shannen. "'Moteurs Action! Stunt Show Spectacular' and Buffalo Bill's Wild West Show Now Closed Forever at Disneyland Paris." *WDW News Today*, November 24, 2020. <https://wdwnt.com/2020/11/moteurs-action-stunt-show-spectacular-and-buffalo-bills-wild-west-show-permanently-cance led-at-disneyland-paris/>.

Nesterak, Max. "Uprooted: The 1950s Plan to Erase Indian Country." *American Public Media Reports*, November 1, 2019. <https://www.apmreports.org/epis ode/2019/11/01/uprooted-the-1950s-plan-to-erase-indian-country#:~:text= In%20the%201950s%2C%20the%20United,Country%20are%20still%20of elt%20today>.

Nicholson, Jenny. Twitter Post. March 18, 2022, 5:23 a.m. <https://twitter.com/Jenn yENicholson/status/1504750444744126469>.

Ohmer, Susan. "Disney's *Peter Pan*: Gender, Fantasy, and Industrial Production." In *Second Star to the Right: Peter Pan in the Popular Imagination*, edited by Allison Kavey, 151–87. New Brunswick, NJ: Rutgers University Press, 2009.

Peter Pan in Disney's Return to Never Land. PlayStation Video Game. Lyon: Disney Interactive and Sony Computer Entertainment and Doki Denki Studio. 2002.

"Peter Pan, with Wendy Grown Up: When She Can No Longer Fly He's Just as Happy with Her Children." *New York Times*, October 22, 1911, LS650.

"Peter Pan: Real Disney Magic; Real Animals Also Make Money." *Newsweek*, February 16, 1953, 96–99.

"Pocahontas Indian Village." *DLP Guide: Disneyland Paris Discovered*. 2022. <https://www.dlrpmagic.com/guidebook/disneyland-park/frontierland/poc ahontas-indian-village/>.

Purdy, John L. "The Baby Boom Generation and the Reception of Native American Literatures: D'Arcy McNickle's 'Runner in the Sun.'" *Western American Literature* 43, no. 3 (Fall 2008): 233–57.

Rebello, Stephen. *The Art of Pocahontas*. New York: Disney Enterprises, 1995.

Shale, Richard. *Donald Duck Joins Up: The Walt Disney Studio During World War II*. Ann Arbor, MI: UMI Research Press, 1982.

Smith, Clay Kinchen. "Problematizing Piccaninnies, or How J. M. Barrie Uses Graphemes to Counter Racism in *Peter Pan*." In *J. M. Barrie's Peter Pan in and*

Out of Time: A Children's Classic at 100, edited by Donna R. White and C. Anita Tarr, 107–26. Lanham, MD: Scarecrow Press, 2006.

Sperb, Jason. "'Take a Frown, Turn It Upside Down': Splash Mountain, Walt Disney World, and the Cultural De-rac[e]-ination of Disney's *Song of the South* (1946)." *Journal of Popular Culture* 38, no. 5 (August 2005): 924–38.

"The Terrifying German 'Revenge Weapons' of the Second World War." *Imperial War Museums*. 2022. <https://www.iwm.org.uk/history/the-terrifying-german-revenge-weapons-of-the-second-world-war>.

"Walt Disney's Return to *Neverland* Opens Friday." *Chicago Defender*, February 13, 2002, 24.

"Zip-a-Dee-Doo-Dah." Composed by Allie Wrubel. Lyrics by Ray Gilbert. Sung by James Baskett for *Song of the South*. 1946.

BRENDA AYRES AND SARAH E. MAIER

8 Neo-Disney's Reconstruction of Masculinities

Just as Disney has had a powerful, decades-long investment in the perpetuation of stereotypes that have relegated its princesses to stereotypical roles of passivity, so, too, have those same films given us a conservative representation of hegemonic masculinity to match. Emblematic of patriarchal power and patrilineal control, the early men of Disney include multiple Prince Charmings beginning with *Snow White and the Seven Dwarves* (1937), through *Cinderella* (1950) and *Sleeping Beauty* (1959) to *The Little Mermaid* (1989) and even *Beauty and the Beast* (1991). While the female protagonists have been enshrined in the Disney Princess Line,[1] discussed at length in critical studies,[2] and revisioned as to what might make a modern "princess," less attention has been paid to the changes in Disney's sense of changing masculinity in its live-action films or in the films under its extended umbrella of animated films.

Jack Zipes, a prolific critic of Disney's spell over the world of fairy tales, makes a salient point that such princess-focused narratives create a parallel conundrum for male characters and "perpetuate a male myth" (1995, 37) that confines men to historical versions of heteronormative masculinity that may or may not have cultural relevance today. Questions of LGBTQ2+ and gender fluidity are quickly outstripping traditional binaries of male and female or even the constructedness of gender eloquently delineated by Judith Butler and others. In dealing with gender in fairy tales that originated in earlier centuries, to broach the possibility of a new man or a neo-Prince is, to say the least, difficult when the twenty-first century is welcoming the representation of transgenderism, discourse on pronoun choices, and expression of non-gendered clothing. Shannon R. Wooden and Richard Gilliam advocate for boy culture studies to recognize that "the landscape is changing for masculinity, that it needs to change, and that it is time to borrow from feminism the practices of theoretically informed cultural interrogation" to continue developing and interrogating "theories of gendered selves to keep pace with the changing cultural landscape" (2014, xiii). The conversation about genders has to be "both/and—interrogating the spectrum of identities and social performances" (xvii) to avoid the either/ or positions of binary oppositions and to open the potential for a wider range of individual experience. The definition of masculinity, in cultural and artistic representations, must expand into multiple possibilities because culture "can no longer presume that masculinity develops within a psychically specific heteronormative ... story" (Corbett 2009, 10). Transmedia adaptations, like those on screen by Disney, must present a prince who, if not progressive, is at least capable of understanding the need for change to occur in his world.

Most Disneyists have addressed the following perceived shortcomings of Disney films: the reductive, normalizing portrayal of females, an emphasis on heterosexual marriages as if no happiness is possible outside of such a union, endings that are unrealistic visions of "happily ever after," efforts to promote traditional "American" values, a conservative way of life and/or right-wing politics, and an exclusion of the Other—be it ethnic and national groups that are not WASP and/or genders that do not conform to the bipolar traditional concept of male versus female. One cannot overstate the effect that Disney films have on the "cultivation of a child's values, beliefs, dreams, and expectations, which shape the adult identity a child will carry and modify through his or her life" (Swindler 1986, 311). Although the predominant focus has been on Disney's treatment of females and the resulting AMBER alerts[3] that decry Disney's "Kardashian" models of femininity,[4] there have been a few scholars concerned also about stereotypical male models in their influence on perceptions and expectations of children (Signorielli 2001; Leaper et al. 2006; Steyer 2014).

In Disney's historical replication of stereotypes of both females and males, each implicates the other: The female is supposed to deny herself (Zipes 2011, 227–33), and the male is supposed to protect her. Disney films teach viewers that the selflessness and charity of females "can transform the world" (Davis 2006, 194). Paradoxically, noble females play at being saviors of the world (Davis 2013, 6) all the while they require being rescued by males.[5] Whereas beauty is more important than brains in desirable female characters, it is the men who are depicted as possessing competency to resolve conflicts hoisted upon females (Witt 2000, 323) by the world, evil creatures, and nasty forces.

Most Disney plots are driven by the female's quest to find and marry her prince (Zipes 2011, 224–51), with this yearning expressed by Snow White as she sings "Someday my prince will come" and telling boys and girls that their major goal in life is to marry. Before marriage, females are like Snow White, asleep in a glass coffin, needing to be brought to life by a male deemed worthy by other people. Disney's males are "strong, protective, powerful, commanding,"[6] but this patriarchal ideology often becomes "their own evil curse" such as demonstrated in both versions of Disney's *Beauty and the Beast* when the Beast literally gives up his life to save Belle (Jeffords 1995, 171). In a study of fairy tales, Jeana Sommer Jorgensen discovered that males are vulnerable and likely to end up dead or maimed or threaten from some violent source.[7] Hence "The privilege that comes with masculinity is fraught with anxiety, rife with competition, and always subject to revocation if one disobeys the rules" (Attebery 2018, 319).

Further, within Disney's marriage plots, males are usually undeveloped characters and serve merely as ploys to rescue the damsel in distress. Sheldon Cashdan, for one, has noticed that the male figures in Disney are generally minor characters and that the "prince tends to be a cardboard character, almost an afterthought, who materializes at the end of the story to ensure a happy ending" (1999, 28).[8] In the three classic princess films—*Snow White, Cinderella*, and *Sleeping Beauty*—women dominate the screen and dialogue, but with what has been called the Disney renaissance era (1989–99; Roberts 2020, 4), the princess movies are male dominated with men speaking 90 percent of the time in *Aladdin*, and even 68 percent of the time in a movie named for the female protagonist, *The Little Mermaid*.[9] Besides lack of equality between the two genders, there has been very little representation of characters outside of the gender binary.

Past Princes v. Ella's New Man

The first prince to capture a Disney audience arrived in 1937 with the release of *Snow White and the Seven Dwarves*; Prince Charming is young
and, yes, charming, but merely as a backdrop and aspirational partner of
sorts for the story of the young girl forced from home by her evil stepmother, the Queen. Other Disney princes follow, many of whom were
depicted only in physical terms without emotional interiority or unique
personalities. They also lack control over their desires, but they do exude
potential heroism. It is not until more recently that "representations of
men do appear to have evolved and matured over time, not only in relation to themselves" (Hine et al. 2018, 4) but also in their interactions with
and expectations of women. Disney's recent move to live-action adaptations creates a combination of their own earlier animated films but with
new material with broader development of characters, including child-
hoods that account for their evolution into dashing heroes and handsome
princes—versions of new men who measure up to stand beside its new,
more individualized young women like Cinderella, Belle, and Mulan.
There are recent males who are neither dashing nor handsome and maybe
ordinary or desirable outside of a Western idealization of male beauty.
They may be heroic or not so heroic, but they are males in ways that are
more realistic and relatable to viewers.

The necessity of change for a new era was immediately apparent to the
men involved in the recreation of Cinderella's prince. Richard Madden,
the actor who plays the newly named Prince Charming, Kit, in Kenneth
Branagh's live-action *Cinderella* (2015), admits he felt a responsibility to
live up to his role and, as the screenwriter Christopher Weitz says, the goal
was "to make [this Prince] not a stuffed shirt" ("A Fairy" 2015, 00:05:05).
To begin with, instead of an impressive, high-born name, the prince goes
by Kit, a nickname given to him by his father when his first name is actually Christopher. The usual Disney prince had no name (Davis 2006,
156) because he was not a person; he was a function. But the neo-Disney
prince has a name, and it is one that lets the viewer believe that he is a
real flesh-and-blood human. The challenge was to explain why, for the

twenty-first-century audience, Cinderella is interesting, and Weitz understands she must be "attracted to the prince other than his enormous wealth and good looks and charm because that's not enough for us nowadays, or at least we can recognize its maybe not the best reason to have a relationship with somebody" (00:05:00).

The traditional Disney male was constructed by assumptions of normative, even toxic, "hegemonic masculinity that allowed men's dominance over women to continue" (Connell and Messerschmidt 2005, 834), and if Disney's live-action and animated films were going to progress to keep up with cultural context, then changes had to be made to the role of princes, beginning with *Cinderella*. For an audience expecting more depth of character and realism in representation in a live-action film, Kit presents the first test of how to balance the expectations of a fairy tale with the modern experience of manhood.

Prince Charming must have the ability to withstand the challenges presented to him by Ella; indeed, their first meeting is an argument over a massive stag the King's party hunts. Riding in the woods, Ella and her horse approach quietly and respectfully, awed at the magnificent beast whom she warns to run or be caught. Ella's horse runs with the stag; the Prince, like a traditional male bred to protect the female, rides to catch up to her, to see if she is in control. Lashing out against him, Ella claims "I'm alright but you've nearly frightened the life out of him … what's he ever done to you that you must chase him about?" (00:27:58). As they circle each other on horseback, both of them astride, there is a seeming equity. Ella refuses to give her name, and he is incredulous that she does not know him. He tells her that he is simply "Kit" and he is an apprentice, which he is—apprentice to becoming a king—but she assumes that he is a man in training for a menial trade. He asks if she is treated well in her situation but her response—"They treat me as well as they are able" (00:29:12)—evokes an apology from him and a sympathetic recognition that her apparent mistreatment is not due to her misbehavior.

In their brief encounter, Ella shares with Kit her mother's wish she should "Have courage and be kind" (00:29:30) and makes Kit promise he will not hurt the stag because "Just because it's what's done doesn't mean it should be done!" (00:29:50), a sentiment Kit later turns on his father regarding the desire for the prince to marry. The king replies, "My father would have told me what I am telling you and I would have listened" (00:31:48), invoking patrilineal and patriarchal privilege all at once to affirm that Kit must bear with tradition especially since they learn the King is dying.

In the next scene, comic relief provides a satirical look at such traditions with the way kings and princes are immortalized. The king asks an artist to make Kit look "marriageable" (00:33:02) in the work, as if the size of the canvas and his very appearance make the man. As Kit sits in his finery for the painter, he argues for freedom of choice in his potential bride but is immediately rebutted by the Grand Duke with "How many divisions will this good honest country girl provide us? How will she make the kingdom stronger?" (00:33:25). The Grand Duke believes it is Kit's role to catch a bride and bring her father's power to the kingdom's advantage; the King reminds Kit of his duty to keep the people safe (00:32:30). An exemplar of conservative tradition, the Grand Duke finds himself now a villain in his exertion of power: His insistence upon a politically advantageous marriage is no longer an acceptable practice to a twenty-first-century viewer, even if the story was set in earlier centuries. As if to make a mockery of the differing views of manliness, an artist is accidentally lowered to the floor on his swing, declaring that the view the floor looking up at the prince is a good angle, not because of his mount or his brawn, but because the prince has "great nostrils" (00:34:36).

The film results in a pairing of a male and female based on individual potential. Kit ignores the Grand Duke. He does not choose Cinderella, nor does he propose; rather, although he recognizes her "spirit, her goodness" (00:38:06) and is smitten with her, when he arrives with the slipper, it is Cinderella who, again, challenges his values. She ignores protocol when she walks by the Grand Duke, then says to Kit, "I have no carriage, no parents, no dowry. I do not even know if that beautiful slipper will fit but, if it does, will you take me as I am, an honest country girl who loves you?" (01:34:40), a proposal that usurps his right to choose when he agrees, then asks, "Will you take me as I am, an apprentice learning his trade?" (01:35:17). As the Grand Duke looks on, the Prince—now King—confirms his love for Cinderella beyond all other considerations. "My Queen" is met with "My Kit" (01:38:19), a man who retains his heteronormative status without risking emasculation by meeting his match, one representative of a fairy-tale world as it "could be" (01:38:50).

What Makes a Man Out of You?

In spite of the fact that Niki Caro's *Mulan* (2020) is a film about a young woman who takes her father's place to battle the Rouran, the film's central consideration is just as much about gender conventions for men as it is for women. The original "The Ballad of Mulan," written sometime in the fourth or fifth century, refers to a young woman and her family, with only a single mention of "comrades" (n.p.). The men in Disney's film are modern add-ins. The young, mischievous Hua Mulan is introduced at the beginning of the film as a girl without fear, like a boy fiercely leaping from rooftops, immune to the inappropriateness of her behavior for a young woman who wishes to bring honor to her family. Her father, Hua Zhou, tells Hua Mulan that her *chi* is very strong, but "it is for warriors, not daughters ... so it is time for you to hide your gift away, to silence its voice. I say this to protect you" (00:05:40). Such a gesture suggests he believes Hua Mulan will encounter many who will not understand the complexity of her gender fluidity and how it will be received by a rigidly patriarchal society. The Matchmaker will be unable to find an auspicious match unless Hua Mulan bows to tradition and accepts conventional gender roles of male and female. There is a scene where she is robed in traditional dress and makeup of an honorable young woman to meet the Matchmaker; Hua Mulan and her friend mock the mask that makes all of her emotions look the same. Once there, the Matchmaker dictates that she must be "Quiet. Composed. Graceful. Elegant. Poised. Polite. These are the qualities we seek in a good wife" (00:16:33). A comedic moment is made of the tea ceremony when Hua Mulan saves her sister from a spider; she is disgraced.

Fate has it that the Huns have attacked, and the emperor needs warriors for the Imperial Army to fight, Böri Khan; conscription demands a male from each family must join in the defense. Hua Zhou, a well-respected but wounded man with no sons, volunteers, but his daughter Hua Mulan knows he would perish if he went. In the darkness of night, she both embraces and rejects tradition; in a scene that parallels the earlier female masquerade, she honors her family's duty to fight for her country by donning her father's armor, his sword, and his beliefs of "loyal, brave, and true" passed from father to daughter and etched on his sword (00:23:33), a right she earns with "devotion to family" (01:43:39). Mulan must embrace her warrior *chi*, embody masculinity, bind her chest to conceal her femaleness, constrain her hair, lower her voice, and build her skills to be courageous for her family. During one close combat exercise with Chen Honghui, we see Hua Mulan finally believe she has a right to be Hua Jun (00:40:01).

The recruits—Chen Honghui, Ling, Yao, Chien-Po, and others—with whom she trains, eats, and jokes are indifferent to (and ignorant of) her sex. The film reveals much of how the young men bond under the leadership of Commander Tung and Sergeant Qiang. The live-action film does not include the original song "I'll Make a Man Out of You," which was refused by Disney and replaced with "Training the Men,"[10] but the assumption that a man can be made—with physical exertion and discipline—no longer is enough. The bonding is emotional as much as physical; some men cry from the pain, some are romantic and poetic about women, while at other times they celebrate each other's success as when Hua Mulan carries her buckets of water to achieve the summit of the mountain rather than devolve into potential jealousy. They are now equals. In the end, their bonding results in Hua Mulan risking her gender secret to save her friend; she is now fully empowered, using all of who she is—being true. The revelation of her gender occurs during an act of heroism (01:10:08) to save Honghui. Apparently when "I'll Make a Man Out of You" first appeared, it became a mantra for not only young millennial males but also for females (Grady 2020).

In a noticeable change to the masculine-defined characters included from the earlier animated version (*Mulan* 1998), Li Shang is absent from the live-action film, a choice that was decried by the LGBTQ2+ community who had always recognized the character as bisexual given his interest in Ping occurs before he realizes s/he is Hua Mulan. Producer Jason Reed said the wise decision was made with compassion for those who expressed the unacceptability for any exploitation of a commanding officer's position over a recruit:

We split Li Shang into two characters. One became Commander Tung (Donnie Yen) who serves as her surrogate father and mentor in the course of the movie. The other is Honghui (Yoson An) who is [Mulan's] equal in the squad .... I think particularly in the time of the #MeToo movement, having a commanding officer that is also the sexual love interest was very uncomfortable and we didn't think it was appropriate. (Szany 2020, n.p.)

Certainly, it would not have been, but the recognition that a partner would need to be Hua Mulan's equal is important, and in more than mere rank. As film critic Soren Hough has pointed out, Disney's "new art was an essential part of growth for a generation that is more fluid (and more free to be fluid) about labels and identity than those that came before us" (2016, n.p.). Hua Mulan's fluid movement between gender positions and performances is welcomed by Li Shang in the animated film; however, the expulsion of Hua Jun/Mulan in the live-action film by the elder generation demonstrates fear of such a breakdown of boundaries and proclaims their "very existence is a lie" (01:18:05) as either a male or a female. It is the next generation of young men who reject such binary oppositions leading Chen Honghui to ask "You would believe Hua Jun. Why do you not believe Hua Mulan?" and choose to follow her for her bravery (01:18:11–36). Indeed, as in "The Ballad of Mulan," "Most people tell the gender of a rabbit by its movement: / The male runs quickly, while the female often keeps her eyes shut. / But when the two rabbits run side by side, / Can you really discern whether I am a *he* or a *she*?" (n.p.). Chen Honghui, from the moment he meets "Hua Jun" to their shared night-time swim (00:41:44), and his ultimate understanding of the young woman, Hua Mulan (01:12:13), loves the entirety of them—all and whomever s/he/they are.

Brave New Animated World(s)

As much as we might have expected the live-action films to explore more readily varieties of masculinities or fluidity of gender, it is the most recent animated films that bring us to a progressive moment, just as Merida in *Brave* (2012) demarcates a break with all of the traditional princesses who came before when she declares, "I am Merida, first born descendent of the clan DunBroch. And I'll be shooting for my own hand!" (2012; 00:26:12). The men of the film are a mess of wimpy, no neck, inarticulate, undisciplined, violent drunkards who remain confused by this new woman. That one moment made it clear that if Disney is going to produce more self-reliant, strong, intelligent women, then the men need to keep up, and alternate non-gendered experiences will need to factor into the screenplays that follow *Brave*.

The more recent Disney films, such as *Moana* (2016), *Coco* (2017), and *Encanto* (2020) belong to "the new Disney era, which started in 2009 with *The Princess and the Frog*" (García de Toro 2021, 79). Despite some criticism that the film is sexist and perpetuates gender stereotypes,[11] the two major male characters in *Moana* are radical departures from earlier Disney men. Beginning with Moana's father, Chief Tui, although overprotective of his daughter like a conventional male, unlike the historical patriarch, he is invested in priming a female to become his successor as chief of their island, Motunui. He is a strong male character as well as a benevolent and wise patriarch of the village, who treats women (his wife, daughter, and mother) as equals to himself. Even though Moana will need to find her own way, define herself, and defy her father by sailing beyond the reef, his concern for her safety is based on his own reckless adventure as a young man when he tried to go beyond the limits of the ocean around his island and nearly lost his life. If Moana had been a boy, then he would have been just as determined to protect him from what he perceived as life threatening. A major theme in the story is that one must take risks and follow one's calling to realize one's full potential, but the chief sings a song that is very wise with these words: "You must find happiness right where you are" (00:09:30 and Scherzinger).

The other male is actually a demigod and hails from Māori mythology. Maui means "to live" or "to subsist" (Westervelt 1910, vi).[12] In a definite neo-Disney film, the male character has been developed with backstory, emotions, and personality: Maui explains his lack of confidence and unwillingness to help Moana and be involved with humans again by relating that he was born of human parents who abandoned him by throwing him into the sea.[13] The gods took mercy on him and changed him into a demigod (01:09:10). The movie opens with a Māori folklore, a creation story where "In the beginning there was only ocean until the Mother Island emerged. Te Fiti [(a goddess)], the greatest power ever known, life itself, shared it with the world. But there were those who sought Te Fiti's heart, that if they possessed it, they would possess power over creation" (00:00:58). Then Maui "the most daring of them all, raced across the vast ocean to take it" (00:00:58–1:33). Gramma Tala, who is telling this story to a gaggle of children that include Moana as a toddler, describes Maui as "a demigod of the wind and sea. He was a warrior, a trickster, a shapeshifter who could change form with the power of his magical fishhook" (00:01:44–3:28). He stole the heart and gave it to mankind so that humans could control their own creation and they would love him, but as much as he did for them, it was never enough (01:10:05). Then Te Kā, the demon of earth and fire stole the heart and his fishhook, and then Maui was never seen again (2:28). Furthermore, in the hands of humans without divine intervention from the goddess of nature, Te Fiti, the coconuts were diseased, and the fish disappeared (00:14:21).

Maui is a parody of the hypermasculine male. As he sings a song that tries to persuade Moana that he is a hero to humans and worthy of her worship and obedience—just like the historical patriarch—and as he flexes his enormous pecs, he boasts that he gave mortals fire (00:38:10), which parallels the myth of Prometheus and made Maui, "beyond question the hero of the largest numbers of nations scattered over the widest extent of territory" (Westervelt 57). Disney's Maui stole the heart to give the islanders so that they can control creation. As Maui sings to Moana, "You're welcome" (00:38:10–41:00 and Fisher) and thinks that she is thunderstruck because she is "facing greatness," which he condescendingly says "is adorable" (38:10). Clearly Moana is very unimpressed and determined to make Maui reclaim the heart and thus restore freedom and posterity to her island. However, Maui has given up on humans and wants to be left alone. He tells Moana that without his fishhook, he is nothing (01:16:50) and that he fears the green stone, the heart of Te Fiti (00:44:25) because humans have become autonomous and no longer needed or wanted any gods. Still, Maui is part human male, and as Edwardo Pérez has observed, the newer Disney males are vulnerable, display emotion, and undergo emotional growth (2020, 78).

Zipes has noted that the typical Disney princes (and here we might extend the term to mean noble, courageous, and handsome males) were "strong admirable characters [who] provide closure to the conflicts of the story and tidy up the mess that is apparently caused" (2011, 28). This is not Maui. His physical appearance as a short, stocky, maybe even obese male with huge flat nose has caused an outrage (Roy 2016; Steiner 2018), even though the US Department of Health and Human Services reported that "Native Hawaiians/Pacific Islanders were three times more likely to be obese than the overall Asian American population" ("Obesity" 2020). Disney's portrait of the demigod holds true to Polynesian culture that traditionally perceived the full-figured body and flat noses as beautiful.

Despite Maui's obvious muscular manhood and exuberant greatness and power, it is Moana who rescues him from Kakamora or coconut pirates, reclaims his magical fishhook from a giant coconut crab (00:59:05–1:02:37), seizes the *pounamu* stone or heart of jade from Te Kā and escapes on her own from the demon, and ultimately is the hero, with a little help that comes late from Maui. Usually the Disney heroine who triumphs is rewarded with the prize of a man as a husband (Davis 2013, 149), but when Moana tries to persuade Maui to return with her to the island to be the Master Wayfinder, he declines (01:33:10), and only after she has gained the victory for him, for Te Fiti, and for her island. The story does not end in a wedding or ballroom dance. Te Fiti transforms from a hideous demon to a beautiful goddess, and all the islands, even the ones that had been only rocks, became full of life (01:31:02). She gives Maui a new fishhook (01:31:48), and transformed into a hawk, he flies away. The women have saved the day, the men are the benefactors, but they also exert their own power separate but equal to that of women. Children who watch films that positively portray egalitarian gender roles are very likely to accept and expect them in real life (Graves 1999, 713).

Maui's voice was provided by Dwayne Johnson, an American-born, Black Nova Scotian-Samoan American wrestler and actor, whose persona— projected through the animated character but also in his role of Frank Wolff in Disney's *Jungle Cruise* (2021)—fits the description of the übersexual male, a contemporary term for modern men (Salzman et al. 2006), as defined by the *Urban Dictionary:*

> They are confident, masculine, stylish, and committed to uncompromising quality in all areas of life. Übersexuals also have depth, subtlety, and individuality. The übersexuals know the difference between right and wrong and will make the right decision regardless of what others around him may think …. [They have] all the good qualities associated with the gender without giving into the negative stereotypes such as chauvinism, emotional unavailability and a brain only filled with sports stats, beer and burgers. Compared with the metrosexual, the übersexual is more into relationships than self. It is a masculinity that combines the best traditional manliness (strength, honor, character) with positive traits traditionally associated with females such as nurturance, communicativeness, and co-operation. (J.A.C. 2005, n.p.)

Although it would be a stretch to credit Maui with all these noble traits, ultimately he does come to respect Moana and selflessly aid her in her quest without dominating and conquering her. The movie ends with her leadership in her village; his own peace, independence, and power; and no mention of marriage and domesticity of the two.

Coco (2017) was released the next year, and similarly had very strong women characters, "depict[ing] the central role that women play in Mexican and Latino family as memory keepers and matriarchs …. They represent Latina women who throughout centuries have worked, raised families, and became integral parts of their communities" (Rodriguez and Duran 2020, 99–105). Even though the title of the film is for the great grandmother, who appears very few times in the story, her ability to stay alive and remember her father is crucial to the father's continued existence in the Land of the Dead and his ability to "cross over" to visit the living family on the Mexican holiday *Día de los Muertos* or The Day of the Dead. This culture believed that if the dead are no longer remembered by the living, they cease to exist.

Coco is mostly about three males: Miguel, the 12-year-old great, great grandson who is a boy who secretly has been playing guitar in secret; Ernesto de la Cruz, "the most famous singer in Mexico" (00:05:15) and who, Miguel thinks, is Coco's father, deceased; and Héctor, also deceased who Miguel discovers is really his father, a song writer who made Ernesto famous. It is discovered late in the story that when Héctor wanted to return to his family, Ernesto seized the opportunity to poison him in order to steal credit for his songs (01:07:08). Miguel enters the Land of the Dead and befriends Héctor and then learns that he, and not Ernesto, is his great, great grandfather and that the family never knew that instead of abandoning the family, he was murdered. Miguel's quest is to return to the Land of the Living to rouse Coco, who seems to be in advanced stages of dementia and cannot remember who is who in the family, to remember her father. If she dies before being able to do this, Héctor will cease to exist even in skeleton form (01:12:19–27).

Like Moana, Miguel lives in a loving family, but he realizes that he is not like them and must take risks and defy the family to be himself, realize his dreams, and develop his gifts (00:04:21). Miguel's family, like Moana's, thought they were under a curse, ever since "music had torn the family apart, but shoes held them altogether" (00:02:46), meaning that the family will remain intact if everyone, including Miguel, works in the family's shoe business. Music is forbidden because the family was torn apart when it was thought that Coco's father abandoned his family for a musical career. Miguel learns that "music has the power to change hearts" (00:13:30). Imelda, Héctor's estranged wife who is also in skeletal form, reconciles with her husband once she learns that he did prioritize his family and did not return only because he was murdered. Miguel learns to prioritize family as well, but when he does, the family's curse is broken when they embrace music. Miguel's song, which he sings a year later at the town's talent show, is joyous:

> When I opened my mouth what came out was a song
> And you knew every word and we all sang along
> To a melody played on the strings of our souls
> And a rhythm that rattled us down to the bone
> Our love for each other will live on forever
> In every beat of my proud corazón. (01:35:12–1:36:00; "Proud Corazón")

The song concatenates music with family by demonstrating musical harmony and remembering that one should find love within one's family and never forget it (01:24:20). In both *Moana* and *Coco*, just as in most Disney movies, "the sanctity of family and the tragic consequences when that sanctity is broken" is a major theme (Eliot 1993, xx). Yet in these two films, the definition of "family" is much more expansive than just a nuclear family of Mom, Dad, kids, and the family's pet. Imitating life, too, *Coco* presents a realistic portrayal of heterosexual marriages in which couples do not always live happily ever after.

Encanto is another Latino film (the setting is Columbia) that emphasizes the importance of family, and it also portrays strong women and an aged, powerful matriarch. The problem is, what do you do when your family does not accept you? What if you wear humongous glasses, seem a bit slow (mentally),[14] and are perceived as not having any gifts (although you do, but they just do not recognize them as such; they do not value for your kindness and generosity of spirit)? What if you are Bruno, the guy that no one is supposed to talk about because he does have a supernatural gift, but it is one that the family disdain; he can see the future, but the prophecies are not what the family wants to hear?

Encanto is not about race; racial difference is negligible. It is a wonderful message to viewers: The color of one's skin simply does not matter. Abuela has triplets: One is very white with red hair, another is Brown with brown hair, and a third is black with black hair. Two children are female, and one is male (01:20:27). Throughout the film, you see every color of skin interacting with each other. Mixed-race couples kiss each other (00:06:35–41). Pepa, Mirabel's red-haired aunt whose moods control the weather, is married to Félix, who has very dark skin and Afro hair, and is shorter than his wife and is stocky. Children of all skin color and physical types play together. Race and the physical appearance of people are a nonissue—this is a strong message to its viewers.

Gender is another nonissue in this movie. Luisa is Mirabel's sister and has been given the gift of supernatural physical strength that exceeds what is possible even for a male. She can easily tote a half-dozen mules and a piano. She is extremely muscular and surely bucks Disney's standard depiction of a young woman with slender waist and a fragile-looking, tiny body. A woman from Bamberg, Germany, wrote: "I saw a bit of myself in her. ... My body type is—how my parents and husband call it—that of a warrior. Growing up, in Disney movies, not very many muscular women were shown and I felt out of place sometime" (quoted in Peters 2022). Like other members in her family with gifts, and not just as the typical Disney female who is self-denying, Luisa generously uses her gift to serve the community. When she fears that she is losing her gifts, however, she weeps like a woman. She is not fixed to any single gender type.

Then there is 15-year-old Camilo who is a shapeshifter; instead, of shifting into animals or objects, he is constantly changing from male to female—he is bigender. More significantly, Disney is telling viewers that gender is not a binary, if indeed there is such a thing as "female" v. "male." Sometimes a woman can act "like a man" and, at other times, "like a woman" as does Luisa, and sometimes a man can do likewise, as does Camilo. In fact, the old Disney womanly ideal, represented in Mirabel's oldest sister Isabela, who is physically beautiful and "perfect" but a "selfish, entitled princess" (01:08:08–22) and who is extremely mean to Mirabel, cries out, "I'm sick of pretty" (01:10:15). The codirector Bryan Howard said, "Isabela is smart and brilliant and so perfect that flowers bloom in footsteps. Anything she attempts to do is a success, which is the opposite of what Mirabel's experience has been in this family" (quoted in Messer 2021, n.p.). One thing Bruno tells Mirabel that she has to do is to embrace Isabela (01:04:55). In short, Mirabel has rejected the beautiful sister, just as Isabela rejected her "giftless" sister with the prominent eyeglasses. For harmony to be restored in the family, even those who were rejected, like Mirabel and Bruno, and who held a grudge, need to forgive and reconcile.

Furthermore, Mirabel and Bruno have the same problem, and it has nothing to do with their ethnicity, race, or gender. They simply are outsiders because they have been rejected by both their family and community in that they do not possess the gifts that people selfishly expect. They are not loved for themselves until the end of the film when the family and community are taught the important lesson that people are more than their gifts; they are miracles in just being who they are (01:25:35). Where Disney's official trailer is posted on YouTube, someone added this comment:

> I just finished watching "Encanto," and I really need to say how relatable Mirabel is. Never being able to fit in, but also never being able to tell anyone. I always feel like this almost anywhere, and especially at school. This movie really gave me a little confidence about sharing the feelings I've been bottling up. (Malflahi 2022, n.p.)

Another commenter wrote: "FIRST DISNEY MOVIE EVER CRIED ABOUT. I love how every character portrays how Maribel feels about being pressured. Part of her feels like she's got too much on her hands, part of her feels like she wants to break free and be herself, parts of her feels she wants to be loved and parts of her wants to be appreciated. I relate to her so much" (Bloo 2022; emphasis in original).

These two comments illustrate how effective is Disney's theme about self-acceptance and acceptance of those who are "different." Grandma Abuela Alma lost her home and her husband in some armed conflict, so when she is given a magical home, she becomes so stalwart about protecting the miracle that she loses sight of whom the miracle is for (01:20:04–09). Mirabel, supposedly the one without gifts, wisely tells her grandmother that in a family, there is "nothing that can be broken that we cannot fix" (01:22:30). A family is like the glass pieces Mirabel finds in Bruno's tower: When she fits them together, the house crumbles and collapses, but it is only then that the family is restored to unity, with all its members present in the picture, including those who do not fit the *status quo*. A house may be a home, but without the family, it can never be a home.

It is not unusual for Disney to grant animation to nonhuman creatures and objects. The ocean is anthropomorphic in *Moana*, just as is the *Casita* in *Encanto*. The supernatural is not an alien world or concept to Disney including the cross over and given the living skeletons in *Coco*. However, in deference to the Latino cultures represented in *Encanto*, the living house follows in the tradition of magical realism found in African and Latino literatures, such as in the novels of Gabriel Garcia Márquez and Isabel Allende. In their collection of essays that identify magical realism in world literatures, Lois Parkinson Zamora and Wendy B. Faris define the term as it

> facilitates the fusion, or coexistence, of possible worlds, spaces, systems that would be irreconcilable in other modes of fiction. The propensity of magical realist texts to admit a plurality of worlds means that they often situate themselves on liminal territory between or among those worlds—in phenomenal and spiritual regions where transformation, metamorphosis, dissolution are common, where magic is a branch of naturalism, or pragmatism. So magical realism may be considered an extension of realism in its concern with the nature of reality and its representation, at the same time that it resists the basic assumptions of post-enlightenment [*sic*] rationalism and literary realism. (1995, 5–6)

It is in the magical world of "Encanto" (that means "magic"), in the *casita*, that all people are equal and loved, even though the character of the house was developed to be "a little bit more opinionated and flawed like a family. It's a house the plays favorites, a house that messes with people," so said codirector Jared Bush (quoted in Reif 2021). Still, it is in the hidden walls and tower that protected Bruno from the rejection of his family, and it is the house that teaches Abuela Alma and the family that they are wrong to reject both Bruno and Mirabel.

Ironically, the family carries the surname of "Madrigal" which is the name of a lyrical poem or group of singers who have different parts but harmonize. The Madrigal family in *Encanto*, like the madrigal family of the human race, does not sing in harmony until it recognizes the magic and the miracle of all individuals, that each contributes in his and her and their ways to enrich the song. It is a strong message to modern families in which the parents may spend such an inordinate amount of time providing for the family through their jobs and efforts that they forget that it is not the *casita* that is important; it is the people who live in the *casita* who are important.

Although the film is rife with strong women, Bruno is the real hero. When he envisions the house as breaking up, he also sees it intact, but in both visions Mirabel stands in front of the house. This prophecy so terrified Abuela, Bruno broke the glass that reflected the visions and then hid himself in the tower so that no one would blame Mirabel for what was to happen. Bruno is not a handsome man, and he is not Mirabel's prince. The song about him, written by the famous Lin-Manual Miranda, became No. 1 on the Billboard Hot 100 Songs Chart, the first from Disney since *Aladdin*'s "A Whole New World" in 1993, and rising higher than *Frozen*'s "Let It Go" (2013). The meaning of "We Don't Talk About Bruno" "has inspired legions of amusing TikToks, creating a viral feedback loop," says Spencer Kornhaber, writing for *The Atlantic*. To him, Bruno could be that family member who has been discarded because of "misunderstood mental health condition, or as someone who just does not below" (2022, n.p.). Kornhaber adds that this song resonates with people who have been shamed by having been marginalized.

Bruno's voice belongs to John Leguizamo, first-generation immigrant from Columbia. When interviewed on the *Today* show, Leguizamo lamented that there were no Latin superheroes even though "we are the largest ethnic group in America" ("John" 2021, 00:02:00–05). He began a comic book titled *Phenom X*, featuring only Latinos and produced only by Latin people (00:02:33–03:03). What is the strip's message? "Inclusion," he replied (00:02:31). In his most recent one-man show titled *Latin History for Morons*, he says to the audience, "If you don't see yourself represented outside of yourself, you feel f—invisible" ("John" 00:06:45–07:04). Bruno—like many males and especially ethnic males—has been hidden in Disney for too long. In *Encanto* Bruno emerges as a real human being with emotional vulnerability but also a nobility that goes way beyond simply kissing some beautiful woman in a glass coffin.

Bibliography

Alexander, Susannah. "Mulan Remake Had an 'I'll Make a Man Out of You' That Disney Passed On." *DigitalSpy*, September 25, 2020. <https://www.digitalspy.com/movies/a34162003/mulan-remake-updated-song/>.

Attebery, Brian. "Reinventing Masculinity in Fairy Tales by Men." *Marvels & Tales* 32, no. 2 (2018): 314–37.

"The Ballad of Mulan." Translated by Philip Naudus. 386–535 AD. <https://mulanbook.com/pages/northern-wei/ballad-of-mulan>.

Bloo. Comment. Disney's *Encanto*/Official Trailer. 2022. <https://www.youtube.com/watch?v=CaimKeDcudo>.

Cashdan, Sheldon. *The Witch Must Die: The Hidden Meaning of Fairy Tales*. New York: Basic Books, 1999.

Coffey, Kelly. "The Kardashians Are Coming to Disney+ with a Brand New Original Series." *ITM*, February 9, 2022. <https://insidethemagic.net/2022/02/the-kardashians-disney-plus-kc1/>.

Connell, R. W., and James W. Messerschmidt. "Hegemonic Masculinity: Rethinking the Concept." *Gender and Society* 19, no. 6 (December 2005): 829–59.

Corbett, Ken. *Boyhoods: Rethinking Masculinities*. New Haven, CT: Yale University Press, 2009.

Davis, Amy M. *Good Girls and Wicked Witches: Women in Disney's Feature Animation*. Eastleigh: John Libbey Publishing, 2006.

———. *Handsome Heroes & Vile Villains: Men in Disney's Feature Animation.* Eastleigh: John Libbey Publishing, 2013.

Eliot, Marc. *Walt Disney: Hollywood's Dark Prince.* New York: Birch Lane Press, 1993.

England, Dawn Elizabeth, Lara Descartes, and Melissa A. Collier-Meek. "Gender Role Portrayal and the Disney Princesses." *Sex Roles* 64 (2011): 555–67. doi:10.1007/s11199-011-9930-7.

"A Fairy Tale Comes to Life." *Cinderella. Extra.* DVD. September 15, 2015.

Frear, Walter F. "Report of the President to the Members of the Hawaiian Historical Society". In *Forty-Eighth Annual Report of the Hawaiian Historical Society or the Year 1939*, 9–10. Honolulu: The Society, February 28, 1940. <http://hdl.handle.net/10524/79>.

García de Toro, Cristina. "Gender Issues and Translation: The Gender of Te Kā Monster in Disney's *Moana.*" *Children's Literature Association Quarterly* 46, no. 1 (2021): 78–93. doi:10.1353/chq.2021.0008.

Grady, Constance. "Why Mulan's 'I'll Make a Man Out of You' Became a Pump-up Playlist Must Have." *Vox*, September 4, 2020.

Graves, Sherryl Browne. "Television and Prejudice Reduction: When Does Television as a Vicarious Experience Make a Difference?" *Journal of Social Issues* 55, no. 4 (1999): 707–25. doi:1.1111/0022-4537.00143.

Hine, Benjamin et al. "The Rise of the Androgynous Princess: Examining Representations of Gender in Prince and Princess Characters in Disney Movies Released 2009–2016." *Social Science* (November 2018): 1–23. doi:10.3390/socsci7120245.

Hough, Soren. "How Disney's *Mulan* Brazenly Challenges Gender and Sexuality." *Robertebert.com*, December 28, 2016.<https://www.rogerebert.com/features/how-disneys-mulan-brazenly-challenges-gender-and-sexuality>.

"I'll Make a Man Out of You." Composed by Matthew Wilder. Lyrics by David Zippel. Sung by Donny Osmond for *Mulan.* 1998.

J.A.C. "Übersexual." *Urban Dictionary*, October 11, 2005. <https://www.urbandictionary.com/define.php?term=Ubersexual>.

Jeffords, Susan. "The Curse of Masculinity: Disney's *Beauty and the Beast.*" In *From Mouse to Mermaid: The Politics of Film, Gender, and Culture*, edited by Elizabeth Bell and Lynda Hass, 161–72. Bloomington: Indiana University Press, 1995.

"John Leguizamo Talks New Latino Superhero Comic, Starring in *Encanto.*" *Today*, October 31, 2021. <https://www.today.com/video/john-leguizamo-talks-new-latino-superhero-comic-starring-in-encanto-125028421607>.

Jorgensen, Jeana Sommer. "Gender and the Body in Classical European Fairy Tales." PhD diss., Indiana University, 2012.

Kornhaber, Spencer. "The Biggest Reason 'We Don't Talk About Bruno' Is a Hit." *The Atlantic* (February 3, 2022): n.p. <https://www.theatlantic.com/culture/archive/2022/02/encanto-disney-music/621475/>.

Laman, Douglas. "How *Encanto* Captures the Experiences of Being Autistic in a Neurotypical Family." *Collider*, December 29, 2021. <https://collider.com/encanto-autistism-representation-explained/>.

Leaper, Campbell, Lisa Breed, Lauri Hoffman, and Carly Ann Perlman. "Variations in the Gender-Stereotyped Content of Children's Television Cartoons Across Genres." *Journal Applied Social Psychology* 32 (2006): 1653–62. doi:1.1111/j.1559-1816.2002.tb02767.x.

Li-Vollmer, M., and M. E. LaPoint. "Gender Transgression and Villainy in Animated Films." *Popular Communication* 1 (2003): 89–109. doi.1.1207/S15405710PV0102_2.

Malflahi, May. Comment. Disney's *Encanto/*Official Trailer. 2022. <https://www.youtube.com/watch?v=CaimKeDcudo>.

Messer, Lesley. "*Encanto:* All the Details of Disney's New Film Revealed." *GMA Newsletter: Culture*, September 10, 2021. <https://www.goodmorningamerica.com/culture/story/encanto-details-disneys-film-revealed-79927992>.

Neill, Carrie. "Field Report: The Princess Problem: Karen Eisenhauer Breaks Down What the Dialogue *Really* Says in Disney's Princess Films." *DSCOUT: People Nerds*. <https://dscout.com/people-nerds/field-report-the-princess-problem>.

"Obesity and Native Hawaiians/Pacific Islanders." OMH: U.S. Department of Health and Human Services, Office of Minority Health. March 26, 2020. <https://minorityhealth.hhs.gov/omh/browse.aspx?lvl=4&lvlid=85>.

Pérez, Edwardo. "From Snow White to Moana: Understanding Disney's Feminist Transformation." In *Disney and Philosophy: Truth, Truth, and a Little Bit of Pixie Dust*, edited by Richard B. Davis and William Irwin, 71–80. Hoboken, NJ: Wiley-Blackwell, 2020.

"Proud Corazón." Written by Adrian Molina and Germaine Franco. Sung by Anthony Gonzalez for *Coco*. Walt Disney Music Company, 2017. <https://www.google.com/search?client=firefox-b-1-d&q=lyrics+for+proud+corazon>.

Reif, Alex. "Meet Casita, the Anthropomorphic House from Disney's *Encanto*." *Laughing Place*, November 24, 2021. <https://www.laughingplace.com/w/articles/2021/11/24/disney-encanto-casita-house-behind-the-scenes/>.

Roberts, Sharon. Introduction to *Recasting the Disney Princess in an Era of New Media and Social Movements*, 3–20, 2020.

——, ed. *Recasting the Disney Princess in an Era of New Media and Social Movements*. Lanham, MD: Lexington Books, 2020.

Rodriguez, Alberto, and Veronica Nohemi Duran. "Elena of Avalor and Mama Coco: Latina Sheroes and Knowledge Keepers." In *Recasting the Disney Princess in the Era of New Media and Social Movements*, edited by Sharon Roberts, 2020, 99–116. Lanham, MD: Lexington Books, 2020.

Roy, Eleanor Ainge. "Disney Depiction of Obese Polynesian God in Film *Moana* Sparks Anger." *The Guardian*, June 27, 2016. <https://www.theguardian.com/world/2016/jun/27/disney-depiction-of-obese-polynesian-god-in-film-moana-sparks-anger>.

Salzman, Marian, Ira Matathia, and Ann O'Reilly. *The Future of Men: The Rise of the Übersexual and What He Means for Marketing Today*. New York: St. Martin's Publishing, 2006.

Signorielli, Nancy. "Television's Gender-Role Images and Contribution to Stereotyping: Past, Present, and Future." In *Handbook of Children and the Media*, edited by Dorothy G. Singer and Jerome L. Singer, 341–58. Thousand Oaks, CA: Sage, 2001.

"Some Day My Prince Will Come." Composed by Frank Churchill and Lyrics by Larry Morey for *Snow White*. 1937. <https://www.youtube.com/watch?v=Qg73_Yt_F2I>.

Steiner, Candice Elanna. "*Moana*." *Gale Business Insights: Global*. 2018. GALE|A523394037.

Steyer, Isabella. "Gender Representations in Children's Media and Their Influence." *Campus-Wide Information Systems* 31 (2014): 171–80.

Streiff, Madeline, and Lauren Dundes. "From Shapeshifter to Lava Monster: Gender Stereotypes in Disney's *Moana*." *Social Sciences* 6, no. 3 (2017): 1–12.

Swindler, A. "Culture in Action: Symbols and Strategies." *American Sociological Review* 51 (1986): 273–86.

Szany, Wendy Lee. "*Mulan*: Why Captain Li Shang Isn't in the Live Action Remake." *Collider*, February 27, 2020. <https://collider.com/mulan-li-shang-not-in-live-action-remake-reason-why/>.

Towbin, Mia A. et al. "Images of Gender, Race, Age, and Sexual Orientation in Disney Feature-Length Animated Films." *Journal of Feminist Family Therapy* 15, no. 4 (2004): 19–44. doi:10.1300/j086v15n04_02.

"Training the Men." Composed by Harry Gregson-Williams. Soundtrack for *Mulan*. 2020. <https://www.youtube.com/watch?v=vxv5BOo8xys>.

Westervelt, William Drake. *Legends of Ma-ui—A Demi God of Polynesia and of His Mother Hina*. Honolulu: The Hawaiian Gazette Company, 1910. <https://books.google.com/books?id=v7LfAAAAMAAJ>.

"Where You Are." Written by Lin-Manuel Miranda. Sung by Nicole Scherzinger for *Moana*. 2016. <https://www.youtube.com/watch?v=RTWhvp_OD6s>.

Witt, Susan D. "The Influence of Television on Children's Gender Role Socialization." *Childhood Education: Infancy Through Adolescence* 76, no. 5 (2000): 322–24. <http://www2.lewisu.edu/~gazianjo/influence_of_televisi on_on_child.htm>.

Wooden, Shannon R., and Ken Gilliam. *Pixar's Boy Stories: Masculinity in a Postmodern Age*. Lanham, MD: Rowan and Littlefield, 2014.

"You're Welcome." Written by Jordan Fisher. Sung by Dwayne Johnson for *Moana*. 2016. <https://www.youtube.com/watch?v=79DijItQXMM>.

Zamora, Lois Parkinson, and Wendy B. Faris. "Introduction: Daiquiri Birds and Flaubertian Parrot(ie)s." In *Magical Realism: Theory, History, Community*, 1– 11. Durham, NC: Duke University Press, 1995.

Zipes, Jack. "Breaking the Disney Spell." In *From Mouse to Mermaid: The Politics of Film, Gender, and Culture*, edited by Elizabeth Bell et al., 21–42. Bloomington, IN: University Press, 1995.

———. *The Enchanted Screen: The Unknown History of Fairy Tales*. New York: Routledge, 2011.

BRENDA AYRES

9 Disney's New Dance at the Ball: *Beauty and the Beast* and Bowing to Difference

According to the biblical account, God "created man in His own image, in the image of God He created him; male and female He created them" (Gen. 1:27). Thus Adam, the first human, was hermaphroditic in a world void of ethnicity, nationality, age, class, and religion. After God formed the woman from Adam, there was no enmity between man and woman or God until they disobeyed God. The consequence was dissension between humans and God, humans and Satan, man and woman, and humans with each other (3:15). One outcome of this was the first act of discrimination—the prejudicial treatment of a person or group based on individuals' differences from the discriminator. In Adam's case, he discriminated against Eve based on her gender; he blamed God for giving him "the woman" who caused him to sin (3:12)[1] Between that time and Christ's sacrifice that made redemption possible for humans,[2] most people have refused to humble themselves and own up to their own sins. They are bent on self-exoneration, autonomy, and self-aggrandizement, all the while judging other people's behavior and aptitudes. They allow their biases to derail the two greatest biblical commandments: to love God and to love their neighbor as themselves.[3] This failure is the very definition and idiosyncrasy of discrimination. To distinguish between individuals and groups and treat them with inequity is a human inclination that has produced illimitable suffering and bloodshed, beginning when the firstborn son of all humans, Cain, murdered his brother Abel (Gen. 4:1–18). Envy, rivalry, and hatred have never been enacted with God's approbation or initiation, for Galatians 3:28 makes this declaration: "There is neither Jew nor Greek, there is neither slave nor fee man, there is neither male nor female; for you are all one in Christ Jesus." Discrimination is a human desecration.

The Bible and the Church did set the standards for morality in the Western world, but fairy tales also emerged to instruct humans how to behave toward fellow humans, animals, and their environment in ways that if followed, would promote peace, harmony, and well-being. Jack Zipes, arguably the foremost expert on fairy tales, theorizes their purpose:

> At their best, fairy tales constitute the most profound articulation of the human struggle to form and maintain a civilizing process. They depict metaphorically the opportunities for human adaptation to our environment and reflect the conflicts that arise when we rail to establish civilizing codes commensurate with the self-interests of large groups within the human population. (2011, 1)

There is at least one tale that addresses the human propensity to discriminate against others; it is a major theme in "Beauty and the Beast."

Published in 1740, "La Belle et la Bête" was written by Gabrielle-Suzanne Barbot de Villeneuve. Many scholars think it is a retelling of the Greco-Roman myth of Psyche and Cupid (Craven 2002, 126) and is replete with allegorical signifiers. The story is about the love between a beautiful mortal, Psyche (which means "soul") and Cupid, a god of erotic love who was the son of Venus (goddess of love) and of Mars (the god of war). Cupid (a force of discord caused by the concurrent existence of love and hatred) has sex (unites) with Psyche (the human soul) at night and then takes her to reside in a magnificent palace (earth), which causes her sisters (others) to be envious (struggle for hegemony). Because Psyche has never seen Cupid, the sisters convince her that he is a winged monster, thus tempting her not only to discriminate against him but also to kill him. In the middle of the night, equipped with a lantern and a dagger and fully committed to destroy someone who is different, Psyche (the human soul) sees—really sees him (erotic love), for the first time, only to discover that he is gorgeous.[4] Love triumphs over hatred, and knowledge and familiarity trump discrimination.

Villeneuve wrote "La Belle" as a lesson for aristocratic young women who were to become or were "brides-to-be" in what was then commonly arranged marriages (Craven 2016, 189). In Villeneuve's story, Beauty is just one of twelve children but the only one who is not cruel, selfish, and vain. The merchant father plans to purchase expensive gifts for each child on his next travel, but Beauty says she wants only his safe return. Like Maurice in the two Disney renditions of "Beauty and the Beast" (1991 and 2017), he promises her a rose. On his way back, his cargo is seized to pay for debt— a frequent problem for many eighteenth-century aristocratic males with title but little money and an unwillingness to live within their means. In a horrific storm, the father takes refuge in a palace. Like Maurice, uninvited, he partakes of food and drink and then picks a rose. The Beast confronts him and learns that the rose is for the man's daughter. The Beast offers the man his freedom in exchange for Beauty. If he declines, the Beast will destroy his entire family, mirroring a realistic and frequent situation for many eighteenth-century families in debt with the only solution being to marry a daughter to a wealthy man. Beauty volunteers to live with the Beast. The Beast lavishes her with riches, clothing, and libraries; but each night, she refuses to allow him to bed her. Since she is homesick, the Beast allows her to visit her family for two months as long as she promises to come back to him. She goes, but upon feeling apprehensive for the Beast, she returns to the palace and finds him dying of a broken heart. When she weeps for him and regrets her discrimination against him, he turns into the prince of her dreams—just as Cupid becomes beautiful to Psyche. In the fairy tale, he had become a beast or was one already because he discriminated against an enchantress. Like the Disney renditions, the spell is broken when he succeeds in vanquishing someone else's discrimination though love.

The message to the eighteenth-century girl was that a man's appearance and age did not matter; it was her duty, for the sake of her family, to marry him and allow him conjugal visits. If she endured, received his love and kindness, and showed him kindness in return, he would become her Prince Charming, and they would live happily ever after.

Zipes figured that the fairy tale spoke also to men about arranged marriages. The Beast was punished for rejecting an old ugly woman (the enchantress); men were also expected to marry a woman for the sake of the family, regardless of her age and physical appearance (227). Gaston is also punished in the Disney versions for judging a woman by what he sees on the surface. Both Gaston and the Beast were guilty of discrimination that cost them and those around them dearly; they failed to appreciate the full value of individuals. In Gaston's case, he saw only a physically beautiful woman who defied his notion of womanhood by being an intellectual and for having dreams unbefitting a female. As for the prince, not only did he fail to respect a poor, old woman who came to his door, but also he surrounded himself with beautiful women and glitter and gold, and most likely regarded his servants as if they were nothing but things or animals before they were magically turned literally into things and animals. Furthermore, as Amy Davis observed, when the Beast first met Belle, he treated her like a servant (2006, 194), as if she were some beast of burden, an animal, like the animated footstool that once had been a pet dog. Ironically it was the Beast himself who was acting like an animal, measuring others in terms of where they fit in relation to himself and his food chain.

The 1756 version by Jeanne-Marie Leprince de Beaumont in *Magasin des Enfants* is similar, but the cast of characters is reduced, and rather than Beast's attempts to have intercourse with Beauty, he allows her to be his asexual mistress, and like the animal he is, he obeys her. She does get to go home where her nasty sisters entice her to stay longer than the allotted time so as to antagonize the Beast to the point of his devouring her—a ploy born out of their discrimination against him and their sister. As in Villeneuve's and Disney's stories, she restores the Beast to life and to his humanity, and then they live happily ever after. The message is almost Victorian: Women may not have the power and authority to choose careers and husbands, but if they play their cards right, because men are so controlled by their bestial, sexual instincts (a Victorian stereotype), women can use their physical allure to get what they want. A pre-Victorian, Mary Wollstonecraft mentions this power play in *A Vindications of the Rights of Woman*: "Women ... boast of their weakness, cunningly obtaining power by playing on the *weakness* of men; and they may well glory in their illicit sway, for, like Turkish bashaws, they have more real power than their masters; but virtue is sacrificed to temporary gratifications, and the respectability of life to the triumph of an hour" (1794 [1792], Ch. 3, 66).

Of course such a tale with its overt sexual references would not have been acceptable for a Victorian audience. It was first sanitized before appearing in Andrew Lang's *Blue Fairy Book* published between 1889 and 1913. In more traditional fashion of Victorian didacticism and its regard for such biblical pronouncements as "Pride goeth before destruction, and a haughty spirit a fall" (Prov. 16:18), where pride is the root of discrimination (assuming that one is better than another), Beauty's father is punished for prioritizing status and wealth and for overly indulging his children with materialism. His house burns down and with it, all his furnishings, gold, silver, and worldly goods. His ships are lost at sea either to pirates or the elements. Then he discovers that his clerks have been stealing from him. The story reads almost like the biblical book of Job (when "Job" is Hebrew for "persecuted or hated") that ends with the realization and recognition that the physical is temporal and under the dominion of God; good gifts are not granted to those because they are deserving but because God is gracious and merciful, which is to say that no one is justified in thinking that he/she is superior to anyone else.

The rest of "Beauty" is similar in details to the other versions but more tailored to a Victorian audience. Through it all, it is Beauty who sacrifices herself to save her family and the Beast. The moral of the story is that if a woman denies herself, she will be blessed with a husband who adores her and will prove to be the prince of her dreams. Impediments to love (like discrimination) can be overcome through self-denial. This is a biblical principle as well, as stated by Christ: "Greater love has no one than this, that a person will lay down his life for his friends" (John 15:13). Beauty's beauty is not just physical; she is spiritually and psychologically beautiful.

Most scholars see self-denial as uniquely expected of the Victorian woman and of Disney's Belles. Davis contends that it is Belle's selflessness and her use of intelligence to support men that result in her reward of the love of a prince (2006, 194). Villeneuve's message to women is that for them to realize the desires of their hearts, they must deny themselves first (Zipes 227–28). Zipes argues that Disney's early *Beauty* film is not feminist, that it is the old story of a woman who sacrifices herself and is rewarded by acquiring a man who will protect her (233). Such a theme is rather nonsensical since it is usually from men that women needed protection.

Satisfying Victorian literary conventions, Beauty cries over the Beast as he is dying, asking, "What can I do to save you?" His answer is to marry him, which she agrees to do, without any mention of love (Summerly 1845 [1843], 34). That's when he turns into a handsome prince, and her selfish sisters transform into stone statues, to remain in that state until they are willing to become more self-denying like their sister (34), although how they are supposed to be able to change when they are in a non-changeable state of being a stone is problematic. Regardless, the transformation into stone is a metaphor for spinstership. Being a spinster was considered one of the worst things that could befall a woman in the nineteenth century. Clearly the Victorian tale is a lesson to girls about the virtue of self-sacrifice and the danger of being selfish.

Another Victorian message has been identified as "the eternal quest of women for love/marriage" as women are "associate[d ...] with reproduction, the inside, passivity, dependence, and emotionality" (Martinez 2016, 31). Even though bookworms, Disney's Belles sing that their favorite part is that the female character meets Prince Charming but "won't discover that it's him until Chapter 3" (2017, 00:07:30–42). When Belle sings, "I want adventure in the great wide somewhere" ("Belle" 1991, 2017), she may or may not realize that that is impossible for single women in the early centuries. Only through men can they live a "fulfilling life" (Martinez 31). George Eliot pronounced this unfairness in *Daniel Deronda* through Gwendolen's complaint: "We women can't go in search of adventures—to find out the Northwest passage or the source of the Nile, or to hunt tigers in the East. We must stay where we grow, or where the gardeners like to transplant us" (1900 [1876], 133–34). The only adventure awaiting young women was domesticity, and so Joyce Inman and Kelli M. Sellers deduce Disney's Belle (1991) to be a "heterosexual, young woman who is coming of age with a wish to be rescued and domesticated" (2016, 40).

Kellie Bean likewise argues that *Beauty* (1991) follows a typical paradigm of a woman's coming to a point of satisfaction only after she falls in love with a prince (2003, 54). She insists that Belle (and Esmerelda and Jasmine) are portrayed as "politically correct" females in that they are "independent, unconventional, even feminist," but "in the Disneyfied world, independence functions not as an indication of female power or self-determination, but rather as a strategy for seduction"; her "lure with titillating resistance, from *The Little Mermaid* to *Mulan*" leads her to where women should be, and that is married to a heterosexual male (54).

Ideologically, Victorian men also put women on pedestals as being more highly evolved in their spirituality and more likely to guard and invoke morality. Exposed to Charles Darwin's theories of evolution, Victorians prided themselves in being high on the chain of being; however, they did articulate a concern that men could behave beastly if they relapsed into the behavior of their ancestors, the apes. It was believed that men were controlled by their animal instincts, especially in the area of sexuality. Victorian women were conditioned to believe that sex was a bestial act and surely must be dreaded for their marriage night. They were told by their culture that women simply could not and did not enjoy sex. Dr. William Acton, then considered an expert on gynecology, stated: "The majority of women (happily for society) are not very much troubled with sexual feeling of any kind. What men are habitually, women are only exceptionally" (1875 [1857], 212). "Just close your eyes and think of England" is marital advice that has been widely quoted and its originator often attributed to Queen Victoria (Keyes 2006, 32). Both Beast and Gaston, therefore, must have been sexually intimidating to Victorian women readers. Although a modern, Allison Craven perceived the Beast as a "grotesquely phallic character" (2016, 191). Similarly, Davis discussed Gaston's hypermasculinity as a dangerous villain who comes very close to raping Belle, a shocking danger pronounced in a Disney film (2013, 232–33).

Because Belle is a woman, she is expected to tame the Beast and convert him into a man who can control his sexual yearnings; this is her sole role. Consequently, "Beauty" is not about the female; it is a story only about the men (Jeffords 1995, 167–68). Victorian women were expected to, as Martha Vicinus described it, "suffer and be still" and be invisible.[5] It may be true that the prince does not have a name in the Disney's version and is simply called the Beast and that Belle does have a place in the title, but she is objectified for her beauty, and she is defined by the Beast, the villagers (who think she is so strange because she loves to read), Gaston, and even her father. Disney does attempt to avoid stereotyping her as a Victorian young lady who does nothing but wait for her prince by having both Belles' rescuing their fathers, and the more recent Belle's inventing a primitive washing machine. However, the reality is that she still is a Victorian type who denies herself to serve the men in her life, including taking care of the wash while she attempts to teach a village girl how to read. Mrs. Sarah Stickney Ellis wrote three books that were bestsellers in England and in

America, titled *The Women of England, The Daughters of England,* and *The Wives of England* through which she advises women to take care of the men in that they have a tendency to let their "animal nature hold[] pre-eminence over the spiritual" (*Wives* 1843 [1840], 149). Thus, Disney's Belles become Beasts' teachers, civilizing them in how to eat with silverware, react with other animals like birds and horses, and dance. Susan Jeffords sees the Beast as "the image of unloved and unhappy [W]white men who need kindness and affection, rather than criticism and reform, in order to become their 'true' selves again" (1995, 165), but it is the sacrificial care of Belle who achieves this for him. Nevertheless, it is a strong endorsement of how to treat all people that is antithetical to discrimination.

It does appear that the male characters in Disney's films are not the typical Prince Charming who rescues the damsel in distress. The prince, because he was selfish and unkind, taxing the village to secure his own creature comforts (00:01:00), was a beast before he looked like a beast. And it is the woman who rescues him instead of the proverbial romance story in which the man rescues the damsel in distress. Historian Miriam Forman-Brunell remarked: "The original folk tales spring from medieval and early modern European cultures that faced all kinds of economic and demographic upheaval—famine, war, disease, terror of wolves. Girls played savior during economic crisis and instability."[6]

As for Gaston, even though he is tall, dark, handsome, and masculine with his bulging muscles, and even though he ostensibly intends to rescue Belle from the Beast, Belle says that the beast is not the monster; Gaston is (01:36:00). Eleanor Byrne and Martin McQuillan have noticed that Gaston's lodging is ornamented with only dead animals, his animal trophies, whereas the Beast's castle is inhabited by live animals, as if this is a good thing (1999, 68). To capture Belle as his wife would add one more dead trophy to his collection. The term "trophy wife" was not used before the 1970s ("trophy," 2021), and the Victorians would never consider their women as animals even if some of them were treated worse than men's dogs and horses, but to reduce a woman to an object and a conquest is a point of discrimination that would be conspicuous to modern audience.

To view Disney's *Beauty* films as further advocacy for only female altruism is to ignore the moral implication of the consequences of selfish acts by men: (1) Maurice, whether willing or otherwise, exchanges his freedom for his daughter, thus risking the loss of the last person who loved and took care of him. (2) Gaston, in his obsession to possess Belle, loses his life in his efforts to kill the Other, the Beast, someone he has hated without knowing who he really is and with fearing that the Beast threatens his hegemonic position. (3) The prince acts like a beast because of his selfishness and self-centeredness and turns into someone or something he disdains. It is only after the Beast grants Belle her freedom and later sacrifices his life to save her, that his acts of humanity change him from a beast to not only a human, but a prince. At the end of both films, Beast shows mercy and kindness to Gaston, even though Gaston was a hateful racist who led the village, like some American lynch mob,[7] to storm the castle for the purpose of destroying what they didn't understand. Gaston's discrimination against the Beast escalates to his stabbing the Beast, who then loses his balance, which in turns causes Gaston to fall to certain death. It is the way of discrimination; it inevitably destroys not only the object of discrimination but also the ogre who feeds on human flesh.

Surely the messages about discriminating between beautiful and beastly behavior would have been apparent to children and adults throughout the tale's history. "Beauty" became very popular during the nineteenth century, appearing in "chapbooks, toy book series, and nursery tale pamphlets" (Hearne 1989, 33). From 1804 to 1900 more than 20 versions "Beauty" were published (33). Felix Summerly (pseudonym for Sir Henry Cole), who was the inventor of the commercial Christmas card in 1843 (O'London 1908, 857), reproduced the tale to suit Victorian demands beginning with a preface that states: "Every age modifies the traditions it receives from its predecessor, and hands them down to succeeding ages in an altered form, rarely with advantage to the traditions themselves. The Modern English versions of Beauty and the Beast, adapted 'to the manners of the present period,' are filled with moralizings on education, marriage, &c." (Summerly 1845 [1843], iii–iv).

Besides marriage and romance,[8] these major versions produced by Disney repudiate discrimination that is "as old as time" (the words to Disney's theme songs in both 1991 and 2017); the tale has to do with attitudes of someone and groups that are different from the "norm." The antecedent for "it" in the second line of the theme song, "True as it can be," most likely refers to romantic love or *eros*, but the films invite us to interpret it as *agape*, the love that Christ identified as the greatest commandment, the love of God and one's neighbor (Matt. 22:39). As the song continues with "somebody bends," it offers the key to tolerance, acceptance, and love (*philos, agape, and eros*).

Betsy Hearne offers another view that deals with discrimination, that the tale "offers the promise that for all our human ugliness and brutality, we can be acceptable, even lovable, to another human being." Its "continued relevance" with "a modern theme stems from this fearful knowledge that we are each beastly, juxtaposed with the hopeful knowledge that we are each beautiful" (133). It may be a significant note that Disney's Beauty is called Belle, but the Beast is not called "Bête." In the French "bête" is feminine. It begs the question as to who/what exactly is the beauty in Disney's films and who/what exactly is the beast. Must we assume that Belle is Beauty and that the prince is the Beast? Significantly both characters do not receive names other than descriptive nouns, and the prince does not get even that. They are symbolic figures that represent perceptions of people that are polarized and oversimplified, as if Others are either beautiful or beastly, based solely on physical appearance.

In 1946, the French filmmaker Jean Cocteau rewrote and produced "Beauty and the Beast." Interestingly, actor Jean Marais, Cocteau's lover, played both Avenant (Disney's Gaston) and the Beast/Prince. Cocteau's ending is psychologically rich in meaning. Avenant penetrates the palace to retrieve Belle when he is shot by an arrow by an animated statue of the Roman goddess of hunters and fertility. He turns into a beast, while Belle is sobbing over the Beast who has died of a broken heart. The Beast then transforms back into the human Prince Ardent and Belle will become his Queen. Because the two beasts and the two men are played by the same actor, one must question again just what is it that makes a person a beast.

By 1991 Disney's first *Beauty* iterated many of the gendered stereotypes of the precursors while complicating the very act of reducing others into subalterns. Another form of discrimination toward women can be found throughout the history of "Beauty" and also in Disney's first version of *Beauty*, as well as in many Disney's films. One would expect stories directed to an audience of children to exalt mothers. There simply is no mention of mothers in the early renditions and none in Disney's 1991 version. As Mark Axelrod pointed out in "Beauties and Their Beasts," in most of the traditional Disney film animations there are no mothers, which is surprising given the prolific heterosexual romances that promise the formation of a nuclear family. If there are stepmothers, they are evil characters (29).[9] Sheldon Cashdan has also examined the plethora of toxic witches, godmothers, stepmothers, and other older females in fairy tales that are used to teach children the difference between good and evil, that they learn from such bad mothers what "negative tendencies" within themselves they should restrain (1999, 28). More specific to Disney is Byrne and McQuillan's theory is that mothers are a threat to Disney's phallogocentrism (72). And certainly there have been those who commented on the phallicism of are Gaston and the Beast[10] and how Disney often uses phallic structures to exterminate bad women.[11]

Axelrod's concern about this idiosyncrasy is that for 50 years, "from *Snow White* (1937) to *Beauty and the Beast* (1991), "Walt Disney's predilection for commodifying virtue by selling products that either ignore or dehumanize the role of woman and/or mother" and that has become a "Disney trademark" (32). In the later version, we *do* see Belle's mother on her deathbed, dying from the plague. The doctor urges Maurice to take his daughter and flee Paris to avoid the plague, and the mother selflessly tells Maurice, "quickly before it takes her too" (01:17:20–19:25). Although we do not learn much about the wife, we are told that Maurice loved her dearly and thought of her enough to sing a song about her, that she was a "love" that "lives on inside our hearts and always will." That love "protects, proceeds, and perseveres / And makes us whole" ("How Does" 2017). Granted, the song does not specify motherly love, but Maurice certainly is singing about a woman who was and continues to be the love of his life (2017, 00:11:33–40). When Belle asks him if he thinks that she herself is odd, he says that her mother was "different" because she was "ahead of her time" (00:13:20). Belle, who knows what tools Maurice needs before he asks for them (00:12:40) and invents a washing machine (00:14:35), is a female capable of scientific invention with left-brain efficacy that the movie indicates that she acquired not just from her father but also from her mother.

Then there is the prince who was beloved and well brought up by his mother, but after she died, his father "made him twisted up like him" (01:04:12). This gives credit and respect for the virtue of a woman in contrast to the selfishness and unkindness of a patriarch.

Additionally, the premier mother in the movie is Mrs. Potts in her maternal treatment of Chip and all residents of the castle. Her presence and influence are palpable in both films, but given that she is portrayed as a teapot, her existence as a representation of motherhood might be overshadowed by being reduced to a domestic icon (a tea pot) known for giving comfort (tea) but being restricted from doing anything else (although in 2017 she was able to scald assailants with hot tea).

Another area of discrimination in Disney's films that has been oversimplified and reductive has been Disney's portrayal of religion and in particular, of witches and enchantresses, a subject that is addressed in other chapters of this book. Just as the historian may have trouble with the historical accuracy of Disney's adaptation of *Beauty and the Beast*, many Christians may have trouble with the following observation: The 2017 enchantress, though she may appear as an old hag in the early scenes of both versions, transforms into a beautiful woman, which causes the prince to realize his error in judgment—which is a major theme of the story: One must not judge a book by its cover or not judge people by their appearance.

This enchantress then becomes Agnes, the poor spinster who begs for provision in the village. Gaston points to her when he warns Belle what will happen if she does not marry. Agnes, as a beggar, however, is most likely testing people in their village as to their empathy for those who are in hardship. Generosity is a sign of love, an attribute that the Beast was missing before he met Belle. Later, Agnes finds Maurice tied to a tree, compliments of Gaston, releases him, and nurses him back to health (01:02:55–07:47). Biblically, there is never such a thing as a good witch; witchcraft is unreservedly condemned in the Bible[12]—despite the later emergence despite Glenda in *The Wizard of Oz* (1900). Nevertheless, instead of the traditional depiction of witches and other enchantresses as being ugly, old, and evil, *Beauty* diversifies with inclusion a group of people whose spiritual/religious proclivities were previously vilified.

Notwithstanding one's perception about witchcraft, viewers will agree that the enchantress is a wise woman who warns the Prince (and by extension, readers) "not be deceived by appearances for beauty is found within" (00:02:46–58). Similarly, the other positive female mentor in the tale, Mrs. Potts, exhorts Belle (and by extension, readers) not to assume that the Beast is a beast. "Somewhere deep in his soul," she reassures Belle, "is a prince of a fellow just waiting to be set free" (00:54:41–55:04). This promise echoes Belle's earlier amazement that the attractive male in her book is revealed as Prince Charming only later in Chapter 3.

Cynthia Erb raises additional questions however. The animal body of the Beast does result in a "destabilization of the terms of traditional masculine heroism" (1995, 55). Cocteau's revision of "the Avenant/Beast relationship" allows viewers to a "dyadic relation as a complex, double-edged bond, characterized at the visual level by an eroticized comparison of male bodies and at the narrative level by tensions and rivalry" (55). As such, "Beauty" is a "thwarting of what otherwise appears to be a traditional heterosexual romance" (55). Sean Griffin then understands all versions of "Beauty and the Beast" as a focus on two males and is not about heterosexual love. Beauty or Belle is the "outsider" in the way that homosexuals have usually been depicted in films (2000, 142–44). In Disney's 1991 film, during the mob song, Gaston imitates the beast as he sings. In the 2017 version, LeFou sings that he knows well there is a "beast running wild," but who exactly is the beast is something he is no longer sure about. Significantly in this last version, Père Robert, who has lent books to Belle from his library, who is played by Ray Fearon, a British Black actor, does not join the mob. The look on his face shows that it is not the Beast that terrifies him; it is the beastly mob.

When the rioting villagers sing, "We don't like what we don't understand. In fact it scares us. And this monster is mysterious at least! Bring your guns, bring your knives, save your children and your wives! We'll save the village and our lives … we'll kill the beast!" ("The Mob Song" 1991 and 2017). The mob scene, to Erb, is "the film's most explicit reference to AIDS panic" (65). The lyrics insinuate a threat of AIDS to people in general, symbolized by the girth and ferocity of a beast—but that threat is not really the Beast, but the beast of a man that is Gaston with his weapons of destruction (66). Griffin noted that when Disney's first *Beauty* was released in 1991, it was during the AIDS epidemic and panic (134–35). A 1991 article in the *New York Times* warned that by 2000, 40 million people would be infected with HIV (Altman 1991, n.p.). In 1992, Dan Rather identified *Beauty* as a metaphor for the AIDS' panic. He invited us to interpret the spell of enchantment is that the Beast has been afflicted with AIDS and now suffers "with the same arbitrary and harshly abbreviate limitations on time and you feel the Beast's loneliness and desperation a little more deeply."[13]

Besides Cocteau's homosexuality,[14] Erb mentions that the lyrics for songs in Disney's *Beauty* were written by Howard Ashman, who died of AIDS during the 1991 production (59). Erb sites "gay strands of the film" (59). Like Cocteau's decision to conflate the Beast and Avenant into the same person portrayed by his lover actor, so Erb sees Disney's Gaston and Beast as a "doubling" (61). She emphasizes that Gaston and the Beast each is "comically 'phallic,' top-heavy figure who rises and swells when he is angered" (63). Additionally, she considers Gaston's self-voyeurism and narcissism possibly emblematic of filmatic portrayals of gay males. However, she also sees Gaston as a straight male who is antagonistic to the gay Beast (64).

In the 2017 scene when the village invades the castle, Madame Garderobe throws dresses upon three men and says, "Be free, be free!" Two of them are horrified, but Stanley is delighted as if finally having been released from his own closet and now can enjoy himself as he is, a gay man. Immediately before this scene, Cogsworth, calls the three, "third-rate Musketeers" (01:43:03;30). This is an interesting reference. Alexandre Dumas, *The Three Musketeers* would not be published until 1844, but the Musketeers (so called because they used muskets) were created in 1622 to fight in the infantry and in the cavalry as dragoons. But the Musketeers of the Guard were primarily bodyguards for the royals. The three musketeers in Dumas' novel, although anachronistic to *Beauty* set in the eighteenth century, were quite enamored with women and were portrayed with hypermasculinity, as models of what a manly man should be, even if Porthos often dressed and acted like a dandy, and even though Artemis in the 1973 version was played by Richard Chamberlain, who was the heart throb of the 1960s when he played Dr. Kildare and Allan Quatermain in the 1980s; Chamberlain was gay although he did not make that public until 1989 (Carvajal 2020, n.p.). Michael York, who played the gay writer in *Cabaret*

(1972), was d'Artagnan. Disney produced another version of *The Three Musketeers* in 1993.

In the final scenes of *Beauty* (2017), Stanley dances with LeFou, and they both act freely as gay men. LeFou is "the antithesis of hegemonic masculinity" epitomized by Gaston; he "is indicative of effeminate, homosexual, or even hyposexual masculinity" (Macaluso 2019 [2018], 221). An article in the British gay men's lifestyle magazine *Attitude* suggested that the recent *Beauty* may "seem like the ultimate celebration of heterosexual love" but "it's actually harbouring a treasure trove of gay secrets—and is set to make history with Disney's first ever 'exclusively gay moment' on film" ("World Exclusive" 2017, n.p.). In an interview the director of the film, Bill Condon, said, "LeFou is somebody who on one day wants to be Gaston and on another day wants to kiss Gaston …. He's confused about what he wants …. But it is a nice, exclusively gay moment in a Disney movie." In a press conference, Condon addressed the queerness of Le Fou and the director's determination to translate this film into representations of inclusivity. He said that it was important to him that Le Fou have a crush on Gaston:

> I talked before about how we translate this into live-action. That means building out the characters. It's also a translation to 2017, you know? … And what is the movie about? What has this story always been about for 300 years? It's about looking closer, going deeper, accepting people for who they really are … and in a very Disney way, we are including everybody. I think this is for everybody, and on the screen we'll see everybody. And that was important to me. (quoted in Petit 2017, n.p.)

The editor-in-chief of the magazine, Matt Cain, praised the gay representation as "normal and natural" is a "watershed moment for Disney." The "moment" was not welcomed by both sides of those with strong feelings against and for acceptance of homosexuality. There were those who wrote that they would not show the movie in their theaters and others who would not allow their children to review it. Russia threatened to ban it (Romano 2017, n.p.). At the other end of the spectrum were those who complained that the "bumbling, sniveling sidekick of a villain … gets a mere seconds-long 'exclusively gay moment' in the background of a straight couple's happy ending" (quoted in Rosewarne 2019, 194).

The 2017 version defies negative discrimination in other ways as well. Many of the debutantes who dance in the opening ballroom scene are Black such as Koko Basigara, Ava Brennan, Sophia Brown, Cassie Clare, Lily Frazer, Leah Hill, Chelsea Inez, Abiona Omonua, and Lucy St. Louis. Another debutante is Jennifer Leung is of Chinese descent. Several other cast members who were debutantes were of a variety of ethnicities. Albeit historically inaccurate to have debutantes and other villagers of diverse races represented in a film with a setting in the mid-1700s, Disney's animation is fantasy directed to children. A historian might have qualms about such inclusivity, but to send a message to children that people in general do include those of a variety of races, ethnicities, and genders is an invaluable concept for them to grasp.

Though they have no major roles, they do contribute to a twenty-first-century message of antidiscrimination. In addition to the other-than-White actors listed above, I noted one person of Asian descent in the bar scene (00:38:39). The 2017 cast also includes (as far as I can tell from the IMDb website); see Table 9.1.

Table 9.1. Multi-ethnic Cast of *Beauty and the Beast* (2017)

Actor	Ethnicity	Role
Ray Fearon	Black British	Père Robert, the priest who shares his library with Belle
Audra McDonald	Black American	Madame Garderobe
Gugu Mbatha-Raw	Black British	Plumette who is in love with the White Lumière
Obioma Ugoala	Black British	Flirtatious farmer
Dean Street	Black British	Dick
Clive Rowe	Black British	Cuisinier
Timia Julien-Box	Black British	Little girl
Yasmin J. James	Black British	Debutante's mother
Alona Leoine	Black American	Market shopper
Tyrone Love	Black British	Village gent

Although there are definite messages in *Beauty* about discrimination regarding gender roles and ethnicity, the ending of the two Disney films do not follow either eighteenth- or nineteenth-century English or American literary conventions. Despite the overt readings of the importance of finding and rehabilitating mates, the Disney tales do not end in a wedding, and marriage is not always extolled as a happily ever after, as demonstrated by Cogsworth. When he becomes human again and his wife, Clothilde cries out, "Henri? Henri! I've been so lonely," Cogsworth says to himself, "Turn back into a clock … Turn back into a clock" (01:56:12). As for Beauty and the Prince and the other characters, they dance a waltz. At the beginning of the Regency, the British would think this dance unseemly because of the proximity of partners. That scandalous writer, Lord Byron, wrote a poem about the waltz and its scandal, but he also writes: "Thus all and each, in movement swift or slow, the genial contact gently undergo" (208–9). Aside from any impropriety, however, the waltz was a significant ending to *Beauty* in its metaphorical display of being in sync with another person with no discrimination separating them. Mark Knowles describes the "more subtle and profound meanings" of waltzing: "In order to accomplish the rapid spinning of the waltz," both partners must "lean back" and trust in each other's support as they "surrender[] to the motion of turning." They have to "share a common axis" and "hold a continuous point of contact, and at the same time maintain self-sufficiency." One must not "overpower[]" the other or else they will both "spin out of control." Both must "share a common center without losing identity or individuality." Knowles concludes that the waltz in a "powerful metaphor" for demonstrating" woman's ability to contribute equally and a man's need to share power" (2009, 179–80). In the same manner, the waltz is a metaphor not only for heterosexual couples—for in the 2017 film gay couples are dancing as well—it is also a metaphor for overcoming discrimination and humans dancing and twirling harmoniously with each other not only despite differences but maybe just because of them.

Bibliography

Acton, William. *The Functions and Disorders of the Reproductive Organs in Childhood, Youth, Adult Age, and Advance Life*. 1862. 6th edn. London: J. and A. Churchill, 1875. <https://books.google.com/books?id=3hwDAAAAQAAJ>.

Allan, Robin. *Walt Disney and Europe*. Bloomington: Indiana University Press, 1999.

Altman, Lawrence K. "W.H.O. Says 40 Million Will Be Infected with AIDS Virus by 2000." *New York Times*, June 18, 1991. <https://archive.nytimes.com/www. nytimes.com/library/national/science/aids/061891sci-aids.html>.

Altmann, Anna E., and Gail de Vos. *Tales, Then and Now: More Folktales as Literary Fictions for Young Adults*. Englewood, CO: Libraries Unlimited, 2001.

Axelrod, Mark. "Beauties and Their Beasts & Other Motherless Tales from the Wonderful World of Disney." In Ayres 2003, 29–38.

Ayres, Brenda, ed. *The Emperor's Old Groove: Decolonizing Disney's Magic Kingdom*. New York: Peter Lang, 2003. New York: Scribner's and Sons, 1918. <https:// books.google.com/books?id=s1gVAAAAYAAJ>.

Barbot de Villeneuve, Gabrielle-Suzanne. "Beauty and the Beast." 1740. Translated by James Robinson Planché. Los Angeles, CA: Enhanced Media, 2017.

Bean, Kellie. "Stripping Beauty: Disney's 'Feminist' Seduction." In Ayres 2003, 53–64.

"*Beauty and the Beast*: Full Cast and Crew." *IMDb*. 2017. <https://www.imdb.com/ title/tt2771200/fullcredits/?ref_=tt_cl_sm>.

Beaumont, Jeanne-Marie Leprince de. *The Story of Beauty and the Beast*. 1756. Glasgow: Good Press, 2020.

"Beauty and the Beast." Composed by Alan Menken. Lyrics by Howard Ashman, Theme Song for *Beauty and the Beast*. 1991 and 2107.

"Belle." Composed by Alan Menken and Lyrics by Howard Ashman for *Beauty and the Beast*. 1991 and 2017.

Brode, Douglas, and Shea T. Brode, eds. *Debating Disney: Pedagogical Perspectives on Commercial Cinema*. Lanham, MD: Rowman and Littlefield, 2016.

Byrne, Eleanor, and Martin McQuillan. *Deconstructing Disney*. London: Pluto Press, 1999.

Carvajal, Edduin. "Richard Chamberlain Once Got Candid About Why He Came Out as Gay at 68." *Am*, April 22, 2020. <https://news.amomama.com/204639-richard-chamberlain-once-got-candid-why.html>.

Cashdan, Sheldon. *The Witch Must Die: The Hidden Meaning of Fairy Tales*. New York: Basic Books, 1999.

Craven, Allison. "Beauty and the Belles: Discourses of Feminism and Femininity in Disneyland." *European Journal of Women's Studies* 9, no. 2 (2002): 123–42.

———. "'Upon a Dream Once More': Beauty Redacted in Disney's Readapted Classics." In Brode and Brode 2016, 187–97.

Davis, Amy M. *Good Girls and Wicked Witches: Women in Disney's Feature Animation*. Herts, UK: John Libbey Publishing, 2006.

———. *Handsome Heroes & Vile Villains: Men in Disney's Feature Animation*. Herts, UK: John Libbey Publishing, 2013.

Eliot, George. *Daniel Deronda*. 1876. Boston: Little, Brown, and Company, 1900. <https://books.google.com/books?id=o5c9AQAAMAAJ>.

Ellis, Sarah Stickney. *The Wives of England: Their Relative Duties, Domestic Influence, and Social*. 1840. New York: D. Appleton and Company, 1843. <https://books.google.com/books?id=GzQEAAAAYAAJ>.

Erb, Cynthia. "Another World or the World of an Other? The Space of Romance on Recent Versions of 'Beauty and the Beast.'" *Cinema Journal* 34, no. 4 (Summer 1995): 50–70.

Garlen, Julie C., and Jennifer A. Sandlin, eds. *Teaching with Disney*. New York: Peter Lang, 2016.

Griffin, Sean. *Tinker Belles and Evil Queens: The Walt Disney Company from the Inside Out*. New York: New York University Press, 2000.

Griswold, Jerry. *The Meanings of "Beauty and the Beast": A Handbook*. Peterborough, ON: Broadview Press, 2004.

Hearne, Betsy Gould. *Beauty and the Beast: Visions and Revisions of an Old Tale*. Chicago: University of Chicago Press, 1989.

"How Does a Moment Last Forever." Composed by Alan Menken and lyrics by Tim Rice. For *Beauty and the Beast*. 2017.

Inman, Joyce Olewski, and Kelli M. Sellers. "The Disney Princess Dilemma: Constructing, Composing, and Combatting Gendered Narratives." In Garlen and Sandlin 2016, 39–50.

Jeffords, Susan. "The Curse of Masculinity: Disney's *Beauty and the Beast*." In *From Mouse to Mermaid: The Politics of Film, Gender, and Culture*, edited by Elizabeth Bell, Lynda Haas, and Laura Sells, 161–71. Bloomington: Indiana University Press, 1995.

Keyes, Ralph. *The Quote Verifier: Who Said What, Where, and When*. New York: St. Martin's Press, 2006.

Knowles, Mark. *The Wicked Waltz and Other Scandalous Dances: Outrage at Couple Dancing in the 19th and Early 20th Centuries*. Jefferson, NC: McFarland, 2009.

Lang, Andrew. "Beauty and the Beast." In *The Blue Fairy Book*, 79–93. London: Longmans, Green, and Company, 1889. <https://www.arvindguptatoys.com>.

Macaluso, Michael. "Postfeminist Masculinity: The New Disney Norm?" 2018. In *The Psychosocial Implications of Disney Movies*, edited by Lauren Dundes, 192–201. Basel, Switzerland: MDPI, 2019.

Martinez, Alejandra. "Awakening Rebellion in the Classroom: Analyzing and Performing Disney." In Garlen and Sandlin 2016, 27–38.

"The Mob Song." Composed by Alan Menken. Lyrics by Howard Ashman for *Beauty and the Beast*. 1998. <https://www.disneyclips.com/lyrics/lyrics118.html>.

O'London, John. "Christmas Cards." *T. P.'s Weekly* 12 (December 25, 1908): 857. <https://books.google.com/books?id=gJlFAQAAMAAJ>.

Orenstein, Peggy. "What's Wrong with Cinderella?" *New York Times*, December 24, 2006. <https://www.nytimes.com/2006/12/24/magazine/24princess.t.html>.

Petit, Stephanie. "*Beauty and the Beast* Director on His Decision to Make LeFou Gay: 'In a Very Disney Way, We Are Including Everybody.'" *People* (March 6, 2017): n.p. <https://people.com/movies/beauty-and-the-best-lefou-gay-decision-director-bill-condon-including-everybody/>.

Rather, Dan. "The AIDS Metaphor in *Beauty and the Beast*." *Los Angeles Times Calendar*, March 22, 1992, 42.

Romano, Nick. "*Beauty and the Beast* Director Says 'Exclusively Gay Moment' Was 'Overblown.'" *Entertainment*, March 4, 2017. <https://ew.com/movies/2017/03/04/beauty-and-the-beast-gay-lefou-overblown/>.

Rosewarne, Lauren. *Sex and Sexuality in Modern Screen Remakes*. Cham: Palgrave Macmillan, 2019.

Sells, Laura. "'Where Do the Mermaids Stand?': Voice and Body in *The Little Mermaid*." In *From Mouse to Mermaid: The Politics of Film, Gender, and Culture*, edited by Elizabeth Bell, Lynda Haas, and Laura Sells, 175–92. Bloomington: Indiana University Press, 1995.

Summerly, Felix. "Beauty and the Beast." In *The Traditional Faëry Tales of "Little Red Riding Hood", "Beauty and the Beast" & "Jack and the Bean Stalk"*, edited by Felix Summerly, i–35. 1843. London: Joseph Cundall, 1845. <https://books.google.com/books?id=zOIHAQAAMAAJ>.

"trophy, n." *OED Online*. December 2021. Oxford University Press. <https://www-oed-com.ezproxy.liberty.edu/view/Entry/206698?redirectedFrom=trophy+wife>.

Veness, Susan. *The Hidden Magic of Walt Disney World: Over 600 Secrets of the Magic Kingdom, Epcot, Disney's Hollywood Studios, and Disney's Animal Kingdom*. 2nd edn. New York: Adams Media, 2015.

Vicinus, Martha, ed. *Suffer and Be Still: Women in the Victorian Age*. York, UK: Methuen, 1972.

Wollstonecraft, Mary. *A Vindication of the Rights of Woman.* 1792. Philadelphia, PA: Mathew Carey, 1794. <https://openlibrary.org/books/OL7025001M/A_vindication_of_the_rights_of_woman>.

"World Exclusive: *Beauty and the Beast* Set to Make Disney History with Gay Character." *Attitude*, March 1, 2017. <https://attitude.co.uk/article/world-exclusive-beauty-and-the-beast-set-to-make-disney-history-with-gay-character-1/13725/>.

Zipes, Jack. *The Enchanted Screen: The Unknown History of Fairy-Tale Films.* New York: Routledge, 2011.

10 "You must go on": The Neo-Disney Female and Her Mental Health

As Disney's entertainment monopoly continues to grow in the twenty-first century, so too does its portrayal of young female characters as they navigate challenging experiences. Disney's "changes in content and the changes in market and technology are closely related to consumerism" (Yang et al. 2021, 608), and, after facing criticism over its treatment of mental health, "often in ways that aimed to denigrate or set apart characters" (Gray 2019), Disney created female characters much more complex than princesses of the past as they actively work to learn about, and manage, their emotional well-being. One of the ways mental health is examined in recent animated Disney films is through song; music has proven effective not only at helping people calm down in crisis (Silverman 2015, 3) but also to help break down stigma that still surrounds open discussion of mental health. Destitute in her darkest hour, Anna sings, "You must go on / And do the next right thing" to motivate herself to persevere through challenges and free the people of the Enchanted Forest in Disney's *Frozen II* ("The Next Right Thing" 2019), and it is by working through her fears within that song that she tells young people it is important to learn from one's mistakes and do better next time. When young female Disney characters work through their mental health challenges, they provide young viewers with ways upon which to work through their own problems.

The World Health Organization (WHO) describes mental health as "A state of well-being in which the individual realizes his or her own abilities, can cope with the normal stresses of life, can work productively and fruitfully, and is able to make a contribution to his or her community" ("Promoting" 2004, 12), and, according to the Canadian Mental Health Association (CMHA), "one in five people in Canada will experience a mental health problem or illness in any given year" ("Mental Health Learning" 2022), while in the United States, one in six children of the ages of 12 to 17 experience a major depressive episode and one in three young adults, from ages 18 to 25) suffer from mental illness ("Mental Health 2020" 2022). Given that young people were experiencing the highest levels of suicidal ideation and serious psychological distress ever recorded prior to the Covid-19 pandemic according to research from the Centre for Addiction and Mental Health (CAMH) ("Suicidal" 2020), an examination of what the animated Disney films can contribute to the well-being of their viewers is more beneficial now more than ever.

Lavinia Rebecchini argues: "By promoting physical and psychological health, music can be an effective treatment option suitable for every environment and people of every age, race, and ethnic background" (2021, 100,374), and thus the songs of Disney's recent animated films help protagonists work through their challenges in a positive manner. This study aims to analyze the depiction of young female characters as they process challenges in a healthy manner, oftentimes through the use of music, and thereby these depictions normalize and destigmatize caring for one's mental health. Since "the public's misunderstanding of mental illness perpetuates stigma, delays treatment for those who desire or require it, and hinders social progress" (Silverman 2), it is vital to have media texts that promote healthy and positive ways of dealing with challenging emotions and/or situations to help children and young people learn strategies for maintaining their well-being. "Animation movies targeting children constitute an entertainment platform with great potential to boost sociocognitive learning among younger audiences" (Neira Piñeiro et al. 2021, 606), so it is excellent to see recent Disney films garnering great success with films like *Encanto* where depictions of working through one's mental health challenges are framed in a constructive light.

How Far We've Come: A Look Back

To say that animated Disney films have come a long way in regard to positive portrayals of mental health representations since their first full-length animated feature film, *Snow White and the Seven Dwarfs* (1937), is an understatement. Early female Disney characters often made light of domestic servitude and aimed for heterosexual marriage as their singular life's aspiration. Marriage as a main goal in one's life can be considered mentally unhealthy as it centers the person's life entirely around someone else. For example, Snow White cleans and takes care of the dwarfs and later marries a prince after he kisses and awakens her from a curse. Although it is wonderful that the prince saves her, Snow White does not know anything about the prince or if their personalities might be compatible; their suitability is never questioned. Similarly, essentially a domestic prisoner to her stepmother and stepsisters, Cinderella completes her chores while singing with her animal friends and marries the prince despite little interaction with him in *Cinderella* (1950). Finally, although much less macabre than the insemination by rape evident in early versions of *The Sleeping Beauty* (1959), Aurora is pricked by a spinning wheel's spindle, arguably a curse of domesticity against a noble-born woman; she too marries White male royalty who awakens her with a kiss but without courtship that would give them time to know each other. These early animated Disney films present passive women whose mental health is not nurtured as there is little beyond the impetus to marry a prince. These renderings of femininity are indeed bleak, but later stories offer glimpses of women peering outside their expected role of domesticity, and that desire for autonomy is a positive mental health trait reflected in Ariel in *The Little Mermaid* (1989), Belle in *Beauty and the Beast* (1991), and *Pocahontas* (1995).

Maria del Rosario Neira Piñeiro et al. (2021) propose that over time, the heroines grew to demonstrate a "rebellious attitude toward the social conventionalisms of their time and break with the prevailing rules ... while maintaining the emotional side of their leadership" (608). In *The Little Mermaid*, Ariel does achieve autonomy in that she is able to make her own choices and live outside the mermaid life she was born into; however, personal goals disappear at the end of the film with her marriage to Prince Eric. Belle demonstrates interest in books and reading rather than beauty but falls in love with the Beast who imprisons her. Even though the Beast does take on more endearing qualities as he works through his own mental health challenges, there is hardly a second thought given to the trauma Belle endures as she is held captive and is thus unable to help her father when he is attacked. Finally, Pocahontas is arguably the most offensive of all depictions within this time period as Pocahontas essentially marries her captor (though Belle marries her captor as well, he is not responsible for the murder of Belle's entire family and culture). There is nothing to be said for Pocahontas' mental health at losing so much when she chooses to be with the man who forced himself on her community in a violent manner. It is evident that "despite being the title characters, women speak just 32% of the time in *The Little Mermaid*, while they have just 24% of lines in *Pocahontas*" (Gray), and so although each of the young female characters is more autonomous and demonstrates more aspects of positive mental health than their precursors, their journey is still overshadowed by the male characters. It is not until the arrival of *Frozen* (2013) that female characters within animated Disney films start to achieve independence not only from the confines of a heterosexual marriage but also from a multitude of antiquated stereotypical behaviors.

"You must go on": A New Era of Female Empowerment

As social understanding of mental health increases, so too do their representations across all media. Most noteworthy are the depictions of mental health as young female protagonists shift into more powerful positions than they occupy at the start of their respective story. Under analysis are Disney's *Frozen*, *Inside Out* (2015), *Zootopia* (2016), *Moana* (2016), *Frozen II* (2019), *Raya and the Last Dragon* (2021), and *Encanto* (2021). Samantha Seybold (2020) posits that "this contorted, postfeminist definition of agency allows Disney to leverage socially appropriate, commodification-friendly messages of equality to its benefit while avoiding any major alteration of its traditional storylines" (83), thereby allowing a space for these young female characters to work through challenges in ways never before imagined as, prior to 2013, almost all of Disney's animated films culminated in heterosexual marriage. While not inherently problematic, marriage is hardly the only significant milestone in a woman's life, and as such it is enjoyable to see Disney's latest animated films focus more on growth, community-building, and working through mental health challenges.

The most positive portrayal of female mental health to date in animated Disney films is their latest release, *Encanto*, as it offers a rich variety of mental health maintenance. At the beginning of the story, Alma, later Abuela after the arrival of her grandkids, and her husband Pedro run from vigilantes with their newborn triplets and, unfortunately, Pedro is killed defending the family as they escape. Alone with their triplets, Abuela is gifted a magical home safe from persecution and, as the family expands, each individual is to receive a magical gift to serve the family and the community. When it is Abuela's granddaughter Mirabel's turn to receive a gift, Abuela says to her, "Whatever gift awaits will be just as special as you" (00:03:44), but when Mirabel turns the doorknob, it dissolves without providing her with a gift. Since she lacks a magical gift, a divide grows between Mirabel and her Abuela.

In order to achieve and maintain good mental health, Joseph M. Sirgy says that levels of mental health, including physiological, emotional, cognitive, metacognitive, developmental, and social-ecological, must be in balance (2020, 8). At the physiological level, the body experiences positive emotions related to a preponderance of neurochemicals like dopamine, serotonin, and oxytocin (8). That is to say, any time people do what they enjoy, the brain releases chemicals that increase their happiness, thereby helping them maintain mental well-being. In *Encanto*, several of the family members believe that their gift is entirely what brings them joy, and that that joy is who they are. For example, Mirabel's sister Luisa is gifted with super strength, and she enjoys carrying loads of donkeys, propping houses back up when they tip, and so on (00:33:32). Luisa's physical appearance, muscular and feminine at the same time as she is very physically fit and also wears a dress, has been a huge hit with young audiences who clamored to find merchandise of her ("Disney Fans" 2022). It is interesting that Luisa's super strong physique almost did not make it into the film, as illustrator and character modeling supervisor Dylan Ekren relates that it was very difficult to convince Disney executives that Luisa's body type should be muscular rather than petite and slim (quoted in Wasalamudalige 2022). However, despite her strength and confidence, Luisa begins to feel weak as the family's magic fades, and the first sign of trouble comes from her eye twitching, a physical indication that she is no longer experiencing positive mental health due to feeling emotionally overwhelmed as the strength of the family. Luisa explains to Mirabel she feels too much pressure to be strong when she sings, "Give it to your sister, your sister's older / Give her all the heavy things we can't shoulder / Who am I if I can't run with the ball? / If I fall to … / Pressure like a grip, grip, grip and it won't let go, whoa / Pressure like a tick, tick, tick 'til it's ready to blow, whoa" ("Surface Pressure" 2021). From there, Mirabel pushes Luisa to be open about her challenges, and it is through song that they work together to better understand what Luisa deals with. The use of music to benefit mental health is clear, that "to maximize support for recovery, a focus on social participation, inclusion, and participation in music activities can help develop positive relationships with others, expand social networks, support personal recovery, and strengthen social participation as well as create positive, joyful experiences" (Damsgaard and Jensen 2021, 6,648), and after working through her challenges in song, Luisa better understands that her magical gift is not the only important part of her existence.

Next, one's emotional level, one's positive emotions like happiness, serenity, and contentment, must be taken care of to balance mental well-being (Sirgy 8–10). Elsa attempts to balance her mental health with leadership of Arendelle in *Frozen II*, and officially abdicates responsibility of their kingdom to sister Anna so that Elsa can live with their mother's family, the Northuldra people. It is likely that Elsa cannot exist in the same space where she was once emotionally imprisoned within the castle as a child when her parents expected her to conceal, not feel her magical powers, arguably symbolic of her out-of-control emotions (Vargová 2021, 63–64). Therefore, Elsa makes the best choice for her mental health and transfers leadership to Anna who does not have the same type of emotional connection to the castle as Elsa.

In order for one's mental health to be in good condition, one must maintain balance at the cognitive level through domains such as family, work, and social life (Sirgy 6). In *Frozen*, Anna and Elsa lack satisfaction in multiple domains—their parents die when they are very young and they do not seem to have any other family members, they cannot do the work needed to run the kingdom because Elsa is unable to control her magical gift, and neither young woman is able to socialize within the community. The major conflict of *Frozen* arises from Elsa's emotional outburst when she freezes the entire kingdom. Based on Hans Christian Andersen's tale *The Snow Queen* (1845), Elsa was originally developed as the villain of the story to match the Snow Queen character (Hill 2019); however, the focus shifted to a story about two young sisters grappling with a shift in power from their deceased parents to Elsa. Despite her misguided formative learning and the outrageous outburst of emotion that freezes the kingdom, Elsa works with her sister and allies to learn to control her magical ability, and thereby her emotions, a sign of positive mental health.

Within *Encanto*, Mirabel is very much loved by her entire family despite her lack of magical gift. In fact, even *casita*, the house with a life of its own, is in sync with Mirabel at the start of the story as it helps Mirabel get dressed and put her shoes on in a playful and rhythmic fashion. The vibrant Colombian community seems to move with Mirabel as she sings about the family's magical gifts to young villagers: "This is my family / A perfect constellation / So many stars and everybody gets to shine" ("Family Madrigal" 2021), and the stars are referenced several times throughout the story to support the message that family members will grow and change over time, and that that is reflective of the natural world around them. One of the most fascinating aspects of *Encanto* is in its portrayals of various types of femininity and masculinity, an excellent step forward in the representation of well-being. Bruno, Abuela's only male child, locks himself away within the walls of Casita in order to help protect the family, and thus asserts his masculinity in a unique way as he quietly patches the cracks forming from the break in the family's magic from literally behind the family's walls. Abuela's daughters, Julieta and Pepa, are both gifted magically but marry nonmagical villagers, Agustín and Félix, who also demonstrate unique forms of masculinity as they support the women, evident when Agustín suffers many bee stings despite his allergies in order to support Mirabel, and when Félix supports wife Pepa as she sings about their wedding day. In addition, the men respect and care for Mirabel despite her lack of magical gift and, in fact, her parents tell her she has nothing to prove (00:11:25). It is because of the family's support for each other that they are able to work through their mental health challenges and regain well-being.

At the metacognitive level, one must be satisfied about one's life compared to their past life, the life of family members, and social circle (Sirgy

6). In *Raya and the Last Dragon*, Raya must work through the severe break in mental health that occurs when she is a child. From the start of the story, Raya is a strong, independent young woman when she successfully dodges traps on her way to visit her family's portion of the broken dragon gem and, in retaliation to the traps, launches forward and says, "Let's show them what clever really looks like" (00:04:14). Raya has a loving relationship with her father, Chief Benja, whose dream is to unite the land of Kumandra as one rather than continue as a fractured society divided into separately governed areas. In fact, her father protects her from the Druun, a force later described by Sisu as "A plague, born from human discord" (00:41:42) after they are betrayed by members of the communities he was trying to unite as Kumandra. Though Raya is saved when her father pushes her into the river, Chief Benja is turned into stone by the Druun. As a result of the betrayal and subsequent loss of her father, Raya suffers from a severe lack of trust: "Trust is a fundamental human experience. It is necessary for society to function. It can play a significant role in happiness. Without it, fear rules" (Wulan et al. 2021, 70), and so Raya must work through her trust issues in order to succeed at uniting the communities and banish the Druun. Raya spends the following six years searching for a way to speak to the last dragon, Sisu, in order to revive her father and the others who were turned to stone due to the Druun's effect. Sisu is reborn through the power of Raya's family's dragon gem, and as Raya and Sisu travel to reclaim the remaining dragon gems, they work with allies from each community in a way that blurs static gender roles of the past. Even Tong, a tough bulk of a man, displays feminine qualities, especially evident when he reveals to the group that he is alone and that he too wishes "to join this fellowship of Druun butt-kickery!" (01:02:35), and thus mental health improves when one is able to express themselves freely.

When the group runs into enemy and betrayer Namaari, Sisu helps them escape by using her powers to create a blinding fog; interestingly, the fog is swirls of blue and pink, conventionally gendered colors representing male and female, possibly indicating that the best combinations are those where male and female identities weave together (01:01:13).

As Sisu acquires the power of her siblings, spirits come together and strengthen the whole being of each. The strength of this friend and familial bond are reflected in *Encanto* as well, as Mirabel is a blend of each of her family member's strengths. Although Raya really struggles to forgive and trust Namaari as the key to bring Kumandra together, Sisu pushes her and says, "It may feel impossible, but sometimes you just have to take the first step even before you're ready" (01:10:42). Raya makes a final stand to assist the community when she gives up her family's portion of the dragon gem to Namaari. Then, when the rest of the group also relinquishes their parts of the gem, Namaari is able to push against her mother's nefarious desire to hoard the gems and, instead, combine them to save the kingdom and restore well-being to the community.

Sisu acts as a bond between the two young women, a bridge between differing ideological approaches to leadership. Raya and Namaari are able to work together to bring peace back to their land. Raya's story concludes with the song "Lead the Way," which reminds the audience to "Put the past behind / Learn from life this time / We can start brand-new … When we just trust / Trust and believe it / You'll see that, we'll lead the way" ("Lead the Way" 2021). Raya's strong leadership capabilities, evident through her ability to forgive in even the most challenging of circumstances, is an example of Disney's recent animated films depicting female characters who learn to manage their mental health.

Because Abuela refuses to admit that the family's magic is in danger in *Encanto*, she lashes out in frustration at Mirabel's lack of gift, which she seems to believe is potentially responsible for the magic breaking down. She even tells Mirabel to step aside and give the task of decorations to one of her gifted siblings and to "let the rest of the family do what they do best" (00:12:20). Their relationship is further strained after Antonio, Mirabel's cousin, receives his magical gift and Abuela asks him if he will use his gift to "serve this community and strengthen our home" (00:19:38), inadvertently indicating that Mirabel will not be able to do, due to her lack of magic. Abuela is unable to recognize her family members as more than their magical gift or Mirabel's lack thereof, and it is the matriarch's negative mental health that deepens the cracks of the Madrigal home. Mirabel and Abuela's relationship reaches a tense moment when Mirabel says to her "I will never be good enough for you" (01:12:44), and it is not until the entire house breaks that Abuela realizes the damage she has done not only to her granddaughter but also to the entire family. This fracturing within the family causes the fracturing of the foundation of the house; it can no longer support the family and collapses. It is only when Abuela sets out to find Mirabel outside their family's area that Abuela realizes the family is broken because of her, not Mirabel or the other family members (01:21:39). Even Mother Nature celebrates when Abuela and Mirabel reconnect and when Mirabel is taken inside the memory of Abuela's original journey that led to the creation of their Encanto and Casita, as scores of butterflies rise around them as they embrace. By working through their challenges together in song, Mirabel and Abuela are able to bring the family, and, with the help of the community, the house, back to a state of well-being.

At the developmental level, positive psychological traits are maintained through self-acceptance, personal growth, purpose in life, environmental mastery, autonomy, and/or positive relations with others (Sirgy 6). A film within Disney's Pixar banner *Inside Out* (2015) transports audiences into the mind of young Riley, whose emotions, personified as Anger, Sadness, Fear, and Disgust, are micromanaged by Joy as she leads them through Riley and his family's tumultuous move to San Francisco. "Joy and Poppy especially stand out from the rest for their contagious vitality and optimism, which heighten everyone else's mood in adverse circumstances" (Neira Piñeiro et al. 612) as Joy attempts to uplift everyone around her. That said, the main message of the film is to be able to appreciate sadness as well as joy, for each emotion has a time and place. Although they bicker a great deal, the Emotions help Riley through the challenging move.

Joy, who struggles at first with her feelings about the other Emotions as she does not feel they are as significant as herself, eventually comes to learn the importance of all emotions working together to create a balanced life. *Inside Out* helps young people work on emotional regulation in order to promote positive mental health. Working with others may be challenging at times, but it is in the best interests of one's mental health to be self-aware and maintain positive relations with others.

Strong and confident in the lack of magic as she appears to be in *Encanto*, Mirabel struggles under the weight of difference when her family takes a photo with Antonio after he receives his gift as she is left out of the shot; she sings, "Don't be upset or mad at all / Don't feel regret or sad at all / Hey, I'm still a part of the Family Madrigal / And I'm fine I am totally fine / I will stand on the side as you shine" ("Waiting for a Miracle" 2021). Although she is confident in who she is despite a lack of magical gift, of course Mirabel wishes to be on the same level as that of her magical family members. Mirabel comes to realize that nothing she does will ever be as good as a magical gift, and that Abuela does not recognize the impact of her rejection on Mirabel. The young girl moves and dances with fireworks and golden glitter as she sings, almost as though she is a part of the light; later, the fireworks at the end of the song match the colors in her dress. Her colorful presence, especially evident when she sings, "Come on, I'm ready! / I've been patient and steadfast and steady! / Bless me now as you blessed us all those years ago" ("Waiting for a Miracle"), reflects Mirabel's attempt to manage her emotions even when they overwhelm her, and it is this confidence in herself that helps her work through her challenges.

Mirabel's sister Isabela must also learn self-acceptance in order to regain well-being as she agrees to a marriage proposal that she does not want in order to support the family. When Isabela's proposal is ruined because it is revealed that Mirabel works to understand Bruno's prophecy, Mirabel must work to reconnect with Isabela. Although the conversation does not begin well, Isabela's emotional outburst at Mirabel leads her to create a cactus (Isabel's gift is magically producing plants) for the first time, and Isabela sings that she "just made something unexpected / Something sharp, something new / It's not symmetrical or perfect / But it's beautiful and it's mine / What else can I do?" While Isabela sings and creates all sorts of new plant life, she asks, "What could I do if I just grew what I was feelin' in the moment? / What could I do if I just knew it didn't need to be perfect? / It just needed to be / And they'd let me be," and later, "What can you do when you are deeply, madly, truly in the moment? / What can you do when you know who you wanna be is imperfect?" ("What Else Can I Do?" 2021). Isabela does not want to be in the heterosexual relationship planned by her family and finally declares: "I never wanted to marry him! I was doing it for the family!" (01:08:29). Although Isabela seems to represent stereotypical feminine gender roles with her perfection and beauty, as the story progresses, Isabela may be a member of the queer community in her rejection of a heterosexual relationship. This identity transformation is evident in Isabela's shift from typically feminine pinks and purples to a rainbow of color that reflects the gay pride flag. In the song "We Don't Talk About Bruno," while cousin Dolores sings, "[Bruno] told me that the man of my dreams would be just out of reach / Betrothed to another," Isabela sings, "He told me that the life of my dreams would be promised, and someday be mine / He told me that my power would grow, like the grapes that thrive on the vine" ("What Else Can I do?"), thereby removing a promised heterosexual future for one focused on herself and her newfound colorful identity Isabela learns more about what she can do outside her expected role as the beautiful and perfect sister and comes to better understand herself and thus her mental well-being improves.

Mirabel empathetically pays attention to the emotional aspects of her family's challenges, and leaders like her are "better predisposed to change because of their innovative style and their sense of quality, along with their person-centered, flexible, communicative, and persuasive approach" (Neira Piñeiro et al. 608). Despite her dislike of Isabela, Mirabel still works to connect with her and thus demonstrates positive leadership qualities while taking care of her—and her sister's—mental well-being. Both of the young women are able to find greater success and love, not only for each other but also for themselves.

At the social-ecological level, positive social resources—like social acceptance, actualization, contribution, integration, harmony, belonging, and attachment to family—must be balanced in order to maintain mental health (Sirgy 6). In Disney's *Zootopia*, young female bunny Judy Hopps struggles as she navigates the traditionally male-dominated profession of policing. Although storylines of Disney past "repeatedly normalize female submission to male interests, expectations, power, and leadership [while] it preserves, idealizes, and values male dominance, rather than gender equality" (Seybold 73), *Zootopia* pushes boundaries as Judy does not allow dominant male ideology prevent or limit her from reaching her goals, and thereby maintains mental well-being.

As she is a small rabbit and there has never been a bunny policeperson before her, Judy's dream to become a police officer is certainly discouraged by her parents, as well as the police force, as everyone believes she is too small to succeed in the role. Even after she is accepted and placed in the city center of Zootopia, Judy is placed on parking meter duty rather than given serious police work; however, she surpasses ticketing goals and investigates crime on her own. Her determined spirit is evident from the start of the film when she announces, "Well he's right about one thing: I don't know when to quit!" (00:05:42) after a young fox argues with her over whether she will succeed as an officer in the city. She is not discouraged and decides to leave behind her parents and siblings to work toward her dreams. In fact, as she rides the train into the city, she listens to the song "Try Everything" on her musical device, the lyrics of which encourage her to keep trying even when she fails because "Birds don't just fly / They fall down and get up / Nobody learns without getting it wrong .... I want to try even though I could fail" (2016). However, late she listens to several depressing songs (00:26:22) in her apartment as she bemoans her encounter with Nick, a thief and fox—a natural enemy to rabbits, who tells her that she will never be a cop. Nevertheless, Judy gets right back to work the next day with a positive attitude, thereby reminding audiences to persevere. By the end of the story, Judy and Nick form a platonic relationship where Judy learns how to be more flexible and therefore better at her job, and Nick becomes a cop officially by studying and getting certified. Seybold observes: "The absence of heterosexual romance in both characters' stories represents important progress within the Disney canon, because Judy Hopps and Moana are the first animated Disney heroines whose stories depict female fulfillment solely in terms of friendship and personal goals, rather than marriage" (77), and so their relationship as friends, rather than love interests, allows Judy the independence to work on her professional goals rather than marriage. In fact, Seybold further argues that "both relationships actually support, rather than subvert, patriarchal norms because they operate on one overarching dynamic in which Nick and Maui constantly challenge Judy and Moana's roles as autonomous heroines" (77).

Proud of her growth as a leader, Judy declares, "I thought Zootopia was this perfect place where everyone got along and anyone could be anything. Turns out real life's a little bit more complicated.... Real life is messy. We all have limitations. We all make mistakes.... We all have a lot in common, and the more we try to understand one another the more exceptional each of us will be" (01:33:32–34). Judy learns to take care of herself emotionally and physically, and as a result her well-being improves as she learns to work with others and contribute in unique ways despite of and perhaps due to her small stature.

Seybold also mentions Moana, the "autonomous heroine" who confronts her family's fear of the unknown in order to take her place as chief of the village when her father passes (77). A unique aspect of *Moana* is that the community already looks to Moana as a leader, even as she trains as a young person and gives advice to both men and women; in fact, "nobody rejects her as a leader.... She is able to celebrate femininity and exercise power and authority over her people through her uncontested leadership" (Ali 2021, 233–36). This lack of opposition to Moana's right to step into the role as the village chief indicates a step forward in the representation of female leadership, which should encourage female viewers to have more confidence to pursue ambitions and male viewers to be more accepting of females in leadership positions—both benefits to peaceful mental health for all concerned.

Although there is no question that Moana will lead the village despite her gender, her father, Chief Tui, is very angry with Moana when she expresses the desire to explore the waters beyond their land in an effort to save their community when villagers tell them about the dying coconuts and lack of fish (00:13:49). Rather than support her proposal of an innovative solution to the community's impending environmental catastrophe, Chief Tui instead "wields the power of his privileged place and position within the community only moments after telling Moana that her place is 'right where you are.' ... Just as the misogyny of rewarding obedience can turn, quickly, into the misogyny of punishing disobedience, Chief Tui makes way for Moana only as long as she obeys. When she disobeys, he shifts from clearing her path to obstructing it" (Hollowell 2021, 766). Chief Tui's support of Moana disintegrates when she does not behave in the manner that he expects, which results in Moana's separation from the family in order to fulfill her goals—a step that many young people may have to take for similar reasons and for personal growth. Chief Tui's " labor and attention are oriented toward Moana's power rather than away from it, and there is no juxtaposition between his responsibility to the community and to her" (767). By the end of the film, they repair their broken relationship, which regains an equitable and harmonious state of well-being for themselves and their community.

Moana's desire for autonomy is evident when she sings, "See the line where the sky meets the sea? / It calls me / And no one knows / How far it goes / If the wind in my sail on the sea stays behind me / One day I'll know / If I go, there's just no telling how far I'll go" ("How Far I'll Go" 2016) and sets off on her own to return goddess Te Fiti's heart to her. That Moana is willing to venture far beyond her own waters to explore and bring resources to her people demonstrates strong leadership and a positive depiction of mental health as she works, steadfast, through challenges. As Moana ventures across the ocean, she "stresses the fact that she is connected to the island and ocean as elements of nature" (Ali 233), and it is arguably this feminine connection with the Earth and water that assists her even as she sometimes fails to exert her leadership with foe-turned-travelling-companion Maui. An incredibly powerful demigod, Maui represents an abundance of masculinity that struggles to collaborate with the much younger, smaller, and female Moana. There is a shift in that power dynamic when Moana "saves Maui from Tamatoa, a giant-monster crab, to help him retrieve his hook, which signifies his male power as he former [*sic*] admits that he is nothing without his magical fishhook" (234); in fact, Moana tries desperately to find a way for them to work together when she says "we can find a way around" (01:15:50), but Maui refuses and states, "Without my hook, I am nothing" (01:16:51) before he flies away. Maui's identity is representative of toxic masculinity, or a set of attitudes and ways of behaving that are, or were, stereotypically associated with or expected of men, often believed to have a negative impact on men and society as a whole ("Toxic Masculinity" 2022), as he struggles to acknowledge the damage he did to Te Fiti when he stole her heart. As he works with Moana throughout the story, Maui eventually acknowledges his mistakes and joins her to return Te Fiti's heart. By the end of the film, " Moana [is] celebrated by her tribe signaling her future leadership as an heir to her father without referring to the issues of any love story, marriage or prince as a savior" (Ali 233). Moana's social acceptance through her undisputed right to the chiefdom and her strong qualities of mental health as she harmonizes relationships with goddess Te Fiti, demigod Maui, her father Chief Tui, and entire community demonstrates a mentally healthy individual.

After she speaks with Luisa in *Encanto*, Mirabel is convinced that she must work to restore the family's disintegrating magic; Mirabel collects pieces from the prophecy that led Bruno to leave the family and is caught in the act by her father Agustín as she attempts to figure out the prophecy's message. Rather than admonish or punish Mirabel, Agustín tries to protect her and says they will not tell anyone; unfortunately, Cousin Dolores overhears them as her gift is enhanced hearing, and the family falls apart during Isabela's proposal dinner when it becomes clear that Luisa cannot lift the table, and an animal scurries away with a portion of Bruno's prophecy (00:52:26).

Later when Abuela and Mirabel return with Bruno to the Casita at the end of the film, they openly discuss the family's emotional and physical struggles and begin to rebuild their home. In addition to praising their family's differing abilities, Mirabel sings that "the stars don't shine, they burn / And the constellations shift / I think it's time you learn / You're more than just your gift" ("All of You" 2021), thus reminding them that their value is not tied to their gift alone; rather, it is who they are as a whole person that counts.

Finally, an appreciation for all forms of personality and types of mental well-being, symbolized through a rainbow of color, is reflected in Mirabel's dress. While other characters have more pronounced, singular identities at the start, Mirabel's dress reflects each of her family members through color and symbol. There is a candle that symbolizes Abuela, flowers for Isabela, a chameleon for Cousin Camilo, a hand lifting a weight to represent Luisa, a sun and cloud for aunt Pepa, musical notes for Dolores, *arepas* (a corn pancake) for Mirabel's mom Julieta, and animals for Antonio. The butterflies on Mirabel's dress represent not only her connection to the entire family but also that she may one day become the matriarch of the house; Mirabel and Abuela are followed by butterflies on numerous occasions, most notably at the end, and there are also several spots throughout the Casita where butterflies appear frequently (Smith 2022). The butterfly symbol also acts as a connection between Abuela and her lost husband Pedro, as he used to sing to a song to her entitled "*Dos Oruguitas*" ("Two Caterpillars"), a song about their family's rebirth and transformation, as well as hope for the future; his song further enhances the film's main theme of transformation as he sings, "It's your time to grow / To fall apart, to reunite / Wonders await you / Just on the other side / Trust they'll be there / And start to prepare / The way for tomorrow" (*"Dos Orguitas"* 2021). Sebastián Yatra, the performer of the song, was proud to point out that although the song was recorded in both Spanish and English, they kept the song in Spanish in all versions of the movie so that "even if you are listening to the movie in Chinese, when the part of 'Dos Oruguitas' comes in, you hear it in Spanish, which is the first time this has happened in the history of Disney movies" (quoted in Ratner-Arias 2022). Through its portrayal of a blend of positive feminine and masculine well-being, as well as its positive depiction of the family as they work through mental health challenges together, *Encanto* provides viewers with an incredibly uplifting story that pushes the potential for even greater female leadership and mental health portrayals in future Disney films, and, thereby, within cinema as a whole.

Conclusion

It is fitting that all these films tackle leadership and mental health challenges faced by young women as health organizations in North America continue to push for the destigmatization of mental health (Heflinger and Hinshaw 2010, 68). As Neira Piñeiro et al. suggest, "The emotional impact of cartoons is bound to influence the perception of minors and to determine their social learning too" (2021, 605); thus, these positive representations of gender, leadership, and mental health, often in song, are invaluable, especially given Disney's pervasive influence on popular culture. The Disney Company has made great strides to better project means to good mental health, as Neira Piñeiro et al. indicate that their "analysis … highlights that the most recent animation films have incorporated active, assertive, and independent protagonists who take control of their lives, even if that entails a clash with traditions" (615–16), and from here it is hopeful that Disney's future animated films featuring young female will continue to progress and develop in their depiction of mental health in a post-pandemic world (if such a dream is possible). Hard as it may have been to imagine only two decades ago, neo-Disneyism portrays young women as strong, creative leaders who work hard to maintain their mental well-being, evidence that indicates that representations of mental health, and working through challenges to maintain positive mental well-being, is becoming normalized in in Disney's animated films.

Bibliography

Ali, Asmaa Ibrahim. "The Development of Stereotypical Representations of Gender in Selected Disney Films: A Feminist Reading." *Journal of the Faculty of Education—University of Alexandria* 31 (2021): 223–38. <https://jealex.journ als.ekb.eg/article_159297_66f90c9ffc07792ce3079bb806310722.pdf>.

"All of You." Written by Lin-Manuel Miranda. Sung by Stephanie Beatriz and Cast for *Encanto*. 2021. <https://music.apple.com/ca/album/encanto-original-mot ion-picture-soundtrack/1594677532>.

Damsgaard, Janne Brammer, and Anita Jensen. "Music Activities and Mental Health Recovery: Service Users' Perspectives Presented in the CHIME Framework." *International Journal of Environmental Research and Public Health* 18, no. 12 (2021): 1–14. <https://doi.org/10.3390/ijerph18126638>.

"Disney Fans Are Obsessed with Luisa from *Encanto* but Where's the Merch?" *Yahoo! Movies*, January 24, 2022. <https://ca.movies.yahoo.com/disney-fans-obsessed-luisa-encanto-182200427.html>.

"*Dos Orguitas*" ("Two Caterpillars"). Written by Lin-Manuel Miranda. Sung by Sebastian Yatra for *Encanto*. 2021. <https://music.apple.com/gb/album/dos-oruguitas-from-encanto-single/1609633487>.

"The Family Madrigal." Written by Lin-Manuel Miranda. Sung by Stephanie Beatriz, Olga Merediz, and Cast for *Encanto*. 2021. <https://music.apple.com/ca/album/encanto-original-motion-picture-soundtrack/1594677532>.

Gray, Richard. "Did Disney Shape How You See the World?" British Broadcasting Corporation, July 31, 2019. <https://www.bbc.com/worklife/article/20190 724-did-disney-shape-how-you-see-the-world>.

Heflinger, Craig Anne, and Stephen P. Hinshaw. "Stigma in Child and Adolescent Mental Health Services Research: Understanding Professional and Institutional Stigmatization of Youth with Mental Health Problems and Their Families." *Administration and Policy in Mental Health and Mental Health Services Research* 37 (2010): 61–70. <https://doi.org/10.1007/s10488-010-0294-z>.

Hill, Cooper. "Elsa Was Originally *Frozen*'s Villain (& Had A Different Look)." *Screenrant*, August 11, 2019. <https://screenrant.com/frozen-elsa-original-vill ain-different-look/#:~:text=The%20Frozen%20story%20is%20loosely,ant agonist%20of%20the%20original%20story>.

Hollowell, Adam. "Chief Tui Makes Way: Moana, Misogyny, and the Possibility of a Profeminist Ethic." *Men and Masculinities* 24, no. 5 (2021): 760–79. <https:// doi.org/10.1177/1097184X20954265>.

"How Far I'll Go." Written by Lin-Manuel Miranda. Sung by Auli'I Cravalho for *Moana*. 2016. <https://music.apple.com/us/music-video/how-far-ill-go-from-moana/1593130833>.

"Lead the Way." Written and Sung by Jhené Aiko for *Raya and the Last Dragon*. 2021. <https://music.apple.com/ca/music-video/lead-the-way-from-raya-and-the-last-dragon/1556305827>.

"Mental Health 2020: Youth and Young Adults." *Nami* (National Alliance on Mental Health). 2022. <https://www.nami.org/mhstats>.

"Mental Health Learning Series." Canada School of Public Service (CSPS). Government of Canada. 2022. <https://www.csps-efpc.gc.ca/mental-health-eng.aspx>.

Neira Piñeiro, Maria del Rosario et al. "Female Leadership Represented in Animation for Children and the Sociocognitive Learning of 21st-Century Girls." *International Journal of Communication* 15 (2021): 605–24.

"The Next Right Thing." Written by Kristen Anderson-Lopez and Robert Lopez. Sung by Kristen Bell for *Frozen II*. 2019. <https://music.apple.com/us/album/the-next-right-thing/1487738280?i=1487738500>.

"Promoting Mental Health: Concepts, Emerging Evidence, Practice." World Health Organization (WHO) in collaboration with The University of Melbourne. Geneva: WHO, 2004. <https://www.who.int/mental_health/evidence/en/promoting_mhh.pdf>.

Ratner-Arias, Sigal. "Oscars 2022: Sebastián Yatra Calls *Encanto* a Gift from God." ABC News, February 10, 2022. <https://abcnews.go.com/Entert ainment/wireStory/oscars-2022-sebastin-yatra-calls-encanto-gift-god-82800 511#:~:text=NEW%20YORK%20%2D%2D%20Sebasti%C3%A1n%20Ya tra,film%20and%20best%20original%20music>.

Rebecchini, Lavinia. "Music, Mental Health, and Immunity." *Brain, Behavior, & Immunity. Health* 18 (2021): 1–6. <https://doi.org/10.1016/j.bbih.2021 100374>.

Seybold, Samantha L. "'It's Called a Hustle, Sweetheart': *Zootopia, Moana*, and Disney's (Dis) Empowered Postfeminist Heroines." *International Journal of Politics, Culture, and Society* 34, no. 1 (2020): 69–84. <https://doi.org/ 10.1007/s10767-019-09347-2>.

Silverman, Michael. *Music Therapy in Mental Health for Illness Management and Recovery*. 1st edn. Oxford: Oxford University Press, 2015.

Sirgy, M. Joseph. *Positive Balance: A Theory of Well-Being and Positive Mental Health*. 1st edn. Cham: Springer International Publishing, 2020. <https://doi.org/10.1007/978-3-030-40289-1>.

Smith, Katie Louise. "Encanto Fans Spot Incredible Easter Eggs on Mirabel's Dress." *Popbuzz*, January 7, 2022. <https://www.popbuzz.com/tv-film/news/encanto-easter-eggs-mirabel-dress/>.

"Suicidal Ideation at Record Levels Among Ontario Students." Centre for Addiction and Mental Health (CAMH), November 23, 2020. <https://www.camh.ca/en/camh-news-and-stories/suicidal-ideation-at-record-levels-among-ontario-students>.

"Surface Pressure." Written by Lin-Manuel Miranda. Sung by Jessica Darrow for *Encanto*. 2021. <https://music.apple.com/ca/album/encanto-original-motion-picture-soundtrack/1594677532>.

"Toxic Masculinity." Dictionary.com. 2022. <https://www.dictionary.com/browse/toxic-masculinity>.

"Try Everything." Written by Tor Hermansen, Mikkel Eriksen, and Sia Furler. Sung by Shakira for *Zootopia*. 2016. <https://music.apple.com/us/music-video/try-everything-from-zootopia/1445003400>.

Vargová, Veronika. "Time to Let It Go: Redefining Gender and Social Stereotypes in Disney's *Frozen*." Master's thesis, Czech Republic: Masaryk University, 2021.

"Waiting on a Miracle." Written by Lin-Manuel Miranda. Sung by Stephanie Beatriz for *Encanto*. 2021. <https://music.apple.com/ca/album/encanto-original-motion-picture-soundtrack/1594677532>.

Wasalamudalige, Hansini. "Encanto Artists Had to Fight Disney for Luisa's Fan-Favorite Muscular Frame." CBR.com, January 21, 2022. <https://www.cbr.com/disney-encanto-artists-fought-for-luisa-muscles/>.

"We Don't Talk About Bruno." Written by Lin-Manuel Miranda. Sung by Stephanie Beatriz and Cast for *Encanto*. 2021. <https://music.apple.com/ca/album/encanto-original-motion-picture-soundtrack/1594677532>.

"What Else Can I Do?" Written by Lin-Manuel Miranda. Sung by Stephanie Beatriz and Diane Guerrero for *Encanto*. 2021. <https://music.apple.com/ca/album/encanto-original-motion-picture-soundtrack/1594677532>.

Wulan, Sri, Nur Latifah, and Sofia Sahana Sitorus. "Development of the Trust Issue in the Movie *Raya and the Last Dragon*." *International Journal of English and Applied Linguistics (IJEAL)* 1, no. 2 (2021): 69–80. <https://doi.org/10.47709/ijeal.v1i2.1042>.

Yang Xiao, Ziqi Xiao, and Zhuyanyan Xue. "The Study on the Transformation of Disney Animated Films Based on Consumerism." *Advances in Social Science, Education and Humanities Research* 571 (2021): 608–13.

DALILA FORNI

11 New Gendered Representations in Contemporary Disney-Pixar Villains

Many Disney-Pixar films have come under fire by critics for their efforts to normalize bipolar gender to young viewers.[1] Some key features are associated with femininity or masculinity in a binary characterization: Girls and women are supposed to be beautiful, romantic, and domestic, while boys and men are supposed to be strong, heroic, and unemotional. The ideal is expressed in these films mostly through princesses and princes as two opposing poles forged by their genders (Forni 2019 and 2020).

Among those characters that indirectly deconstruct gender norms in Disney-Pixar films, villains—intended as characters in the story who oppose the hero or heroine—are the most powerful and intriguing figures as they confound Disney's gender stereotypes performing identities that differ from male and female standards. Even in classics, villains deconstruct gender norms and sometimes reinterpret gender canons through a queer or nonbinary approach such as Ursula in *The Little Mermaid* (1989). In relation to gender standards and social codes, antagonists have been presenting more daring personalities if compared to positive characters, and their gender identity is usually more fluid. Disney villains show off their personality through a theatrical and dramatic style that differs from social norms related to traditional portrayals of static masculinity and femininity. Thus, villains encourage viewers to challenge and rethink the supposed naturalness of gender norms (Griffin 2011, 73), and therefore, their representation in Disney-Pixar films exerts a strong impact on the social perception of gender, especially in such films designed to present gendered models and standards that should be followed (Forni 2019). That these nonnormative gender identities are presented as evil may foster a misleading message to young viewers: Villains are evil models not to be followed and they usually do not encourage an empathic contact or identification with young viewers. Therefore, their non-stereotypical identity is presented as a characteristic that should not be desired or imitated.

Villainesses v. Princesses

Villains are characters who oppose the hero or heroine and show evil intentions and/or actions. The hero or heroine is intended as the principal character in the story whose actions and intentions are usually positive, good (Campbell 1990). Very young audiences can easily identify with positive or negative intentions in most of the Disney-Pixar films because they are often marked by determined tropes that make them immediately decipherable and mirror Western social standards in their representation of gender identities. For instance, villains are usually associated with dark colors and settings, theatrical gestures and poses, or bodies that do not conform to beauty standards and gender canons. Princesses and heroines are clearly opposed to Disney villains, who perform deviant and non-traditional gender roles and features (Ayres 2003, 19; Wellman 2020, 2). This trend represents the opposition between evil and good, where evil is related to nonconformity (the villain) and good to conformity (the princess), both physically and psychologically such as Ursula who opposes Ariel in *The Little Mermaid*, both in her physical appearance and her behavior, as they are both depicted as nonconforming to social standards and ideals.

    Ironically, Disney female villains offer a more interesting and compelling image of femininity than do princesses: Villains are active characters, with precise objectives that go beyond marriage, and they often present a "diva" temper. Female villains are sometimes depicted as *femmes fatales*, which is to say, fascinating, mysterious, and transgressive women looking for power. These characters appear as fascinating despite their negative role in the story while, at the same time, their attitude is associated with evil and, for this reason, their behavior is meant to be rejected as it represents a negative model of femininity that is not to be followed. Princesses preserve the norm, with some alterations from the Renaissance era of Disney (the 1990s), while villains have been disrupting it starting from earlier full-length films (Putnam 2013, 151; Lester 2017, 195).

If on the one hand Disney princesses have been sharing specific beauty standards, then on the other hand villains are portrayed through contrasting characteristics. They are often ugly like Cinderella's stepsisters (1950) and Madam Mim in *The Sword in the Stone* (1963), old like the evil Queen/witch in *Snow White* (1937), overweight or curvy like Ursula in *The Little Mermaid* and Mother Goethel in *Tangled* (2010), or with asymmetrical and harsh features like Maleficent in *Sleeping Beauty* (1959) (Wellman 6). Although their appearance contrasts with Western standards of beauty, villains are particularly self-confident about their bodies and are often "preoccupied with their appearance, exhibiting a kind of vanity" (Li-Vollmer and LaPointe 2003, 102).

From the very start of Disney's full-length films, the Queen in *Snow White* offers an unconventional gender representation compared to Snow White. She wears dark-colored clothes that totally cover her body, showing just her face and hands. Her face presents sharp traits and heavy makeup: These elements create a contrast with the pure, naïve style chosen for Snow White and princesses' portrayals in general (Griffin 73; Wellman 6). Maleficent, in *Sleeping Beauty*, follows the same features both in her clothing and in her physical design as she presents a bony, emaciated face and very dark clothes covering her body. The dark colors of black, blue, green, or brown, in Western cultures, are often associated with aggression, rage, mourning, strain, and power (Wellman 6). Cruella de Vil in *One Hundred and One Dalmatians* (1961) shares the same physical and facial patterns, with extremely skinny traits and flat chest. Villains' portrayals nonverbally convey specific messages that further enrich their personality with negative auras, opposing them to positive, beautiful, and normative characters (5).

Similarly, *The Sword in the Stone* presents the character of Madam Mim, a short, ugly, old woman with purple hair. The witch displays her happiness in using her magic for evil purposes: She has the ability to change her body but sometimes prefers to make herself even uglier. When she turns herself into a beautiful woman, she does it for two main reasons: to charm and deceive her audience through her fake physical appearance. In her most beautiful form, she briefly flirts with Merlin and Arthur as a *femme fatale* but then goes back to her original form to shock the two men and the viewers with her real shape and traits, which do not conform to Western beauty standards. When Madam Mim yells, "I'm an ugly old creep!" she seems frustrated by her body, but she also seems proud and joyful because of her power to scare her enemies. Madam Mim performs transgressive behavior based on her body—used as a sexual weapon to defeat her enemies—and in doing so she opposes the virginal, gentle, and naïve portrayal of Disney princesses (Lester 202).

Another key characteristic of Disney villains is their voice and posture. Villains usually speak with "enormous style and panache" (Griffin 74), so that they often overshadow the main character. Their voices are high-pitched, cold, well-paused, and show superiority. The voice is sometimes accompanied by slow, elegant, sweeping movements and theatrical poses, with specific music that emphasizes their magnificence that offers the viewer stunning stage entrances, as Maleficent does when arriving at the King's party to which she was not invited (00:07:40). Villains walk slowly, purposefully, solemnly with posture that further highlights their importance, elegance, and, consequently, power. Movements further characterize Disney villains' personalities: Villains present dramatic, exaggerated gestures and their movements easily catch the viewers' attention thanks to their noticeable performances (Wellman 5). Cruella DeVil, for one, always smokes her long cigarettes and uses them as tools to give emphasis to her gestures (Griffin 73). Villains' dramatic call to attention is presented as an unpleasant characteristic, not to be imitated and should be linked to a bad personality.

As pointed out by Natalie Wellman, villains often see the main characters' beauty as something to envy (10–11). The Evil Queen in *Snow White* is jealous of her stepdaughter's beauty and looks for the mirror's approval to be sure of her own appearance, and Lady Tremaine, who is envious of Cinderella's beauty and kindness. Mother Gothel too seems to disapprove Rapunzel's beauty in a constant desire to overshade her. Significantly, all these figures are evil, manipulative stepmothers, women who are not related to nurturing and care: They not only deconstruct female standards, but they also revise the supposedly "natural" relation between femininity and innate motherhood.

Another important difference between princesses and female villains is that princesses appear smaller and present in submissive positions, while villainesses appear bigger or taller and present in dominating positions. Wellman provides the example of Rapunzel and Mother Gothel, where the former is often depicted while sitting on a chair, while the latter stands in front of her. Similarly, Ursula appears in a massive physical appearance, in strong contrast to Ariel's tiny body, and Lady Tremain looks much taller than Cinderella. Later films project similar contrasts as well: In *Brave* (2015) Merida is tinier than Mor'du, the bear; and in *The Princess and the Frog* (2009), Dr. Facilier is taller than Tiana. The characters' appearances create a power gap where princesses are usually not as physically strong as their evil counterparts, both male and female. As noted by Wellman, in many films princesses would not be able to defeat the villain on their own (12). A man's help is often essential to rescue the main character: Prince Charming saves Snow White, Cinderella, and Aurora; the Seven Dwarfs kill the Queen/witch, while Maui actively supports Moana in her fight with Te-Ka. The message given to young audiences is clear: "The only female characters within Disney films that are able to do things completely on their own are the villains. Consequently, girls who look up to the princesses are not seeing independent role models" (15).

Hegemonic Masculinities, Sissy Villains, and Drag Queens

Early Disney classics present only female villains: From 1937 to 1967, the only male villain in Disney films was Captain Hook in *Peter Pan* (1953) (Davis 2014, 189). The 1990s saw an increasing production of male villains: During the last decade of the twentieth century, most of the antagonists were men. In early films the hero represented the hegemonic man[2] and was opposed to an evil woman (*Snow White*; *Sleeping Beauty*; *Little Mermaid*, and so on); successively, the hegemonic masculinity of the hero was juxtaposed to the minor masculinity of the male villain such as in *Aladdin* (1992) and *The Lion King* (1994) (Al-Jbouri and Pomerantz 2020, 52). The relationship between villains and masculinity was complex and differed from the qualities related to female antagonists.

Some studies noted recurrent depictions of male villains, while female villains display a minor range of characteristics in relation to their look, as noted above, as being ugly, old, unattractive, and wear dark colors (Sharmin and Sattar 2018, 54). Reasons for being bad also differ: Female antagonists become villains for reasons such as jealousy, vanity, and inherent evil. These motives are far less present in male villains, whose motivators are mostly power and wealth. These representations of binary genders reassert persistent stereotypes to reinforce social gender perceptions. However, Wellman notices an evolution in female villains' reason to be evil: A recurrent tendency sees recent antagonists becoming bad because a man has taken something from them. In *Moana* (2016) Te-Fiti/Te-Ka had her heart stolen, while in *Tangled* (2010) Mother Goethel, although acting for vanity, sees her main tool to be young—Rapunzel—stolen by a man (13).

Some antagonists go back to hegemonic masculinities as they exhibit physical strength, violent behaviors, power, and extreme self-esteem (Al-Jbouri and Pomerantz 52). Gaston in *Beauty and the Beast* (1991) represents one of the most explicative examples of toxic masculinity: He is full of himself and shows off his masculine traits in a song entirely dedicated to himself. In the song, he highlights his physical appearance, his success with women, his love for hunting, and his superiority in the village. The same features are presented in characters like Shan Yu in *Mulan* (1998) and Clayton in *Tarzan* (1999).

However, other evil characters create a new archetype where the villain is effeminate. Meredith Li-Vollmer and Mark LaPointe give the examples of *Peter Pan*'s Captain Hook, Scar in *The Lion King*, Jafar in *Aladdin*, and Hades in *Hercules* (1997). These characters represent a different interpretation of what being male means: They show a drag-queen style, an excessive display of femininity that defines them as deviant, different, and, therefore, evil. So, in these films we see a hypermasculine hero punishing and defeating a womanish villain: The message conveyed is that men who do not adhere to specific male standards have to be ridiculed, punished, or marked as evil (52).

Scar represents a weak male figure if we consider his body; he repels the concept of heterosexual family and bonds and acts with elegance and swishing movements (Griffin 211). Similarly, Jafar communicates through theatrical movements and elegant gestures that could be associated with femininity, mostly if compared with Aladdin's behavior and appearance (143). In addition, Hook could be explored in relation to the figure of Father. Father presents some feminine qualities and gestures that are exaggerated by Hook, as noted by Adelia Brown: "Father stumbles about without a confident masculine gait, while Hook glides girlishly across the floor. Father worries a little too much about his cufflinks, while Hook dresses with impeccable style" (2021, 4). Even if Hook's clothes are related to traditional male clothes of the time, nowadays his outfit recalls a female style not only because of his pink shirt, the fluffy feathers in his hat, and his cape but also because of his melodramatic and exaggerated speaking and gestures (Griffin 76). These details amplify both his femininity and masculinity, giving the idea of a feminine man who is trying to perform a masculine role (4). Sean Griffin states that "how theatrically [he performs] gender roles [indicates that] the naturalness of gender can be called into question" (73).

Another example of an effeminate villain is Governor John Ratcliffe in *Pocahontas* (1994). In his first appearance, he dresses in pink and purple, shows pigtails tied with pink bows, wears a pink feathered boa, dances, and drinks tea effeminately, putting his finger up. He contrasts with two the virile figures of John Smith, the male hero of the story; and Kocoum, the Indian warrior (Putnam 157). Again, the queer overtone chosen to depict a villain fosters a negative vision of minorities and social differences: "Rather than hiding this [queer] potential leaning in the character, … Disney chose to highlight the behavior, taking pains only to portray it as villainous. Disney could portray queerness without risking their moral reputation, so long as that queerness involved objective harm and unquestionable evil" (Brown 6).

Queerness[3] is not exclusively related to antagonists labelled as male. One of the most emblematic villains often interpreted through a queer perspective is Ursula in *The Little Mermaid*. She is partially human and partially octopus, is overweight, and presents very large breasts, wears heavy makeup, and her lips and nails are long, painted red. These elements construct a female figure, but her traits are so exaggerated that together with her deep voice and her flirting movements they "suggest something much more masculinized" (Putnam 154). Indeed, her gestures and movements resemble a theatrical show: She swings and shakes her hips with slight sexual overtones. It is no coincidence that Ursula was inspired by a drag-queen star, Divine. This choice was intentional, and codirector John Musker, who worked at the character's design, explained that he "really [wanted] to get some of Divine's big, campy, overweight diva" (Brown 7). Ursula was modelled looking at a real queer person, even if most of the young viewers would not have recognized her (quoted in Griffin 146); however, this queer-coding collocates the character once more in the evil side of the plot, connecting queerness to evil (Brown 7). The drag performance created by Ursula develops on different levels. Besides her first, queer appearance, the villainess impersonates a beautiful feminine character who tries to marry Prince Eric, break Ariel's romance, and gain King Triton's powers. In this case too, Ursula's drag is presented as negative, evil:

> She laughs maniacally as she transforms, emphasizing the villainy of dressing up as a feminine woman. When her disguise dissolves at the wedding, she turns back into her masculine self, with rolls of fat bursting out of the wedding dress. A bigger, masculine character emerging from a feminine dress resembles a negative perception of drag queens, and the dark lighting and horrified reactions portray the behavior as evil. (7)

Cinderella's stepsisters use a similar approach. Their masculine image is strongly opposed to Cinderella's beauty and gentleness, to her feminine figure. Drizella and Anastasia have no breasts and look square-bodied: "The complete absence of their breasts makes them appear both mannish and non-reproductive, contrasting strongly with Cinderella and other princess figures, with their heterosexual reproductive agendas" (Putnam 152). Moreover, they have big, round eyes, round noses, big brows, and extremely big feet: Their faces and bodies are boyish and unpleasant, unfeminine for Western beauty standards so that "with their flat chests, huge bustles, and awkward curtsies, [the stepsisters] could as well be read as comic drag acts in this balletic fantasy" (Bell et al. 1995, 20).

Another example is Cruella DeVil, who displays male attributes— both in her physical being as well as in her personality—and does it through an exaggeration that resembles a caricature (Maltin 1987, 98), thus deconstructing feminine standards in a villain that could be easily turned into a male character. This point is noted by Griffin as well, who states that Cruella's inflections "seem to be attempts by the character to show her astounding chic and cultured femininity. Yet, in her attempts to be the epitome of feminine glamour (which is why she wants the Dalmatian coat that spurs the narrative), she consistently and quite hilariously points out the concept of gender-as-role-playing" (74). Cruella clearly differs from any Disney princess, but also from her female counterpart, Anita, who displays a more domestic and gentle kind of femininity.

Disney filmography has presented a few queer characters like LeFou in *Beauty and the Beast* (2017); however, many characters have been interpreted both by critics and viewers through a queer lens. In particular, villains often undergo a queer interpretation (Brown 6). Many Disney villains share some characteristics with queerness and specifically with drag queens as they often overperform and transgress gender norms.

However, their gender transgression gives a prefigured interpretation of their behavior as well: "By performing gender outside of normative expectations, individuals may therefore draw into question much more than their gender: in a culture with firmly naturalized constructions of gender, gender transgression may also cast doubt on a person's competence, social acceptability, and morality" (Li-Vollmer and LaPointe 91). Thus, not all villains possess or display queer characteristics, but most of the queer characters are villains: Disney sends a specific message related to what is considered noncanonical, usually associated with evil (Putnam 149). Another interesting fact is that villains are usually depicted alone, without partners or close friends; they do not have love stories or other relationships, except for their sidekicks, who are usually highly subordinated. Queer and/or evil characters are usually outsiders with no affection for any other character; they totally stand in their own, rejected from society. Ursula has no friends except her sidekicks, two moray eels, and she is exiled from King Triton's royal palace. Cruella DeVil lives alone in a mansion, Hell Hall, far from the city. Maleficent lives in her castle with her henchmen and a raven as a friend. Villains are depicted as lonely, nonconforming characters that are not included into society, outcasts that will not stimulate identification with young viewers because of their diversity.

Recent Trends in Heroines and Villains

The 1990s offer a first change in the construction of Disney princesses/ heroines. Figures such as Ariel, Belle, Mulan, Jasmine, and Pocahontas present new traits like agency, willfulness, independency, and wisdom (Lester 196). Then, after a decade where lead characters were mainly male, Disney returned to female protagonists with films such as *The Princess and the Frog, Tangled, Brave*, and *Frozen* (2013) These films further work on a new approach to femininity: New, positive female relationships are considered such as between a biological mother and daughter or between sisters (Wellman 4).

Currently, Disney-Pixar films are trying to adapt old tropes to current times, changing their main figures' physical aspect, behavior, and attitude. New bodies or new skin colors and traits are presented, such as embodied by Mirabel in *Encanto* (2021), Miguel in *Coco* (2017), or Tiana in *The Princess and the Frog*, and so on. This transformation is also occurring through a series of live-action films that are deconstructing gender roles for both heroes and villains. For example, princesses show new empower-ment, usually lacking in the original, animated version, while antagonists are often given a backstory so as to understand the reasons why they acted as villains. Consequently, the definition of what is good or evil is on the wane: *Moana* (2016) constructs a villain who, at the end of the narrative, proves to be good. Princesses or princes and villainesses or villains are not black and white anymore, but they share some in-the-middle shades (Wellman 12–13).

Regardless of gender, antagonists had a key transformation at the end of the twentieth century. Jens Kjeldgaard-Christiansen and Sarah Helene Schmidt divide villains into two main categories, partially chrono-logical: overt and covert villains. Initially, overt villains were more common as they were portrayed and perceived as deviant characters right from the beginning of the film. Their villainy was mainly conveyed by their phys-ical, nontraditional appearance: They were extremely fat or skinny, ugly, nonconforming to beauty canons. Moreover, they often spoke with low pitches and sadistic laughter to highlight their attitude. They were also linked to specific minorities in order to highlight their anomaly inside the plot or linked to queer or foreign stereotypes, so that "they represent salient aspects of groups and individuals that diverge from an idealized norm" (2019, 6). In addition, villains announced their evil intentions from their first appearance in the movie.

Recent films present a different pattern because most of their villains do not overtly display their evil intentions. An exception is Mother Goethel, but many other antagonists do not present clear signs of evil and the viewer is not immediately encouraged to suspect their wickedness. Thus, Kjeldgaard-Christiansen and Schmidt define them as covert villains (2) and give the following as examples:

> The anthropomorphized ewe, Bellwether, from *Zootopia* [(2016)] is, so to speak, a wolf in sheep's clothing. As the right hand of the mayor, a literal lion, Bellwether feigns submissiveness and good intentions. She eventually reveals herself as the mastermind of a scheme to cull the city of Zootopia's predator population, including her own boss. She wants his power. Similar arcs—a benign-seeming character turns out to be the film's true villain—also feature in *Wreck-It Ralph* (2012), *Frozen* and *Big Hero 6* (2014). (6)

In order to highlight recurrent structures in Disney contemporary villains and examine their evolution in relation to gender norms, the analysis offered by Kjeldgaard-Christiansen and Schmidt is particularly useful. In their opinion, some villains are characterized by four recurrent elements, defined as "non-stigmatizing antipathetic cues": predatory likeness, dark environing, angry expressivity, and oblique communication of feeling. These elements are not linked to minorities and victimized groups. Through these attributes, films avoid social prejudice and do not harm progressive sensibilities in their representations of villains (9). Predatory likeness associates the villain to one or more predators through physical similarities, producing fear or disgust in viewers. Many villains turn into animalistic predators. For instance, Jafar transforms into a snake and Maleficent turns into a dragon. Disney villains are mainly presented in dark environments, creating a fearful scenario. For example, Lady Tremaine is presented lying in a dark bedroom as an obscure figure and, similarly, Mother Goethel is often depicted in dark spaces. Angry expressions usually produce fearful responses in viewers, encouraging a sense of untrustworthiness. Anger creates a sort of warning: The villain is representing a threat, and anger is their default condition, mostly in classic Disney films. Last, through oblique communication an emotion is shown directly to the audience, for instance, through unnatural or unmotivated measures, such as exaggerated gestures or facial expressions, or monologues where to give specific information about past or future plans. These components act as a clue to unravel the antagonist's real intentions.

Analysis of Ten Case Studies

Disney-Pixar movies from 2012 to 2021 notably exhibit a different kind of villain than in earlier films, reflecting changing attitudes toward gender and diversity. Of these, the following 10 films illustrate this change: *Wreck-It Ralph* with King Candy, *Brave* with Mor'du, *Big Hero 6* with Yoki, *The Good Dinosaur* with Thunderclap (2015), *Zootopia* with Miss Bellwether, *Moana* with Te-Ka (2016), *Coco* with Ernesto De La Cruz (2017), *Raya and the Last Dragon* with Namaari (2021), *Luca* with Ercole (2021), and *Encanto* with (Abuela Alma Madrigal (2021).[4]

Out of ten main characters, one in each film, six of them are overtly "male," while four are "female." Female villains were mostly opposed to female heroines, and male villains to male heroes, with the only exception of Mor'du, opposed to Merida in *Brave*. This intra-gender fight further highlights different gender performances between good and evil characters. Moreover, villains were divided into covert and overt, following Kjeldgaard-Christiansen and Schmidt's definition, and presented very similar trends: Five out of ten characters were overt—three males (Thunderclap, Mor'du, and Ercole) and two females (Namaari and Te-Ka), and five were covert—again, three males (Yoki, Ernesto, and King Candy) and two females (Alma Madrigal and Dawn Bellwether) (Kjeldgaard-Christiansen and Schmidt 2).

Some villains perform traditional gender roles both regarding masculinity and femininity. Male villains present one or more elements usually related to toxic masculinity, such as strong and virile bodies (Mor'du), bossy leadership (Ercole), inability to express emotions (Yoki), and overambitious traits with an obsession for power (Ernesto). Female villains with traditional gender identities exhibit qualities often related to femininity, such as being gentle, kind, harmless (Dawn Bellwether), and showing strong love but also anxieties for family (Abuela Alma Madrigal). The two conventional female villains, despite their evident differences from each other, both have been created with traditional physical aspects and clothes, like a long dress, a black mourning shawl, and pearl earrings for Abuela Alma Madrigal, and a black jacket and gray and pink skirt for Dawn Bellwether.

In their gender identity, villains that present canonical gender models are more common than noncanonical ones. In regard to physical appearance, dressing, gesture, and personality traditionally prescribed to polarized genders, seven out of ten antagonists presented gender norms (Mor'Du or Dawn Bellwether) and three of them nontraditional characteristics. Namaari can be considered nontraditional both for her physical appearance (short hair and muscular figure and clothes not marked by gender) and her personality (strong, active, a leader). Although these traits partially belong to Raya too, Namaari contrasts with the main female character as she visually performs different gender dynamics that make the villain appear more masculine and more anti-canonical. Te-Ka can be considered nontraditional for similar reasons: Her traits go beyond gender expectations as she is depicted as a lava monster that could be easily defined as male as well. The nontraditional King Candy wears nonconventional clothes and light colors and apparently manifests a gentle, benevolent personality.

Another aspect of neo-Disney genderfication with villains can be identified by their settings, which are quite diversified, unlike in early films with dark elements when presenting a villain, both male and female. Little children were left in no doubt at how evil was Maleficent in *Sleeping Beauty* for her anger was always reinforced by thunder and lightning. However, in the recent *Encanto*, Alma Madrigal acts in different spaces, but when she is first presented at the beginning of the movie, she is represented in Mirabel's room with feeble light and dark undertones (00:02:57). A very common strategy with the latest covert villains is to place them in neutral or sunny places when they are considered good by the viewer/character, and then move them in darker, obscure settings when they come out as villains or act as villains (Bellwether, Yoki, Ernesto, and King Candy). Following a similar strategy, when the latest overt villains reach the climax of their actions, bright places are replaced by darker atmospheres: Ercole acts in Portorosso, a sunny city, but the last duel between the villain and the main characters is depicted in a rainy, gray context (01:13:50). No specific gender-based differences were found in relation to this aspect, which goes back to older Disney films and helps convey a specific atmosphere when dealing with dangerous situations and evil characters. Thus, if villains were immediately recognizable in earlier Disney films, viewers now assist to a multifaceted dilemma about what is perceived as good or evil, a dilemma that is conveyed through different environments and traits that deconstruct canonical villain types. *Zootopia* offers an effective example: Nick Wilde, a fox, should be the main villain being that Judy is a bunny and foxes are known to eat rabbits, but Nick becomes partner and best friends with her. So, heroes and villains both present more complex personalities, displaying both good and bad features and their portrayal evolves following a new perception of what is socially considered positive or negative (Campbell; Orrin and Berger 2004).

The villains in these 10 films present a variety of characteristics and bodies. Three out of 10 villains are (or are directly related to) animals, from Nyctosaurus Thunderclap to white sheep Bellwether, up to Mor'du, mostly portrayed in his bear form. In addition, three villains are old or middle-aged (Alma Madrigal, King Candy, and Robert) and show typical and realistic traits of seniority, such as wrinkles or gray hair and old-fashioned attire. These aspects are far less highlighted, far less caricatured if compared to previous films, where old, evil characters were portrayed as incredibly ugly and repulsive, like *Snow White*'s Queen in her witch form and Madam Mim in *The Sword and the Stone*. A new sensibility about old age is emerging, portraying characters that go beyond fixed labels to present multifaceted identities. However, considering beauty standards, even if villains are not necessarily portrayed as ugly, positive characters still tend to be more attractive according to contemporary cultural standards, to enlist the audience's attention and sympathy: Viewers are encouraged to identify with and support characters that adhere to aesthetic standards and moral values, while villains are given nonstandard qualities related to appearance and personality.

Other villains display heterogeneous gendered bodies: Namaari counteracts female standards with her agender physicality, while Ernesto presents canonical, virile masculinity. In *Luca*, Ercole, despite his toxic behavior, shows an atypical body, totally disconnected from virility as he is small, thin, physically fragile. Compared to Stella's father, Massimo, who physically relates to masculine standards, with a huge body, big muscles, tattoos, thick moustache, and eyebrows; Ercole appears much less virile in his visual image but is far crueler in his attitude. These two opposing models reveal a new depiction of masculine characters: Ercole looks harmless, but hides an evil personality, while Massimo may look potentially dangerous, but his attitude is calm, benevolent, warm. Following a new common direction, villains (both overt and covert, both male and female) often create a contrast between an inoffensive appearance and sometimes dismantle gender standards, like Ercole. They operate with evil intentions and exhibit a sadistic personality. The misleading, innocent appearance is the reason why power gaps are not so common as in previous films, where villains sometimes appeared physically bigger, stronger, or more powerful in their postures. A clear example is Dawn Bellwether who is characterized by a tiny physicality and wears elegant and old-fashioned clothes. Even if she is presented as an advocate for Judy, she turns out to be the main villain, in contrast with her small size and her innocent appearance, further symbolized by her animal species, the ewe, known for its meekness. Regarding colors, dark shades are still presented, both in overt and covert villains: Alma Madrigal wears a long, dark red dress with a black mourning shawl. Yoki wears a black coat and gloves, with a white kabuki mask with red markings, clearly evoking blood and rage, and yellow eyes that could remind fierce animals. Mor'du is characterized by dark colors both in his human and animal shape. Thunderclap and Te-Ka present dark tones as well. However, light-colored clothes are selected too: Ernesto wears completely white clothes, such as a white jacket and a white hat; Turbo wears a white racing suit, although his appearance changes when he is presented as King Candy, who wears a red papillon, a purple tailcoat, yellow trousers, and a white shirt, so as to disguise his evil intentions through a harmless appearance.

Moreover, most of the villains wear everyday outfits: Some of them are covert villains that change their everyday clothes when turning into the antagonist, like Yoki, while others always present the same ordinary look, like Ercole Visconti or Dawn Bellwether. The same goes for Alma Madrigal and Ernesto, who present typical clothes of their cultures. Thus, new villains' clothes present many different aspects but seem to lose some of the elegance and queerness related to older antagonists, previously mentioned in the chapter, to select everyday outfits that put them in close relation to everyday life and make it more difficult to identify the villain right from the beginning of the film. Overall, physical appearance becomes more and more variegated, presenting different traits, bodies, and clothes from several cultures (Asian, Mexican, Colombian, Italian, and so on). This aspect applies both to villains and heroes or heroines. Villains are not portrayed as a different social or ethnic group with elements that create a contrast with the protagonist but share the same cultural background with the main character, erasing the past link between diversity and evil. If movies as *Snow White* or *Sleeping Beauty* presented a strong visual contrast between positive and negative characters and did it displaying villains as eccentric and peculiar in their clothes and manners, then new villains generally fit in a variegated group of people and do not emerge so strongly. Many characters could not be labelled as villains simply by looking at their appearance. Disney-Pixar gives its viewers a new message: Evil may be found anywhere and does not necessarily match with specific personal or physical characteristics.

Each of the villains have strong personalities, desires, and abilities. Antagonists are often relentless, savage, selfish, harsh, and express emotions related to rage in violent ways or through indirect clues, such as frowning or showing their teeth. Mor'du is one of the clearest examples, but also less ferocious characters, as Namaari or Ercole, show their teeth to express anger. Nevertheless, some characters present contrasting aspects of their personalities during the narrative: Bellwether initially appears cheerful, shy, innocent, but when her evil plan is discovered, she reveals her true nature. She is selfish, heartless, revengeful, arrogant, clever but manipulative, and racist (Beaudine et al. 2017, 231). Similarly, King Candy gives the impression of being a funny old man, a positive and warm character, but he is actually selfish, jealous, vindictive, and violent. Namaari is depicted as a shy girl when she is young but becomes hot-tempered and pitiless when she grows up. She is portrayed as an active, strong, and loyal leader and her character could not be considered totally bad, as she is moved by reasons similar to Raya's. In *Coco*, Ernesto initially appears as a charming, encouraging, sensible, and intelligent man, but he successively demonstrates to be extremely selfish, overambitious, and evil. Yoki presents a similar evolution: At the beginning he is a smart professor, he loves science and robotics, he is good-hearted, but successively becomes revengeful, selfish, and cruel. However, Yoki demonstrates to be a more complex figure as he commonly manifests his moral dilemmas, understanding the impact of his action on other people. Other characters (mostly overt villains) do not evolve in the narrative and stay negative. For instance, right from the beginning, Ercole is presented as a selfish, bossy, proud, and materialistic boy.

If female villains have been encouraging new interpretations related to gender norms, showing innovative characteristics for femininity as agency and leadership, then several male villains are based on hegemonic masculinities that are difficult to deconstruct. For instance, although Ercole does not visually represent toxic masculinity, his traits adhere to this concept. He fears what is different and wishes to kill the sea monsters as they symbolize diversity. In his racist, close-minded attitude and aversion to diversity, he resembles Gaston from *Beauty and the Beast*. Like Gaston, he is not given a backstory to explain his unpleasant attitude. Another character who represents toxic masculinity is Mor'du, in his human form, whose actions are extremely violent, and his appearance goes back to a canonical standard of masculinity. Furthermore, *Coco* offers one of the most complex representations of male identity. Ernesto De La Cruz represents hegemonic masculinity both considering his physical appearance (body, stature) and his personality (desire for power, bossy attitude). He is opposed to Miguel, an emotional boy who deconstructs gender standards, and to Hector, who represent a very different male identity:

> De la Cruz's masculinity (like Gaston's in Beauty in the Beast) is intertwined with his villainy, portrayed by his willingness to use physical and social assets to maintain the illusion of his success .... While de la Cruz is motivated by ambition, Hector is motivated by the love of his family. Hector's nonhegemonic masculinity makes Coco's representations of manhood unique in how Hector embodies a thickly described

lifeworld with nuance and gender relativity.... Hector presents an alternative masculinity that is both heroic and vulnerable; principled but flawed. (Al-Jbouri and
Pomerantz 57–58)

As these elements demonstrate, contemporary villains present multiple
traits. Most of them are based on recurrent qualities (aggressiveness,
egoism, violent attitudes, and so on). If compared to the past, many
stories focus on the evolution of the antagonist, for instance, telling how
a character became evil or how he or she chose to be good, understanding
his or her actions. In the sample, villains are not simply cruel: They
became evil for a reason and consequently their personality undergoes
an evolution through the plot. Again, characters are more complex and
explored in depth: Evil and good are not opposed features, but both can
be found in different characters and for different reasons. The most recurrent motif is power (four characters: Thunderclap, Dawn Bellwether,
Ercole, and Mor'du), followed by popularity (Ernesto, King Candy), protect and preserve their family or people (Alma Madrigal and Namaari),
and revenge/rage after a loss (Te-Ka, whose heart was stolen, and Yokai,
whose daughter was killed). Thus, power and popularity are motives for
being evil for mostly male characters, while protecting a family or group
of people is exclusively female, going back to traditional female standards.

Some characters are moved by reasons that are not merely evil. For
example, Alma Madrigal has no real intention of harming her family. She
could be defined as a villain only because of her antagonistic attitude against
Mirabel and because of her calculating, programming, strict character. The
film clearly tells the story of Alma's past traumas, explaining the reasons
why she is so worried about her family and her *casita*. At the end of the
film, she admits her faults and tries to find a new balance with her relatives.
Alma rediscovers the true value of family, forgetting her obsession for magic
and talents. Alma represents the culmination of a new Disney tendency
that sees the villain as a character to be redeemed, a character whose true
nature has to be discovered, as in the case of Te-Ka.

Another key point in the analysis of villains is how the films end
and what antagonists do when the story is over. This component allows
giving a moral or educative perspective on evil figures, whose punishment is quite indicative of how other characters, but also society, look at

them. Villains could be killed, punished, or admitted in a group, they may evolve during the narrative and understand the implications of their evil actions. In the sample, just one villain is killed at the end of the narrative, King Candy in his virus form. King Candy is one of the few cases where villains die in recent films, together with Dr. Facilier in *The Princess and the Frog* and Mother Goethel in *Tangled*, who were not considered in the sample. For what concerns other characters, Thunderclap is carried downstream in a river but survives, while Ernesto is crushed by a giant bell, but as he is already dead, he is presumably not damaged. Other antagonists admit their guilt or make amends and are accepted as good characters, like Alma Madrigal or Namaari, or end up in prison, like Dawn Bellwether or Yoki (who admits his faults and shows regret but is punished with prison anyway). In the other two cases, the villain's spirit or true nature is released, as in Mor'du and Te-Ka, who are liberated from their torment and portrayed as not-so-negative characters at the end of the film. Considering this aspect, there are no specific gender differences in the selected sample, as male and female villains face similar conclusions. Women appear to be more willing to admit their faults, but the sample was too small to detect a consistent inclination.

The Disney Villain of the Future

Disney-Pixar is working on characters who are considered and depicted as complex human beings rather than simply male or female representations (Al-Jbouri and Pomerantz 56). Villains are no exception and engage in different actions regardless of gender, a feature already present in older films, which saw bad characters as more open to gender fluidity. However, some traits are evolving: If in previous films villains were the most extrovert and nonconforming to gender expectations, including performing queerness, this element was not found as strongly in the contemporary reference sample of 10 selected films. This phenomenon does not mean that the antagonists no longer revise gender norms, but their transgression has become less eccentric and peculiar, leading the villain toward less eclectic performances in comparison to the past. Villains are now much more tied to daily life, and their emotional and personal spheres are more important than aesthetic. Their psychological depth expands while their visual richness flattens considering queerness and transgression. This phenomenon might be connected to postmodernism: Its influence on Disney films lead to a different construction of characters that now avoid essentialism in order to present a larger variety of qualities and traits.

The evolution of villains must be compared to the transformations of the protagonists. For example, with regard to femininity, Disney-Pixar is proposing more modern and innovative models, giving new characteristics to its heroines and princesses who are no longer calm and gentle, but determined, active, bold, with new goals. The contrast with the strong personalities of the villainesses is now softened, and the gap between good and bad characters is less evident. The villainesses no longer stand out for their anti-canonical determination precisely because they are juxtaposed with characters who are moving in this direction, dismantling the female dichotomy between good-passive and bad-active. Judy from *Zootopia* has great ambitions and is dynamic, resolute, determined, characteristics that outline her nemesis too, Bellwether. The same goes for Raya or Merida, who follow precise goals and desires.

Furthermore, Disney's villains are supposed to be models not to be imitated. Even in the past, when they represented queerness, they were presented as reproachable, not to be followed, despicable even if fascinating. Today, the characters in the selected films tend to represent a kind of wickedness that is inherent and hidden in everyday life, more distant from attitudes and identities considered deviant and eccentric. Some films hide the villain behind misleading everyday aspects, such as Bellwether's sweet appearance; other films, such as *Coco* or *Luca*, use the villain to obscure and criticize overly traditional and harmful models, such as toxic masculinity, in favor of a more sensitive character. Others use the villain to enact a deconstruction of the canon, as in *Raya*, where the villain appears more fluid than the protagonist. When villains have aesthetic peculiarities, these are related to the context, which has been opened up in recent films to multiple cultural representations. Thus, it is not the villain who is classified as different in reference to ethnicity, an accent, or a particular attire, but these characteristics are integrated into the population described in the story, thereby being more realistic. Further, what Kjeldgaard-Christiansen and Schmidt called "non-stigmatizing antipathetic cues" (1) are increasingly recurring: To emphasize the badness of a character, clues are given such as expressions of anger, dark atmospheres, and references to dangerous animals like predators, factors that have nothing to do with a specific discrimination related to race or gender.

Many trends can be detected, and while Disney-Pixar films continue to present villains that subvert the gender norms, this subversion is less conspicuous and less in contrast to the positive figures of the story. Furthermore, if queer characters seemed inherently evil, many contemporary antagonists present background stories that can explain where their temperament comes from, giving depth to these characters as well, resisting prefixed labels.

Bibliography

Al-Jbouri, Elizabeth, and Shauna Pomerantz. "A New Kind of Monster, Cowboy, and Crusader? Gender Hegemony and Flows of Masculinities in Pixar Animated Films." *Boyhood Studies* 13, no. 1 (2020): 43–63.

Ayres, Brenda. "The Wonderful World of Disney: The World That Made the Man and the Man That Made the World." In *The Emperor's Old Groove: Decolonizing Disney's Magic Kingdom*, edited by Brenda Ayres, 15–25. New York: Peter Lang, 2003.

Beaudine, Gregory, Osibodu Oyemolade, and Aliya Beavers. "Disney's Metaphorical Exploration of Racism and Stereotypes: A Review of Zootopia." *Comparative Education Review* 61, no. 1 (2017): 227–34.

Bell, Elizabeth, Linda Haas, and Laura Sells, eds. *From Mouse to Mermaid: The Politics of Film, Gender, and Culture*. Bloomington: Indiana University Press, 1995.

Brown, Adelia. "Hook, Ursula, and Elsa: Disney and Queer-Coding from the 1950s to the 2010s." Baltimore, MD: Johns Hopkins University, 2021.

Campbell, Joseph. *The Hero with a Thousand Faces*. New York: Harper and Row, 1990.

Connell, Raewyn. *Masculinities*. Stanford, CA: Stanford University Press, 2005.

Davis, Amy. *Good Girls and Wicked Witches: Women in Disney's Feature Animation*. Eastleigh, UK: John Libbey, 2006.

————. *Handsome Heroes & Vile Villains: Men in Disney's Feature Animation.* Bloomington: Indiana University Press, 2014.

Forni, Dalila. "Genere e Cartoni Animati. La Formazione dell'Immaginario Femminile attraverso i Cartoon." In *Le Donne si Raccontano. Autobiografia, Genere e Formazione del Sé,* edited by Simonetta Ulivieri, 405–16. Pisa: ETS, 2019.

————. "Il Cinema d'Animazione per l'Infanzia e l'Adolescenza. Filoni Narrativi tra Studi Cinematografici e Sguardi D'autore." In *Frontiere. Nuovi Orizzonti della Letteratura per l'Infanzia,* edited by Maria Teresa Trisciuzzi, 109–30. Pisa: ETS, 2020.

Griffin, Sean P. *Tinker Belles and Evil Queens: The Walt Disney Company from the Inside Out.* New York: New York University Press, 2011.

Jagose, Annamarie. *Queer Theory: An Introduction.* New York: New York University Press, 1996.

Kimmel, Michael, ed. *The Politics of Manhood.* Philadelphia, PA: Temple University Press, 1994.

Kjeldgaard-Christiansen, Jens, and Sarah Helene Schmidt. "Disney's Shifting Visions of Villainy from the 1990s to the 2010s: A Biocultural Analysis." *Evolutionary Studies in Imaginative Culture* 3, no. 2 (2019): 1–16.

Lester, Catherine. "Frozen Hearts and Fixer Uppers: Villainy, Gender, and Female Companionship in Disney's *Frozen.*" In *Discussing Disney,* edited by Amy Davis, 193–216. Bloomington: Indiana University Press, 2017.

Li-Vollmer, Meredith, and Mark LaPointe. "Gender Transgression and Villainy in Animated Film." *Popular Communication* 1, no. 2 (2003): 89–109.

Maltin, Leonard. *Of Mice and Magic: A History of American Animated Cartoons.* New York: Plume, 1987.

Orrin, E. Klapp, and Arthur Asa Berger. *Heroes, Villains, & Fools. The Changing American Character.* New York: Routledge, 2004.

Putnam, Amanda. "Mean Ladies: Transgendered Villains in Disney Films." In *Diversity in Disney Films: Critical Essays on Race, Ethnicity, Gender, Sexuality and Disability,* edited by Johnson Cheu, 147–62. Jefferson, NC: McFarland, 2013.

Sharmin, Tania, and Sanyat Sattar. "Gender Politics in the Projection of Disney Villains." *Journal of Literature and Art Studies* 8, no. 1 (2018): 53–57.

Wellman, Natalie. "Disney's Portrayal of Women: An Analysis of Female Villains and Princesses." *Concordia Journal of Communication Research* 7, no. 1 (2020): 1–20.

12 Maleficent's Rage

The animated *Sleeping Beauty* (1959) introduced Disney's audience to a malevolent being who arrives uninvited at Princess Aurora's christening, full of anger and vindictiveness for the slight. The black-cloaked, horned woman is an enchantress who dooms an innocent girl-child to a living death: Aurora must sleep until kissed by her true love. Usually interested only in the innocent child's outcome and a happy ending, viewers of the film rarely question who the enchantress is and why she is so full of rage. In the live-action creation *Maleficent* (2014), the viewer is confronted with a dark fantasy narrative that investigates her character to create a fully realized being rather than a caricature that allows the viewer to re-vision the feminist potential in the new adaptation.

Perhaps Maleficent was simply righteously angry, not at the lack of invitation, but with the assumption that one life has more value than another, or that perceived evil deserves alienation and punishment while unproven innocence is assured of protection in Disney's kingdom. Following the idea borrowed from Ann Heilmann and Mark Llewellyn on neo-Victorianism, here neo-Disney might also be *"self-consciously engaged with the act of (re)interpretation, (re)discovery and (re)vision"* (2010, 4; emphasis in original), or at least as a critical reader of the film, one might find value in doing so. Georges Letissier, in his review of their work, reminds us that "the prefix 'neo,' when used in conjunction with genre, means new, modified, and fostering more or less radical changes" (2016, n.p.) to the original narrative(s); certainly, *Maleficent* is a radical undertaking in relation to Disney's previous tale.

Reinterpreting folklore is Disney business and the story of a sleeping young woman arises from its earliest inceptions as *La Belle au Bois Dormant* or *Dornröschen*, and its inclusions in the narrative *Perceforest* (14th C), Giambattista Basile's *The Pentamerone* (1634), The Grimm Brothers' *Little*

Briar Rose (1812), and Charles Perrault's *La Belle au Bois Dormant* (1697) or its translation into dance in *The Sleeping Beauty* ballet by Pyotr Tchaikovsky and Marius Petipa (1890). In all of these iterations, the narrative contains a princess who falls into a nonvoluntary sleep just as she enters young womanhood. *Sleeping Beauty* is Disney's version of the heteronormative love story between Aurora and her charming Prince Phillip who seeks to free her from her sleeping spell with his sword of virtue. The patriarchal conventions are clear; a young virginal woman can only be saved by a young man of honor, prestige, and power. Fairy-tale scholars understand that these tales have been told, historically, for a purpose where they are "a form of social education" wherein they "imagine dilemmas and offer a range of permissible solutions, leveling socially acceptable and unacceptable behavior, demarcating good and evil, exploring existential questions, and binding the teller and the audience into a common understanding of community identity," which is why it is important to "pay close attention to what stories people are telling our children" (Justice 2014, 194).

Sleeping Beauty has been through continual transmedia adaptation since she first appeared. Most viewers think of Disney's *Sleeping Beauty* as the traditional or original version of the story, but it is an animated, already heavily adapted version that has been altered from the first oral and literary versions of the folkloric beauty who sleeps. Disney "has not only dominated a market sector; it has also, to some degree, defined modern cultural iterations of classic narrative tropes" (Shapiro 2014, n.p); indeed, some early versions of such folktales are far more disturbing than most viewers realize. This film, *Maleficent*, returns to the darkness of the earlier tales to upend those expectations even when "an indicated genre will already predispose a reader" (Zipes 2015, 204) or viewer to certain points of view whether it be of Aurora as innocent or Maleficent as evil.

Twentieth- and twenty-first-century transmedia adaptations sanitize the story to omit the adultery, bigamy, murder, rape, and cannibalism of the original tales. For example, in "Sun, Moon, and Talia" by Giambattista Basile, Talia has pricked her finger on flax and has fallen "dead upon the ground"; one day, when the king "beheld Talia, who seemed to be enchanted, he believed that she was asleep, and he called her, but she remained unconscious. Crying aloud, he beheld her charms and felt his blood course hotly through his veins. He lifted her in his arms, and carried her to a bed, where he gathered the first fruits of love. Leaving her on the bed" (2017 [1634], para. 4) where she unconsciously gives birth to twins who awaken her by sucking the splinter from her finger (para. 5). By any definition, the king's act is rape without consent. His wife finds out, and orders the children killed and fed to him while she plans to throw Talia into a pit of fire; although these acts do not come to pass, none are chosen for reproduction by Disney for its adaptation.

While retellings allow for such changes, they also offer the possibility to rediscover previously silent characters or fill in gaps with new readings of a character. Just as the horrific acts in the folkloric tales have been erased, and "the negative representation of Sleeping Beauty's [young] prince has been mitigated in canonical versions of the tale, female villainy and rivalry have been preserved" (Brugué and Llompart 2020, 110). There has long been interest in the vulnerable sleeping princess, but very little attention has been given to her supposed nemesis. Unnamed in original tales, Disney's enchantress has now come to be known as Maleficent. Jack Zipes points to what he calls the "Disney Spell," which is, in part, created by the reinforcement of social conventions because although "the plots varied and the themes and characters were altered, the classical fairy tale for children and adults reinforced the patriarchal symbolic order based on rigid notions of sexuality and gender" including elitism and separation (1995, 26). In many such narratives it is older women who unleash their evil on the young and beautiful, like Disney's crone of an evil queen upon Snow White, or Ursula upon Ariel.

While modern readership/viewership has preferred the "happily ever after" storyline that may strengthen the sense of morality of fairy tales, there is a definite problem in that the "evil principle is embodied by a woman," which "inevitably reinforces and perpetuates the sexual stereotyping and the misogyny" that consistently pits "female characters as rivals or enemies" in intra-female hostilities (Brugué and Llompart 110). More recent fictional representations of Sleeping Beauty narratives, like those by poet Anne Sexton or author Angela Carter, "exemplify a cultural shift in audiences' expectations of how women are represented" (107) in fairy tales.

Revisioning Maleficent in Sleeping Beauty's story provides the viewer with a name and narrative for the enchantress, Maleficent, who is no longer just the villain of story; rather, she is presented as both powerless and powerful. The film begins with a voice-over from the now elderly Aurora, who acts as a frame narrator. Aurora, as a voice of experience, challenges the viewer to revisit previous expectations with "Let us tell an old story anew and see how well you know it" (00:00:35) because "So you see, the story is not quite as you were told" (01:27:18). Aurora's challenge to her listener is to confront our assumptions because we have not, to this point, understood Maleficent's narrative because we have been more interested in Aurora's own tale.

Linda Woolverton, the screenwriter, when asked how one can update an iconic villain, replied twofold; first, she was surprised when doing her research that Maleficent was "a fairy, not a witch" (quoted in Couch 2014) and second, she reminds us that the "world has changed in the 50 years since the original movie, and hopefully we're more open to all aspects of womankind, whether they're good *or* evil. She's kind of both." She adds: "I love the idea of depicting all aspects of her, including the dark and wicked parts, like making a bad mistake in a moment of anger—which we've all done—and saying something we can never take back" (quoted in Rathe). The voice-over narration by Aurora tells us there is "one who was both hero and villain. And her name was Maleficent" (01:28:14). A woman can be both, not limited to either/or in a binary opposition between good and evil, or innocent and knowing. *Maleficent* is, in part, of a trend in fantastic narratives toward the "craving" for and "exaltation of fantastic otherness, the anthropomorphization of and identification with supernatural beings, and the rehabilitation of classic fairy-tale villains" (Schwabe 2019, 4). Much more importantly, Maleficent is a commentary on the violence inflicted as a means of control upon a woman who refuses to be silenced. With its focus on Maleficent, not as a scorned woman but as a woman grievously wronged, the film gives the viewer insight into the motivation for a seemingly unfeminine and indefensible act against a baby girl-child. *Maleficent* complicates the narrative with two such acts against two innocent, vulnerable girl-children: Aurora and Maleficent.

The world of *Maleficent* contains two specific societies, one clearly of the natural world of the Moors, full of fairies and fairy folk set against a world full of men in a realm of entitlement and overreaching power.[1] The narrative voice begins with the expected opening of "Once upon a time," which quickly shifts to "there were two kingdoms that were the worst of neighbors. So vast was the discord between them that it was said only a great hero or a terrible villain might bring them together" (00:00:52). Maleficent is one of those fairy folk. She is young, energetic, compassionate, and kind. She is described as a "spirit you might take her for a girl but she was not just any girl. She was a fairy" (00:01:27) with healing powers (00:02:04).

Figure 12.1. Maleficent as a child fae (00:02:08).

Maleficent, the girl-fae, is just as happy and playful as she is magnificently horned, winged, and wide-eyed at the beauty of her world. Her beautiful, powerful wings define her as she grows into a woman (see Figure 12.1). Tentative yet searching as they express her emotions, protective yet fearless as she explores her surroundings, and glorious yet a gift as she matures, Maleficent's wings are the embodiment of her self-definition, showing her feelings, intentions, and confidence with their majesty (00:08:31).

Figure 12.2. Maleficent at approximately age 16 (00:09:02).

In her idyllic childhood, Maleficent experiences a far-reaching moment of change when a young boy, Stefan, wanders far afield from the kingdom and into her moor world. The Moor people live as a communal culture with mutual support and trust; when she catches Stefan stealing a gem that could ease his poverty and lift his social status, Maleficent becomes intrigued with his brazen act. They grow together and learn about each other as well as their respective societies through their secret visitations; mutual trust becomes an integral part of their relationship. Stefan is less present for her when social pressure increasingly demands that he should seek advancement in his own patriarchal society. A servant in the castle without a father of his own, he follows the hypermasculine, toxic example of King Henry who is restless to expand his empire and powerfully charismatic. Unable to resist the draw of temptation, King Henry seeks to extend his colonial boundaries to coerce other peoples and lands to submit to his will. The King has "heard of a growing power in the moors" and demands his military forces "to strike it down" (00:09:28). King Henry sets out, leading his men on horseback, to declare war.

Solitary and compelling, the young Maleficent (see Figure 12.2)—now the protector of the Moor people—comes confidently forward to stand fast in her refusal to be subservient to the oppression of men. She raises a wall of thorns to protect the Moor folk's borders and then, accompanied by the Earth, personified by the Ent-like Balthazar and his compatriots, they rise together to combat the unprovoked invasion intended to "crush" (00:10:27) the folk, not negotiate with them. Even the battle scene reinforces the difference in the patriarchal, linear, aggressive thought process in the lines of the soldiers who continually attack, versus Maleficent's more skillful and nuanced mode of defense in the multi-layered and strategic appearance of the various Moor folk (00:10:00); indeed, she asks—not demands—the Moor folk who are "every manner of strange and wonderful creature" (00:1:06) to "Arise and stand with me" (00:11:20). At her request, the Earth awakens when she decries to the invaders, "You will not have the moors, not now, not ever" (00:13:18).

With the combination of Maleficent's unique fae power[2] to control nature, as well as the trees' and roots' mutual respect for her,[3] and the Moorish desire for self-determination, the Moor folk accomplish their righteous cause to remain an entity unto themselves outside of patriarchal control. They are not interested in the human world; that said, Maleficent is no longer merely curious and content. She has had to become a warrior (00:13:00) in the image of the Amazons or Boudicca[4] to protect her people. Maleficent now "fully embraces her role as mother of the Moors, crafting a new maternal identity as a warrior mother" wherein she "reclaims classically masculine attributes of fierceness, assertiveness, and power" and "with license to speak, act, and defend like her male counterparts in the human kingdom" (Wehler 2019, 104). Maleficent casts off Disney's old, conventional expectations of mature womanhood and motherhood—mothers are notoriously dispensed of in Disney films—and repels the invaders with violence and magic. Both *Maleficent* and Maleficent challenge the social convention and long-standing Disney acceptance that men are the ones who are to hold strategic power. For her insolence, she is deemed to be "maleficent," a person with a disposition given to evildoing or even criminal (*OED* 2020) when, in fact, she begins as a nurturing being of nature.

In response to the Moor people's victory, King Henry is deeply offended by his loss but even more so by his defeat by a nonhuman but obviously female warrior. Maleficent has transgressed all normalized boundaries of femininity to threaten his own masculinity. He is humiliated by Maleficent's mastery over the field of war and declares, in his arrogance, that a King "does not take orders from a winged elf" (00:10:50), completely missing the point—and race—of her preservation of independence for the Moor folk. King Henry places a blood bounty onto Maleficent when he gives the ultimatum: "Bring me her head!" (00:11:07). Unable to accept defeat by a woman and/or fae, he sends forth his top male commanders to assert, by proxy, his patriarchal prerogative to conquer. King Henry directly and deliberately asks: "Who among you is worthy? Kill the winged creature and avenge me" (00:15:01). Having challenged their collective manhood, it is to the man who can control or emasculate the usurping, bold, non-subservient, aggressive, powerful female fae that will go the spoils of war—that man will be named heir and successor to the throne.

The Disneyfied animated version of Prince Phillip is not the central con-cern of *Maleficent*; rather, the male character here is Maleficent's childhood friend, Stefan, who is ambitious but made constantly aware of his status as merely a servant to King Henry. Although neither a soldier nor a nobleman, he overhears this promise from the King to the man who avenges his loss. In pursuit of power, Stefan is ruthless. He intentionally trades on his friendship with Maleficent and after a long absence appears to her on the Moors, sup-posedly to warn her of the King's plan for invasion. Nostalgic for an earlier, less complicated time, Maleficent is pleased to spend time with him on her sixteenth birthday. Maleficent, in her kindness and her willingness to for-give his absence, does not see that the ambition and greed of her erstwhile friend have left no room for their shared past. Stefan and Maleficent share her first kiss—indeed, she believes it is "true love's kiss" (00:06:08)—and he demands her allegiance afterward if he is to protect her from the humans who mean to kill her: "You have to trust me" (00:16:09).

Unbeknownst to Maleficent, Stefan gives her a sleeping draught that soon creates an image where Maleficent is now the sleeping beauty (00:17:06). Once she is unconscious and unable to consent, he raises his knife to kill her as a sacrifice to his lust for power. Unable to consummate his quest for her death (00:17:30) because his ambition is stronger than his ability, in the significant filmic elision that follows, Stefan viciously dismembers Maleficent from her wings. His act is unrepresentable for its inhumanity. He makes the deliberate, sadistic choice to rip away the self and life she has known, fully aware of her wings integral part in her self-conception of who she is.

What follows is a soul-wrenching portrait of the aftermath of predacious sexual violence. The medieval atmosphere of the narrative suits its content; atrociously, Maleficent's trauma is the "story of wartime rape *feels* ancient and familiar" (Baaz and Stern 2013, 16). King Henry sanctions any act that results in the disempowerment of Maleficent, including an act of rape as a weapon of war. Woolverton's screenplay is, then, connected to issues in our own world in which, on June 19, 2008, the United Nations Security Council passed Resolution 1820 that recognizes, among other points, that "women and girls are particularly targeted by the use of sexual violence, including as a tactic of war to humiliate, dominate, instill fear in, disperse and/or forcibly relocate civilian members of a community or ethnic group" (1). This resolution is the first action to be "overtly and solely justified by the observation that sexual violence can be a deliberate tactic or weapon of war; this understanding of sexual violence compelled states to act in response to one aspect of gender based violence" (Crawford 2017, 92–93) found in the atrocities of late twentieth- and early twenty-first-century conflicts. Maleficent's context is both imperative and irrelevant; to be sexually victimized is barbaric in any time or in any war.

Stefan, in his desire to please King Henry and elevate himself, enacts a militarized and mythologized masculinity used in gender-based violence of war to attain "the attendant promises and entitlements associated with inhabiting these masculinities" (Baaz and Stern 20). In such a wartime, rape does not have to "be a direct order for it to be strategic" because "implicit condoning or encouragement of rape can also serve" (47). The action Stefan takes, mutilating Maleficent and stealing her wings and her sense of self is, as in all war conflicts, a means to "punish, humiliate or torture seemingly 'subversive' women for threatening" (21) the Kingdom's national security. Such an act is aimed at destroying the very fabric of the Moor society, literally bringing its leader to her knees in pain. The male-dominated, warmongering society of the king has decided that a woman like Maleficent—strong, defiant, protective—is " 'in need of punishment' challenge the notion of femininity that is 'worthy of protecting' " (21). In *Maleficent*, the men believe the fae must be dominated and destroyed.

The morning after Stefan's zealous violence for his cause, the beautiful Maleficent wakes into brokenness, devastation, and pain (00:18:10). Both betrayed and bleeding, the young fae on the cusp of womanhood realizes that she has been emotionally and physically violated (see Figure 12.3), as well as crucially, excruciatingly separated from her self with the loss of her wings (see Figure 12.3). The "re/visioning of the fairy-tale heroine" or here, the assumed villain, "intersects with an acute knowledge of rape culture, a pervasive threat that is inscribed on the bodies of girls and women who are under constant attack by social and political forces that desire to possess them and contain them" (D'Amore 2017, 386–87). Maleficent's trauma is all-encompassing and long-term. Her clothing demonstrates the changes in her self-image; previously dressed in lightweight, nature-colored clothing (00:01:31) with flowing hair that allows her to be one with the landscape begins to shift in purpose and tone. Maleficent wraps her horns in snakeskin or dark leather

Figure 12.3. Angelina Jolie as Maleficent at the moment of waking into trauma in *Maleficent* (00:18:40).

(00:29:00) until even her hair is tightly controlled and her body coverings become oversized and made of protective material, a symbol indicator, or armor, for the need she feels to protect her body and to erase it from sight.

The film narrative demonstrates the dark fae's anger and how the intentionality of Stefan's actions effect particular outcomes. After the elided scene, Maleficent is always on guard for danger and, tragically, often overwhelmed with guilt; she immediately internalized the self-destructive belief that she is at fault for trusting her abuser. The Earth, refusing to leave her lost in shock and guilt, and in return for her unfailing protection, responds to Maleficent's obvious pain and creates for her a powerful walking staff to help her move forward (00:20:30). This fundamental scene of man's misuse of woman not only reclaims the cruelty of the past folk-loric narratives and gives justification to the animated Maleficent's anger but, in keeping with an abused woman's dissociation, portrays a realistic moment of literal lost balance significant to who Maleficent becomes as a woman. She sits—and hides—in the dark among the ruins (00:21:30). Stefan's act of unconscionable assaultive violence results in Maleficent having to withdraw into herself where she "revel[s]n the sorrow that her curse had wrought" (00:34:18) as she darkens the Moors with her intern-alized sense of shame.

A transitional moment demonstrates the goodness that remains in Maleficent and, in many ways, begins her recovery. As she walks back to the Moors, she encounters a raven trapped in a net. A raven's "black appear-ance can be read as symbolic of ill portent and potential death" (Bowman 2011, 94), but there is no indication that this particular raven has been any problem at all but is merely a focus of male sport. Angered by the men who laugh at the bird's inability to fly away and the trauma they are inflicting, Maleficent changes the raven into a man, the shape-shifting Diaval. In return, he is angry and demands immediately, "What have you done to my beautiful self?" (00:22:46) before he thanks her for saving him. Diaval vows to Maleficent that, "in return for saving my life, I am your servant. Whatever you need;" in a recognition of important kinship, Maleficent asks him to be her "wings. I need you to be my wings" (00:23:15). It is from Diaval that Maleficent learns Stefan "did this to [her] so he would be king" (00:24:07). Her rage erupts in green fire in a declaration of vengeance while the fear of the Moor folk demonstrates they feel her rising power.

A new addition to the Sleeping Beauty narrative arc, Diaval is both compatriot in battle and confidante in life to the dark fae. With his constant, often silent, companionship, he implicitly seems to know that Maleficent must regain "trust, autonomy, initiative, competence, identity and intimacy" (Herman 1997, 145) if she is to heal from the disempowerment and disconnection she feels since the trauma. Diaval has an innate understanding of the freedom and selfhood she has lost with her wings because he, too, is without his own at times when he shapeshifts into a different guise. Diaval is the only being with whom Maleficent lets down her guard—he quietly comforts her and encourages her to heal in both body and spirit; that said, he cannot cure her. Maleficent must, like other traumatized women, "be the author and arbiter of her own recovery" (145) even if he is frustrated when she holds him at a distance.

The other young woman in the filmic narrative is Aurora, the young princess whom Maleficent curses. Unlike the reasoning in the earlier stories that the curse is in retaliation for lack of a party invitation, here Maleficent acts in kind—just as now King Stefan took away her young womanhood, Maleficent takes his young daughter's womanhood away in a sleeping curse that will last until true love's kiss (00:32:44) might awaken her. Clearly, this specificity is ironic and cruel; the same kiss the chaste Maleficent had experienced with Stefan as a 16-year-old has now turned to seal the horror of Aurora's fate. The look of disbelief on the obsessive King Stefan's face is twofold; first, he had expected Maleficent to conform to social expectations of woman's passivity, stay privately silent, and shamefully hide on the Moors but, instead, she confronts him in public as the predator he is. Seeing his fear, she admits, "I like you begging ... do it again" (00:32:01). Second, King Stefan surely knows that her curse is poetic justice; to see an innocent loved one harmed is far more excruciating than suffering personal harm.

In the wake of Aurora's birth and using all means at his disposal such as wealth and power, King Stefan convinces three pixies—Knotgrass, Thistlewit, and Flittle—to leave the palace with baby Aurora to keep her from harm until the day after her sixteenth birthday. The pixies' names are another interesting change to female figures. In the original Disney film, they are named Flora, Fauna, and Merryweather, clearly directly associated with unthreatening nature; conversely, in *Maleficent*, their names are more aggressive and less nurturing in tone. The viewer learns that Queen Leila—the daughter King Henry gives to Stefan for (he believes) killing Maleficent—is dead, much to the indifference of her husband. As an exchange of female chastity for male power, Queen Leila is written out of the story even before her death, possibly from postpartum depression deepened by her child being removed from her; she is an example of proper but invisible, invalid/ated womanhood. Leila, despite her class and status as a royal, is another woman silenced by King Stefan. The King's actions prompt Maleficent's curse, but Aurora is Queen Leila's daughter too. Stefan takes Maleficent's wings, and he similarly takes Leila's child from her. As the archetype of traditional femininity under patriarchy, Leila's child is the most important piece of her selfhood just as Maleficent's sense of self is in the freedom of her wings. Her wings had allowed her to be a protective mother to the Moors and its people, but King Stefan strips her of them; likewise, he removes Leila's ability to be a mother by sending away her child. It is against this lingering social construction of the beatified, wronged paragon of passive virtue that the other women—Aurora and Maleficent—will be judged.

Any argument that maternalism is instinctive to female beings is challenged in this transmedia adaptation; the female pixies are unable to sustain even the health of the girl-child. Maleficent—although she directly admits "I hate you" to the child whom she calls "Beasty" (00:36:00)—must step in, with Diaval's assistance, to insure Aurora's survival with milk and food. At one point, Maleficent saves the "curious little Beasty" (00:44:10) from falling to her death while the pixies petty quarrel and Maleficent even steps in to rock her cradle when they have ignored her cries (00:37:20). What begins as Maleficent's observation that "it's so ugly you could almost feel sorry for it" (00:35:45) becomes, over time, a presence felt to be a guide and confidant as Aurora grows. Maleficent watches from the shadows where, to counter the nuclear family demanded by heteronormative and patriarchal society, Maleficent constructs a nonnormative family of choice for the young girl. Aurora is a birth child of the Kingdom but a kindred spirit child of the Moors, and she easily moves between the two worlds. Maleficent's understanding of her in-betweenness is complemented with Diaval's caregiving, to create an odd couple of parenthood who share Aurora's joys and her challenges.

Unintimidated by the massive wall of thorns Maleficent has constructed to protect both herself and her community from the attacks of the King's forces, Aurora openly explores the land as she learns about herself. She spends increasing time on the Moors, learning the ways of the Moor folk while the two as-yet-unseen guardians are unfailing in their attention to and protection of Aurora. There is a point when Aurora asks Maleficent to come out of the shadows: "I know who you are. You are my fairy godmother. You have been watching over me my whole life" (00:49:00). Her belief in Maleficent as her fairy godmother suggests a conflation of magical power and parental love. Who Maleficent is to Aurora has nothing to do with her damaged body; that said, Maleficent's growing love for the girl-child allows her to move forward in her recovery. Although Aurora tells Maleficent, "Don't be afraid" to come out of the shadows, Maleficent feels that if she does come forward, "Then you [Aurora] will be afraid" (00:48:38–50) as she projects her self-hatred through Aurora's potential response to her appearance. Again, Woolverton refuses to provide a caricature of a "man-hating feminist" but offers instead "a woman forged by destruction, war, and revenge, [who] finds love again, but not in the form of a lover but rather in the form of a daughter" (Wehler 102). Aurora feels she is the child of Maleficent's heart; indeed, Aurora's love of the moors and its people is the proof of the fae's own compassion and love.

In a devastating exchange, the young Princess Aurora asks Maleficent about her absent wings. Aurora asks a prescient question of Maleficent: "Why don't you [fly]? The other fairies fly" (00:54:40). Maleficent's desire to be truthful with Aurora is caught by her promise to be her protectress; Maleficent settles for a narrative a girl-child can understand without psychological harm and that is one she will be able to articulate. With a complex reaction of longing, sadness, and rage, Maleficent tells the persistent Aurora, "They were stolen from me" (00:54:55). Maleficent laments that her wings were "so big they dragged behind me when I walked" and that they "were strong. They could carry me above the clouds into the headwinds. They never faltered. Not even once. I could trust them" (00:55:02). She can only answer, "There is an evil in this world. And I cannot keep you from it" (00:57:32).

Maleficent is as much about the simplicity of a girl-child's perspective versus the complexity of woman's lived experience as it is about challenging the social expectation that a person—particularly a woman—should be selfless and forgiving. Initially, Aurora is not able to comprehend what caused a young woman (Maleficent at her same age of 16) to move from naïveté to malevolence; rather, Aurora must be later shocked into the realization that her father, King Stefan, is the man who caused Maleficent's pain, but does not yet have the understanding to be awed by how this dark fae has knowingly and with great love, quietly but unfailingly, adopted her rapist's daughter.

Told of Maleficent's curse by the kingdom-complicit pixies, Aurora flees in her own anger and disappointment from her Moor mother back to the male-centric society that deserted her. Aurora has internalized the false dichotomy of patriarchy that casts women as either heroine or villain in a replication of the traditional good girl/bad girl stereotype of women on a continuum of purity to fallen. Expecting a protective welcome, once there, for her disobedience of the order to stay away and because she is an inconvenient disruption when the men are making war, Aurora's own father instantly, physically has his men constrain her (01:06:12). King Stefan's arrogant lack of guilt over his predatory behavior, then his indifference to Aurora's fear and pleading leads to the execution of the curse. Seeking escape from imprisonment, Aurora is drawn to a spinning wheel where she pricks her finger and falls into magical sleep (01:08:40); however, it is Maleficent's self-awareness and honesty that lead to Aurora's—and Maleficent's—salvation.

Maleficent tries repeatedly and with extreme guilt but she cannot break the curse. She realizes the stakes for Aurora and her family are high, so she transfigures Diaval into a great black warhorse to take them toward the Kingdom, ready to wreak havoc with all her powers on those who stand in between them and their beloved daughter. Diaval reminds Maleficent that she is in physical, mortal jeopardy from King Stefan, but maternal fear overrides any personal concerns. The story speaks of "the strength of women and the things they feel between one another" with "all this strength and all this feminism," says Jolie (quoted in Wieselman 2014). Even though she brings the new young Prince to try to wake Aurora, she knowingly admits to Diaval that the curse is predicated on its necessary fallibility. The mythologies of heterosexual "love at first sight" and "true love's kiss" are deconstructed when the Prince's attempt has no effect.

Despondent at her failures, Maleficent significantly does not ask anyone for forgiveness for her past act. She owns her actions. As Maleficent speaks to the sleeping girl-child, she emanates a warm gold aura and admits her grave mistake: "I will not ask your forgiveness because what I have done to you is unforgivable. I was so lost in hatred and revenge. Sweet Aurora, you stole what was left of my heart. And now I have lost you forever. I swear, no harm will come to you as long as I live. And not a day shall pass that I don't miss your smile" (01:16:00). When Maleficent kisses Aurora on the head, the curse breaks. Maleficent has come to terms with her trauma; her own curse is lifted, and a by-product of that love is her maternal love for Aurora. True love's kiss "came from the person who really didn't believe she was capable of any kind of goodness of love—that she would in any way be loved or have love is something she'd long ago dismissed from her life. So the thing is not only that she does express it, but it's the shock" for Maleficent "that is beautiful" (in Wieselman). True love's kiss is enacted simultaneously with a promise of truthfulness and protection by a mother of choice who loves her child unconditionally. Aurora awakens.

Sarah Bowman articulates the preference within "Disney movies [to] code socially preferable characteristics—such as humility, obedience, nurturing, and innocence—as 'good,' offering the reward of 'happily ever after'" (82). Any other potential archetypes of womanhood seem to cast the villainess against the female protagonist where "selfishness, vanity, seduction, cruelty, and am- bition are coded as 'evil,' promising rejection, expulsion from society, and even death" and these "'evil' aspects of the Feminine may also prove dangerous to both mates and offspring in terms of reproductive success" (82). This dichotomy between a princess and her mother figure is, at least in *Maleficent*, false; indeed, in this film narrative, the protagonist is no longer only one sleeping beauty— they have both been cast in that role—but the film's narrative refuses the idea of the traditional feminine as silent victims of male aggression.

In scenes overwhelmed by heat and flames, it is the connection be- tween the fae and the princess that empowers them to combat the patri- archal forces that seek to contain them. Caught in iron chains that burn her and unable to protect Aurora, Maleficent transforms Diaval into a fire-breathing dragon, but they are surrounded by iron shields until they are confronted by the mad King (01:21:05). Unhinged, King Stefan ignores Maleficent's defiance and mocks her as a "fairy creature without wings in a world where you don't belong" then assaults her again by ripping off her protective cloak to expose and shame her (01:22:27). His tyranny is now the embodiment of evil, not Maleficent. The punishment of King Stefan in the scenes that follow is justified in the absence of any court of law; he was a rational subject who "who intend[ed] evil for particular purposes, and therewith can be held accountable" (Baaz and Stern 52). King Stefan is culpable for his actions and, when confronted, he sees Maleficent's suppressed rage become an earth-shaking manifestation of green fire and light.

The green smoke and fire that surrounds Maleficent is significant; her firelight is, at first, golden, but after her trauma, it turns green (see Figure 12.4.). The green of nature might refer to a regained sense of harmony so perhaps it is a reminder of Maleficent's Moor heritage; this interpretation seems likely if taken alongside folklore that aligns green with fairies and spirits. More recently, the monstrous is associated with green to assert nonhumanness.[5]

Figure 12.4. Maleficent as she appears to King Stefan at the christening (00:31:43).

Aurora chooses to act in solidarity with Maleficent and actively comes into her own maturity when, under attack, she must trust her most basic instincts and the strength she has earned. She turns to her mother—of choice, not biology—and acts to save their relationship just as Maleficent had once saved their bond. The foregrounding of the love between the two women is a "story unimaginable in the world of fairytales: Maleficent, a woman forged by destruction, war, and revenge, finds love again, but not in the form of a lover but rather in the form of a daughter" (Wehler 102). The mother-daughter relationship gives both women strength and compassion as well as determination and comfort.

Aurora's courage to act frees Maleficent's wings from the King's trophy case where he has kept them as a kind of *momento mori* of his act of violence (01:20:40). The wings rise in exultation to reunite with the dark fae (01:22:42). This act is "more than just a climactic plot twist, more than just character redemption, and way more than revenge" (Swiz 2020); Aurora and Maleficent stand together—matriarch of the Moors and her heiress—against an aristocratic patriarchy that would divide mother and daughter as inconsequential spoils of war.

The trauma experienced by Maleficent, and Aurora, reflects the much larger issue of how "in wars and post-conflict situations … rape and other forms of sexual violence are used as a tactic of war and terrorism in conflicts around the world" (Maas and Jolie 2019) with impunity. The moment Maleficent reunites with her wings, power radiates from her; she has reclaimed her body and her spirit.

Some critics refuse to see this neo-Disney adaptation as a positive step to increase awareness on so many woman-focused issues. For example, because he is uncomfortable with the insertion of sexual politics into a "fairy tale" film, Jordan Shapiro ridiculously claims that "most writers are stuck on the gender implications and, therefore, missing the real point. The scene is not about rape. It is a social commentary arguing that any hierarchical rise to power inherently happens through the exploitation of others" before he turns his analysis to why Maleficent is "an oppressive ruler of the Moors" (2014). In *The Federalist*, Libby Emmons claims that the film has been "Grotesquely Distorted" by what she sees as "that ghastly contemporary distraction, identity politics" (2019). Emmons argues that the main problem with the narrative is that there is no love in the story because "a classic Disney romance means there's true love, so much that the princess gets to go simply gaga over it. True love in a Disney story means being blissed out on the joy of being with another person, totally enthralled and delighted" and where "fairies spin around the princess's head like stars, and sweet songs erupt from her throat unbidden" (Emmons). Richard Corliss, writes in *Time* magazine, "This dashing lad won Maleficent's love and, ambition overwhelming ardor, clipped and stole her wings to become the king of a neighboring realm. Bastard!" (2014). Although this piece is not intended as a review of the filmic merits of *Maleficent*, it should be noted how appalling the flippancy is in how a major film critic reads this story of two women. *Maleficent* refuses any simplistic vision of unthinking, passive womanhood and those critics who reject the increasingly independent, progressive, strong women in cinematic narratives will be disappointed.

In *Maleficent*, it is the healing love of mother and daughter that creates true joy for both women. Creating the powerful herstory of Maleficent's trauma is a calculated choice by two powerful women: Woolverton is the writer who has infused woman-centered and alternate perspectives into Disney's *Beauty and the Beast* (1991, 2017) and Jolie is United Nations High Commissioner for Refugees as well as executive producer, actor, and mother. From her multiple perspectives, Jolie confirms that "we were very conscious, the writer [Linda Woolverton] and I, that it was a metaphor for rape" (2014) during an interview with BBC *Woman's Hour*.

Speaking at the Global Summit to End Sexual Violence in Conflict, Jolie demanded the end of rape as a weapon of war because it "is a myth that rape is an inevitable part of conflict" because "there is nothing inevitable about it" (quoted in Rich 2014). Maleficent's devastating experience parallels how "women and girls are still the majority of the victims of war" because of acts of degradation based on the "abuse of power, gender bias, violence and lack of justice," said Jolie (quoted in Lederer 2019). While these statements were made about women and children in war zones, they are applicable to the female-centric perspectives in *Maleficent*. As critic Katey Rich comments, it is "one thing to speak in front of global dignitaries about the need to combat rape; it's quite another to slip that message into a global blockbuster" (2014). Certainly, the young Maleficent's trauma intentionally resonates with Jolie's statement to the United Nations that parts of humanity "seem incapable of upholding minimum standards of humanity in many parts of the world" (quoted in Lederer 2019). Such unspeakable acts do not result in tidy, self-effacing fairy tales of forgiveness; instead, all that was lacking in the Disney animated feature with its one-dimensional gorgon of an evil fairy is replaced in *Maleficent* by an exposition of the vindicated enchantress. Jolie offers:

> To read *Maleficent* and its complexity is to consider what can fairy tales offer to an empathetic understanding of modern life, and how in an age of Me Too and #MeToo they might speak to the various traumas of womanhood. To feel "different, marginalized, bullied, or abused—so we change… harder, we become meaner, we make terrible choices, and can, like Maleficent, take it out on someone innocent. But we can also identify with being in that dark space but finding the things in life that remind us that we still have a humanity" where there are "things that can bring us back and open us up again after feeling so dark and so lost and so angry." (quoted in Wieselman 2014)

It is not enough to create strong female characters; this trope is not progressive because it usually involves selflessness and self-sacrifice. She reflects on her own version of Maleficent's character: "We are impacting generations and culture around the world [via Disney]. What are we saying?"; Woolverton, too, believes what a strong woman should mean is

> somebody who is proactive in their world, who affects their world, isn't a victim … or if they are victimized by it, they take action to change that for themselves. They look at the world in interesting ways, maybe another way than the culture does. That makes a strong woman if she's vocal about it, or even goes about trying to make changes without being vocal about it. There are so many interesting ways to describe women besides just strong, even this pure difficult strength. It's strong-*willed*. (quoted in Erbland 2019)

While a female "villain" may behave in a manner conventionally deemed unfeminine, self-interested, or destructive, her actions often provide the needed impetus for the protagonist "to ascend to the next level of consciousness" (Bowman 95). In this case, of Maleficent and Aurora, is the will of these strong women to be seen and empowered that motivates *Maleficent* (see Figure 12.5). The humanity embodied in the posthuman fae as flawed protector of the Moors and Aurora as a no-longer-naïve Queen of the Moors is set in healthy opposition to the ethical depravity

Figure 12.5. The crowning of Aurora as Queen of the Moors before Maleficent and Diaval (01:27:14).

of the male-centered, repressive kingdom as well as the irresponsibility of complicit women represented by the "good" fairy triumvirate.

As Joan Acocella suggests, Maleficent is both "a badass and a paragon" (2014), but she fails to explain why Maleficent is one or the other or both. Although she refers to Angelina Jolie, the question of who Maleficent is—from fae child to matriarchal paragon and the clear justification of her badass righteous wrath—is fundamental in the age of #MeToo, a movement based on the ability to speak one's truth and name the perpetrator who has exercised violence over others. In this filmic adaptation, the narrative develops an original herstory of Maleficent, from childhood to woman-hood, who is less evil enchantress and more dark fae, less cruel stereotype and more nurturing, fiercely protective maternal matriarch. The Beasty and the Badass embrace their unique family founded in a chosen mother's love; the women's solidarity reiterates the new *Maleficent's* exploration of the woman/women of the natural world who empower a new generation of women both in and without the film. They are "themselves protectors. As mothers. As peacekeepers. As human rights defenders" (Maas and Jolie) as allies, as survivors, as protectors, as mothers, and as daughters. All powerful. All women.

Bibliography

Acocella, Joan. "Love's True Kiss: *Maleficent*'s Complex Sexual Politics." *The New Yorker* (July 2014): 2. <https://www.newyorker.com/culture/culture-desk/loves-true-kiss-maleficent-s-complex-sexual-politics>.

Baaz, Maria Eriksson, and Maria Stern. *Sexual Violence as a Weapon of War?: Perceptions, Prescriptions, Problems in the Congo and Beyond*. London: Zed Books, 2013.

Basile, Giambattista. "Sun, Moon, and Talia." 1634. Translated and edited by D. L. Ashliman. 1998–2013. <https://sites.pitt.edu/~dash/type0410.html#basile>.

Bowman, Sarah Lynne. "The Dichotomy of the Great Mother Archetype in Disney Heroines and Villainesses." In *Vader, Voldemort and Other Villains: Essays on Evil in Popular Media*, edited by Jamey Heit, 80–97. Jefferson, NC: McFarland, 2011.

Brugué, Lydia, and Auba Llompart. "The Strongest of the Fairies: Reworking Gender and Villainy in Walt Disney's *Maleficent*." In *Contemporary Fairy-Tale Magic: Subverting Gender and Genre*, edited by Lydia Brugué and Auba Llompart, 107–115. Amsterdam: Rodopi, 2020.

Corliss, Richard. Review: "*Maleficent*: Sympathy for the Rebel." *Time*, May 29, 2014. <https://time.com/136170/maleficent-movie-review-angelina-jolie/>.

Couch, Aaron. "*Maleficent* Writer: I Cried Writing Angelina Jolie's Big Moment." *The Hollywood Reporter*, June 2, 2014. <https://www.hollywoodreporter.com/news/maleficent-movie-screenwriter-cried-writing-708353>.

Crawford, Kerry F. *Wartime Violence: From Silence to Condemnation of a Weapon of War*. Washington, DC: Georgetown University Press, 2017.

D'Amore, Laura Mattoon. "Vigilante Feminism." *Marvels & Tales: Journal of Fairy-Tale Studies* 31, no. 2 (2017): 386–405.

Emmons, Libby. "The New Maleficent Movie Is Grotesquely Distorted by Identity Politics." *The Federalist*, October 22, 2019. <https://thefederalist.com/2019/10/22/the-new-maleficent-movie-is-grotesquely-distorted-by-identity-politics/>.

Erbland, Kate. "Disney's Most Valuable Screenwriter Has Had Enough of the 'Strong Female' Trope." *IndieWire*, October 17, 2019. <https://www.indiewire.com/2019/10/linda-woolverton-disney-screenwriter-lion-king-beauty-beast-maleficent-1202182354/>.

Heilmann, Ann, and Mark Llewellyn, *Neo-Victorianism. The Victorians in the Twenty-First Century, 1999–2009*. Basingstoke: Palgrave, 2010.

Jolie, Angelina et al. "Angelina Jolie, William Hague, and Sexual Violence in Conflict." *Woman's Hour*. BBC Radio 4. BBC. June 11, 2014. <https://www.bbc.co.uk/programmes/b0460hz8>.

Justice, Benjamin. "Maleficent Reborn: Disney's Fairytale View of Gender Reaches Puberty." *Social Education* 74, no. 4 (2014): 194–98.

Lederer, Edith M. "Angelina Jolie: Equality for Women Key to Peaceful World." *AP News*, March 29, 2019. <https://apnews.com/article/ed9bd5eba9684210b0ce4777c820eeb7>

Letissier, Georges. "Ann Heilmann and Mark Llewellyn, *Neo-Victorianism. The Victorians in the Twenty-First Century, 1999–2009*." *Cahiers Victoriens et Édouardiens* 83 (Spring 2016). <http://journals.openedition.org/cve/2644>.

Maas, Heiko, and Angelina Jolie. "Sexual Violence Is Rife in War Zones. We Must Take Action." *The Washington Post*, April 22, 2019. <https://www.washingtonpost.com/opinions/2019/04/22/sexual-violence-is-rife-war-zones-we-must-take-action/>.

"maleficent, adj." *OED Online*. Oxford University Press. September 2020. <www.oed.com/view/Entry/112857>.

"Post-Traumatic Stress Disorder." *Mayo Clinic*. <https://www.mayoclinic.org/diseases-conditions/post-traumatic-stress-disorder/symptoms-causes/syc-20355967>.

Rathe, Adam. "The Making of Maleficent: How Linda Woolverton Created the Movies' Most Terrifying Villainess." *Dujour*. n.d. <https://dujour.com/culture/maleficent-screenwriter-linda-woolverton-interview/>.

Rich, Katey. "Angelina Jolie Confirms a Key *Maleficent* Scene Was About Rape." *Vanity Fair*, June 12, 2014. <https://www.vanityfair.com/hollywood/2014/06/angelina-jolie-maleficent-rape>.

Schwabe, Claudia. *Craving Supernatural Creatures: German Fairy-Tale Figures in American Pop Culture*. Detroit, MI: Wayne State University Press, 2019.

Shapiro, Jordan. "Why Disney's *Maleficent* Matters." *Forbes*, June 5, 2014. <https://www.forbes.com/sites/jordanshapiro/2014/06/05/why-disneys-maleficent-matters/?sh=51723f3f3901>.

Swiz, Alicia. "Yes, the *Maleficent* Rape Scene Matters for All Women." *Daily Dot*, June 17, 2020. <https://www.dailydot.com/unclick/maleficent-rape-scene-yes-all-women/>.

United Nations Security Council. "Resolution 1820." June 19, 2008. <https://documents-dds-ny.un.org/doc/UNDOC/GEN/N08/391/44/PDF/N0839144.pdf?OpenElement>.

Wehler, Melissa. "'Hello, Beasty': Uncompromising Motherhood in Disney's *Maleficent*." In *Fourth Wave Feminism in Science Fiction and Fantasy Volume 1: Essays on Film Representations, 2012–2019*, edited by Valerie Estelle Frankel, 102–14. Jefferson, NC: McFarland, 2019.

Wieselman, Jarett. "Angelina Jolie Explains the Twist Ending of *Maleficent*." *BuzzFeed*, May 31, 2014. <https://www.buzzfeed.com/jarettwieselman/angel ina-jolie-explains-the-twist-ending-of-maleficent>.

Zipes, Jack. "Breaking the Disney Spell." In *From Mouse to Mermaid: The Politics of Film, Gender, and Culture*, edited by Elizabeth Bell et al., 21–42. Bloomington: Indiana University Press, 1995.

———. "Media-Hyping of Fairy Tales," In *The Cambridge Companion to Fairy Tales*, edited by Maria Tatar, 202–19. Cambridge: Cambridge University Press, 2015.

13 Beyond Perfection: Inclusion and Self-Exploration of Neo-Disney "Beauties," "Beasts," and "Monsters"

Children in their early stages of development seek life-like figures to emulate and then incorporate their behavioral lessons into the growth of their own psyche. As new and more sophisticated types of media have been produced and made available to the general public, the influence of media on children has exponentially increased. According to "Some Media Effects on Children—A Review," the average Canadian child spends 14 hours watching television each week (a result similar to that of a survey of American children), and this excessive exposure to the virtual world of television programs makes the children assume it to be the real world, establishing a false image in their minds (Ahandani and Taasobi 2015, 49). Therefore, they should be exposed to only age-appropriate television programs, which necessitates parental supervision (48). Walt Disney's world-famous media company has continued to produce films that have been perceived to be suitable for the young audience, establishing itself as the best-known purveyor of family entertainment in the twentieth and twenty-first centuries. Whether a movie or merchandise, Disney products offer consumers a visual representation of their childhood desires and fantasies, as well as tangible objects that let them live out that fantasy. As a result, it is fair to claim that Disney has an obvious impact on the formation and shaping of countless children's personalities.

Critics have good reason to analyze and question television media that communicate powerful messages to children. This includes Disney products; they should be more inclusive of diverse physical types and ethnicities of people and avoid propagating stereotypes so that young consumers have the opportunity to develop their ideas without bias. Major themes in Disney movies have promoted a strong familial bond, irrespective of the composition of the family, where all the family members share a deep understanding of each other, despite the differences among them, and the father continues to be portrayed as the head of the family (Cheung et al. 2021). These representations of the families provide children with information about family constructions, hierarchies, and roles (Zurcher et al. 2018, 7). Children tend to accept these Disney family structures as the norm and therefore are often conflicted when their own family dynamics diverge. They are susceptible to accepting stereotypes as desirable models to emulate, and the films teach children how to treat those who do not match those shown in the films, for better and for worse. Such preconceptions create not only a psychological bias for children that can be detrimental to their self-realization and identity but also a misunderstanding of how to deal with others. The restrictive constraints of Disney's normalizing indoctrination hinder children's development and individualism.

Moreover, the Disney's folkloric depiction of body types that are supposed to be considered beautiful and handsome, and are rewarded for being so in the stories, reinforces their acceptance, expectations, and desirability while rejecting those with characteristics that do not measure up to such standards. Preferable characters are young and slender (Rowe 2019, 29). As for behavior, females are to act as though they are delicate, and males, resilient (Towbin et al. 2008 [2004], 21). Because of these stereotypes, Disney's films have come under much critical attack and have since increased its inclusivity of diverse cultures and genders. More recent films project bodily imperfections, like obesity and physical handicaps, in characters that the stories ask for either sympathy or acceptance, and ultimately, send the message that one should value all people as individuals instead of types. Disney has also made a concerted effort to faithfully render multiple ethnicities and nonnuclear family formations with approbation. It appears that the benefits of acceptance and tolerance have become an urgent impetus embraced by Disney as indicated in the Walt Disney Company's "Stories Matter" website, with its stated declaration: "Stories shape how we see ourselves and everyone around us. So as storytellers, we have the power and responsibility to not only uplift and inspire, but also consciously, purposely and relentlessly champion the spectrum of voices and perspectives in our world" (2022). The efforts are apparent in such recent releases as *Moana* (2016), *Raya and the Last Dragon* (2021), and *Encanto* (2021). Furthermore, the psychosocial struggle for young people to discover their true selves is the major theme that drives *The Lion King* (2019), *Frozen II* (2019), and *Luca* (2021). Nevertheless, Disney has far to go to fully "champion the spectrum of voices and perspectives in our world."

The Body Dynamic and Femininity

Amanda Rutherford and Sarah Baker placed the following 11 female characters in the "Princess Bubble": Cinderella (1950), Aurora (1959), Snow White (1965), Ariel (1989), Jasmine (1992), Tiana (2009), Belle (2010), Rapunzel (2011), Merida (2012), Elsa (2013), and Anna (2013), emphasizing Disney's covetable physical traits, over a span of 60 years (2021, n.p.). Nine of the eleven princesses are Caucasian with the exception of Jasmine who has a brown skin tone and Tiana who has "too light" African American complexion (Lester 2010, 299). Disney's inclination toward picturing princesses with light-colored skin stems from a long-prevailing bias in parts of American culture (Azmi et al. 2018, 687). Most of the princesses have blue eyes and blonde hair, implying White supremacy and an inadequate representation of people of color (Rutherford and Baker). Tiana—being the daughter of a maid at the palace instead of being a princess—problematizes the first-ever portrayal of her ethnicity into the princess franchise (Lester 299) by suggesting that African Americans are primarily lower class. Only after she marries the lighter-skinned Prince Naveen can she become a princess. It is as if Disney is saying to African-American children that only through partnering with generous hegemonic races can they find happiness instead of being able to realize their dreams on their own or with others of their same race.

Furthermore, Beth A. Wiersma concludes that the traditional Disney holds a very patriarchal view of women (2000, 30) with the females designed to satisfy the male gaze in that they are given sensual hourglass figures that have tiny waists and curvy breasts and hips (51; Rowe 28). Additional sexual objectification of their bodies has included big eyes, pointed noses, long necks, thin arms and wrists, and long fingers (Xu 2021, 328), with little regard for what these projections intentionally or unintentionally instill in the minds of their audiences. Even Disney's more recent attempts to avoid stereotypes send the message that Tiana's larger lips (a feature of Black women) are less attractive than the other White princesses (Laemle 2018 n.p.), and her metamorphosis as a frog in much of the film minimizes the screen time for a Black princess. Being portrayed as a nonhuman throughout the formative stage of her relationship with Prince Naveen, Tiana is not treated as an object of desire by the handsome Prince. Disney's uniform representation of princesses restricts a child's imagination and behavior (Uppal 2019, 8), and even more significantly, inculcates children to believe that beauty and success for females are dependent upon their physical attractiveness. For those women with imperfect bodies, there is no hope for happiness in this life (Rowe 26).

Beauty, which in itself is a relative ideological and cultural concept in modern times for it cannot be universally defined in absolute terms, was a prized possession in the Disney universe before its transformation into neo-Disneyism. Only the characters who were moral and good were allowed by Disney to be beautiful, as opposed to villains who were depicted and repeatedly asserted as ugly (Azmi et al. 687; Xu 326). As a result, physical appearance induces a psychological dimension and encoding for viewers, associating the physical with good or evil. The young and good-hearted Cinderella was so beautiful that even after she was forced to do the house chores and live in misery, she retained her beauty (1950, 00:26:31). Her stepsisters were unattractive due to their selfish nature and cruel treatment toward Cinderella—they verbally degraded her and forced her to do extra work, as shown in the film, so that she could not attend the ball in the palace (00:31:54). Wiersma points out: "Even though Anastasia and Drizella are young and somewhat thin, they have unattractive faces and exaggerated body parts. These girls have lines on their faces … big noses, big feet, and protruding butts. Their voices are loud and have a screeching sarcastic tone to them" (53–54). In *Sleeping Beauty*, the good fairy Flora blesses Princess Aurora with the "Gift of Beauty," which is "Beauty rare, Gold of sunshine in her hair / Lips that shame the red, red rose / She'll walk with springtime wherever she goes" (00:05:59), whereas Maleficent, the film's antagonist, is presented as a figure of darkness with protruding horns on her head and two large black wings, who arrived at the ceremony uninvited and cursed the princess. Beauty also serves as a driving force behind the evil deeds of the villainous characters—Mother Gothel in *Tangled* in search of beauty and youth kidnaps little Princess Rapunzel and keeps her hidden from the world in a secluded tower amidst the forest. She exploits the magical powers contained in Rapunzel's hair to regain and retain her youth, hence her immortal beauty (00:11:04). *Sleeping Beauty* and *Tangled* convey to the young audience that the only ways to appear beautiful are either to be virtuous and obtain the valuable beauty as a reward or to be outwardly evil and snatch it away from the group of conventionally beautiful individuals.

Some Disney princesses such as Anna, Aurora, Ariel, Snow White, and Cinderella, fall in love at first sight—exemplifying Disney's obsession with physical beauty, for the princesses do not bother with getting to know the men they are to marry, and the females, like the males, are focused on only each other's external appearance, which is a dangerous message to send to children. Tiana is an exception in that her main objective is not to find a husband; she is determined to open her own restaurant. Despite being depicted as a girl supposedly not concerned about physical appearance, she despises her slimy body after she is transformed into a frog (00:29:34) and wishes to revert to being the young girl, with the dark yet perfect figure, that she once used to be.

Apart from physical beauty, the other conventional feminine virtues such as purity, kindness, and virginity are also noticeable personality traits of the older Disney princesses: "These princesses have an average age of sixteen years and are naïve, most without formal education or worldly experience, and they have additional distinctive traits which include poise, elegance, and other desired feminine characteristics—like kindness and purity" (Rutherford and Baker). The qualities of characters are inextricably tied to how they look. Because of the princesses' lack of experience and tiny bodies, as well as their vulnerability, passivity, and fragility, they are dependent upon male characters—fathers, brothers, or spouses—to protect them, to provide for them, and to prevent them from having any agency or freedom for self-identification. Flynn Rider, for one, rescues Rapunzel from a secluded tower and restores her to the palace. The Prince saves Snow White's life with a kiss. Prince Naveen helps Tiana open her restaurant. On Ariel's behalf, Eric defeats Ursula and thus ends her reign of terror.

In contrast, since 2016, the neo-Disney heroines in *Moana*, *Raya and the Last Dragon*, and *Encanto* are unconventional and independent; they not only are capable of rescuing themselves but also rescue entire populations of people including males. Although a Disney princess, Moana the daughter of Motunui's Chief, has been trained, not to be someone's wife and trophy, but to assume the responsibilities as chief over the village. Moana is a neo-Disney young woman who is focused on earning the princess title for herself by saving their island. She is a leader instead being the traditionally submissive young Disney princess. Her heroism takes place in a hostile world outside of what used to be a restricted sphere of domesticity. Her brand of femininity is that she cares for her people, is brave enough to take risks, and is able to motivate others to save lives. Significantly and relevantly, she mirrors and affirms the value of modern working women. Moana is the chosen one tasked with retrieving Te Fiti's heart and saving her village (which is essentially her entire world for she has never stepped out of the island), from being devoured by the darkness (the stereotypical association of darkness with evil remains). Moana sets off into the vast ocean without human company, heedless to any potential risks and in defiance of her father who has repeatedly warned her against going beyond the reef (00:31:15). She is passionate about completing her duty as the up-and-coming chief and saving her people's island, which seems to have come under a curse. The mainstays of the villagers' industry, the coconuts, have become diseased, and their main food source, fish, has receded. Unlike her princess predecessors, she is a tribal, brown-skinned girl with thick, black, wavy hair (see Figure 13.1). Moana bursts the "Princess Bubble" (Rutherford and Baker). Her physique is strong with arms and legs that are thick and muscular, with a personality that is equally resolved and capable. She represents a more positive image than the usual Disney body type; rather, Moana's natural appearance encourages a new generation of young girls to find themselves reflected in characters whom they can admire and emulate. Her clothes lack the refinement of any aristocracy, and she is the only princess to remain barefooted throughout the film. She is a true princess and heroine worthy to emulate because of her courageous and challenging feat in saving her people's world. She is purely motivated by her responsibility toward her people for she describes herself in the song "I am Moana": "I am a girl who loves my island … I am the daughter of the village chief / We are descended from voyagers / Who found their way across the world … I've delivered us to where we are / I have journeyed farther / I am everything I've learned and more" (01:20:48).

Figure 13.1. Moana.

Prior to the debut of Moana, the princesses' lives are largely reliant on the male members of their families. The fathers of Ariel and Jasmine oppress their daughters either violently or tactically, forcing them to make decisions that impede their personal growth and desire. These princesses are denied their freedom, which makes the young women face difficulties in negotiating with their adolescent selves (Wynns and Rosenfeld 2003, 99). When they do rebel, it is primarily driven by their desire to explore love (95), thus substituting one patriarch for another. In contrast, Moana's rebellion is motivated, not by a love interest, but firstly by an innate allure for adventure beyond the restricted world bounded by the reef, and then secondly by a sacred trust to restore Te Fiti's heart. Despite Tui's best efforts to keep her away from the ocean, Moana's curiosity, and her sense of responsibility gets the better of her, and she does not hold back from exploring the vastness of the ocean. As a theme for Disney, familial dominance over meek and defenseless female characters is nothing new, and it blurs the line between love and abuse of power. In practically every film, family members strive to exert control over the lives of young characters, but Moana has the obligation of performing a manly task, which is why she does not wait for a man to save her and why she does subvert patriarchal control. She saves Maui, a demigod, several times and persuades him to return Te Fiti's heart.

The physical traits of the neo-Disney characters are diverse and therefore unique in the Disney family. The 2021 fantasy adventure film *Raya and the Last Dragon* features mainly two female characters—Raya, the princess of the kingdom of Heart, the proud yet responsible guardian of the Dragon Gem; and Namaari, the cunning yet capable daughter of the leader who is in charge of Kingdom of Fangs. Namaari is brown with a Southeast Asian appearance. Like Moana, she has a muscular body, and her outfit does not accentuate her bodily curves; instead, it emphasizes her broad shoulders and muscular arms (see Figure 13.2). About the early depiction of Asians in Disney films, Alan Spector complained that they were "often tended to lump ethnic groups into a kind of undifferentiated mass—Asians, Chinese, Japanese, Siamese" (1998, 46), and Sheng-mei Ma, likewise, censored Disney for over-simplifying the "exotic Other" (2003, 150). Neo-Disney characters are much complex and individualized than those created previously.

Figure 13.2. Namaari.

Figure 13.3. Virana.

Namaari's asymmetrical hairstyle, with one side of her head shaved, is identical to her mother Virana's style, and is quite similar to the hairstyles that some women have today. It is worth noting that Virana's hair is platinum blonde throughout the film (see Figure 13.3), a color that people from Southeast Asia rarely have. The blonde hair suggests the possibility of her having it dyed, which as per the research by Rutherford and Baker, can be interpreted as Disney's emphasis on White supremacy and the Asian culture's predisposition to internalize the Western influences. One can also consider it a subtle indication that a woman from the Disney universe is exercising autonomy over her own body, as well as confounding stereotypes. The half-shaved head also symbolizes Namaari's breaking free from the princess frame in which the length of the hair is associated with femininity. Most of the princesses' long hair contribute to their feminine strengths, with the exception of Cinderella and Snow White who have shoulder-length hair yet embody the feminine stereotype (Wiersma 51). Rapunzel's hair is her strength, which she apparently loses after it is cut by Flynn Rider toward the end of *Tangled* (01:24:15).

Namaari wears an ear-cuff on only one ear, defying the conventional girly appearance. She is a warrior who wants to defeat Raya, the protagonist of the film, but unlike the negative characters depicted in older movies such as Maleficent, Ursula, and Lady Tremaine (Cinderella's stepmother), Namaari is not pictured in the dark. Considering that Disney connects evil with darkness, Namaari's casting in light is the director's declaration that she is not wicked. The actual evil is the rivalry between the five kingdoms of Kumandra, which is fuelled by the greed and fear of the people—physically manifested in the film as the blackish-purple phantom, Druun, that lurks in the dark and converts whomever it comes into contact with into stones (Leroy 2021, n.p.).

Most critics describe traditional Disney princesses as "naïve" and quick to trust strangers (Rutherford and Baker), as well as "not resistive towards difficulties" (Liu and Yang 2021, 1036) who fall in love quickly, do not protest oppression, and forgive others easily (for instance, Cinderella, Rapunzel, Ariel, and Snow White). In *Raya and The Last Dragon*, none of the female characters trust each other easily. At a young age, when Raya shows Namaari the Dragon Gem, Namaari betrays her, resulting in the gem's being broken into pieces and bringing back the distrust and greed, symbolized by the Druun. At the beginning of the film, young Raya can be seen overcoming obstacles and reaching up to the Dragon Gem, while Namaari uses the bait of friendship to achieve it. Deception and distrust are not conventionally heroic feminine traits that Disney features in its films. Raya, Namaari, Virana, Tong, Dang Hu, and even Noi, a baby, is led by skepticism and deception and live in an unfortunate "dystopian world" (00:00:42) where no one can be trusted. Sisu's extremely trusting disposition pushes her into dangerous situations; for instance, there is deception in her encounter with Dang Hu—who appears to be a nice elderly lady but is horribly devious and selfish in reality. Although Dang Hu is a minor character, she tricks Sisu into believing her, locks her out amidst the darkness scattered with Druuns, and abandons her to die (00:51:50). Raya saves her life, but it gives her yet another reason to keep her trusting side hidden from the world. Near the end of the film, Sisu succeeds in convincing Raya and Namaari to trust each other once more (01:24:11). Rather than just a reference to classic princess qualities, the neo-Disney heroine gives others the benefit of the doubt, thus demonstrating that she is a character of strength, patience, and ethics. Although the pre-Renaissance Disney women are typically gentle, trusting, and forgiving, they are usually gullible and easily hurt, but the neo-Disney woman can handle challenges and betrayals; like Disney males, they are "independent, unique and strong" (Xu 330), and they can also be gentle and caring when necessary.

Released in December 2021, *Encanto* is another neo-Disney film that hosts a diverse cast of powerful female characters. Based in Colombia, the film accurately depicts the country's profound Indigenous, European, and African culture and traditions. Members of the large Madrigal family each has a unique body along with a unique gift that is essentially a superpower, except for Mirabel, who does not receive a gift from the Miracle Candle. The three daughters of Julieta and Agustin Madrigal—Luisa, Isabela, and Mirabel—possess magical powers associated with their physical characteristics. Mirabel's elder sister Luisa is big with incredible strength and is capable of lifting anything from barrels and donkeys to the entire *casita* (house). Luisa's imposing muscular physique visually validates her gift of strength. She has stronger biceps than any of the male characters in the film, is the tallest of the daughters (see Figure 13.4), and is considered "the beauty and the brawn" (00:07:34). She feels obligated to carry the load (quite literally) of the family, even when she is exhausted, typifying many older siblings who go beyond their limits and usual responsibilities to support the family. Her song "Surface Pressure" reveals her "disneyfied" feminine side when she confesses that she pushes her limits in order to be validated by her family, and exclaims, "I'm pretty sure I'm worthless if I can't be of service" (00:53:55). Luisa's statement connects her to classic Disney princesses like Rapunzel and Cinderella, who seek validation from their families in the same way. Further, the pressure that Luisa feels to meet the family expectations worries her especially when she is afraid that she is losing her gift of physical strength.

Figure 13.4. Luisa's muscular figure.

No matter how Luisa's unconventional character was conceived, the character designers faced difficulties with regard to presenting a girl with such a heavily muscular figure. In *Comic Book Resources* (CBR.com), it is made clear that "Dylan Ekren, an illustrator and character modeling supervisor who worked on *Encanto*, said that it was incredibly difficult to convince the House of Mouse that Luisa should forgo the petite and slim build of many other Disney women to have a muscular frame instead" (Wasalamudalige 2022). *Inside the Magic* also notes that in the context of a tradition that has showcased petite women regardless of how strong they are, this image of Luisa was not considered "commercially beautiful" by Disney (Paris 2022), and, as a result, Disney did not initially approve of the diversified appearance of this character (Wasalamudalige; Paris). Although the theatrical release of the film portrays Luisa's body as sturdy and muscular, the initial lack of approval within the Disney Company indicates that Luisa's appearance was not universally accepted as a Disney brand.

Mirabel's eldest sister, Isabela Madrigal, is "the perfect golden child" (00:07:28). She makes flowers bloom with every step she takes and decorates their home with them. She has been portrayed as a woman who embodies some of the more conventional Disney attributes. In contrast to Luisa, she exhibits a more feminine image with brown skin, long, black hair, sharp features, and a petite figure (see Figure 13.5).

Figure 13.5. Isabela.

Isabela sacrifices her desires for the sake of the family when she agrees to marry Mariano Guzman, despite the fact that she never wanted to marry him. Isabela is the ideal daughter though she does not want to be so. She expresses her frustrations during her argument with Mirabel and screams, "I've been stuck being perfect my whole entire life, and literally the only thing you have ever done for me is mess it up" (01:09:06). She further exhibits her vexation by creating a cactus instead of a beautiful flower. This is the first time she contradicts her perfect nature and goes against her family's expectations. Soon, she is surrounded by large darkish plants, which evokes imagery of the wild, while she plays with colors. Her physical appearance also changes—bright colors quickly cover her monotonously purple clothes. Isabela was so perfect before that she never had a "bad hair day" (00:46:53)—neatly done hair symbolizes the unnaturally perfect image that she has to maintain to live up to her Abuela's expectations—but once she gains control of her body and explores her individuality, Isabela appears wild, defying all conventional beauty standards.

Mirabel has received no tangible gift from the Miracle Candle, but she remains hopeful and loves her magical family dearly. She is a 15-year-old girl who takes up the responsibility of protecting the family's magic after Abuela Alma; thus, she is the successor and princess of *Encanto*. Disney princess movies have a huge influence on their target young audience, especially girls (Azmi et al. 687), and Mirabel is the princess most young girls can readily relate to for her short wavy hair, not-so-slender body, and messy lifestyle, which presents herself to be more human among the other miraculous members of the Madrigal family (see Figure 13.6). She is also the first Disney Princess to wear glasses, which is a significant indication that the Disney company is working toward highlighting and normalizing the bodily imperfections in its movies. The audience has paid close attention to the characters' clothing in *Encanto*; a Twitter post has pointed out that each character's attire has a symbol that represents their magical abilities, but Mirabel's skirt has all of them, depicting her as the embodiment of the magic and highlighting her natural gift of keeping the family together with love (Menachips 2022).

What also distinguishes Mirabel from the other characters is her down-to-earth attitude in finding a solution to problems and her strong desire to save their *casita* so that her family never becomes homeless again. The Miracle Candle did not provide her with any of the magical powers because she had already been gifted by Nature with the gifts of love and passion. Alma Madrigal, Mirabel's grandmother, becomes so afraid of losing the magical gifts of her family that she overlooks Mirabel's innate power of love and passion until the time when their home fell into pieces and none of the magical gifts could heal the damage.

Figure 13.6. Mirabel.

Recognition of Self

Madeleine Binkley writes, "Modern day mass media is an element where children gain knowledge and expertise, and ultimately form an identity for themselves" (2016, 13). Disney influences the development of children's psyches by providing the young audience a gateway through which their imaginations can run wild among the colorful surroundings that reflect their own fantasies, for a person's psychological development is greatly influenced by the formative experiences he or she is exposed to at a young age (13). Citing Lasisi Ajayi's claim, Binkley asserts that "Disney has become one of the most prevalent educators of its time, educating children how to express cultural notions of race, gender, sexuality, and ultimately, a discourse of the self" (quoted in 13). Mary-Catherine Harrison agrees: "Empathy for fictional characters can prompt ethical behavior in the extra-fictional world" (2011, 257), which again points to Disney's important role in assisting children in forming their identities.

Disney's children's films frequently include images of societal Others and mentally ill individuals to maintain an apparent inclusive stance and to project an image that the company is not prejudiced; however, they do not always do so with compassion; they often treat such characters unfairly as discovered by Andrea Lawson and Gregory Fouts who have analyzed 34 films produced by Disney between 1937 and 2001, aimed largely at children, that contain references to mental illness (2014, 312). They found that 21 percent of the primary Disney characters are mentally ill, and "the average number of mental illness references per film was 4.6, with the 3 most prevalent words being … 'crazy,' 'mad' or 'madness,' and 'nut' or 'nutty'" (312). They concluded that "these references were commonly employed to segregate, alienate, and denote the inferior status of the character(s) to which they referred—a finding consistent with the overwhelmingly negative portrayal of mental illness found in adult media … implying that to be mentally ill is to be different in a negative and inferior way" (312).

The frequency of mental health issues depicted in the Disney children's films requires the analysis of coping mechanisms adopted by the fictional characters, which influence the general development of children who watch the films. James A. Graham, Hope Yuhas, and Jessica L. Roman deduced that children acquire coping mechanisms in real life while trying to adapt to stressful circumstances such as death and that the development of adequate coping mechanisms in childhood is crucial to a person's overall physical, mental, and emotional health (2018, 19). They examined the mechanisms used by various Disney characters, including Simba (in *Lion King* (1994) and Moana (25–27) in dealing with the deaths of their close relatives (in this case, Mufasa and Tala). The familial and societal expectations imposed on children should be considered such a source of distress, failing to conform to which might have grave impacts on a child's psyche. It has already been established that children are unable to build their coping skills on their own and require the assistance of their families and support networks (Graham et al. 19), implying that family as a social unit has a direct impact on a person's psychological well-being but could very well be the trigger to distress, such as the isolation and low self-esteem experienced by Coco and Mirabel because they don't conform to their families' expectations. A vivid picture of societal expectations put on children and adolescents is conveyed through almost all the children's animated films, including recent ones such as *Frozen*, *The Lion King*, *Raya and the Last Dragon*, *Luca*, and *Encanto*, where even the neo-Disney characters struggle to cope.

Although Disney has incorporated more wide-ranging body images and gender constructs in their recent children's films, its characters lack personal freedom, which hinders their development of identities independent of society, leading the young audience to anticipate a world that does not validate the authenticity of the self. Characters such as Elsa, Simba, Namaari, Luca, Alberto, Luisa, Isabela, Pepa, and Camilo suffer psychological stress as a result of their lack of personal freedom, but they conceal their stress from others, thereby suggesting to children that deception should be used to mask trouble instead of dealing with mental distress.

Expectations are linked with people's lives right from their childhood, which at times become too heavy a burden for them. Jiryung Ahn insists that it is crucial for children to fit into specific social categories (2011, 415), but it necessarily restricts their ability to make their own choices and to maintain individuality. It is natural that this restriction takes a toll on the mental well-being of children as they grow up to become adults who cannot form their identity out of the social norms and thus remain trapped in a societal category. These conditions are not always severe enough to be classified as "illness," but do pose difficulties. With the exception of Moana, Disney's prominent trends in children's films do not allow for self-exploration, as evidenced by the wide range of its films that disregard the individuality of its characters while alienating them and projecting them as the social Other to serve as a good example of what not to do. Even Moana was forbidden by her father from following her dream to discover what was "out there" (00:10:56), but with her grandmother's support, she shows the courage to push past the boundaries (00:31:15). However, when Moana is apparently fulfilling her desire, she is actually serving her community, saving her village people from dying of hunger due to the coconut crisis and fish shortages. This tradition of creating characters solely for the purpose of serving the family and the community continues to exist, and almost any character who attempts to venture beyond social conventions and family responsibilities is developed as someone who is not as fortunate as Moana to earn acceptance from the family or society.

Elsa's special powers must remain concealed from the rest of the world, lest she harms others. Even after being crowned Queen, she is not validated for her individuality; as a result, she runs away from everyone and builds her own castle made of ice, where she lives alone embracing her powers and her true self. Anna, the only living member in Elsa's family after their parents died, takes on the responsibility to convince her to return to Arendelle and serve her purpose as the queen, to which Elsa responds, "I never knew what I was capable of … I belong here, alone, where I can be who I am without hurting anybody" (2013, 00:55:21). The fear that Elsa faced throughout her childhood after Anna was injured because of her powers magnifies the fear of not getting accepted by society for who she was, thus she kept herself hidden. Elsa's anxiety mirrors today's young generation who are afraid of rejection for being "different" from the rest. Elsa is finally compelled to leave the comfort that she had found in her solitude, to save her sister, which makes her come back to Arendelle, but Elsa continues to feel lonely and unsettled as observed in *Frozen II*. An organized society does not validate Elsa's powers and she feels alienated it her palace in Arendelle. She eventually returns to the Enchanted Forest because "she belongs to nature" (Wu 2020, 35). In Yan Wu's opinion, "Elsa shows the awakening of female self-awareness in the twenty-first century, independent in personality and spirit" (36), but can she actually become "independent" of the society? She learns to accept who she is, and her magic turns from "negative" to "positive" (35), but Arendelle cannot provide her a place to belong, and she remains an outsider in her motherland. Anna, who serves as traditional Disney's spokesperson in a way that she fulfils her duties toward her sister and countrymen, sets an example for what a queen should be: She grows out of her naïveté that she once displayed in selecting a husband like Hans, and remains committed to her people. Because Anna is more "normal" than her sister with mystical powers, the people of Arendelle accept her as their queen more readily. Therefore, Elsa's return to nature is not much of a favorable outcome for the people in the audience struggling to accept their true selves.

Mobility, in terms of fleeing away from an organized society or culture, is a recurring trait of the characters in Disney children's movies, and it is often associated with escaping from a situation. Escaping as a way of dealing with a situation should be problematic for a young audience. In the 1998 film *Mulan*, the young female protagonist goes off to take her father's place in the army so he will not die. It may be argued that it is a vivid depiction of selflessness, a stereotypical feminine quality; however, her voluntary escape to an unknown place where she will get to train in the Chinese military and experience the life of a warrior can be interpreted as her attempt to accomplish the quest for her real self. Mulan is unhappy living the life that society has planned for a girl like her. In the song "Reflection," she does not see her authentic self-reflected while conventionally dressed as a woman, asking, "Who is that girl I see, staring straight back at me? Why is my reflection someone I don't know?" (1998, 00:13:44). Mulan is intelligent, but it is not the quality she requires to be the "perfect bride" (00:13:25), and this "failure to bring honor to her family … marks Mulan as a disgrace according to the standards of her traditional Chinese culture" (Dunn 2019, 13). Thus, Disney's practice of not acknowledging the qualities of its characters that are beyond societal norms has persisted even in the earlier films back in the late twentieth century. This dissatisfaction makes Mulan escape the land where she originally belongs in order to overcome the obstacles set up by societal expectations for her to act like a woman. Mulan's mobility can be regarded as a method for her to break free from the typical image of a woman, and it is necessitated by the people around her in a way that they have forced her to constantly fight with herself, obstructing the development of her identity using social standards.

When Simba in *The Lion King* believes that he is unwanted by his own people and flees to save himself, he is subjected to a similar force. Scar convinces Simba that he failed to live up to his father's expectations, blaming the young cub as the cause of his father's death (00:45:38). This incident terrifies Simba to an extent that he runs away from all his loved ones, fearing that they will despise him now, and isolates himself with Timon and Pumbaa. While Simba's coping mechanism for dealing with his father's death costs him his childhood as a lion, Scar, is not welcomed as a king, by the pride of lions. The underprivileged sections of society, especially persons with nonheterosexual orientations, have traditionally been underrepresented in Disney films. Scholars have tried to analyze Scar based on the traits that he displays in order to distinguish him from the heterosexual population. Georgia Vraketta is one of them and produces several proofs to support her claim (2022, 4). She insists that Scar was outraged because his brother (who symbolized the epitome of masculinity) did not acknowledge Scar's powers that might be seen as the hostility of oppressive heterosexual forces (2022, 4). He transforms into a villain who murders Mufasa in order to establish himself to be as powerful as his brother. He does not, however, carry out the murder with his bare claws (4), as is typical for lions. Although Scar is the only standing male in their tribe after Mufasa's death, he continues to feel isolated, as he is not accepted by his community. This theory is plausible, given Scar's effeminate demeanor and no female partner depicted in the film. However, Scar approaches Sarabi to be his queen, so that the other lions do not reject him (01:02:40). Nevertheless, projecting a presumably homosexual character as a social outcast and villain, who belongs with the hyenas representing the lower classes of the society, demonstrates a lack of sympathy for the queer individuals on Disney's part.

Another such instance is the relationship between Luca and Alberto, two young sea monsters featured in the coming-of-age fantasy *Luca*. They share a strong bond that can be considered homosexual in nature. They take care of each other and want to get a Vespa so that they can live on their own (00:56:52). It makes Alberto jealous when Luca spends time with Giulia (00:56:02) and talks about the telescope that Guilia has taught him about (00:56:16). Luca used to live in the ocean until he met Alberto and discovered the outside world. His parents refer to the land (a place unknown to them and all other sea creatures) as a place packed with "bloodthirsty lunatics" (00:42:39), but once Luca steps outside the confines of the ocean, he realizes that he can explore more about himself without the fear of rejection because nobody above the surface of water knows him. Despite the fact that the land is not depicted as a place for sea monsters and that the sea monsters evoke a sense of fear among the human beings, Luca gets the opportunity to pursue his goal of education (00:55:59). Going beyond the established limit of the ocean opens up an entirely new world for Luca, but it poses some difficulties in terms of hiding his identity because he cannot afford to risk his life by revealing himself as a sea monster—a foreign being—trespassing into the homogenous human community. Alberto, though enjoying his life on his own terms, had to live in isolation; he used to live alone on a tower near the seashore, presumably abandoned by his father because he was so different from other sea monsters, was obsessed with a "Vespa," and failed to conform to the rules set by his ocean culture that hates humans and their lives above the surface. Alberto finds a companion in Luca and shares a glimpse of his alienated life of solitude with Luca, which surprisingly resonates with the latter. Both young sea monsters desire to go beyond their pre-established realm, which is demonstrated by their practice of collecting human belongings. The director, Enrico Casarosa, revealed that there is a hint of romance in the development of the relationship between Luca and Alberto, but he has declared that the film is about "friendship" between the two boys who feel like outsiders in their community: "I think the reason probably we didn't talk about ... [a romantic relationship] as much ... is that we were really focusing on *friendship* and so *pre-romance*" (quoted in Taylor 2022; emphasis added). The lack of depictions of homosexual relationships in the children's film is a marketing strategy keeping the commercial picture of American culture in mind in which some consumers prefer not to discuss homosexuality since it tarnishes their religious convictions. When it comes to themes like homosexuality and the societal Other, there has always remained a sense of discomfort in the films produced under the Disney banner.

Namaari is designed to attract the eyes of a queer audience. She exhibits a strong masculine physique with an asymmetrical hairstyle and has no friends. She finds a friend in Raya, only for a short period of time before she must sacrifice her friendship to serve her kingdom and fulfil the expectations of her people. At a very young age, she uses friendship as bait to deceive her only friend and tries to seize the Dragon Gem under her mother's control (00:15:15). Namaari betrays Raya for the second time, accidentally killing Sisu, the last remaining dragon because she does not "have any other choice" (01:16:28). All her actions are efforts to avoid becoming a social outcast. She expresses the guilt, fear, and helplessness emphatically in order to indicate to the audience that she is only doing what her community expects of her and that she "never meant for anyone to get hurt" (01:11:43). Namaari's unfortunate condition reveals itself when it becomes apparent from her mother's words that she may harm Raya to protect their people: "We're not going to give her a choice" (01:12:03), and she is observed isolating herself in her room (01:13:18), concerned about her friend. The complicated nature of these two girls' friendship might also be seen as romantic because, even though they are against each other due to Namaari's betrayal, they still care for each other. However, none of the Disney staff has made any such statement on this subject. In turn, Namaari is constantly portrayed as rejecting Raya's friendship, as well as her true self as a young girl, because of her responsibilities as a chief's daughter, implying to the young audience that commitments toward the community take precedence over individual freedom.

In the Disney films for children, each family being a social unit represents a hierarchy based on "worth, ability, authority, or some other attribute" (Artz 2002, n.p.), and those belonging to the lower strata (usually children) have to comply with the norms established by the authoritarian member of that family. Because "Abuela runs the show" in the Madrigal family of *Encanto* (00:06:02), all her children and grandchildren must follow her codes of conduct. She does not allow anyone to open up about their mental distresses, preserving a picture of a "fantastical and magical" family (00:06:25). Pepa clearly struggles to maintain a positive attitude throughout the film, but because others are unwilling to discuss it, she reminds herself to have "clear skies" (00:46:19), which is a technique of suppressing emotions. She portrays a depressed woman whose feelings are not acknowledged by her family. Bruno is compelled to pretend to flee from his room and remain hidden in the walls of the *casita* so that he does not face anyone because his visions were considered to be incapable of being put to any good use. Everyone in the *Encanto* community dismisses his ability to foresee the future and its many possible interpretations as being dangerous prophecies, so they "don't talk about Bruno" (00:06:50). The family had high expectations for Isabela and Luisa, which made them feel exhausted and constrained. Camilo's shapeshifting may be regarded as his quest for his original self; Dolores is not allowed to speak of "the man of [her] dreams" (00:49:16) because he has been chosen as the groom for her cousin by the family, and Antonio needs to "serve this community and strengthen [their] home" (00:20:29) at the age of 5.

Every younger member must meet the family's expectations and serve his/her community. It is a recurring trait of Disney animated films for children, as can be seen in the older films of *The Little Mermaid* and *Mulan*, among others. Mulan is made to realize "if I were truly to be myself, I would break my family's heart" (00:13:44), just like Moana's father decides for her that "the village of Motunui is all" she needs (00:08:56). If these young characters do not conform to these rules, then the family has the authority to punish them; for example, King Triton destroys Ariel's treasured Grotto for not obeying the rules made by a "responsible merman" like him (00:36:13); and Luca's parents decide to send him deep in the ocean where he might suffer from a lack of oxygen, and "no sunlight ... [and] nothing to see anyway" (00:25:39).

Neo-Disney Needs to Be More Neo-Disneyistic

Twenty-first-century Disney children's films have been inclusive enough to finally acknowledge bodily imperfections as an acceptable trait and to grant their female characters autonomy over their bodies, as evidenced by the depictions of Mirabel—a princess with glasses, Luisa—a brawn teenager girl, Virana—a blonde-headed South Asian woman, and Namaari—a "Princess Undercut" (00:59:04). However, the characters' innate individualism—their perspective of the world—remains underrepresented. The family and community, as well as the restrictions imposed by these hierarchical structures, have remained major driving forces of the plots in these films, for which the characters are often compelled to make sacrifices. More strong and opinionated girls, such as Moana, and more sensitive and compassionate boys, such as Luca and Alberto, need to be represented to assist young girls to learn their worth, and boys to grow out of the tough and heroic image created by sociocultural standards and express their delicate selves without fear of societal judgment. Disney may then be able to reflect the real or at least endorse a more human-friendly world to its young audience, rather than making people feel obligated to submit to traditional, outdated norms.

Bibliography

Ahandani, Ebrahim Alinia, and Roghayyeh Taasobi. "Some Media Effects on Children." *International Journal of Innovation and Research in Educational Sciences* 2, no. 2 (March 2015): 48–53. <https://www.researchgate.net/publicat ion/273574534_Some_Media_Effects_on_Children-A_Review>.

Ahn, Jiryung. "Review of Children's Identity Construction via Narratives." *Creative Education* 2, no. 5 (December 2011): 415–17. doi:10.4236/ce.2011.25060.

Ajayi, Lasisi. "A Multiliteracies Pedagogy: Exploring Semiotic Possibilities of a Disney Video in a Third Grade Diverse Classroom." *Urban Review* 43, no. 3 (2011): 396–413. doi:10.1007/s11256-010-0151-0.

Artz, Lee. "Animating Hierarchy: Disney and the Globalization of Capitalism." *Global Media Journal* 1, no. 1 (December 2002): n.p. <https://www.globalm ediajournal.com/archive/gmj-volume-1-issue-1-year-2002.html>.

Azmi, N. J., Radzuwan Ab Rashid, and Zanirah Wahab. "Young Girls' Perception of Beauty in Disney Princess Movies." *International Journal of Asian Social Science* 8, no. 9 (July 2018): 686–693. doi:10.18488/journal.1.2018.89.686.693.

Binkley, Madeleine. "An Argument on Disney and Psychological Development." *URJ-UCCS: Undergraduate Research Journal at UCCS* 10, no. 1 (December 2016): 11–18. <https://urj.uccs.edu/index.php/urj/article/view/232>.

Cheung, Monit, Carol A. Leung, and Yu-Ju Huang. "Absentee Parents in Disney Feature-Length Animated Movies: What Are Children Watching?" *Child and Adolescent Social Work Journal* (2021): 1–14. doi:10.1007/s10560-021-00799-0.

deCordova, Richard. "The Mickey in Macy's Window: Childhood, Consumerism, and Disney Animation." In *Disney Discourse: Producing the Magic Kingdom*, edited by Eric Smooden, 202–205. New York: Routledge, 1994.

Dunn, George A. "'True to Your Heart' Honor and Authenticity in Mulan." In *Disney and Philosophy: Truth, Trust, and a Little Bit of Pixie Dust*, 1st edn, edited by Richard B. Davis, 11–23. Hoboken, NJ: John Wiley and Sons, 2019.

Graham, James A., Hope Yuhas, and Jessica L. Roman. "Death and Coping Mechanisms in Animated Disney Movies: A Content Analysis of Disney Films (1937–2003) and Disney/Pixar Films (2003–2016)." In *The Psychosocial Implications of Disney Movies*, edited by Lauren Dundes, 17–30. Basel, CH: SMDPI, 2018, doi:10.3390/socsci7100199.

Harrison, Mary-Catherine. "How Narrative Relationships Overcome Empathic Bias: Elizabeth Gaskell's Empathy Across Social Difference." *Poetics Today* 32, no. 2 (Summer 2011): 255–88. doi:10.1215/03335372-1162686.

"I Am Moana." Written by Lin-Manuel Miranda. Sung by Auli'I Cravalho and Rachel House for *Moana*. 2016. <https://www.youtube.com/watch?v=HEiS F8HpyDg>.

Laemle, Jessica L. "Trapped in the Mouse House: How Disney Has Portrayed Racism and Sexism in Its Princess Films." *Student Publications*. Fall 2018. <https://cup ola.gettysburg.edu/student_scholarship/692/>.

Lawson, Andrea, and Gregory Fouts. "Mental Illness in Disney Animated Films." *Sage Journals* 49, no. 5 (May 2004): 310–14. <https://journals.sagepub.com/ doi/abs/10.1177/070674370404900506>.

Leroy, Kath. "*Raya and the Last Dragon*: The Main Characters, Ranked by Intelligence." *Screenrant*, March 10, 2021. <https://screenrant.com/raya-and-the-last-dragon-smartest-characters/>.

Lester, Neal A. "Disney's *The Princess and the Frog*: The Pride, the Pressure, and the Politics of Being a First." *The Journal of American Culture* 33 (December 2010): 294–308. doi:10.1111/j.1542-734X.2010.00753.x.

Liu, Yuze, and Mo Yang. "The Transformation of Female Images in Disney Animated Films from the 20th to the 21st Century in the Context of the American Feminist Movement." *Proceedings of the 2021 4th International Conference on Humanities Education and Social Sciences (ICHESS 2021)*, 1034–9. The Netherlands: Atlantis Press, December 2021. <https://doi.org/10.2991/ass ehr.k.211220.177>.

Ma, Sheng-mei. "Mulan Disney, It's Like, Re-Orients: Consuming China and Animating Teen Dreams." In *The Emperor's Old Groove: Decolonizing Disney's Magic Kingdom*, edited by Brenda Ayres, 149–64. New York: Peter Lang, 2003.

Menachips. Twitter. January 3, 2022, 12:56 a.m. <https://twitter.com/menachips/ status/1478085375927238663>.

Paris, Lindsey. "Disney Didn't Want Luisa with Muscles, and Now She's Outselling Isabela." *Inside the Magic*, January 24, 2022. <https://insidethemagic.net/ 2022/01/disney-didnt-want-luisa-muscles-outselling-isabella-lp1/>.

"Reflection." Written by Matthew Wilder and David Zippel Sung by Lea Salonga for *Mulan*. 1988.

Rowe, Rebecca. "Shaping Girls: Analyzing Animated Female Body Shapes." *Sage Journals* 14, no. 1 (March 2019): 22–36. <https://doi.org/10.1177/174684771 9829871>.

Rutherford, Amanda, and Sarah Baker. "The Disney 'Princess Bubble' as a Cultural Influencer." *Media Culture Journal* 24 (2021). doi:10.5204/mcj.2742.

Spector, Alan. J. "Disney Does Diversity: The Social Context of Racial-Ethnic Imagery." In *Cultural Diversity and the U.S. Media*, edited by Yahya R. Kamalipour and Teresa Carilli, 39–49. Albany, NY: SUNY Press, 1998.

"Stories Matter." The Walt Disney Company. 2022. https://storiesmatter.thewaltdi sneycompany.com/>.

"Surface Pressure." Written by Lin-Manuel Miranda. Sung by Jessica Darrow for *Encanto*. Walt Disney Studio, 2020. <https://www.youtube.com/watch?v= ErY3eeRFTFg>.

Taylor, Drew. "*Luca* Director Enrico Casarosa on LGBTQ+ Themes in Pixar Film." *TheWrap*, January 5, 2022. <https://www.thewrap.com/luca-enrico-casarosa-is-luca-gay/>.

Towbin, Mia Adessa et al. "Images of Gender, Race, Age, And Sexual Orientation." 2004. *Journal of Feminist Family Therapy* 15, no. 4 (September 2008): 19–44. <https://www.tandfonline.com/doi/abs/10.1300/J086v15n04_02>.

Uppal, Charu. "Over Time and Beyond Disney—Visualizing Princesses Through a Comparative Study in India, Fiji, and Sweden." In *The Psychosocial Implications of Disney Movies*, edited by Lauren Dundes, 1–16. Basel: MDPI, 2019, <https://doi.org/10.3390/socsci8040105>.

Vraketta, Georgia. "The Representations of Gender, Sexuality and Race in Disney's The Lion King." *Academia*, February 7, 2022. <https://www.academia.edu/4893757/The_Representations_of_Gender_Sexuality_and_Race_in_Disney_s_The_Lion_King>.

Wasalamudalige, Hansini. "*Encanto* Artists Had to Fight Disney for Luisa's Fan-Favorite Muscular Frame." *CBR.com*, January 21, 2022. <https://www.cbr.com/disney-encanto-artists-fought-for-luisa-muscles/>.

Wiersma, Beth A. "The Gendered World of Disney: A Content Analysis of Gender Themes in Full-Length Animated Disney Feature Films." *Open PRAIRIE: Open Public Research Access Institutional Repository and Information Exchange.* 2000, 14–68. <https://openprairie.sdstate.edu/cgi/viewcontent.cgi?article= 2925&context=etd>.

Wu, Yan. "The Analysis of Elsa's Growth from the Perspective of Ecofeminism." *Open Journal of Social Sciences* 8, no. 6 (June 2020): 30–36. doi:10.4236/jss.2020.86003.

Wynns, Scarlet L. and Lawrence B. Rosenfeld. "Father-Daughter Relationships in Disney's Animated Films." *Southern Communication Journal* 68, no. 2 (March 2003): 91–106. <https://doi.org/10.1080/10417940309373253>.

Xu, Mo. "Analysis on the Influence of Female Characters in Disney Films." *Proceedings of the 2021 5th International Seminar on Education, Management and Social Sciences (ISEMSS 2021)*. The Netherlands: Atlantis Press, August 2021, 327–31. <https://doi.org/10.2991/assehr.k.210806.061>.

Yao, Jia. "Research on Marketing Strategy: Case Study of Disneyland." *Proceedings of the Second International Conference on Economic and Business Management (FEBM 2017).* The Netherlands: Atlantis Press, October 2017, 473–81. <https://doi.org/10.2991/febm-17.2017.63>.

Zurcher, J. D., S. M. Webb, and Tom Robinson. "The Portrayal of Families Across Generations in Disney Animated Films." In *The Psychosocial Implications of Disney Movies*, edited by Lauren Dundes, 1–16. Basel, CH: MDPI, 2018. doi:10.3390/socsci7030047.

SARAH E. MAIER

Epilogue: Neo-Disney's Multifaceted Rainbow World

To write a book about Disney, neo or otherwise, is a treat, like grabbing some Twizzlers while checking out at the grocery store. Nevertheless, we wanted to make sure that we left our fangirl selves behind to create a collection that would critically engage with the latest Disney films entertainment identifying the progress toward inclusivity that we applaud as well as interrogate it with rigor. While recognizing that the original Walt Disney world has expanded and continues to move toward an increasingly inclusive, multinational representation of gender fluidity, lived experience, and imaginative intelligence, it is also true that Disney has only begun to touch on the full spectrum of human—and nonhuman—life. Mental health issues, LGBTQ2+ identities, BIPOC cultures, animal worlds, environmental issues, and posthuman worlds and possibilities, are all part of this next phase of neo-Disneyism which is both necessary and engaging for fans and scholars alike.

Given the current academic interest in ecocentrism, bioethics, animal studies, thing theory, posthumanism, transhumanism, instead of traditional analysis of Disney's depiction of plants, animals, and other nonhuman entities as anthropocentric, these tools of theory can open a "whole new world" when viewing the latest version of, say, *The Jungle Book* (2016) or *The Lion King* (2019). Besides perhaps offering a perspective from the animals, we should consider what such movies teach people about the value of nature and the urgency to preserve animals that are growing extinct (like elephants and tigers) and protect our environment.

This one volume cannot remotely capture all there is still to do on the subject of neo-Disneyism. Sequels, pirates, monsters, cars, superheroes, droids, rats, emotions, dinosaurs, fish, authors, jungles, jazz, and religion have yet to be investigated through academic critical inquiry. Sequels—unlike remakes, adaptations, or live-action films—try to prolong a story and its merchandising not just of princes and princesses but of monsters, cars, planes, and a plethora of other beings. Another facet of scholarship that begs attention is a comparison of Disney's storytelling techniques with those of other narrators of the same original source. One example is Eleanor Porter's *Pollyanna* of 1913; an inquiry into its adaptation and appropriation might consider what and why the differences between it and Disney's famous *Pollyanna* of 1960 are set in Vermont and, then again in *Pollyanna* of 2008, set in an English village. The endings have changed with the times and requirements of context; such reworkings are worthy of a volume of their own.

One might even consider films that began as a Disney ride like *Jungle Cruise* (2021) or *Pirates of the Caribbean*, which is a classic example of where a popular ride became an even more popular film series with swashbuckling action and odd characters like Captain Jack Sparrow, Davy Jones, and Captain Elizabeth Swann-Turner. Disney has shown it is able to have an understanding of multiple directionality from product to film and merchandise; the movement is fluid, not linear, and it would be worth consideration to decide if the impact on the viewer changes with the tide.

Musicology is an understudied part of the Disney canon; work could be done on how Disney songs contain messages that promote positive mental health, and many more Disney songs have yet to be analyzed for their social influence. The songs have real-world use; in one instance, Massachusetts firefighters sang "Let it Go" to a girl to calm her while stuck in an elevator (McGlensey 2014), and in a more recent, incredibly poignant moment, a young Ukrainian girl—Amelia Anisovych—sang the same song while sheltering in a subway station from the falling Russian bombs during the War on Ukraine (Cooper 2022). In each case and across the world, the song about power and release has given comfort to those in need, children and adults alike.

One might explore the history of rewrites such as "You've Got a Friend in Me" for the *Toy Story* franchise. Some Disney songs have been banned and still others considered quite controversial. Tori Brazier says, "As Disney releases its documentary *Howard* on Disney+, celebrating the life and career of the late lyricist, we look back at times when famous Disney songwriters, despite the hits, didn't always hit the right notes" (2020). It might also be interesting to consider why many of the Disney songs have become Billboard successes and deemed classics or have become viral moments in the Twitterverse. Further, it would be an interesting conversation to find out why were some songs retained or altered or replaced from an early to a later Disney film such as "He's a Tramp" in *Lady and the Tramp*, and the replacement of "Training the Men" for "I'll Make a Man Out of You" in *Mulan*.

More work can be done on "friendship" and its depictions throughout the Disney canon. Children can learn to build friendships with those individuals who are "different," by appreciating the unlikely friendship between two monsters, one big, popular, scary, and blue, while the other is small, round, hardworking, not scary, and green, like Sully and Mike in *Monsters, Inc.* (2001) and *Monsters University* (2013), where nerds win over frat boys. Buzz and Woody surpass jealousy and explore differing masculinities to become intergalactic pals in the *Toy Story* franchise (1995–2019). Resonating with very modern teenagers is the relationship between Luca, the geek and Alberta, a cool type. Cars with existential crises, back tattoos, law degrees, artistic ability, and spy skills offer the possibility of subjective belief in one's own self rather than what the world expects when the underdog McQueen wins the race and, more importantly and to his great relief, attains the brainy girl—Sally's—respect.

LGBTQ2+ issues continue to arise in relation to Disney, from the films' increasingly rainbow flag to its lack of initial action on important social issues like Florida's attempt to pass a "Don't Say Gay" bill. The president of Disney, Bob Chapek, initially tried to step aside from the fray with his statement: "The biggest impact we can have in creating a more inclusive world is through the inspiring content we produce, the welcoming culture we create here and the diverse community organizations we support, including those representing the LGBTQ2+ community" (quoted in Shanfeld 2022) until a backlash of public opinion required a corporation that influences perhaps the most children of any one company take a stand. In addition to the political ramifications, an internal letter from Disney employees alleges that the company censors same-sex affection in Pixar films:

> We at Pixar have personally witnessed beautiful stories, full of diverse characters, come back from Disney corporate reviews shaved down to crumbs of what they once were …. Even if creating LGBTQIA+ content was the answer to fixing the discriminatory legislation in the world, we are being barred from creating it. (Vary and Jackson 2022)

On another front, and nearly five years after he played Le Fou, Josh Gad has very recently said,

> We didn't go far enough to say, "Look how brave we are." My regret in what happened is that it became 'Disney's first explicitly gay moment' and it was never intended to be that. It was never intended to be a moment that we should laud ourselves for, because frankly, I don't think we did justice to what a real gay character in a Disney film should be. (Pollard 2022, n.p.)

In spite of public demand, Elsa was not to have a relationship with another young woman to make her Disney's first animated openly lesbian character and provoking disappointment in the young people who had hoped to see themselves represented on screen (St. James 2019).

With such access to children and young adults (in addition to adults!), Disney has the capacity to bring important subjects to the attention of and to explore ideas increasingly relevant to its audiences. Although our collection has made progress in addressing Disney's increasingly positive portraits of BIPOC persons and Indigenous Cultures, there is still a great deal of critical work to be done on where Disney began in its films and recompense to be made for those racist and culturally insensitive portrayals of the past. "Black Lives Matter" has prompted overdue, important conversations and confrontations on race relations in the United States, while the Indigenous Truth and Reconciliation Commission is at the forefront of Canadian concern. Horrific war against the Ukrainian people forces those with power to address issues of diasporic individuals rather than rest in the comfort of middle-class whiteness. Future critical work should emphasize how Disney does or does not sidestep these issues but engages their audiences in meaning possibilities of understanding.

The nonjudgmental discussion of mental health challenges, particularly for youth, have long since been needed so that viewers do not measure themselves as failures in relation to what they see on screen. *Inside Out* (2015) opened increased awareness on mental health in Pixar films with the emotional characters of Joy, Fear, Anger, Disgust, Sadness, Bing Bong and their person, Riley, who—like many young people—experiences a move away from what is comfortable and known to a new home. The recent live-action *Cruella* (2021) has a small girl witness the death of the woman who has been her mother. The extensive backstory of Ella's life—the very horridness of it all—sees her run away from the killer to the streets, live with equally young but caring thieves in a family of choice, and then grow into an overlooked, mistreated young woman emphasizes how unaddressed trauma might eventually manifest in her alter ego, Cruella, due to mental illness and violence.

Questions should be asked about what Disney might do to prepare the young generations for a future full of technology and such endearing robots like WALL-E (Waste Allocation Load Lifter-Earth-Class; 2008) or Baymax, the deuteragonist, prototype healthcare robotic nurse in *Big Hero 6* (2014), or the malevolent, multi-eyed creature with mechanical tentacles in *Amphibia* (2019) or Turbo/King Candy, a villain in a video game in *Wreck-It Ralph* (2012). Neo-Disneyism's acquisition of new universes, as well as the human, posthuman, nonhuman, and alternative beings who inhabit those worlds in the form of the MARVEL and *Star Wars* characters/franchises indicates there are off-planet new directions of future generations it wishes to illustrate in animated and non-animated forms. Robots with emotions (C3PO and R2-D2, Jarvis/Vision), mythic gods (Thor, Loki), strong women (Pepper Potts, Natasha Romanov/ Black Widow, Wanda Maximoff/Scarlet Witch) who now include a lesbian woman (Carol Danvers/Captain Marvel), have joined the Disney family while men of character (Steve Rogers/Captain American, Tony Stark/Ironman, Bruce Banner/Hulk) who include men of integrity and color (Nick Fury, T'Challa/Black Panther) fight for the conscience of the Universe. Continued narratives in the past, present, or the alien future, off-planet arenas, and multiverses should, we hope, continue to evolve these gems of possible scholarly interests in the many worlds of neo-Disneyism.

Bibliography

Brazier, Tori. "From 'Arabian Nights' to 'Zip-a-Dee-Doo-Dah': Disney's Most Controversial Songs." *Yahoo Movies*, August 10, 2020. <https://www.yahoo.com/video/disneys-most-controversial-songs-140540432.html>.

Cooper, Anderson. "Girl's Singing Inside Kyiv Bomb Shelter." *CNN: Anderson Cooper 360*, March 7, 2022. <https://www.cnn.com/videos/world/2022/03/07/let-it-go-frozen-kyiv-shelter-ukraine-ac360-wknd-sot-intl-ovn-vpx.cnn>.

"He's a Tramp." Sung by Janelle Monáe for *Lady and the Tramp*. Written by Sonny Burke and Peggy Lee but lyrics were altered. 2019. <https://www.youtube.com/watch?v=tgI9QrD22cc>.

———. Written by Sonny Burke and Peggy Lee. Sung by Peggy Lee for *Lady and the Tramp*. 1955. <https://www.youtube.com/watch?v=KhJcyrkfjQg>.

"I'll Make a Man Out of You." Composed by Matthew Wilder. Lyrics by David Zippel. Sung by Donny Osmond for *Mulan*. 1998.

McGlensey, Melissa. "Firefighters Sing 'Let It Go' to Calm Scared Child During Rescue." *Huffington Post*, March 26, 2014. <https://www.huffpost.com/entry/frozen-rescue_n_5028290>.

Pollard, Alexandra. "The Saturday Interview: Josh Gad." *The Independent*, February 26, 2022. <https://www.independent.co.uk/arts-entertainment/tv/features/josh-gad-interview-disney-gay-b2024275.html>.

Pollyanna. Directed by Sarah Harding. Carlton Television. 2003.

Porter, Eleanor H. *Pollyanna*. 1913. Adapted by Marion Leighton. Ilust. Gual. New York: Baronet Books, 1995.

Shanfeld, Ethan. "After 'Don't Say Gay' Bill Backlash, Disney CEO Expresses 'Unwavering Support' for LGBTQ Community." *Variety*, March 7, 2022. <https://variety.com/2022/film/news/disney-ceo-bob-chapek-support-lgbtq-1235197938/>.

Spanos, Brittany. "Janelle Monáe Frees Herself. *Rolling Stone* (April 26, 2018). <https://www.rollingstone.com/music/music-features/janelle-monae-frees-herself-629204/>.

St. James, Emily. "Why Elsa from Frozen Is a Queer Icon—And Why Disney Won't Embrace That Idea." *Vox*, November 22, 2019. <https://www.vox.com/culture/21418282/mulan-ill-make-a-man-out-of-you-disney-animated-1998>; <https://www.vox.com/culture/2019/11/22/20975178/frozen-2-elsa-girlfriend-lesbian-queer-review>.

"Training the Men." Composed by Harry Gregson-Williams. Soundtrack for *Mulan*. 2020. <https://www.youtube.com/watch?v=vxv5BOo8xys>.

Vary, Adam B. and Angelique Jackson. "Disney Censors Same-Sex Affection in Pixar Films, According to Letter from Employees." *Variety*, March 9, 2022. <https://variety.com/2022/film/news/disney-pixar-same-sex-affection-censorship-dont-say-gay-bill-1235200582/>.

"You've Got a Friend in Me." Written and sung by Randy Newman for *Toy Story*. 1996. <https://www.youtube.com/watch?v=Zy4uiiyoqgA>.

Cited Disney Filmography

The Adventures of Ichabod and Mister Toad. Directed by Jack Kinney, Clyde Geronimi, and James Algar. Walt Disney Productions. 1947.

Aladdin. Directed by Ron Clements and John Musker Walt Disney Pictures. 1992. <https://www.disneyplus.com/movies/aladdin/2SngByljXESE>.

Alice in Wonderland. Directed by Clyde Geronimi, Wilfred Jackson, and Hamilton Luske. RKO Radio Pictures. 1951.

Alice Through the Looking-Glass. Directed by James Bobin. Walt Disney Studios Motion Pictures. 2016.

Alice's Adventures in Wonderland. Directed by Tim Burton. Walt Disney Studios Motion. 2010.

Amphibia. Created by Matt Brady. Disney Television Animation. 2019–present.

Aristocats. Directed by Wolfgang Reitherman. Walt Disney Productions. 1970.

The Avengers. Directed by Joss Whedon. Marvel Studios. 2012.

Beauty and the Beast. Directed by Gary Trousdale and Kirk Wise. Screenplay by Linda Woolverton. Walt Disney Pictures. 1991.

———. Directed by Bill Condon. Screenplay by Stephen Chbosky and Evan Spiliotopoulos. Walt Disney Pictures. 2017.

Big Hero 6. Directed by Don Hall and Chris Williams. Walt Disney Pictures. 2014.

Black Panther. Directed by Ryan Coogler. Marvel Studios. 2018.

Brave. Directed by Mark Andrews and Brenda Chapman. Walt Disney Pictures. 2012.

Cars. Directed by John Lasseter. Walt Disney Pictures and Pixar Animation Studios. 2006.

Cinderella. Directed by Clyde Geronimi, Wilfred Jackson, and Hamilton Luske. Walt Disney Pictures. 1950. <https://www.disneyplus.com/movies/cinderella/VJPw3bEy9iHj>.

———. Directed by Kenneth Branagh. Walt Disney Studios Motion Picture. 2015.

Coco. Directed by Lee Unkrich. Walt Disney Pictures-Pixar Animation Studios. 2017.

Cruella. Directed by Craig Gillespie. Walt Disney Pictures, Mar Platt Productions, and Gunn Films. 2021.

Dumbo. Directed by Ben Sharpsteen. Walt Disney Productions. 1941.

Encanto. Directed by Jared Bush, Byron Howard, and Charise Castro Smith. Walt Disney Pictures. 2021. <https://www.disneyplus.com/movies/encanto/33q7DYirtHQH>.

Enchanted. Directed by Kevin Lima. Walt Disney Pictures. 2007.

Fantasia. Directed by Joe Grant and Dick Huemer. Walt Disney Productions. 1940.

Fantasia 2000. Directed by Don Hahn et al. Walt Disney Pictures. 1999.

Frozen. Directed by Chris Buck and Jennifer Lee. Walt Disney Pictures. 2013. <https://www.disneyplus.com/movies/frozen/4uKGzAJi3ROz>.

Frozen II. Directed by Jennifer Lee. Walt Disney Pictures. 2019. <https://www.disneyplus.com/movies/frozen-2/28vdy71kJrjb>.

The Good Dinosaur. Directed by Peter Sohn. Walt Disney Pictures-Pixar Animation Studios. 2015.

Hercules. Directed by Ron Clements and John Musker. Walt Disney Pictures. 1997.

The Hunchback of Notre Dame. Directed by Gary Trousdale and Kirk Wise. Walt Disney Pictures. 1996.

The Incredibles. Directed by Brad Bird. Walt Disney Pictures. 2004.

Inside Out. Directed by Pete Doctor and Ronnie Del Carmen. Pixar Animation Studios. 2015. <https://music.apple.com/us/music-video/try-everything-from-zootopia/1445003400>.

Iron Man. Directed by Jon Favreau. Marvel Studios. 2008.

The Jungle Book. Directed by Wolfgang Reitherman. Walt Disney Productions. 1967.

———. Directed by Stephen Sommers. Walt Disney Pictures. 1994.

———. Directed by Jon Favreau. Walt Disney Studios. 2016.

The Jungle Book 2. Directed by Steve Trenbirth. Walt Disney Pictures. 2003.

Jungle Cruise. Directed by Jaume Collet-Serra. Walt Disney Pictures. 2021.

Lady and the Tramp. Directed by Clyde Geronimi, Wilfred Jackson, and Hamilton Luske. Screenplay by Ward Greene, Erdman Penner, and Joe Rinaldi. Walt Disney Productions. 1955.

———. Directed by Charlie Bean. Screenplay by Kari Granlund and Andrew Bujalski. Walt Disney Pictures. 2019.

Lilo and Stitch. Directed by Chris Sanders and Dean DeBlois. Walt Disney Pictures. 2002.

The Lion King. Directed by Roger Allers and Rob Minkoff. Walt Disney Pictures. 1994.

———. Directed by Jon Favreau. Walt Disney Pictures and Fairview Entertainment. 2019.

The Little Mermaid. Directed by Ron Clements and John Musker. Walt Disney Pictures. 1989. <https://www.disneyplus.com/movies/the-little-mermaid/5MpPFhS8FTXh>.

Luca. Directed by Enrico Casarosa. Walt Disney Pictures and Pixar Animation Studios. 2021.

Make Mine Music! Directed by Jack Kinney et al. Walt Disney Productions. 1946.

Maleficent. Directed by Robert Stromberg. Screenplay by Linda Woolverton. Performed by Angelina Jolie, Sharlto Copley, Elle Fanning et al., Walt Disney Pictures. 2014.

Maleficent: Mistress of Evil. Directed by Joachim Rønning. Screenplay by Linda Woolverton, Noah Harpster, and Micah Fitzerman-Blue. Performed by Angelina Jolie, et al. Walt Disney Pictures. 2019.

The Many Adventures of Winnie the Pooh. Directed by John Lounsbery and Wolfgang Reitherman, Walt Disney Productions. 1977.

Mary Poppins. Directed by Robert Stevenson. Walt Disney Productions. 1964.

Mickey's Man Friday. Directed by David Hand. Walt Disney Productions. 1935.

Mickey's Nightmare. Directed by Burt Gillett. Walt Disney Productions. 1932.

Midnight in a Toy Shop. Directed by Wilfred Jackson. Walt Disney Productions. 1930.

Moana. Directed by Ron Clements, John Musker, and Don Hall. 2016. <https://www.disneyplus.com/movies/moana/70GoJHflgHH9>.

Monsters, Inc. Directed by Peter Docter. Walt Disney Pictures and Pixar Animation Studios. 2001.

Monsters University. Directed by Dan Scanion. Walt Disney Pictures and Pixar Animation Studios. 2013.

Mosby's Marauders. Directed by Michael O'Herlihy. Walt Disney productions. 1967.

Mulan. Directed by Niki Caro. Performed by Yifei Liu, Donnie Yen, and Li Gong. Walt Disney Pictures. 2020.

———. Directed by Tony Bancroft and Barry Cook. Performed by Ming-Na Wen, Eddie Murphy, and BD Wong. Walt Disney Pictures. 1998.

———. Directed by Yuxi Li. Performed by Chuxuan Liu and Mo Li. iQIYI. <https://www.iq.com/play/owds1dsqvg>.

Nutcracker and the Four Realms. Directed by Lasse Hallström and Joe Johnston. Walt Disney Pictures. 2018.

Old Yeller. Directed by Robert Stevenson. Walt Disney Productions. 1957.

Once Upon a Time. Season 4. Episode 23. "Operation Mongoose (Part 2)." Directed by Ralph Hemecker. ABC Studios. May 10, 2015.

One Hundred and One Dalmatians. Directed by Clyde Geronimi, Hamilton Luske, and Wolfgang Reitherman. Walt Disney Productions. 1961.

Peter Pan. Directed by Clyde Geronimi, Hamilton Luske, and Wilfred Jackson. Walt Disney Productions. 1953.

Pinocchio. Directed by Ben Sharpsteen and Hamilton Luske. RKO Radio Pictures. 1940.

Pocahontas. Directed by Mike Gabriel and Eric Goldberg. Walt Disney Pictures. 1995. <https://www.disneyplus.com/movies/pocahontas/2WjLTJt9dM5C>.

Pocahontas II: Journey to a New World. Directed by Tom Ellery and Bradle Raymond. Walt Disney Premiere. 1998.

Pollyanna. Directed by David Swift. Walt Disney Productions. 1960.

The Princess and the Frog. Directed by Ron Clements and John Rusker. Walt Disney Pictures. 2009.

Raya and the Last Dragon. Directed by Don Hall, Carlos López Estrada, and John Ripa. 2021. <https://www.disneyplus.com/movies/raya-and-the-last-dragon/6dyengbx3iYK>.

Red Sorghum. Directed by Zhang Yimou. Performed by Gong Li and Jiang Wen. Xi'an Film Studio. 1988.

Rescuers Down Under. Directed by Hendel Butoy and Mike Gabriel. Walt Disney Pictures and Walt Disney Feature Animation. 1990.

Return to Never Land. Directed by Robin Budd. Walt Disney Pictures. 2002.

Robin Hood. Directed by Wolfgang Reitherman. Wolfgang Reitherman. 1973.

Santa's Workshop. Directed by Wilfred Jackson. Walt Disney Productions. 1932.

Sleeping Beauty. Directed by Eric Larson and Les Clark. Walt Disney Productions. 1959. <https://www.disneyplus.com/movies/sleeping-beauty/1rc2EavpNV7U>.

Snow White and the Seven Dwarfs. Directed by William Cottrell, David Hand, and Wilfred Jackson. Walt Disney Productions. 1937. <https://www.disneyplus.com/movies/snow-white-and-the-seven-dwarfs/7X592hsrOB4X>.

So Dear to My Heart. Directed by Harold D. Schuster and Hamilton Luske. Screenplay by John Tucker Battle. Walt Disney Productions. 1948. <https://www.youtube.com/watch?v=JmQgUxLReTE>.

Song of the South. Directed by Harve Foster and Wilfred Jackson. Walt Disney Productions. 1946.

Squanto: A Warrior's Tale. Directed by Xavier Koller. Walt Disney Pictures. 1994.

Star Wars. Directed by George Lucas. Lucasfilm Ltd. 1977.

The Suite Life of Zack and Cody. Created by Danny Kallis and Jim Geoghan. Disney Channel. 2005–8.

The Suite Life on Deck. Created by Danny Kallis and Jim Geoghan. Disney Channel. 2008–11.

Swiss Family Robinson. Directed by Ken Annakin. Walt Disney Productions. 1960.

The Sword in the Stone. Directed by Wolfgang Reitherman, Walt Disney Productions. 1963.

Tangled. Directed by Nathan Greno and Byron Howard. Walt Disney Pictures. 2010.

Tarzan. Directed by Kevin Lima and Chris Buck. Walt Disney Pictures. 1999.

The Three Caballeros. Directed by Norman Ferguson et al. Walt Disney Productions. 1944.

The Three Musketeers. Directed by Stephen Herek. Walt Disney Pictures. 1993.

The Tigger Movie. Directed by Jun Falkenstein. Walt Disney Pictures. 2000.

Toby Tyler; or, Ten Weeks with a Circus: A Radio Dramatization. Audible Audiobook. The Colonial Radio Theatre on Brilliance Audio. January 2, 2012.

Toby Tyler or Ten Weeks with a Circus. Directed by Charles Barton. Performed by Kevin Corcoran. Walt Disney. 1960.

Toy Story. Directed by John Lasseter. Walt Disney Pictures and Pixar Animation Studios. 1995.

Toy Story 2. Directed by John Lasseter. Walt Disney Pictures and Pixar Animation Studios. 1999.

Toy Story 3. Directed by Lee Unkrich. Walt Disney Studios and Pixar Animation Studios. 2010.

Toy Story 4. Directed by John Colley. Walt Disney Studios and Pixar Animation Studios. 2019.

Treasure Island. Directed by Byron Haskin. RKO-Walt Disney British Productions. 1950.

"Ugly Duckling." *A Silly Symphony*. Written by Hans Christian Andersen (1843) and Vernon Stallings. Walt Disney Productions. 1939. <https://www.youtube.com/watch?v=RCX-mPstrPU>.

Wall-E. Directed by Andrew Stanton. Walt Disney Pictures. 2008.

Winnie the Pooh and the Honey Tree. Directed by Wolfgang Reitherman. Walt Disney Productions. 1966.

Wreck-It Ralph. Directed by Rich Moore. Walt Disney Pictures. 2012.

Zootopia. Directed by Byron Howard, Rich Moore, and Jared Bush. Walt Disney Pictures. 2016. <https://www.disneyplus.com/movies/zootopia/1QOxl dhm1sKg>.

Notes

Introduction: Walt Disney's Wonderful World of Color

1. For studies on the influence of Disney on developing Children's perceptions see Schickel (18); Graves (1999); Meredith Li-Vollmer and Mark E. LaPoint (2003); Mia Towbin et al. (2004); Campbell Leaper, Lisa Breed, Lauri Hoffman, and Carly Ann Perlman (2006); Campbell Leaper, Lisa Breed, Lauri Hoffman, and Carly Ann Perlman (2006); A. L. Singer (2017); Lauren Dundes (2019), and Andreas Müller-Hartmann (2007).
2. Additionally, the authors of *Animating Difference* praise the movie for having neither prince nor princess that needs rescue; however, they also criticized the film for its emphasis on whiteness and heterosexuality (King et al. 2010, 3–4).
3. See Ayres and Maier's works on neo-Victorianism, neo-Victorian things, and neo-Gothicism listed in the bibliography.
4. By "the Other," I am referring partially to Georg Wilhelm Friedrich Hegel's concept of those people other than oneself that helps one identify one's self (1988 [1807], 109–11), but also to Gayatri Chakravorty Spivak's theory of alterity that separates self from not-self and implies discrimination against those who are different from self in regard to gender, race, ethnicity, and class. See Spivak's chapter titled "Who Claims Alterity" 2012, 57–72. *Alter* is Latin for the "other," the latter being a term that will appear often in *Neo-Disneyism* and will be capitalized.
5. About Disney and colorblindedness, see Sarah Turner (2013, 83–98 and 2014, 237–60), Chávez (2018, 209–18), and Jill Anne Morris (2019, 213–28).
6. BIPOC stands is an acronym for "Black, Indigenous, (and) People of Color." LGBTQ2+ refers to lesbian, gay, bisexual, transgender, queer, two-spirited, and a number of other identities.
7. About his nostalgia, besides what Ayres writes in the first chapter, see Schickel (209–10), Robin Allan (1999, 3), Svetlana Boym (2001, 16), and Zornado (2017, 23).

Neo-Victorianism and Neo-Disneyism

1. See Ayres (2021, 3).
2. Quoted in Schaffer (2016, 33) from *The Globe* (1994, C14).
3. Quoted in Allan (1999, 18) from Arndt (1982, 16).

4. By 1933, 13 million Americans were out of work (Kennedy 1999, 163).

5. In the 1950s in America, milkmen used to deliver milk in glass bottles directly to customers' houses. Typically, women were housewives and mothers who would have been alone through the day, having contact only with the milkman (and possibly a postman). Hence the milkman joke became a euphemism for adultery and illegitimate paternity.

6. The line is from "A Boy Like That," warning Maria, a Puerto Rican, not to be involved with White Tony. See Stephen Sondheim (1957).

7. The Claremont House certainly could have inspired the creation of Lady's house, but it is much more elaborate. See "Claremont House."

8. To learn more about the Italian American anti-defamation activity against the show, see Kenna (2016).

9. Quoted in Salvato (640) from the *OED* (see bibliography).

Transmedial Paratexts and Ideology in Disney's *Brave*, *Pocahontas*, and *Mulan*

1. See Pallant's Chapter 6, "The Disney Renaissance" (89–110) for a full description.

2. See Eduardo Bonilla-Silva and David Dietrich (2011), Sarah Turner (2013), Neal Lester (2010), and Ajay Gehlawat (2010).

3. Disney placed a warning for some of its earlier films that had drawn flak for their racist content, like *Lady and the Tramp* (1955), *Dumbo* (1941), and *The Jungle Book* (1967). A content advisory notice was placed on these films saying that they contain negative depictions and stereotypes of certain cultures and that they are wrong ("Disney Updates" 2020, n.p.).

4. Jonathan Gray built his concept of paratextual material by expanding on Gerard Genette's notion of paratexts—materials that accompany a text such as the title, illustrations, introduction, preface, illustrations, and so on. Gray added to the list paratexts action figures, DVD/ Blu-ray extras, and franchise material in general and argued that they should not be brushed off as mere marketing add-ons to the text (2010, 8).

5. Transmedia games, transmedia adaptation, transmedia franchising, and transmedia branding and marketing are some of the most common forms of transmedial expression as pertaining to films (Kennedy 2019; Dena 2019; von Stackelberg 2019; and Giovagnoli 2019).

6. The scale and reach of its corporate holdings make it economically expedient; according to Joseph L. Zornado, "Theme parks, a cruise ship fleet, a major television

network, a major sports cable network, among a host of other holdings, including toys and consumer product tie-ins, account for a lion's share of corporate earnings" (2017, 180). Another significant portion of its profits come from the control of media distribution because "Walt Disney Studios, Touchstone Pictures, Hollywood Pictures, Marvel Studios, and Lucasfilm, among others, produce fantasy film projects capable of reaching nearly every audience demographic in almost every corner of the world" (180).

7. Jenkins explains the term as "the flow of content across multiple media platforms, the cooperation between multiple media industries, and the migratory behavior of media audiences who would go almost anywhere in search of the kinds of entertainment experiences they wanted" (n.p.).

8. Sarah Coyne, Jennifer R. Linder, Eric Rasmussen, and David A. Nelson conducted a study on a group of 3-to-4-year-olds to examine how exposure to princess media and its products affected gendered behavior in children, its impact on body image and prosocial behavior in children. Participants consisted of 198 children, who were tested at two time points (approximately one year apart). Data consisted of parent and teacher reports, and child observations in a toy preference task. The results revealed that when the children are left to play with the dolls without any active parental intervention, it made girls engage in girly-girl behavior (2016, 1,909).

9. This understanding of what it means to be a princess is tied to the notion of post-feminism, which will be dealt with later in this chapter.

10. The "new" movies that are the main focus of his study were released from 2000s to 2010s: *The Princess and the Frog, Tangled* (2010), *Brave* (released under Pixar), *Frozen* (2013), and *Moana* (2016). The older ones referred to in the study are the remaining princess movies released prior to 2000 (Hine et al. 4).

11. Brenda Ayres, coeditor of this volume, made this association.

12. The emphasis here is on the idea of self-empowerment through consumption rather than gender equity.

Imagineered Neo-Victorian American Real Estate: "A clean, unspoiled spot"

1. Quoted in Allan (1999, 2) from *The Marceline News*, September 2, 1938.

2. See Steven Watts' *The Magic Kingdom: Walt Disney and the American Way of Life* (1997).

3. It is ironic that the singer sued the British National Party for using the song in 2009 as an anti-immigration album ("Dame Vera Lynn" 2009).

4. A term coined between 1888 and 1890, bindle is a sack that carries one's belongings wrapped in a loth or blanket and then tied to a stick. It was usually associated with hobos that would hop the railway trains during the early 1900s and then increasing during the Great Depression in the 1930s. *Toby Tyler; or, Ten Weeks with a Circus* was written in 1880 by James Otis Kaler. Disney made it into a movie that first aired in 1960, starring Kevin Corcoran. In the book and in the Disney movie, Toby carries a sack of all his possessions without a stick, but the 2012 cover of the radio dramatization shows him holding the bindle almost like a boy grasping a baseball bat. Norman Rockwell's famous *The Runaway* (1958) portrays the back of a police officer and a runaway boy eating at a soda shop, with the bindle lying on the floor.

5. See Eker (2020).

6. See Gibson (2012).

7. The poem is reproduced in the Forbes' article on Stuart (410). I was unable to find the author of the poem; it is reproduced in print in a variety of places and the author listed as anonymous. The first that I found it in print is in the *Masonic Review* about the pluckiness of Mrs. William Emerson, the widowed mother of Ralph Waldo Emerson and his five siblings (Moore 1888, 21–22). The second is in *The Biographical Dictionary* (1893, 404) in a description of another "sturdy western self-made man," Asaph Buck (401). Republished from the *Woman's Herald* (1891–3), "Pluck" appears in *Life* (1905, 653).

8. In a letter to Robert Lawson, at Edinburgh in answer as to the admission of females to the medical university (Wylie 1881, 100–101).

9. I discuss this in depth in Chapter 1 in this volume.

10. "Tin Pan Alley" represents publications of music in New York City that were popular in the late nineteenth and early twentieth century. See Marcuse (1959, 236, 300, 330, and 379).

11. The line previous to this is "Buy me some peanuts and Cracker Jack."

12. Quoted in paperbacklou from *Evening Star* (August 23, 1867) that quotes from *The Nantucket Inquirer and Mirror* (2021, n.p.).

13. Quoted in Watts 23 from Schickel (1968, 323).

14. The quotes are in an anonymous article published by Thunderbird, the American Graduate School of International Management (2006), from Turner and Gumbel (1992, A1).

Eastern Witch from the West: Xianniang in Niki Caro's *Mulan*

1. A portion of this paper was previously published in the *Journal of Asia Pacific Studies* 6, no. 2 (August 2021): 187–96.

The Hybrid Alice: Framing the Imperial Gothic in Tim Burton's *Alice's Adventures in Wonderland*

1. In an interview with *Grazia Magazine*, Colleen Atwood, costume designer for *Into the Looking Glass*, discusses Alice's costume in this sequence. Referring to the piece as a "lavender organza Oriental top," Atwood notes that the costume was inspired by Chinese embroidery and period fabrics. Notably, though, her inspiration for the costuming of *Looking Glass* overall was a hybrid of John Tenniel's illustrations from Carroll's *Alice* texts and nineteenth-century Japanese designs. Given the lack of reference to Japan in the imperial nexus of Burton and Bobin's *Alice* films, these costuming choices profess a Pan-Asian Orientalism in themselves (Bailey 2016).

2. In a *Looking Glass* press roundtable, Bobin and Burton discuss the extensive influence that Burton had on Bobin's sequel, ensuring a cohesive cinematic universe across both films ("Alice Through the Looking Glass Press Conference" 2016).

3. Kara M. Manning (2011), Catherine Siemann (2012), and Sonya Fritz and Sara Day (2018) agree that Burton's method of bringing Alice to the twenty-first century is the concern with female autonomy that is evinced by her imperial career.

4. Emma D. Graner demonstrates the connections between *Alice* and Victorian travel narratives, claiming that Carroll's text satirizes the way nineteenth-century travelogs engage with colonial Others (2014); Laura Ciolkowski similarly argues that Alice actively forms her domesticized British identity against the colonial landscape of Wonderland (1988).

5. While this imperial overtone is present in Disney's 1951 animated adaptation, wherein Alice abandons a history lesson about William the Conqueror (1028–1087) in order to follow the White Rabbit, the alterations made by this adaptation negate the protofeminist spirit of Carroll's texts. Deborah Ross has written extensively on this topic (2004 and 2000).

6. See Cannon Schmitt's work with Said (1997, 13).

7. In Carroll's *Looking-Glass*, this line is said by the White Queen (177). That it is said by Charles Kingsleigh in Burton's film emphasizes the entanglements between the imperial quest, the colonized Other, and Alice's role as a hybrid of both subjectivities.

8. While the phrase "Great Game" originated in 1840 from a letter between two British political agents, Captain Arthur Conolly and Major Henry Rawlinson, in which Conolly writes: "You've a great game, a noble game before you," it was popularized by *Kim* (Yapp 2001, 181).

9. Mercury exposure from felt was a risk in the nineteenth century for hat makers and was the inspiration for Carroll's creation of the Mad Hatter ("Alice Through the Looking Glass Press Conference").

10. While physiognomy is more widely applicable to the strange denizens of Underland, the Red Queen's bulbous head would attract the attention of Victorian phrenologists. Phrenology, a pseudoscience that correlated human mental traits with the

shape of their skulls, was popularized by Johann Spurzheim and Franz Josef Gall in *The Physiognomical System of Drs. Gall and Spurzheim* (1815).

11. While issues surrounding race are one of the larger areas of Disney scholarship, and therefore an extensive field survey is too big for this project, an excellent starting selection of essays regarding Disney's insensitive handling of race can be found in Johnson Cheu (2012).

12. Quoted in Mouzakis 63 from Pells 152.

Peter Pan After the Blitz: Finding What Remains in *Return to Never Land*

1. It is notable that we cannot reduce the racism in Disney's *Peter Pan* to a simple extension of the racism in J. M. Barrie's Peter Pan play and novel. See Clay Kinchen Smith for a fascinating breakdown of how Barrie's revisions to *Peter Pan* deconstruct easy racialization of the native Neverlanders, along with a convincing argument that the Disney version "overtly [obscures] Barrie's problematizing construction with a veneer of 'play' and covertly by erasing the tribe's specificity and replacing it with a more invidious history of erasure" (2006, 121).

2. For further details on Congressional efforts in the 1950s to erase Indigenous rights and cultures in the United States, see Max Nesterak (2019). For a compelling argument on *Peter Pan*'s complicity in these efforts through their dehumanizing depiction of Native peoples, see John L. Purdy.

3. For example, Susan Ohmer provides a survey of both positive and negative contemporaneous reviews, but ultimately positions the film as "a huge success at the box office … increasing [Disney's] revenue more than 10 percent over the previous year" (176). Donald Crafton quotes many of the same reviews but argues the film is "usually associated with Disney's 'lackluster' postwar films," and "received little attention from animation historians or film historians specializing in the 1950s" (1989, 33).

4. <https://disney.fandom.com/wiki/Return_to_Never_Land/Gallery>.

5. While *Return to Never Land* ends with Wendy assuring Peter that she hasn't "really" changed (01:00:42–1:00:55), it is important to note that she is no longer *really* "Wendy Darling." *Return to Never Land* never mentions Jane, Danny, or Wendy's last name, though she would presumably have taken her husband's name when she married. The film does not dwell specifically on Wendy's transformation from Darling child to darling wife, but it is thematically significant that Jane is not a Darling in any sense of the word.

6. The specific poster is an abstracted version of the Abram Games "Blonde Bombshell" poster, withdrawn from circulation in 1941 for being "too glamorous" (Gilbert 2014). During the height of World War II, Walt Disney Studios provided one minute of animation for *It's Your War Too* (1944), a short commissioned by the US Government

to promote the Women's Army Corps (WAC), the American equivalent of the Auxiliary Territorial Service (ATS) that Jane so admires (Shale 1982, 7).

7. Tinkerbell's newfound friendship with Jane hints at the beginning of a project to develop Tinkerbell into a more fully realized character, beginning with Gail Carson Levine's novel *Fairy Dust and the Quest for the Egg* (2005), which sees the fairy developed "as a hard-working innovator with a passion for invention," a move that spurred the launch of the lucrative Disney Fairies franchise (Meyers et al. 2014, 108–9).

8. Noel Brown offers a compelling reading of the Disney live-action feature films of the 1950s as a vehicle for American values and ideologies through the lens of "highly commodified and stereotyped … senses of time, place, and nationality" (2015, 195). *Treasure Island* (1950), another Disney/Bobby Driscoll collaboration, gets special mention as the beginning of Disney's foray into Britishness through a Disney-American lens.

9. *Peter Pan: Adventures in Never Land*, a PlayStation and Windows game released the same year as *Return to Never Land* (and released under the same name in North America), provides an odd alternative explanation. In the game—which features a teepee shop where feathers are currency and multiple visits to "Indian Village" levels—Peter learns from Tiger Lily that a powerful magic hides the entrance (and various falling rocks and spiky obstacles) from all who try to venture into the village. Peter, or "Great Chief Little Falling Eagle," as the Chief calls him, must play his panpipes to gain access to the village (2002).

Neo-Disney's Reconstruction of Masculinities

1. The Princess Line was created in 2001. It is a media franchise and toy line of twelve characters to date: Snow White, Cinderella, Aurora, Ariel, Belle, Jasmine, Pocahontas, Mulan, Tiana, Rapunzel, Merida, and Moana. See Amala Charulatha's chapter in this volume.

2. See Amala Charulatha's chapter in this volume.

3. AMBER is a backronym for America's Missing: Broadcast Emergency Response. This is an alert to the public on smartphones, television, and radio for help to find abducted children.

4. In addition to having created so many female characters with Kardashian figures that are buxom and wear erotic outfits, Disney+ and Hulu will air a new reality series titled *The Kardashians* scheduled for streaming internationally on April 14, 2020 (Coffey 2022).

5. An overview of "climatic rescues" can be found in Benjamin Hine et al. (2018, 5).

6. For an in-depth study of the individual traits of the stereotypical Disney male, see Dawn Elizabeth England, Lara Descartes, and Melissa A. Collier-Meek (2011, 558–62). See also Susan Witt who lists these depictions that were identified by the National Institute

of Mental Health (2000, 322–23). Three more good sources are Mia Adessa Towbin et al. (2004, 21–22), Hine et al. (8–9), and Campbell Leaper et al. (2006, 1655–61).

7. Quoted in Brian Attebery (2018, 319) from Jorgensen (2012, 235).

8. An overview of "happily-ever-after" endings is covered by Hine et al. (5–6).

9. Per research by sociolinguists Karen Eisenhaur and Carmen Fought (Neill n.d., n.p.).

10. According to Susannah Alexander, the song was passed on by Disney because it did not fit the tone of the new film (2020).

11. See Madeline Streiff and Lauren Dundes (2017, 1–2).

12. Dr. Westervelt was a long-standing member and secretary for the Hawaiian Historical Society. He translated several books into the Hawaiian language and wrote five volumes of Hawaiian legends (Frear 1940, 9): *Legends of Maui* (1910), *Legends of Old Honolulu* (1915), *Legends of Gods and Ghost-Gods* (1915), *Hawaiian Legends of Volcanoes* (1916) and *Hawaiian Historical Legends* (1923). According to Westervelt, "The Maui story probably contains a larger number of unique and ancient myths than that of any other legendary character in the mythology of any nation," with the legends originating in New Zealand (in the south), Hawaii (in the north) and the Tahitian and Hervey Islands (in the east) and were shared by Tonga, Fiji, and Samoa (vi).

13. Westervelt explains that Maui was "prematurely born, and his mother, not caring to be troubled with him, cut off a lock of her hair, tied it around him and cast him into the sea. In this way the name came to him, Maui-Tiki-Tiki, or 'Maui formed in the topknot' " (6).

14. In fact, one writer describes how Mirabel reminds him of what it's like to be autistic. One aspect he really appreciated that she "like many autistic people, has long since accepted who she is and the qualities that make her different from her family." Another aspect is family members try to "cure" her autism, which is impossible. Finally, she does not strive to become "superpowered like her siblings" (2022). John Leguizamo, who is the voice for Bruno, was also the voice for Sid, the giant ground sloth in the *Ice Age* series. Sid represents a character who was mentally slow and quirky. No doubt, many viewers connected the two characters.

Disney's New Dance at the Ball: *Beauty and the Beast* and Bowing to Difference

1. They did not need to discern good from evil before their obedience, but once they disobeyed God's one and only commandment and that was not to eat from the tree of the fruit of knowledge of good and evil (Gen. 2:17), "the eyes of both of them were opened," so that they saw evil and not just goodness, the first act of discrimination (Gen. 3:6). Satan/the serpent promised Eve that if she ate the fruit, her eyes would be open and therefore be like God, knowing good from evil (3:5). When confronted by God, Adam blamed God for giving him "the woman," and then Eve blamed the

serpent (Gen. 3:12 and 13). This is the first act of discrimination against God and woman. All scriptures are from the New American Standard.

2. Redemption from Adam's sin is described in Romans 5:12–21: "Therefore, just as through one man sin entered the world, and death through sin, and so death spread to all mankind, because all sinned ... so that, as sin reigned in death, so also grace would reign through righteousness to eternal life through Jesus Christ our Lord."

3. When asked by a lawyer to state the greatest commandment in the Law, Jesus replied, "You shall love the Lord your God with all your heart, and with all your soul, and with all your mind. This is the great and foremost commandment. The second is like it, 'You shall love your neighbor as yourself' " (Matt. 22:35–39).

4. For a more in-depth discussion of the parallels between "Beauty and the Beast" and Psyche and Cupid, and other sources, see Chapter four of Griswold and Craven (2002, 126). For an exploration of the multiple versions of *Beauty and the Beast* including movies, see Chapter 11 of Zipes' *The Enchanted Screen* (2011, 224–51).

5. This is the title of her seminal collection of essays on Victorian women (1972).

6. Forman-Brunell was quoted in Peggy Orenstein's article for the *New York Times* (2006, n.p.).

7. Sean Griffin recollects that Disney's 1991 film was made during the AIDs panic, and the mob scene simulates the panic of Americans (2000).

8. Anna E. Altmann and Gail De Vos offer a history of the various versions of *Beauty* and summaries of its various interpretations (2001, 1–45).

9. He points this out in 2003 with *Snow White* (1937), *Cinderella* (1950), *Sleeping Beauty* (1959), *The Little Mermaid* (1989), and *Beauty and the Beast* (1991), so his argument does not apply to the 2017 version of *Beauty and the Beast*. Eleanor Byrne and Martin McQuillan make this observation citing the same films plus *Aladdin* (1992) and *The Hunchback of Notre Dame* (1996).

10. See my reference to Allison Craven (2016, 191) and Amy Davis (2013, 232–33) above.

11. Such as Ursula in *The Little Mermaid* (1989) who is impaled by "a phallic mast from a ship" (Sells 179–80).

12. Exodus 22:18, Leviticus 19:26, and 20:27 demand that a witch be put to death. Revelations 22:15 says that those who practice magic arts "will not inherit eternal life." These are just a few scriptures that warn against sorcery of any kind.

13. Quoted in Griffin (2000, 134) from *Los Angeles Times Calendar* (1992, 42).

14. Jean Cocteau was openly homosexual. Many of his works have homoerotic imagery and overtones such as his semi-autobiographical *Le Livre Blanc* (1928).

New Gendered Representations in Contemporary Disney-Pixar Villains

1. See, for examples, Davis (2006) and Griffin (2011).

2. Hegemonic masculinity and toxic masculinity are a form of masculinity that encourages or defends men's dominant position, marginalizing different interpretations of gender identity that do not follow dominant standards and expectations. In Western cultures, these male standards usually related to aggressiveness, rage, invulnerability, unemotionality, stoicism, assertiveness, strength. See: Michael Kimmel (1994) and Raewyn Connell (2005).

3. "Queer" is an umbrella term that covers a wide spectrum of meanings. Generally, queerness indicates the rejection of those classifications that try to categorize identity or sexual orientation. Queer indicates "those gestures or analytical models which dramatize incoherencies in the allegedly stable relations between chromosomal sex, gender, and sexual desire" (Jagose 1996, 3).

4. The sample was created following these criteria. Movies produced in a period of time of 10 years (2012–2021) were selected, but prequels, sequels, spin-offs, and live actions were not included. Moreover, films that do not feature a structured villain were not included as well. For instance, Soul was not selected as it does not display a specific villain: The only antagonistic figure may be Terry the accountant, but she is not portrayed as particularly evil in the narrative. Similarly, *Inside Out* and *Onward* were not included as they offer minor antagonistic characters (Jangles the Clown) or final bosses that were not presented as main villains through the story.

Maleficent's Rage

1. The second film, *Maleficent: Mistress of Evil* (2019) creates a third society, that of the dark faes. Reflective of Indigenous cultures of the desert, polar, forest, plain, and othered people's territories, Maleficent finds she is of this elder race that humanity has chased into hiding.

2. It is only in the second *Maleficent* film that the viewer understands that even among the hidden worlds of the dark fae, Maleficent's powers and their strength are unique.

3. After the battle, Balthazar and Maleficent bow in equality and thanks, not subservience, to each other (00:13:56).

4. The Amazon women were a group of warriors who lived without women and defended their way of life; Boudicca, and ancient British queen, stood against Roman rule.

5. For example, in popular culture, think of Marvel's Incredible Hulk, or the incorrect but numerous pictures of Victor Frankenstein's creature, both monstrous and green.

Notes on Contributors

The Editors

BRENDA AYRES AND SARAH E. MAIER coedited and contributed chapters to the following: *The Theological Dickens* (Routledge, 2022), *Neo-Victorian Things: Re-Imagining Nineteenth-Century Material Cultures* (Palgrave, 2022), *Neo-Victorian Madness: Rediagnosing Nineteenth-Century Mental Illness in Literature and Other Media* (Palgrave, 2020); *Neo-Gothic Narratives: Illusory Allusions from the Past* (Anthem, 2020); *Animals and Their Children in Victorian Culture* (Routledge, 2019); and *Reinventing Marie Corelli for the Twenty-First Century* (Anthem 2019). The two cowrote *A Vindication of the Redhead: The Typology of Red Hair Throughout the Literary and Visual Arts* (Palgrave, 2021).

The Contributors

BRENDA AYRES, PhD, retired from full-time residential teaching, currently teaches online nineteenth-century English literature and professional writing for Liberty University. Besides the listing of publications above, her works can be found at the Amazon and Barnes & Noble websites. She was the editor and contributor to several chapters in the 2003 *The Emperor's Old Groove: Decolonizing Disney's Magic Kingdom* (Peter Lang).

MICHELLE CHAN, after receiving her PhD in Royal Holloway, University of London, works in the Department of English Language and Literature of Hong Kong Shue Yan University. She conducts research on the subjects of Victorian studies, children's literature and fantasy. She has published "Bonds and Companionship: The Healing Efficacy of the Picture Books of the 2011 Great East Japan Earthquake" in *Trauma, Memory and Healing in Asian Literature and Culture* (2021).

AMALA CHARULATHA is a PhD candidate in the Department of Indian and World Literatures at The English and Foreign Languages University. Her dissertation is on the ideology of fairy-tale adaptations by Disney where she looks at how fairy tales from a premodern era were transformed to suit a contemporary audience in a capitalist society, and the ideological implications of the changes made to the narrative. Her research interests include myth, folklore and fairy-tale studies, and adaptation studies.

DALILA FORNI, PhD, works in the Department of Education, University of Florence. Her interests include Children's Narratives and Gender Studies. Her doctoral thesis discussed new male and female models in contemporary picture books and has been published in the volume *Raccontare il genere. Nuovi modelli identitari nell'albo illustrato* (2022). She also published a monograph, *Children's Literature Across Media. Film and Theatre Adaptations of Roald Dahl's Charlie and the Chocolate Factory* (2020). Her "LGBTQIA Fairy Tales: Queering *Cinderella* in Lo's *Ash and Doghue's* 'The Tale of the Shoe'" is included in *Adaptation in Young Adult Novels: Critically Engaging Past and Present* (2020).

SHENG-MEI MA (馬聖美) is Professor of English at Michigan State University in Michigan, USA, specializing in Asian Diaspora and East-West comparative studies. He is the author of over a dozen books, including *The Tao of S* (2022); *Off-White* (2019); *Sinophone-Anglophone Cultural Duet* (2017); *The Last Isle* (2015); *Alienglish* (2014); *Asian Diaspora and East-West Modernity* (2012); *Diaspora Literature and Visual Culture* (2011); *East-West Montage* (2007); *The Deathly Embrace* (2000); *Immigrant Subjectivities in Asian American and Asian Diaspora Literatures* (1998); and memoir *Immigrant Horse's Mouth* (2023). He is also the coeditor of five books and special issues such as *Transnational Narratives in Englishes of Exile* (2018). He has also published a collection of poetry in Chinese, *Thirty Left and Right* (三十左右).

SARAH E. MAIER is Professor of English & Comparative Literature at the University of New Brunswick. Besides the works listed above as coeditor and coauthor, she has published extensively on the Brontës; edited special issues on *Sir Arthur Conan Doyle* and *Neo-Victorian Considerations, Charlotte Brontë at the Bicentennial*; and published articles on biofiction and neo-Victorian narratives.

ELAINE MORTON, PhD, is a high school educator whose studies focus on how mental health and emotions affect women. Her dissertation, titled "Emotionally Ever After: A Qualitative Analysis of Socio-Emotional Spaces Inhabited by Female Fairy Tale Characters and their Cinematic Adaptations," explores how gendered emotions affect behavior across classic fairy tales and modern cinematic retellings; recent publications include the chapter "Into the Woods: Mother Nature as Protector of Young Female Survivors in Post-Apocalyptic Film and Television" in *Children and Childhood in Post-apocalyptic Cinema and Television* (Lexington 2022).

KORINE POWERS is a PhD candidate studying violence and masculinity in postwar American film and genre fiction at Boston University. Her dissertation traces the history of serial killer film and fiction back to popular American genre forms like the cowboy and the hard-boiled detective. Her work on Hannibal Lecter as war orphan/avenger appears in *Twentieth-Century Literature*'s Spring 2020 issue. Her chapter in *Critical Essays on Elmore Leonard: If It Sounds Like Writing ...* (Wiley Blackwell 2020) examines the self-conscious, uneasy construction of the White Western protagonist in *Hombre* (1961).

RRITWIKA ROYCHOWDHURY is a postgraduate student of English Literature at Presidency University, Kolkata. Her dissertation explores the reversal of gender essentialism due to the feminist stereotypes prominent in late nineteenth-century New Woman fiction. Additionally, her main research interests lie in representations of childhood in literature and media, the evolution of children's literature, depictions of religion in the books for children, fairy tales, folklores, folk cultures, and fantasy fiction. She tries her hand at writing flash fiction during her free time.

TAYLOR TOMKO is a PhD candidate in the Department of English and Writing Studies at the University of Western Ontario, specializing in the *fin-de-siècle* Gothic. Her dissertation focuses on hypnosis in late Victorian psychical research. Her other interests include nineteenth-century adventure narratives, occult texts and ghost stories, posthumanism, cultural studies, and the Disney theme parks.

Index

www.ingramcontent.com/pod-product-compliance
Lightning Source LLC
LaVergne TN
LVHW051636050326
832903LV00022B/782